2002 SUPPLEMENT TO

THE FIRST AMENDMENT AND RELIGION AND THE CONSTITUTION

CASES AND MATERIALS

By

Arnold H. Loewy
Graham Kenan Professor of Law
University of North Carolina School of Law

AMERICAN CASEBOOK SERIES®

WEST
GROUP

A THOMSON COMPANY

D1411877

Mat #40057174

American Casebook Series, and the West Group symbol
are registered trademarks used herein under license.

COPYRIGHT © 2001 By WEST GROUP
COPYRIGHT © 2002 By WEST GROUP
         610 Opperman Drive
         P.O. Box 64526
         St. Paul, MN 55164–0526
         1–800–328–9352

ISBN 0–314–26439–6

 *TEXT IS PRINTED ON 10% POST CONSUMER RECYCLED PAPER*

Table of Contents

Table of Cases

The principal cases are in bold type. Cases cited or discussed in the text are roman type. References are to pages. Cases cited in principal cases and within other quoted materials are not included.

Chapter III

DISTINGUISHING SPEECH FROM CONDUCT

A. ATTRACTIVE SPEECH

Insert p. 44 (After question 3)

PROBLEM

PLANNED PARENTHOOD OF COLUMBIA/WILLAMETTE, INC. v. AMERICAN COALITION OF LIFE ACTIVISTS

290 F.3d 1058 (9th Cir.2002), amended ___ F.3d ___, 2002 WL 1467678 (9th Cir.2002).

RYMER, CIRCUIT JUDGE.

For the first time we construe what the Freedom of Access to Clinics Entrances Act (FACE), 18 U.S.C. § 248, means by "threat of force." FACE gives aggrieved persons a right of action against whoever by "threat of force . . . intentionally . . . intimidates . . . any person because that person is or has been . . . providing reproductive health services." 18 U.S.C. § 248(a)(1) and (c)(1)(A). This requires that we define "threat of force" in a way that comports with the First Amendment, and it raises the question whether the conduct that occurred here falls within the category of unprotected speech.

Four physicians, Dr. Robert Crist, Dr. Warren M. Hern, Dr. Elizabeth Newhall, and Dr. James Newhall, and two health clinics that provide medical services to women including abortions, Planned Parenthood of the Columbia/Willamette, Inc. (PPCW) and the Portland Feminist Women's Health Center (PFWHC), brought suit under FACE claiming that they were targeted with threats by the American Coalition of Life Activists (ACLA), Advocates for Life Ministries (ALM), and numerous individuals.[1] Three threats remain at issue: the Deadly Dozen "GUILTY" poster which identifies Hern and the Newhalls among ten others; the Crist "GUILTY" poster with Crist's name, addresses and photograph; and the "Nuremberg Files," which is a compilation about those whom the ACLA anticipated one day might be put on trial for crimes against humanity. The "GUILTY" posters identifying specific physicians were circulated in the wake of a series of "WANTED" and

---

1. Michael Bray, Andrew Burnett, David A. Crane, Timothy Paul Dreste, Joseph L. Foreman, Stephen P. Mears, Monica Migliorino Miller, Catherine Ramey, Dawn Marie Stover, Donald Treshman, and Charles Wysong. We refer to them collectively as "ACLA."

"unWANTED" posters that had identified other doctors who performed abortions before they were murdered.

Although the posters do not contain a threat on their face, the district court held that context could be considered. It defined a threat under FACE in accordance with our "true threat" jurisprudence, as a statement made when "a reasonable person would foresee that the statement would be interpreted by those to whom the maker communicates the statement as a serious expression of intent to harm." Applying this definition, the court denied ACLA's motion for summary judgment in a published opinion. *Planned Parenthood of the Columbia/Willamette, Inc. v. ACLA (PPCW II)*, 23 F.Supp.2d 1182 (D.Or.1998). The jury returned a verdict in physicians' favor, and the court enjoined ACLA from publishing the posters or providing other materials with the specific intent to threaten Crist, Hern, Elizabeth Newhall, James Newhall, PPCW, or the Health Center.

A panel of this court reversed. In its view, the standard adopted by the district court allowed the jury to find ACLA liable for putting the doctors in harm's way by singling them out for the attention of unrelated but violent third parties, conduct which is protected by the First Amendment, rather than for authorizing or directly threatening harm itself, which is not. *Planned Parenthood of the Columbia/Willamette, Inc. v. ACLA (PPCW IV)*, 244 F.3d 1007 (9th Cir.), *reh'g en banc granted*, 268 F.3d 908 (9th Cir.2001). The panel decided that it should evaluate the record independently to determine whether ACLA's statements could reasonably be construed as saying that ACLA, or its agents, would physically harm doctors who did not stop performing abortions. Having done so, the panel found that the jury's verdict could not stand.

We reheard the case en banc because these issues are obviously important. We now conclude that it was proper for the district court to adopt our long-standing law on "true threats" to define a "threat" for purposes of FACE. FACE itself requires that the threat of force be made with the intent to intimidate. Thus, the jury must have found that ACLA made statements to intimidate the physicians, reasonably foreseeing that physicians would interpret the statements as a serious expression of ACLA's intent to harm them because they provided reproductive health services. Construing the facts in the light most favorable to physicians, the verdict is supported by substantial evidence. ACLA was aware that a "wanted"-type poster would likely be interpreted as a serious threat of death or bodily harm by a doctor in the reproductive health services community who was identified on one, given the previous pattern of "WANTED" posters identifying a specific physician followed by that physician's murder. The same is true of the posting about these physicians on that part of the "Nuremberg Files" where lines were drawn through the names of doctors who provided abortion services and who had been killed or wounded. We are independently satisfied that to this limited extent, ACLA's conduct amounted to a true threat and is not protected speech.

As we see no reversible error on liability or in the equitable relief that was granted, we affirm. However, we remand for consideration of whether the punitive damages award comports with due process.

I

The facts are fully set out in the district court's order granting injunctive relief, *PPWC III*, 41 F.Supp.2d at 1131–1155, and we shall not belabor them. In sum:

On March 10, 1993, Michael Griffin shot and killed Dr. David Gunn as he entered an abortion clinic in Pensacola, Florida. Before this, a "WANTED" and an "unWANTED" poster with Gunn's name, photograph, address and other personal information were published. The "WANTED" poster describes Gunn as an abortionist and invites participation by prayer and fasting, by writing and calling him and sharing a willingness to help him leave his profession, and by asking him to stop doing abortions; the "unWANTED" poster states that he kills children at designated locations and "[t]o defenseless unborn babies Gunn in [sic] heavily armed and very dangerous." After Gunn's murder, Bray and Paul Hill (a non-party who was later convicted of murdering a different doctor) prepared a statement supporting Griffin's acquittal on a justifiable homicide theory, which ALM, Burnett, Crane, Dodds, Foreman, McMillan, Ramey and Stover joined.

On August 21, 1993, Dr. George Patterson, who operated the clinic where Gunn worked, was shot to death. A "WANTED" poster had been circulated prior to his murder, indicating where he performed abortions and that he had Gunn perform abortions for his Pensacola clinic.

In July 1994, Dr. John Bayard Britton was murdered by Paul Hill after being named on an "unWANTED" poster that Hill helped to prepare. One gives Britton's physical description together with his home and office addresses and phone numbers, and charges "crimes against humanity"; another also displays his picture and states that "he is considered armed and extremely dangerous to women and children. Pray that he is soon apprehended by the love of Jesus!!!" In addition to these items, a third version of the Britton "unWANTED" poster lists personal achievements and Britton's "crimes against humanity," also warning that "John Bayard Britton is considered armed and extremely dangerous, especialy [sic] to women and children." ALM, Bray, Burnett, Crane, McMillan, Ramey and Stover signed a petition supporting Hill.

Many pro-life activists in Operation Rescue condemned these acts of violence. As a result, ALM, Bray, Burnett, Crane, Foreman, McMillan, Ramey and Stover, who espoused a "pro-force" point of view, split off to form ACLA. Burnett observed, "if someone was to condemn any violence against abortion, they probably wouldn't have felt comfortable working with us." Organizational meetings were held in the spring of 1994, and ACLA's first event was held in August 1994. ACLA is based in Portland, Oregon, as is ALM. ALM publishes *Life Advocate*, a magazine that is distributed nationally and advocates the use of force to oppose the delivery of abortion services. Except for Bray, who authored *A Time to Kill* and served time in federal prison for conspiring to bomb ten clinics, the individual defendants were directors of ACLA and actively involved in its affairs. ALM commissioned and published Bray's book, noting that it "shows the connection between the [justifiable homicide] position and clinic destruction and the shootings of abortionists." Wysong and ACLA also drafted and circulated a "Contract on the Abortion

Industry," having deliberately chosen that language to allude to mafia hit contracts.

ACLA presented the Deadly Dozen poster during a January 25, 1995 press conference at the March for Life event in Washington, D.C. Bray, Burnett, Crane, Dodds, Foreman, McMillan, Murch, Ramey, Stover, Treshman and Wysong were there; Dreste later ratified the poster's release. This poster is captioned "GUILTY" at the top (which meant the same thing to Crane, who drafted it, as "wanted"), beneath which in slightly smaller print the poster indicates "OF CRIMES AGAINST HUMANITY." The poster continues: "Abortion was provided as a choice for East European and Jewish women by the (Nazi) National Socialist Regime, and was prosecuted during the Nuremberg Trials (1945–46) under Allied Control Order No. 10 as a 'war crime.'" Under the heading "THE DEADLY DOZEN," the poster identifies thirteen doctors of whom James Newhall, Elizabeth Newhall, and Warren Hern are three. The poster provides Hern's residence and the home address of James Newhall and Elizabeth Newhall; it also lists the name and home address of Dr. George Kabacy, a doctor who provided abortions at PPCW. It offers a "$5,000 REWARD" "for information leading to arrest, conviction and revocation of license to practice medicine." At the bottom the poster bears the legend "ABORTIONIST" in large, bold typeface. The day after the Deadly Dozen poster was released, the FBI offered protection to doctors identified on it and advised them to wear bulletproof vests and take other security precautions, which they did. Knowing this, ALM reprinted the poster in the March 1995 edition of its magazine *Life Advocate* under a cover with the "grim reaper" holding a scythe; Murch printed it in his newsletter *Salt & Light*; and ACLA republished the Deadly Dozen poster at events in August 1995 and January 1996.

ACLA released the Crist poster along with five others in August 1995 at the old federal courthouse in St. Louis where the *Dred Scott* decision had been handed down. Burnett, Crane, Dreste, McMillan, Ramey, Stover and Wysong attended the event. Three of the posters identify doctors; the others identify reproductive health care clinics, one of which was a Planned Parenthood affiliate where Crist worked. The Crist poster has "GUILTY" in large bold letters at the top followed by "OF CRIMES AGAINST HUMANITY" in smaller font. It also gives his home and work addresses; states "Please write, leaflet or picket his neighborhood to expose his blood guilt"; offers a "$500 REWARD" "to any ACLA organization that successfully persuades Crist to turn from his child killing through activities within ACLA guidelines"; and has "ABORTIONIST" in large bold type at the bottom.

At its January 1996 conference, ACLA displayed the Deadly Dozen poster, held a "White Rose Banquet" to honor prisoners convicted of anti-abortion violence, and introduced ALM's Paul deParrie to unveil the "Nuremberg Files." ACLA sent a hard copy of some of the Files to Neal Horsley (a nonparty) to post on the internet, and ACLA's name appeared on the Nuremberg Files website opened in January 1997. Approximately 200 people are listed under the label "ABORTIONISTS: the shooters," and 200 more are listed under Files for judges, politicians, law enforcement, spouses, and abortion rights supporters. Crist, Hern and the Newhalls are listed in the "abortionists" section, which bears the legend: "Black font (working); Greyed-out

Name (wounded); Strikethrough (fatality)." The names of Gunn, Patterson and Britton are struck through.

By January 1995 ACLA knew the effect that "WANTED," "unWANTED," or "GUILTY" posters had on doctors named in them. For example, in a September 1993 issue of *Life Advocate* which reported that an "unwanted" poster was being prepared for Britton, ALM remarked of the Gunn murder that it "sent shock waves of fear through the ranks of abortion providers across the country. As a result, many more doctors quit out of fear for their lives, and the ones who are left are scared stiff." Of another doctor who decided to quit performing abortions after circulation of a "Not Wanted" poster, Bray wrote that "it is clear to all who possess faculties capable of inductive analysis: he was bothered and afraid." Wysong also stated: "Listening to what abortionists said, abortionists who have quit the practice who are no longer killing babies but are now pro-life. They said the two things they feared the most were being sued for malpractice and having their picture put on a poster." And Burnett testified with respect to the danger that "wanted" or "guilty" posters pose to the lives of those who provide abortions: "I mean, if I was an abortionist, I would be afraid."

By January 1995 the physicians knew about the Gunn, Patterson and Britton murders and the posters that preceded each. Hern was terrified when his name appeared on the Deadly Dozen poster; as he put it: "The fact that wanted posters about these doctors had been circulated, prior to their assassination, and that the—that the posters, then, were followed by the doctor's assassination, emphasized for me the danger posed by this document, the Deadly Dozen List, which meant to me that—that, as night follows day, that my name was on this wanted poster ... and that I would be assassinated, as had the other doctors been assassinated." Hern interpreted the poster as meaning "Do what we tell you to do, or we will kill you. And they do." Crist was "truly frightened," and stopped practicing medicine for a while out of fear for his life. Dr. Elizabeth Newhall interpreted the Deadly Dozen poster as saying that if she didn't stop doing abortions, her life was at risk. Dr. James Newhall was "severely frightened" in light of the "clear pattern" of a wanted poster and a murder when there was "another wanted poster with my name on it."

The jury found for plaintiffs on all FACE claims, except for Bray and Treshman on the RICO claims.[2] The district court then considered equitable relief. It found that each defendant used intimidation as a means of interfering with the provision of reproductive health services; that each independently and as a co-conspirator published and distributed the Deadly Dozen poster, the Crist poster, and the Nuremberg Files; and that each acted with malice and specific intent in communicating true threats to kill, assault or do bodily harm to each of the plaintiffs to intimidate them from engaging in legal medical practices and procedures. The court found that the balance of hardships weighed "overwhelmingly" in plaintiffs' favor. It also found that the defendants' actions were not protected speech under the First Amend-

---

2. On the FACE claims, the jury awarded $39,656 to Crist, $14,429 to Hern, $15,797.98 to Elizabeth Newhall, $375 to James Newhall, $405,834.86 to PPCW, and $50,243 to PFWHC from each defendant as compensatory damages and $14.5 million to Crist, $13 million to Hern, $14 million to Elizabeth Newhall, $14 million to James Newhall, $29.5 million to PPCW, and $23.5 million to PFWHC in punitive damages.

ment. Accordingly, it issued a permanent injunction restraining defendants from threatening, with the specific intent to do so, any of the plaintiffs in violation of FACE; from publishing or distributing the Deadly Dozen poster and the Crist poster with specific intent to threaten the plaintiffs; from providing additional material concerning plaintiffs, with a specific intent to threaten, to the Nuremberg Files or similar web site; and from publishing or distributing the personally identifying information about the plaintiffs in the Files with a specific intent to threaten. The court also required defendants to turn over materials that are not in compliance with the injunction except for one copy of anything included in the record, which counsel was permitted to retain.

How should the Court Have decided this case? Why?

Chapter V

OBSCENITY

B. PROTECTING CHILDREN

1. CHILDREN AS CONSUMERS OF SEXUALLY–EXPLICIT MA-TERIAL

p. 332 (after question 4)

ASHCROFT v. AMERICAN CIVIL LIBERTIES UNION
122 S.Ct. 1700 (2002).

Justice Thomas announced the judgment of the Court and delivered the opinion of the Court with respect to Parts I, II, and IV, an opinion with respect to Parts III–A, III–C, and III–D, in which The Chief Justice and Justice Scalia join, and an opinion with respect to Part III–B, in which The Chief Justice, Justice O'Connor, and Justice Scalia join.

This case presents the narrow question whether the Child Online Protection Act's (COPA or Act) use of "community standards" to identify "material that is harmful to minors" violates the First Amendment. We hold that this aspect of COPA does not render the statute facially unconstitutional.

I

After our decision in *Reno v. American Civil Liberties Union*, Congress explored other avenues for restricting minors' access to pornographic material on the Internet. In particular, Congress passed and the President signed into law the Child Online Protection Act. COPA prohibits any person from "knowingly and with knowledge of the character of the material, in interstate or foreign commerce by means of the World Wide Web, mak[ing] any communication for commercial purposes that is available to any minor and that includes any material that is harmful to minors."

Apparently responding to our objections to the breadth of the CDA's coverage, Congress limited the scope of COPA's coverage in at least three ways. First, while the CDA applied to communications over the Internet as a whole, including, for example, e-mail messages, COPA applies only to material displayed on the World Wide Web. Second, unlike the CDA, COPA covers only communications made "for commercial purposes." And third, while the CDA prohibited "indecent" and "patently offensive" communications, COPA re-

7

stricts only the narrower category of "material that is harmful to minors." *Ibid.*

Drawing on the three-part test for obscenity set forth in Miller v. California, 413 U.S. 15 (1973), COPA defines "material that is harmful to minors" as

"any communication, picture, image, graphic image file, article, recording, writing, or other matter of any kind that is obscene or that—

"(A) the average person, applying contemporary community standards, would find, taking the material as a whole and with respect to minors, is designed to appeal to, or is designed to pander to, the prurient interest;

"(B) depicts, describes, or represents, in a manner patently offensive with respect to minors, an actual or simulated sexual act or sexual contact, an actual or simulated normal or perverted sexual act, or a lewd exhibition of the genitals or post-pubescent female breast; and

"(C) taken as a whole, lacks serious literary, artistic, political, or scientific value for minors." 47 U.S.C. § 231(e)(6).

Like the CDA, COPA also provides affirmative defenses to those subject to prosecution under the statute. An individual may qualify for a defense if he, "in good faith, has restricted access by minors to material that is harmful to minors—(A) by requiring the use of a credit card, debit account, adult access code, or adult personal identification number; (B) by accepting a digital certificate that verifies age; or (C) by any other reasonable measures that are feasible under available technology." Persons violating COPA are subject to both civil and criminal sanctions. A civil penalty of up to $50,000 may be imposed for each violation of the statute. Criminal penalties consist of up to six months in prison and/or a maximum fine of $50,000. An additional fine of $50,000 may be imposed for any intentional violation of the statute.

II

"[A]s a general matter, 'the First Amendment means that government has no power to restrict expression because of its message, its ideas, its subject matter, or its content.' " However, this principle, like other First Amendment principles, is not absolute. Obscene speech, for example, has long been held to fall outside the purview of the First Amendment. But this Court struggled in the past to define obscenity in a manner that did not impose an impermissible burden on protected speech. The difficulty resulted from the belief that "in the area of freedom of speech and press the courts must always remain sensitive to any infringement on genuinely serious literary, artistic, political, or scientific expression."

Ending over a decade of turmoil, this Court in *Miller* set forth the governing three-part test for assessing whether material is obscene and thus unprotected by the First Amendment: "(a) [W]hether 'the average person, applying contemporary community standards 'would find that the work, taken as a whole, appeals to the prurient interest; (b) whether the work depicts or describes, in a patently offensive way, sexual conduct specifically defined by the applicable state law; and (c) whether the work, taken as a whole, lacks serious literary, artistic, political, or scientific value."

Miller adopted the use of "community standards" from *Roth*, which repudiated an earlier approach for assessing objectionable material. "[T]he primary concern ... is to be certain that ... [material] will be judged by its impact on an average person, rather than a particularly susceptible or sensitive person—or indeed a totally insensitive one."

III

The Court of Appeals, however, concluded that this Court's prior community standards jurisprudence "has no applicability to the Internet and the Web" because "Web publishers are currently without the ability to control the geographic scope of the recipients of their communications." We therefore must decide whether this technological limitation renders COPA's reliance on community standards constitutionally infirm.

A

In addressing this question, the parties first dispute the nature of the community standards that jurors will be instructed to apply when assessing, in prosecutions under COPA, whether works appeal to the prurient interest of minors and are patently offensive with respect to minors.[1] Respondents contend that jurors will evaluate material using "local community standards" while petitioner maintains that jurors will not consider the community standards of any particular geographic area, but rather will be "instructed to consider the standards of the adult community as a whole, without geographic specification."

In the context of this case, which involves a facial challenge to a statute that has never been enforced, we do not think it prudent to engage in speculation as to whether certain hypothetical jury instructions would or would not be consistent with COPA, and deciding this case does not require us to do so. It is sufficient to note that community standards need not be defined by reference to a precise geographic area. See *Jenkins v. Georgia*, ("A State may choose to define an obscenity offense in terms of 'contemporary community standards' as defined in *Miller* without further specification ... or it may choose to define the standards in more precise geographic terms, as was done by California in *Miller*"). Absent geographic specification, a juror applying community standards will inevitably draw upon personal "knowledge of the community or vicinage from which he comes." Petitioner concedes the latter point and admits that, even if jurors were instructed under COPA to apply the standards of the adult population as a whole, the variance in community standards across the country could still cause juries in different locations to reach inconsistent conclusions as to whether a particular work is "harmful to minors."

---

1. Although the phrase "contemporary community standards" appears only in the "prurient interest" prong of the *Miller* test, see Miller v. California, 413 U.S. 15, 24 (1973), this Court has indicated that the "patently offensive" prong of the test is also a question of fact to be decided by a jury applying contemporary community standards. See, e.g., Pope v. Illinois, 481 U.S. 497, 500 (1987). The parties here therefore agree that even though "contemporary community standards" are similarly mentioned only in the "prurient interest" prong of COPA's harmful-to-minors definition jurors will apply "contemporary community standards" as well in evaluating whether material is "patently offensive with respect to minors."

B

Because juries would apply different standards across the country, and Web publishers currently lack the ability to limit access to their sites on a geographic basis, the Court of Appeals feared that COPA's "community standards" component would effectively force all speakers on the Web to abide by the "most puritan" community's standards. And such a requirement, the Court of Appeals concluded, "imposes an overreaching burden and restriction on constitutionally protected speech."

In evaluating the constitutionality of the CDA, this Court expressed a similar concern over that statute's use of community standards to identify patently offensive material on the Internet. We noted that "the 'community standards' criterion as applied to the Internet means that any communication available to a nationwide audience will be judged by the standards of the community most likely to be offended by the message." The Court of Appeals below relied heavily on this observation, stating that it was "not persuaded that the Supreme Court's concern with respect to the 'community standards' criterion has been sufficiently remedied by Congress in COPA."

The CDA's use of community standards to identify patently offensive material, however, was particularly problematic in light of that statute's unprecedented breadth and vagueness. The statute covered communications depicting or describing "sexual or excretory activities or organs" that were "patently offensive as measured by contemporary community standards"—a standard somewhat similar to the second prong of *Miller*'s three-prong test. But the CDA did not include any limiting terms resembling *Miller*'s additional two prongs. It neither contained any requirement that restricted material appeal to the prurient interest nor excluded from the scope of its coverage works with serious literary, artistic, political, or scientific value. The tremendous breadth of the CDA magnified the impact caused by differences in community standards across the country, restricting Web publishers from openly displaying a significant amount of material that would have constituted protected speech in some communities across the country but run afoul of community standards in others.

COPA, by contrast, does not appear to suffer from the same flaw because it applies to significantly less material than did the CDA and defines the harmful-to-minors material restricted by the statute in a manner parallel to the *Miller* definition of obscenity. These additional two restrictions substantially limit the amount of material covered by the statute. Material appeals to the prurient interest, for instance, only if it is in some sense erotic.[2] Of even more significance, however, is COPA's exclusion of material with serious value for minors. See 47 U.S.C. § 231(e)(6)(C). In *Reno*, we emphasized that the serious value "requirement is particularly important because, unlike the 'patently offensive' and 'prurient interest' criteria, it is not judged by contem-

---

2. Justice STEVENS argues that the "prurient interest" prong does not "substantially narrow the category of images covered" by COPA because "[a]rguably every depiction of nudity—partial or full—is in some sense erotic with respect to minors," (dissenting opinion) (emphasis in original). We do not agree. For example, we have great difficulty understanding how pictures of a war victim's wounded nude body could reasonably be described under the vast majority of circumstances as erotic, especially when evaluated from the perspective of minors. See Webster's Ninth New Collegiate Dictionary 422 (1991) (defining erotic as "of, devoted to, or tending to arouse sexual love or desire").

porary community standards." Thus, the serious value requirement "allows appellate courts to impose some limitations and regularity on the definition by setting, as a matter of law, a national floor for socially redeeming value."[3]

C

When the scope of an obscenity statute's coverage is sufficiently narrowed by a "serious value" prong and a "prurient interest" prong, we have held that requiring a speaker disseminating material to a national audience to observe varying community standards does not violate the First Amendment. In *Hamling v. United States*, 418 U.S. 87 (1974), this Court considered the constitutionality of applying community standards to the determination of whether material is obscene.

Like respondents here, the dissenting opinion in *Hamling* argued that it was unconstitutional for a federal statute to rely on community standards to regulate speech. Justice Brennan maintained that "[n]ational distributors choosing to send their products in interstate travels [would] be forced to cope with the community standards of every hamlet into which their goods [might] wander." As a result, he claimed that the inevitable result of this situation would be "debilitating self-censorship that abridges the First Amendment rights of the people."

This Court, however, rejected Justice Brennan's argument that the federal mail statute unconstitutionally compelled speakers choosing to distribute materials on a national basis to tailor their messages to the least tolerant community: "The fact that distributors of allegedly obscene materials may be subjected to varying community standards in the various federal judicial districts into which they transmit the materials does not render a federal statute unconstitutional."

Fifteen years later, *Hamling*'s holding was reaffirmed in *Sable. Sable* addressed the constitutionality of a statutory provision prohibiting the use of telephones to make obscene or indecent communications for commercial purposes. The petitioner in that case, a "dial-a-porn" operator, challenged, in part, that portion of the statute banning obscene phone messages. Like respondents here, the "dial-a-porn" operator argued that reliance on community standards to identify obscene material impermissibly compelled "message senders ... to tailor all their messages to the least tolerant community." Relying on *Hamling*, however, this Court once again rebuffed this attack on the use of community standards in a federal statute of national scope: "There is no constitutional barrier under *Miller* to prohibiting communications that are obscene in some communities under local standards even though they are not obscene in others. *If Sable's audience is comprised of different communities with different local standards, Sable ultimately bears the burden of complying with the prohibition on obscene messages.*" (emphasis added).

---

3. Justice STEVENS contends that COPA's serious value prong only marginally limits the sweep of the statute because it does not protect all material with serious value but just those works with serious value for minors. His dissenting opinion, however, does not refer to any evidence supporting this counterintuitive assertion, and there is certainly none in the record suggesting that COPA restricts about the same amount of material as did the CDA. Moreover, Justice STEVENS does not dispute that COPA's "serious value" prong serves the important purpose of allowing appellate courts to set "as a matter of law, a national floor for socially redeeming value."

The Court of Appeals below concluded that *Hamling* and *Sable* "are easily distinguished from the present case" because in both of those cases "the defendants had the ability to control the distribution of controversial material with respect to the geographic communities into which they released it" whereas "Web publishers have no such comparable control." In neither *Hamling* nor *Sable*, however, was the speaker's ability to target the release of material into particular geographic areas integral to the legal analysis. In *Hamling*, the ability to limit the distribution of material to targeted communities was not mentioned, let alone relied upon, and in *Sable*, a dial-a-porn operator's ability to screen incoming calls from particular areas was referenced only as a supplemental point. In the latter case, this Court made no effort to evaluate how burdensome it would have been for dial-a-porn operators to tailor their messages to callers from thousands of different communities across the Nation, instead concluding that the burden of complying with the statute rested with those companies.

While Justice KENNEDY and Justice STEVENS question the applicability of this Court's community standards jurisprudence to the Internet, we do not believe that the medium's "unique characteristics" justify adopting a different approach than that set forth in *Hamling* and *Sable*. If a publisher chooses to send its material into a particular community, this Court's jurisprudence teaches that it is the publisher's responsibility to abide by that community's standards. The publisher's burden does not change simply because it decides to distribute its material to every community in the Nation. Nor does it change because the publisher may wish to speak only to those in a "community where *avant garde* culture is the norm," but nonetheless utilizes a medium that transmits its speech from coast to coast. If a publisher wishes for its material to be judged only by the standards of particular communities, then it need only take the simple step of utilizing a medium that enables it to target the release of its material into those communities.[4]

Respondents offer no other grounds upon which to distinguish this case from *Hamling* and *Sable*. While those cases involved obscenity rather than material that is harmful to minors, we have no reason to believe that the practical effect of varying community standards under COPA, given the statute's definition of "material that is harmful to minors," is significantly greater than the practical effect of varying community standards under federal obscenity statutes. It is noteworthy, for example, that respondents fail to point out even a single exhibit in the record as to which coverage under COPA would depend upon which community in the country evaluated the material. As a result, if we were to hold COPA unconstitutional because of its use of community standards, federal obscenity statutes would likely also be unconstitutional as applied to the Web,[5] a result in substantial tension with our prior suggestion that the application of the CDA to obscene speech was constitutional.

---

4. In addition, COPA does not, as Justice KENNEDY suggests, "foreclose an entire medium of expression." While Justice KENNEDY and Justice STEVENS repeatedly imply that COPA banishes from the Web material deemed harmful to minors by reference to community standards, the statute does no such thing. It only requires that such material be placed behind adult identification screens

5. Obscene material, for instance, explicitly falls within the coverage of COPA.

D

Respondents argue that COPA is "unconstitutionally overbroad" because it will require Web publishers to shield some material behind age verification screens that could be displayed openly in many communities across the Nation if Web speakers were able to limit access to their sites on a geographic basis. "[T]o prevail in a facial challenge," however, "it is not enough for a plaintiff to show 'some' overbreadth." Rather, "the overbreadth of a statute must not only be real, but substantial as well." At this stage of the litigation, respondents have failed to satisfy this burden, at least solely as a result of COPA's reliance on community standards. Because Congress has narrowed the range of content restricted by COPA in a manner analogous to *Miller's* definition of obscenity, we conclude, consistent with our holdings in *Hamling* and *Sable*, that any variance caused by the statute's reliance on community standards is not substantial enough to violate the First Amendment.

IV

The scope of our decision today is quite limited. We hold only that COPA's reliance on community standards to identify "material that is harmful to minors" does not by itself render the statute substantially overbroad for purposes of the First Amendment. We do not express any view as to whether COPA suffers from substantial overbreadth for other reasons, whether the statute is unconstitutionally vague, or whether the District Court correctly concluded that the statute likely will not survive strict scrutiny analysis once adjudication of the case is completed below. While respondents urge us to resolve these questions at this time, prudence dictates allowing the Court of Appeals to first examine these difficult issues. Petitioner does not ask us to vacate the preliminary injunction entered by the District Court, and in any event, we could not do so without addressing matters yet to be considered by the Court of Appeals. As a result, the Government remains enjoined from enforcing COPA absent further action by the Court of Appeals or the District Court.

For the foregoing reasons, we vacate the judgment of the Court of Appeals and remand the case for further proceedings.

JUSTICE O'CONNOR, concurring in part and concurring in the judgment.

I agree with the plurality that even if obscenity on the Internet is defined in terms of local community standards, respondents have not shown that the Child Online Protection Act (COPA) is overbroad solely on the basis of the variation in the standards of different communities. Like Justice BREYER, however, I write separately to express my views on the constitutionality and desirability of adopting a national standard for obscenity for regulation of the Internet.

The plurality's opinion argues that, even under local community standards, the variation between the most and least restrictive communities is not so great with respect to the narrow category of speech covered by COPA as to, alone, render the statute substantially overbroad. I agree, given respondents' failure to provide examples of materials that lack literary, artistic, political, and scientific value for minors, which would nonetheless result in variation among communities judging the other elements of the test. Respondents' examples of material for which community standards would vary include such things as the appropriateness of sex education and the desirability of adoption by same-sex couples. Material addressing the latter topic, however, seems highly unlikely to be seen to appeal to the prurient interest in any community, and educational material like the former must, on any objective inquiry, have scientific value for minors.

But respondents' failure to prove substantial overbreadth on a facial challenge in this case still leaves open the possibility that the use of local community standards will cause problems for regulation of obscenity on the Internet, for adults as well as children, in future cases. In an as-applied challenge, for instance, individual litigants may still dispute that the standards of a community more restrictive than theirs should apply to them. And in future facial challenges to regulation of obscenity on the Internet, litigants may make a more convincing case for substantial overbreadth. Where adult speech is concerned, for instance, there may in fact be a greater degree of disagreement about what is patently offensive or appeals to the prurient interest.

Nor do I think such future cases can be resolved by application of the approach we took in *Hamling* and *Sable*. I agree with Justice KENNEDY that, given Internet speakers' inability to control the geographic location of their audience, expecting them to bear the burden of controlling the recipients of their speech, as we did in *Hamling* and *Sable*, may be entirely too much to ask, and would potentially suppress an inordinate amount of expression. For these reasons, adoption of a national standard is necessary in my view for any reasonable regulation of Internet obscenity.

Our precedents do not forbid adoption of a national standard. Local community-based standards originated with *Miller v. California*. In that case, we approved jury instructions that based the relevant "community standards" on those of the State of California rather than on the Nation as a whole. In doing so, we held that "[n]othing in the First Amendment requires" that a jury consider national standards when determining if something is obscene as a matter of fact. The First Amendment, we held, did not require that "the people of Maine or Mississippi accept public depiction of conduct found tolerable in Las Vegas, or New York City." But we said nothing about the constitutionality of jury instructions that would contemplate a national standard—i.e., requiring that the people who live in all of these places hold themselves to what the nationwide community of adults would find was patently offensive and appealed to the prurient interest.

Later, in *Jenkins v. Georgia* we confirmed that "*Miller* approved the use of [instructions based on local standards]; it did not mandate their use." The instructions we approved in that case charged the jury with applying "community standards" without designating any particular "community." In holding that a State may define the obscenity standard by stating the *Miller* standard without further specification *Jenkins* left open the possibility that jurors would apply any number of standards, including a national standard, in evaluating material's obscenity.

To be sure, the Court in *Miller* also stated that a national standard might be "unascertainable," and "[un]realistic." But where speech on the Internet is concerned, I do not share that skepticism. It is true that our Nation is diverse, but many local communities encompass a similar diversity. For instance, in *Miller* itself, the jury was instructed to consider the standards of the entire State of California, a large and diverse State that includes both Berkeley and Bakersfield. If the *Miller* Court believed generalizations about the standards of the people of California were possible, and that jurors would be capable of assessing them, it is difficult to believe that similar generalizations are not also possible for the Nation as a whole. Moreover, the existence of the Internet, and its facilitation of national dialogue, has itself made jurors more aware of the views of adults in other parts of the United States. Although jurors asked to evaluate the obscenity of speech based on a national standard will inevitably base their assessments to some extent on their experience of their local communities, I agree with Justice BREYER that the lesser degree of variation that would result is inherent in the jury system and does not necessarily pose a First Amendment problem. In my view, a national standard is not only constitutionally permissible, but also reasonable.

While I would prefer that the Court resolve the issue before it by explicitly adopting a national standard for defining obscenity on the Internet, given respondents' failure to demonstrate substantial overbreadth due solely to the variation between local communities, I join Parts I, II, III–B, and IV of Justice THOMAS' opinion and the judgment.

JUSTICE BREYER, concurring in part and concurring in the judgment.

I write separately because I believe that Congress intended the statutory word "community" to refer to the Nation's adult community taken as a whole, not to geographically separate local areas. The statutory language does not explicitly describe the specific "community" to which it refers. It says only that the "average person, applying contemporary community standards" must find that the "material as a whole and with respect to minors, is designed to appeal to, or is designed to pander to, the prurient interest...."

In the statute's legislative history, however, Congress made clear that it did not intend this ambiguous statutory phrase to refer to separate standards that might differ significantly among different communities. The relevant House of Representatives Report says:

> "The Committee recognizes that the applicability of community standards in the context of the Web is controversial, *but understands it as an 'adult' standard, rather than a 'geographic' standard, and one that is reasonably constant among adults in America with respect to what is suitable for minors*." (emphasis added).

This statement, reflecting what apparently was a uniform view within Congress, makes clear that the standard, and the relevant community, is national and adult. At the same time, this view of the statute avoids the need to examine the serious First Amendment problem that would otherwise exist. To read the statute as adopting the community standards of every locality in the United States would provide the most puritan of communities with a heckler's Internet veto affecting the rest of the Nation. The technical difficulties associated with efforts to confine Internet material to particular geographic areas make the problem particularly serious. A nationally uniform adult-based standard—which Congress, in its Committee Report, said that it intended—significantly alleviates any special need for First Amendment protection. Of course some regional variation may remain, but any such variations are inherent in a system that draws jurors from a local geographic area and they are not, from the perspective of the First Amendment, problematic.

For these reasons I do not join Part III of Justice THOMAS' opinion, although I agree with much of the reasoning set forth in Parts III–B and III–D, insofar as it explains the conclusion to which I just referred, namely that variation reflecting application of the same national standard by different local juries does not violate the First Amendment.

JUSTICE KENNEDY, with whom JUSTICE SOUTER and JUSTICE GINSBURG join, concurring in the judgment.

I

If a law restricts substantially more speech than is justified, it may be subject to a facial challenge. There is a very real likelihood that the Child Online Protection Act (COPA or Act) is overbroad and cannot survive such a challenge. Indeed, content-based regulations like this one are presumptively invalid abridgements of the freedom of speech. Yet COPA is a major federal statute, enacted in the wake of our previous determination that its predecessor violated the First Amendment. See *Reno*. Congress and the President were aware of our decision, and we should assume that in seeking to comply with it they have given careful consideration to the constitutionality of the new enactment. For these reasons, even if this facial challenge appears to have considerable merit, the Judiciary must proceed with caution and identify overbreadth with care before invalidating the Act.

In this case, the District Court issued a preliminary injunction against enforcement of COPA, finding it too broad across several dimensions. The Court of Appeals affirmed, but on a different ground. COPA defines "material that is harmful to minors" by reference to "contemporary community standards," and on the theory that these vary from place to place, the Court of Appeals held that the definition dooms the statute "without reference to its other provisions." The Court of Appeals found it unnecessary to construe the rest of the Act or address the District Court's reasoning.

This single, broad proposition, stated and applied at such a high level of generality, cannot suffice to sustain the Court of Appeals' ruling. To observe only that community standards vary across the country is to ignore the antecedent question: community standards as to what? Whether the national variation in community standards produces overbreadth requiring invalidation of COPA depends on the breadth of COPA's coverage and on what community standards are being invoked. Only by identifying the universe of speech burdened by COPA is it possible to discern whether national variation in community standards renders the speech restriction overbroad. In short, the ground on which the Court of Appeals relied cannot be separated from those that it overlooked.

The statute, for instance, applies only to "communication for commercial purposes." The Court of Appeals, however, did not consider the amount of commercial communication, the number of commercial speakers, or the character of commercial speech covered by the Act. Likewise, the statute's definition of "harmful to minors" requires material to be judged "as a whole." The notion of judging work as a whole is familiar in other media, but more difficult to define on the World Wide Web. It is unclear whether what is to be judged as a whole is a single image on a Web page, a whole Web page, an entire multipage Web site, or an interlocking set of Web sites. Some examination of the group of covered speakers and the categories of covered speech is necessary in order to comprehend the extent of the alleged overbreadth. The Court of Appeals found that COPA in effect subjects every Internet speaker to the standards of the most puritanical community in the United States. This concern is a real one, but it alone cannot suffice to invalidate COPA without careful examination of the speech and the speakers within the ambit of the Act. For this reason, I join the judgment of the Court vacating the opinion of the Court of Appeals and remanding for consideration of the statute as a whole. Unlike Justice THOMAS, however, I would not assume that the Act is narrow enough to render the national variation in community standards unproblematic. Indeed, if the District Court correctly construed the statute across its other dimensions, then the variation in community standards might well justify enjoining enforcement of the Act. I would leave that question to the Court of Appeals in the first instance.

II

The nub of the problem is, as the Court has said, that "the 'community standards' criterion as applied to the Internet means that any communication available to a nationwide audience will be judged by the standards of the community most likely to be offended by the message." *Reno*. If material might be considered harmful to minors in any community in the United States, then the material is covered by COPA, at least when viewed in that place. This observation was the linchpin of the Court of Appeals' analysis, and we must now consider whether it alone suffices to support the holding below.

The quoted sentence from *Reno* was not casual dicta; rather, it was one rationale for the holding of the case. In *Reno*, the Court found "[t]he breadth of [COPA's predecessor] ... wholly unprecedented," in part because of variation in community standards. The Court also relied on that variation to assess the strength of the Government's interest, which it found "not equally strong throughout the coverage of this broad statute." The Court illustrated the point with an example: A parent who e-mailed birth control information to his 17–year-old child at college might violate the Act, "even though neither he, his child, nor anyone in their home community found the material 'indecent' or 'patently offensive,' if the college town's community thought otherwise." Variation in community standards rendered the statute broader than the scope of the Government's own expressed compelling interest.

It is true, as Justice THOMAS points out that requiring a speaker addressing a national audience to meet varying community standards does not always violate the First Amendment. See *Hamling*, *Sable* (obscene phone messages). These cases, however, are of limited utility in analyzing the one before us, because each mode of expression has its own unique characteristics, and each "must be assessed for First Amendment purposes by standards suited to it." Indeed, when Congress purports to abridge the freedom of a new medium, we must be particularly attentive to its distinct attributes, for "differences in the characteristics of new media justify ... differences in the First Amendment standards applied to them." The economics and the technology of each medium affect both the burden of a speech restriction and the Government's interest in maintaining it.

In this case the District Court found as a fact that "[o]nce a provider posts its content on the Internet and chooses to make it available to all, it generally cannot prevent that content from entering any geographic community." By contrast, in upholding a ban on obscene phone messages, we emphasized that the speaker could "hire operators to determine the source of the calls or engag[e] with the telephone company to arrange for the screening and blocking of out-of-area calls or fin[d] another means for providing messages compatible with community standards." *Sable*. And if we did not make the same point in *Hamling*, that is likely because it is so obvious that mailing lends itself to geographic restriction. A publisher who uses the mails can choose the location of his audience.

The economics and technology of Internet communication differ in important ways from those of telephones and mail. Paradoxically, as the District Court found, it is easy and cheap to reach a worldwide audience on the Internet, but expensive if not impossible to reach a geographic subset. A Web publisher in a community where *avant garde* culture is the norm may have no desire to reach a national market; he may wish only to speak to his neighbors; nevertheless, if an eavesdropper in a more traditional, rural community chooses to listen in, there is nothing the publisher can do. As a practical matter, COPA makes the eavesdropper the arbiter of propriety on the Web. And it is no answer to say that the speaker should "take the simple step of utilizing a [different] medium." (principal opinion of THOMAS, J.). "Our prior decisions have voiced particular concern with laws that foreclose an entire medium of expression.... [T]he danger they pose to the freedom of speech is readily apparent—by eliminating a common means of speaking, such measures can suppress too much speech."

Justice BREYER would alleviate the problem of local variation in community standards by construing the statute to comprehend the "Nation's adult community taken as a whole," rather than the local community from which the jury is drawn.

There is one statement in a House Committee Report to this effect, "reflecting," Justice BREYER writes, "what apparently was a uniform view within Congress." The statement, perhaps, reflects the view of a majority of one House committee, but there is no reason to believe that it reflects the view of a majority of the House of Representatives, let alone the "uniform view within Congress."

In any event, we need not decide whether the statute invokes local or national community standards to conclude that vacatur and remand are in order. If the statute does incorporate some concept of national community standards, the actual standard applied is bound to vary by community nevertheless, as the Attorney General concedes. The national variation in community standards constitutes a particular burden on Internet speech.

III

The question that remains is whether this observation "by itself" suffices to enjoin the Act. I agree with the Court that it does not. We cannot know whether variation in community standards renders the Act substantially overbroad without first assessing the extent of the speech covered and the variations in community standards with respect to that speech.

First, the breadth of the Act itself will dictate the degree of overbreadth caused by varying community standards. Indeed, Justice THOMAS sees this point and uses it in an attempt to distinguish the Communications Decency Act of 1996, which was at issue in *Reno.* To explain the ways in which COPA is narrower than the CDA, Justice THOMAS finds that he must construe sections of COPA elided by the Court of Appeals. Though I agree with the necessity for doing so, Justice THOMAS' interpretation—undertaken without substantial arguments or briefing—is not altogether persuasive, and I would leave this task to the Court of Appeals in the first instance. As this case comes to us, once it is accepted that we cannot strike down the Act based merely on the phrase "contemporary community standards," we should go no further than to vacate and remand for a more comprehensive analysis of the Act.

Second, community standards may have different degrees of variation depending on the question posed to the community. Defining the scope of the Act, therefore, is not relevant merely to the absolute number of Web pages covered, as Justice STEVENS suggests, it is also relevant to the proportion of overbreadth, "judged in relation to the statute's plainly legitimate sweep." Because this issue was "virtually ignored by the parties and the amicus" in the Court of Appeals, we have no information on the question. Instead, speculation meets speculation. On the one hand, the Court of Appeals found "no evidence to suggest that adults everywhere in America would share the same standards for determining what is harmful to minors." On the other hand, Justice THOMAS finds "no reason to believe that the practical effect of varying community standards under COPA ... is significantly greater than the practical effect of varying standards under federal obscenity statutes." When a key issue has "no evidence" on one side and "no reason to believe" the other, it is a good indication that we should vacate for further consideration.

The District Court attempted a comprehensive analysis of COPA and its various dimensions of potential overbreadth. The Court of Appeals, however, believed that its own analysis of "contemporary community standards" obviated all other concerns. It dismissed the District Court's analysis in a footnote:

> "[W]e do not find it necessary to address the District Court's analysis of the definition of 'commercial purposes'; whether the breadth of the forms of content covered by COPA could have been more narrowly tailored; whether the affirmative defenses impose too great a burden on Web publishers or whether those affirmative defenses should have been included as elements of the crime itself; whether COPA's inclusion of criminal as well as civil penalties was excessive; whether COPA is designed to include communications made in chat rooms, discussion groups and links to other Web sites; whether the government is entitled to so restrict communications when children will continue to be able to access foreign Web sites and other sources of material that is harmful to them; what taken 'as a whole' should mean in the context of the Web and the Internet; or whether the statute's failure to distinguish between material that is harmful to a six year old versus a sixteen year old is problematic."

As I have explained, however, any problem caused by variation in community standards cannot be evaluated in a vacuum. In order to discern whether the variation creates substantial overbreadth, it is necessary to know what speech COPA regulates and what community standards it invokes.

IV

In summary, the breadth of the Act depends on the issues discussed above, and the significance of varying community standards depends, in turn, on the breadth of the Act. The Court of Appeals was correct to focus on the national variation in community standards, which can constitute a substantial burden on Internet communication; and its ultimate conclusion may prove correct. There may be grave doubts that COPA is consistent with the First Amendment; but we should not make that determination with so many questions unanswered. The Court of Appeals should undertake a comprehensive analysis in the first instance.

JUSTICE STEVENS, dissenting.

Appeals to prurient interests are commonplace on the Internet, as in older media. Many of those appeals lack serious value for minors as well as adults. Some are offensive to certain viewers but welcomed by others. For decades, our cases have recognized that the standards for judging their acceptability vary from viewer to viewer and from community to community. Those cases developed the requirement that communications should be protected if they do not violate contemporary community standards. In its original form, the community standard provided a shield for communications that are offensive only to the least tolerant members of society. Thus, the Court "has emphasized on more than one occasion that a principal concern in requiring that a judgment be made on the basis of 'contemporary community standards' is to assure that the material is judged neither on the basis of each juror's personal opinion, nor by its effect on a particularly sensitive or insensitive person or group." In the context of the Internet, however, community standards become a sword, rather than a shield. If a prurient appeal is offensive in a puritan village, it may be a crime to post it on the World Wide Web.

The Child Online Protection Act (COPA) restricts access by adults as well as children to materials that are "harmful to minors." COPA is a substantial improvement over its predecessor, the Communications Decency Act of 1996(CDA), which we held unconstitutional five years ago in *Reno v. American Civil Liberties Union (ACLU I)*. Congress has thoughtfully addressed several of the First Amendment problems that we identified in that case. Nevertheless, COPA preserves the use of contemporary community standards to define which materials are harmful to minors. As we explained in *ACLU I*, "the 'community standards' criterion as applied to the Internet means that any communication available to a nationwide audience will be judged by the standards of the community most likely to be offended by the message."

We have recognized that the State has a compelling interest in protecting minors from harmful speech, and on one occasion we upheld a restriction on indecent speech that was made available to the general public, because it could be accessed by minors, *Pacifica*. Our decision in that case was influenced by the distinctive characteristics of the broadcast medium, as well as the expertise of the agency, and the narrow scope of its order. ("[R]egardless of the strength of the government's interest" in protecting children, "[t]he level of discourse reaching a mailbox simply cannot be limited to that which would be suitable for a sandbox") *Sable, Butler v. Michigan*.

Petitioner relies on our decision in *Ginsberg v. New York*, for the proposition that Congress can prohibit the display of materials that are harmful to minors. But the statute upheld in Ginsberg prohibited selling indecent materials directly to children, whereas the speech implicated here is simply posted on a medium that is accessible to both adults and children. Like the restriction on indecent "dial-a-porn" numbers invalidated in *Sable*, the prohibition against mailing advertisements for contraceptives invalidated in Bolger, and the ban against selling adult books found impermissible in *Butler*, COPA seeks to limit protected speech that is not targeted at children, simply because it can be obtained by them while surfing the Web. In evaluating the overbreadth of such a statute, we should be mindful of Justice Frankfurter's admonition not to "burn the house to roast the pig," *Butler*.

COPA not only restricts speech that is made available to the general public, it also covers a medium in which speech cannot be segregated to avoid communities where it is likely to be considered harmful to minors. The Internet presents a unique forum for communication because information, once posted, is accessible everywhere on the network at once. The speaker cannot control access based on the location of the listener, nor can it choose the pathways through which its speech is transmitted. By approving the use of community standards in this context, Justice THOMAS endorses a construction of COPA that has "the intolerable consequence of denying some sections of the country access to material, there deemed acceptable, which in others might be considered offensive to prevailing community standards of decency."

If the material were forwarded through the mails, as in *Hamling*, or over the telephone, as in *Sable*, the sender could avoid destinations with the most restrictive standards. Indeed, in *Sable*, we upheld the application of community standards to a nationwide medium because the speaker was "free to tailor its messages ... to the communities it *chooses* to serve," by either "hir [ing] operators to determine the source of the calls ... [or] arrang[ing] for the screening and blocking of out-of-area calls." (emphasis added). Our conclusion that it was permissible for the speaker to bear the ultimate burden of compliance assumed that such compliance was at least possible without requiring the speaker to choose another medium or to limit its speech to what all would find acceptable. Given the undisputed fact that a provider who posts material on the Internet cannot prevent it from entering any geographic community a law that criminalizes a particular communication in just a handful of destinations effectively prohibits transmission of that message to all of the 176.5 million Americans that have access to the Internet. In light of this fundamental difference in technologies, the rules applicable to the mass mailing of an obscene montage or to obscene dial-a-porn should not be used to judge the legality of messages on the World Wide Web.[6]

6. It is hardly a solution to say, as Justice THOMAS suggests that a speaker need only choose a different medium in order to avoid having its speech judged by the least tolerant community. Our overbreadth doctrine would quickly become a toothless protection if we were to hold that substituting a more limited forum for expression is an acceptable price to pay. Since a content-based restriction is presumptively invalid, I would place the burden on parents to "take the simple step of utilizing a medium that enables," them to avoid this

In his attempt to fit this case within the framework of *Hamling* and *Sable*, Justice THOMAS overlooks the more obvious comparison—namely, the CDA invalidated in *ACLU I*. When we confronted a similar attempt by Congress to limit speech on the Internet based on community standards, we explained that because Web publishers cannot control who accesses their Web sites, using community standards to regulate speech on the Internet creates an overbreadth problem. "[T]he 'community standards' criterion as applied to the Internet means that any communication available to a nationwide audience will be judged by the standards of the community most likely to be offended by the message."[7]

Justice THOMAS points to several other provisions in COPA to argue that any overbreadth will be rendered insubstantial by the rest of the statute. These provisions afford little reassurance, however, as they only marginally limit the sweep of the statute. It is true that, in addition to COPA's "appeals to the prurient interest of minors" prong, the material must be "patently offensive with respect to minors" and it must lack "serious literary, artistic, political, or scientific value for minors." Nonetheless, the "patently offensive" prong is judged according to contemporary community standards as well. Whatever disparity exists between various communities' assessment of the content that appeals to the prurient interest of minors will surely be matched by their differing opinions as to whether descriptions of sexual acts or depictions of nudity are patently offensive with respect to minors. Nor does the requirement that the material be "in some sense erotic" substantially narrow the category of images covered. Arguably every depiction of nudity— partial or full—is in some sense erotic with respect to minors.

Petitioner's argument that the "serious value" prong minimizes the statute's overbreadth is also unpersuasive. Even though the serious value prong limits the total amount of speech covered by the statute, it remains true that there is a significant amount of protected speech within the category of materials that have no serious value for minors. That speech is effectively prohibited whenever the least tolerant communities find it harmful to minors.[8] While the objective nature of the inquiry may eliminate any worry that

material before requiring the speaker to find another forum.

7. Justice BREYER seeks to avoid the problem by effectively reading the phrase "contemporary national standards" into the statute. While the legislative history of COPA provides some support for this reading, it is contradicted by the clear text of the statute, which directs jurors to consider "community" standards. This phrase is a term of art that has taken on a particular meaning in light of our precedent. Although we have never held that applying a national standard would be constitutionally impermissible, we have said that asking a jury to do so is "an exercise in futility," *Miller*, and that "[a] juror is entitled to draw on his own knowledge of the views of the average person in the community or vicinage from which he comes for making the required determination." Any lingering doubts about the meaning of the phrase were certainly dispelled by our discussion of the issue in *ACLU I*

and we presume that Congress legislates against the backdrop of our decisions. Therefore, Justice THOMAS has correctly refused to rewrite the statute to substitute a standard that Congress clearly did not choose. And even if the Court were willing to do so, we would still have to acknowledge, as petitioner does, that jurors instructed to apply a national, or adult, standard, will reach widely different conclusions throughout the country.

8. The Court also notes that the limitation to communications made for commercial purposes narrows the category of speech as compared to the CDA. While it is certainly true that this condition limits the scope of the statute, the phrase "commercial purposes" is somewhat misleading. The definition of commercial purposes covers anyone who generates revenue from advertisements or merchandise, regardless of the amount of advertising or whether the advertisements or products are related to the images that allegedly are harm-the serious value determination will be made by the least tolerant community, it does not change the fact that, within the subset of images deemed to have no serious value for minors, the decision whether minors and adults throughout the country will have access to that speech will still be made by the most restrictive community. The Court also notes that the limitation to communications made for commercial purposes narrows the category of speech as compared to the CDA. While it is certainly true that this condition limits the scope of the statute, the phrase "commercial purposes" is somewhat misleading. The definition of commercial purposes covers anyone who generates revenue from advertisements or merchandise, regardless of the amount of advertising or whether the advertisements or products are related to the images that allegedly are harmful to minors. As the District Court noted: "There is nothing in the text of the COPA, however, that limits its applicability to so-called commercial pornographers only; indeed, the text of COPA imposes liability on a speaker who knowingly makes any communication for commercial purposes 'that includes any material that is harmful to minors.'" In the context of the Internet, this is hardly a serious limitation. A 1998 study, for example, found that 83 percent of Web sites contain commercial content. Interestingly, this same study found that only 1.5 percent of the 2.8 million sites cataloged contained pornographic content.

Justice KENNEDY makes a similar misstep when he ties the overbreadth inquiry to questions about the scope of the other provisions of the statute. According to his view, we cannot determine whether the statute is substantially overbroad based on its use of community standards without first determining how much of the speech on the Internet is saved by the other restrictions in the statute. But this represents a fundamental misconception of our overbreadth doctrine. As Justice White explained in *Broadrick v. Oklahoma* "the overbreadth of a statute must not only be real, but substantial as well, *judged in relation to the statute's plainly legitimate sweep.*" (Emphasis added.) Regardless of how the Court of Appeals interprets the "commercial purposes" or "as a whole" provisions on remand, the question we must answer is whether the statute restricts a substantial amount of protected speech relative to its legitimate sweep by virtue of the fact that it uses community standards. These other provisions may reduce the absolute number of Web pages covered by the statute, but even the narrowest version of the statute abridges a substantial amount of protected speech that many communities would not find harmful to minors. Because Web speakers cannot limit access to those specific communities, the statute is substantially overbroad regardless of how its other provisions are construed.

Justice THOMAS acknowledges, and petitioner concedes, that juries across the country will apply different standards and reach different conclusions about whether particular works are harmful to minors. We recognized as much in *ACLU I* when we noted that "discussions about prison rape or safe sexual practices, artistic images that include nude subjects, and arguably the

ful to minors. As the District Court noted: "There is nothing in the text of the COPA, however, that limits its applicability to so-called commercial pornographers only; indeed, the text of COPA imposes liability on a speaker who knowingly makes any communication for commercial purposes 'that includes any material that is harmful to minors.'" In the context of the Internet, this is hardly a serious limitation. A 1998 study, for example, found that 83 percent of Web sites contain commercial content. Interestingly, this same study found that only 1.5 percent of the 2.8 million sites cataloged contained pornographic content.

card catalog of the Carnegie Library" might offend some community's standards and not others. In fact, our own division on that question provides further evidence of the range of attitudes about such material. Moreover, *amici* for respondents describe studies showing substantial variation among communities in their attitudes toward works involving homosexuality, masturbation, and nudity.

Even if most, if not all, of these works would be excluded from COPA's coverage by the serious value prong, they illustrate the diversity of public opinion on the underlying themes depicted. This diversity of views surely extends to whether materials with the same themes, that do not have serious value for minors, appeal to their prurient interests and are patently offensive. There is no reason to think the differences between communities' standards will disappear once the image or description is no longer within the context of a work that has serious value for minors. Because communities differ widely in their attitudes toward sex, particularly when minors are concerned, the Court of Appeals was correct to conclude that, regardless of how COPA's other provisions are construed, applying community standards to the Internet will restrict a substantial amount of protected speech that would not be considered harmful to minors in many communities.

Whether that consequence is appropriate depends, of course, on the content of the message. The kind of hard-core pornography involved in *Hamling*, which I assume would be obscene under any community's standard, does not belong on the Internet. Perhaps "teasers" that serve no function except to invite viewers to examine hardcore materials, or the hidden terms written into a Web site's "metatags" in order to dupe unwitting Web surfers into visiting pornographic sites, deserve the same fate. But COPA extends to a wide range of prurient appeals in advertisements, online magazines, Web-based bulletin boards and chat rooms, stock photo galleries, Web diaries, and a variety of illustrations encompassing a vast number of messages that are unobjectionable in most of the country and yet provide no "serious value" for minors. It is quite wrong to allow the standards of a minority consisting of the least tolerant communities to regulate access to relatively harmless messages in this burgeoning market. In the context of most other media, using community standards to differentiate between permissible and impermissible speech has two virtues. As mentioned above, community standards originally served as a shield to protect speakers from the least tolerant members of society. By aggregating values at the community level, the *Miller* test eliminated the outliers at both ends of the spectrum and provided some predictability as to what constitutes obscene speech. But community standards also serve as a shield to protect audience members, by allowing people to self-sort based on their preferences. Those who abhor and those who tolerate sexually explicit speech can seek out like-minded people and settle in communities that share their views on what is acceptable for themselves and their children. This sorting mechanism, however, does not exist in cyberspace; the audience cannot self-segregate. As a result, in the context of the Internet this shield also becomes a sword, because the community that wishes to live without certain material not only rids itself, but the entire Internet of the offending speech.

In sum, I would affirm the judgment of the Court of Appeals and therefore respectfully dissent.

QUESTIONS AND NOTES

1. What, if anything, did the Court actually hold?

2. How, if at all, is this case different from *Reno*?

3. To what extent, if at all, is the Court retreating from *Reno*?

4. Does *Ashcroft* raise serious questions about the viability of community standards?

5. Assuming that community standards test remains apart of our jurisprudence, what is (ought to be) the relevant community? Explain.

In the *Playboy* case, a sharply divided Court seemed to indicate even less patience with the "save the children" argument.

UNITED STATES v. PLAYBOY ENTERTAINMENT GROUP, INC.

529 U.S. 803, 120 S.Ct. 1878 (2000).

JUSTICE KENNEDY delivered the opinion of the Court.

This case presents a challenge to § 505 of the Telecommunications Act of 1996. Section 505 requires cable television operators who provide channels "primarily dedicated to sexually-oriented programming" either to "fully scramble or otherwise fully block" those channels or to limit their transmission to hours when children are unlikely to be viewing, set by administrative regulation as the time between 10 p.m. and 6 a.m. Even before enactment of the statute, signal scrambling was already in use. Cable operators used scrambling in the regular course of business, so that only paying customers had access to certain programs. Scrambling could be imprecise, however; and either or both audio and visual portions of the scrambled programs might be heard or seen, a phenomenon known as "signal bleed." The purpose of § 505 is to shield children from hearing or seeing images resulting from signal bleed.

To comply with the statute, the majority of cable operators adopted the second, or "time channeling," approach. The effect of the widespread adoption of time channeling was to eliminate altogether the transmission of the targeted programming outside the safe harbor period in affected cable service areas. In other words, for two-thirds of the day no household in those service areas could receive the programming, whether or not the household or the viewer wanted to do so.

After a trial, a three-judge District Court concluded that a regime in which viewers could order signal blocking on a household-by-household basis presented an effective, less restrictive alternative to § 505. Finding no error in this conclusion, we affirm.

I

Playboy Entertainment Group owns and prepares programs for adult television networks, including Playboy Television and Spice. Playboy transmits its programming to cable television operators, who retransmit it to their subscribers, either through monthly subscriptions to premium channels or on a so-called "pay-per-view" basis. Cable operators transmit Playboy's signal, like other premium channel signals, in scrambled form. The operators then provide paying subscribers with an "addressable converter," a box placed on the home television set. The converter permits the viewer to see and hear the descrambled signal. It is conceded that almost all of Playboy's programming consists of sexually explicit material as defined by the statute.

The statute was enacted because not all scrambling technology is perfect. Analog cable television systems may use either "RF" or "baseband" scrambling systems, which may not prevent signal bleed, so discernible pictures may appear from time to time on the scrambled screen. Furthermore, the listener might hear the audio portion of the program.

These imperfections are not inevitable. The problem is that at present it appears not to be economical to convert simpler RF or baseband scrambling systems to alternative scrambling technologies on a systemwide scale. Digital technology may one day provide another solution, as it presents no bleed problem at all. Indeed, digital systems are projected to become the technology of choice, which would eliminate the signal bleed problem. Digital technology is not yet in widespread use, however. With imperfect scrambling, viewers who have not paid to receive Playboy's channels may happen across discernible images of a sexually explicit nature. How many viewers, how discernible the scene or sound, and how often this may occur are at issue in this case.

In March 1998, the District Court held a full trial and concluded that § 505 violates the First Amendment. It agreed that the interests the statute advanced were compelling but concluded the Government might further those interests in less restrictive ways. One plausible, less restrictive alternative could be found in another section of the Act: § 504, which requires a cable operator, "upon request by a cable service subscriber ... without charge, [to] fully scramble or otherwise fully block" any channel the subscriber does not wish to receive. As long as subscribers knew about this opportunity, the court reasoned, § 504 would provide as much protection against unwanted programming as would § 505. At the same time, § 504 was content neutral and would be less restrictive of Playboy's First Amendment rights.

The court described what "adequate notice" would include, suggesting

"[operators] should communicate to their subscribers the information that certain channels broadcast sexually-oriented programming; that signal bleed ... may appear; that children may view signal bleed without their parents' knowledge or permission; that channel blocking devices ... are available free of charge ...; and that a request for a free device ... can be made by a telephone call to the [operator]."

The means of providing this notice could include

"inserts in monthly billing statements, barker channels (preview channels of programming coming up on Pay–Per–View), and on-air advertisement on channels other than the one broadcasting the sexually explicit programming."

The court added that this notice could be "conveyed on a regular basis, at reasonable intervals," and could include notice of changes in channel alignments.

The District Court concluded that § 504 so supplemented would be an effective, less restrictive alternative to § 505, and consequently declared

§ 505 unconstitutional and enjoined its enforcement. The court also required Playboy to insist on these notice provisions in its contracts with cable operators.

II

Two essential points should be understood concerning the speech at issue here. First, we shall assume that many adults themselves would find the material highly offensive; and when we consider the further circumstance that the material comes unwanted into homes where children might see or hear it against parental wishes or consent, there are legitimate reasons for regulating it. Second, all parties bring the case to us on the premise that Playboy's programming has First Amendment protection. As this case has been litigated, it is not alleged to be obscene; adults have a constitutional right to view it; the Government disclaims any interest in preventing children from seeing or hearing it with the consent of their parents; and Playboy has concomitant rights under the First Amendment to transmit it. These points are undisputed.

The speech in question is defined by its content; and the statute which seeks to restrict it is content based. Section 505 applies only to channels primarily dedicated to "sexually explicit adult programming or other programming that is indecent." The statute is unconcerned with signal bleed from any other channels. ("[Section 505] does not apply when signal bleed occurs on other premium channel networks, like HBO or the Disney Channel"). The overriding justification for the regulation is concern for the effect of the subject matter on young viewers. Section 505 is not " 'justified without reference to the content of the regulated speech.' " It "focuses *only* on the content of the speech and the direct impact that speech has on its listeners." This is the essence of content-based regulation.

Not only does § 505 single out particular programming content for regulation, it also singles out particular programmers. The speech in question was not thought by Congress to be so harmful that all channels were subject to restriction. Instead, the statutory disability applies only to channels "primarily dedicated to sexually-oriented programming." One sponsor of the measure even identified appellee by name. See 141 Cong. Rec. 15587 (1995) (statement of Sen. Feinstein) (noting the statute would apply to channels "such as the Playboy and Spice channels"). Laws designed or intended to suppress or restrict the expression of specific speakers contradict basic First Amendment principles. Section 505 limited Playboy's market as a penalty for its programming choice, though other channels capable of transmitting like material are altogether exempt.

The effect of the federal statute on the protected speech is now apparent. It is evident that the only reasonable way for a substantial number of cable operators to comply with the letter of § 505 is to time channel, which silences the protected speech for two-thirds of the day in every home in a cable service area, regardless of the presence or likely presence of children or of the wishes of the viewers. According to the District Court, "30 to 50% of all adult programming is viewed by households prior to 10 p.m.," when the safe-harbor period begins. To prohibit this much speech is a significant restriction of communication between speakers and willing adult listeners, communication which enjoys First Amendment protection. It is of no moment that the statute does not impose a complete prohibition. The distinction between laws burdening and laws banning speech is but a matter of degree. The Government's content-based burdens must satisfy the same rigorous scrutiny as its content-based bans.

Since § 505 is a content-based speech restriction, it can stand only if it satisfies strict scrutiny. *Sable Communications v. FCC*. If a less restrictive alternative would serve the Government's purpose, the legislature must use that alternative. *Reno v. ACLU*. To do otherwise would be to restrict speech without an adequate justification, a course the First Amendment does not permit.

Our precedents teach these principles. Where the designed benefit of a content-based speech restriction is to shield the sensibilities of listeners, the general rule is that the right of expression prevails, even where no less restrictive alternative exists. We are expected to protect our own sensibilities "simply by averting [our] eyes." *Cohen v. California, Erznoznik v. Jacksonville*. Here, of course, we consider images transmitted to some homes where they are not wanted and where parents often are not present to give immediate guidance. Cable television, like broadcast media, presents unique problems, which inform our assessment of the interests at stake, and which may justify restrictions that would be unacceptable in other contexts. *FCC v. Pacifica Foundation*. No one suggests the Government must be indifferent to unwanted, indecent speech that comes into the home without parental consent. The speech here, all agree, is protected speech; and the question is what standard the Government must meet in order to restrict it. As we consider a content-based regulation, the answer should be clear: The standard is strict scrutiny. This case involves speech alone; and even where speech is indecent and enters the home, the objective of shielding children does not suffice to support a blanket ban if the protection can be accomplished by a less restrictive alternative.

In *Sable Communications*, for instance, the feasibility of a technological approach to controlling minors' access to "dial-a-porn" messages required invalidation of a complete statutory ban on the medium. And, while mentioned only in passing, the mere possibility that user-based Internet screening software would " 'soon be widely available' " was relevant to our rejection of an overbroad restriction of indecent cyberspeech. Compare *Rowan v. Post Office Dept.*, 397 U.S. 728, 729–730 (1970) (upholding statute "whereby any householder may insulate himself from advertisements that offer for sale 'matter which the addressee in his sole discretion believes to be erotically arousing or sexually provocative' "), with *Bolger v. Youngs Drug Products Corp.*, 463 U.S. 60, 75 (1983) (rejecting blanket ban on the mailing of unsolicited contraceptive advertisements). Compare also *Ginsberg v. New York* (upholding state statute barring the sale to minors of material defined as "obscene on the basis of its appeal to them"), with *Butler* (rejecting blanket ban of material " 'tending to incite minors to violent or depraved or immoral acts, manifestly tending to the corruption of the morals of youth' "). Each of these cases arose in a different context—*Sable Communications* and *Reno*, for instance, also note the affirmative steps necessary to obtain access to indecent material via the media at issue—but they provide necessary instruction for complying with accepted First Amendment principles.

Our zoning cases, on the other hand, are irrelevant to the question here. ([contrary to the opinion of] BREYER, J., dissenting). We have made clear that the lesser scrutiny afforded regulations targeting the secondary effects of crime or declining property values has no application to content-based regulations targeting the primary effects of protected speech. The statute now before us burdens speech because of its content; it must receive strict scrutiny.

There is, moreover, a key difference between cable television and the broadcasting media, which is the point on which this case turns: Cable systems have the capacity to block unwanted channels on a household-by-household basis. The option to block reduces the likelihood, so concerning to the Court in *Pacifica,* that traditional First Amendment scrutiny would deprive the Government of all authority to address this sort of problem. The corollary, of course, is that targeted blocking enables the Government to support parental authority without affecting the First Amendment interests of speakers and willing listeners—listeners for whom, if the speech is unpopular or indecent, the privacy of their own homes may be the optimal place of receipt. Simply put, targeted blocking is less restrictive than banning, and the Government cannot ban speech if targeted blocking is a feasible and effective means of furthering its compelling interests. This is not to say that the absence of an effective blocking mechanism will in all cases suffice to support a law restricting the speech in question; but if a less restrictive means is available for the Government to achieve its goals, the Government must use it.

III

The District Court concluded that a less restrictive alternative is available: § 504, with adequate publicity. No one disputes that § 504, which requires cable operators to block undesired channels at individual households upon request, is narrowly tailored to the Government's goal of supporting parents who want those channels blocked. The question is whether § 504 can be effective.

When a plausible, less restrictive alternative is offered to a content-based speech restriction, it is the Government's obligation to prove that the alternative will be ineffective to achieve its goals. The Government has not met that burden here. In support of its position, the Government cites empirical evidence showing that § 504, as promulgated and implemented before trial, generated few requests for household-by-household blocking. Between March 1996 and May 1997, while the Government was enjoined from enforcing § 505, § 504 remained in operation. A survey of cable operators determined that fewer than 0.5% of cable subscribers requested full blocking during that time. The uncomfortable fact is that § 504 was the sole blocking regulation in effect for over a year; and the public greeted it with a collective yawn.

The District Court was correct to direct its attention to the import of this tepid response. Placing the burden of proof upon the Government, the District Court examined whether § 504 was capable of serving as an effective, less restrictive means of reaching the Government's goals. It concluded that § 504, if publicized in an adequate manner, could be.

The District Court employed the proper approach. When the Government restricts speech, the Government bears the burden of proving the constitutionality of its actions. When the Government seeks to restrict speech based on its content, the usual presumption of constitutionality afforded congressional enactments is reversed. "Content-based regulations are presumptively invalid," *R.A.V. v. St. Paul,* and the Government bears the burden to rebut that presumption.

This is for good reason. "The line between speech unconditionally guaranteed and speech which may legitimately be regulated, suppressed, or punished is finely drawn." Error in marking that line exacts an extraordinary cost. It is through speech that our convictions and beliefs are influenced, expressed, and tested. It is through speech that we bring those beliefs to bear on Government and on society. It is through speech that our personalities are formed and expressed. The citizen is entitled to seek out or reject certain ideas or influences without Government interference or control.

When a student first encounters our free speech jurisprudence, he or she might think it is influenced by the philosophy that one idea is as good as any other, and that in art and literature objective standards of style, taste, decorum, beauty, and esthetics are deemed by the Constitution to be inappropriate, indeed unattainable. Quite the opposite is true. The Constitution no more enforces a relativistic philosophy or moral nihilism than it does any other point of view. The Constitution exists precisely so that opinions and judgments, including esthetic and moral judgments about art and literature, can be formed, tested, and expressed. What the Constitution says is that these judgments are for the individual to make, not for the Government to decree, even with the mandate or approval of a majority. Technology expands the capacity to choose; and it denies the potential of this revolution if we assume the Government is best positioned to make these choices for us.

It is rare that a regulation restricting speech because of its content will ever be permissible. Indeed, were we to give the Government the benefit of the doubt when it attempted to restrict speech, we would risk leaving regulations in place that sought to shape our unique personalities or to silence dissenting ideas. When First Amendment compliance is the point to be proved, the risk of non-persuasion—operative in all trials—must rest with the Government, not with the citizen.

With this burden in mind, the District Court explored three explanations for the lack of individual blocking requests. First, individual blocking might not be an effective alternative, due to technological or other limitations. Second, although an adequately advertised blocking provision might have been effective, § 504 as written did not require sufficient notice to make it so. Third, the actual signal bleed problem might be far less of a concern than the Government at first had supposed.

To sustain its statute, the Government was required to show that the first was the right answer. According to the District Court, however, the first and third possibilities were "equally consistent" with the record before it. As for the second, the record was "not clear" as to whether enough notice had been issued to give § 504 a fighting chance. The case, then, was at best a draw. Unless the District Court's findings are clearly erroneous, the tie goes to free expression.

The District Court began with the problem of signal bleed itself, concluding "the Government has not convinced us that [signal bleed] is a pervasive problem." The District Court's thorough discussion exposes a central weakness in the Government's proof: There is little hard evidence of how widespread or how serious the problem of signal bleed is. Indeed, there is no proof as to how likely any child is to view a discernible explicit image, and no proof of the duration of the bleed or the quality of the pictures or sound. To say that millions of children are subject to a risk of viewing signal bleed is one thing; to avoid articulating the true nature and extent of the risk is quite another. Under § 505, sanctionable signal bleed can include instances as fleeting as an image appearing on a screen for just a few seconds. The First Amendment requires a more careful assessment and characterization of an evil in order to justify a regulation as sweeping as this. Although the parties have taken the additional step of lodging with the Court an assortment of videotapes, some of which show quite explicit bleeding and some of which show television static or snow, there is no attempt at explanation or context; there is no discussion, for instance, of the extent to which any particular tape is representative of what appears on screens nationwide.

The Government relied at trial on anecdotal evidence to support its regulation, which the District Court summarized as follows:

"The Government presented evidence of two city councilors, eighteen individuals, one United States Senator, and the officials of one city who complained either to their [cable operator], to their local Congressman, or to the FCC about viewing signal bleed on television. In each instance, the local [cable operator] offered to, or did in fact, rectify the situation for free (with the exception of 1 individual), with varying degrees of rapidity. Included in the complaints was the additional concern that other parents might not be aware that their children are exposed to this problem. In addition, the Government presented evidence of a child exposed to signal bleed at a friend's house. Cindy Omlin set the lockout feature on her remote control to prevent her child from tuning to adult channels, but her eleven year old son was nevertheless exposed to signal bleed when he attended a slumber party at a friend's house.

"The Government has presented evidence of only a handful of isolated incidents over the 16 years since 1982 when Playboy started broadcasting. The Government has not presented any survey-type evidence on the magnitude of the 'problem.' "

Spurred by the District Court's express request for more specific evidence of the problem, the Government also presented an expert's spreadsheet estimate that 39 million homes with 29.5 million children had the potential to be exposed to signal bleed. The Government made no attempt to confirm the accuracy of its estimate through surveys or other field tests, however. Accordingly, the District Court discounted the figures and made this finding: "The Government presented no evidence on the number of households actually exposed to signal bleed and thus has not quantified the actual extent of the problem of signal bleed." The finding is not clearly erroneous; indeed it is all but required.

Once § 505 went into effect, of course, a significant percentage of cable operators felt it necessary to time channel their sexually explicit programmers. This is an indication that scrambling technology is not yet perfected. That is not to say, however, that scrambling is completely ineffective. Different cable systems use different scrambling systems, which vary in their dependability. "The severity of the problem varies from time to time and place to place, depending on the weather, the quality of the equipment, its installation, and maintenance." At even the good end of the spectrum a system might bleed to an extent sufficient to trigger the time-channeling requirement for a cautious cable operator. (The statute requires the signal to be "*fully* blocked" (emphasis added)). A rational cable operator, faced with the possibility of sanctions for intermittent bleeding, could well choose to time channel even if the bleeding is too momentary to pose any concern to most households. To affirm that the Government failed to prove the existence of a problem, while at the same time observing that the statute imposes a severe burden on speech, is consistent with the analysis our cases require. Here, there is no probative evidence in the record which differentiates among the extent of bleed at individual households and no evidence which otherwise quantifies the signal bleed problem.

In addition, market-based solutions such as programmable televisions, VCR's, and mapping systems (which display a blue screen when tuned to a scrambled signal) may eliminate signal bleed at the consumer end of the cable. Playboy made the point at trial that the Government's estimate failed to account for these factors. Without some sort of field survey, it is impossible to know how widespread the problem in fact is, and the only indicator in the record is a handful of complaints. If the number of children transfixed by even flickering pornographic television images in fact reached into the millions we, like the District Court, would have expected to be directed to more than a handful of complaints.

No support for the restriction can be found in the near barren legislative record relevant to this provision. Section 505 was added to the Act by floor amendment, accompanied by only brief statements, and without committee hearing or debate. One of the measure's sponsors did indicate she considered time channeling to be superior to voluntary blocking, which "puts the burden of action on the subscriber, not the cable company." (statement of Sen. Feinstein). This sole conclusory statement, however, tells little about the relative efficacy of voluntary blocking versus time channeling, other than offering the unhelpful, self-evident generality that voluntary measures require voluntary action. This is not to suggest that a 10,000 page record must be compiled in every case or that the Government must delay in acting to address a real problem; but the Government must present more than anecdote and supposition. The question is whether an actual problem has been proven in this case. We agree that the Government has failed to establish a pervasive, nationwide problem justifying its nationwide daytime speech ban.

Nor did the District Court err in its second conclusion. The Government also failed to prove § 504 with adequate notice would be an ineffective alternative to § 505. There is no evidence that a well-promoted voluntary blocking provision would not be capable at least of informing parents about signal bleed (if they are not yet aware of it) and about their rights to have the bleed blocked (if they consider it a problem and have not yet controlled it themselves).

The Government also contends a publicized § 504 will be just as restrictive as § 505, on the theory that the cost of installing blocking devices will outstrip the revenues from distributing Playboy's programming and lead to its cancellation. This conclusion rests on the assumption that a sufficient percentage of households, informed of the potential for signal bleed, would consider it enough of a problem to order blocking devices—an assumption for which there is no support in the record. It should be noted, furthermore, that Playboy is willing to incur the costs of an effective § 504. One might infer that Playboy believes an advertised § 504 will be ineffective for its object, or one might infer the company believes the signal bleed problem is not widespread. In the absence of proof, it is not for the Court to assume the former.

It is no response that voluntary blocking requires a consumer to take action, or may be inconvenient, or may not go perfectly every time. A court should not assume a plausible, less restrictive alternative would be ineffective; and a court should not presume parents, given full information, will fail to act. If unresponsive operators are a concern, moreover, a notice statute could give cable operators ample incentive, through fines or other penalties for noncompliance, to respond to blocking requests in prompt and efficient fashion.

There would certainly be parents—perhaps a large number of parents—who out of inertia, indifference, or distraction, simply would take no action to block signal bleed, even if fully informed of the problem and even if offered a relatively easy solution.

Even upon the assumption that the Government has an interest in substituting itself for informed and empowered parents, its interest is not sufficiently compelling to justify this widespread restriction on speech. The Government's argument stems from the idea that parents do not know their children are viewing the material on a scale or frequency to cause concern, or if so, that parents do not want to take affirmative steps to block it and their decisions are to be superseded. The assumptions have not been established; and in any event the assumptions apply only in a regime where the option of blocking has not been explained. The whole point of a publicized § 504 would be to advise parents that indecent material may be shown and to afford them an opportunity to block it at all times, even when they are not at home and even after 10 p.m. Time channeling does not offer this assistance. The regulatory alternative of a publicized § 504, which has the real possibility of promoting more open disclosure and the choice of an effective blocking system, would provide parents the information needed to engage in active supervision. The Government has not shown that this alternative, a regime of added communication and support, would be insufficient to secure its objective, or that any overriding harm justifies its intervention.

There can be little doubt, of course, that under a voluntary blocking regime, even with adequate notice, some children will be exposed to signal bleed; and we need not discount the possibility that a graphic image could have a negative impact on a young child. It must be remembered, however, that children will be exposed to signal bleed under time channeling as well. Time channeling, unlike blocking, does not eliminate signal bleed around the clock. Just as adolescents may be unsupervised outside of their own households, it is hardly unknown for them to be unsupervised in front of the television set after 10 p.m. The record is silent as to the comparative effectiveness of the two alternatives.

Basic speech principles are at stake in this case. When the purpose and design of a statute is to regulate speech by reason of its content, special consideration or latitude is not accorded to the Government merely because the law can somehow be described as a burden rather than outright suppression. We cannot be influenced, moreover, by the perception that the regulation in question is not a major one because the speech is not very important. The history of the law of free expression is one of vindication in cases involving speech that many citizens may find shabby, offensive, or even ugly. It follows that all content-based restrictions on speech must give us more than a moment's pause. If television broadcasts can expose children to the real risk of harmful exposure to indecent materials, even in their own home and without parental consent, there is a problem the Government can address. It must do so, however, in a way consistent with First Amendment principles. Here the Government has not met the burden the First Amendment imposes.

The Government has failed to show that § 505 is the least restrictive means for addressing a real problem; and the District Court did not err in holding the statute violative of the First Amendment. In light of our ruling, it is unnecessary to address the second question presented: whether the District Court was divested of jurisdiction to consider the Government's postjudgment motions after the Government filed a notice of appeal in this Court. The judgment of the District Court is affirmed.

It is so ordered.

JUSTICE STEVENS, concurring.

Because JUSTICE SCALIA has advanced an argument that the parties have not addressed, a brief response is in order. Relying on *Ginzburg v United States,* JUSTICE SCALIA would treat programs whose content is, he assumes, protected by the First Amendment as though they were obscene because of the way they are advertised. The four separate dissenting opinions in *Ginzburg,* authored by Justices Black, Harlan, Douglas, and Stewart, amply demonstrated the untenable character of the *Ginzburg* decision when it was rendered. The *Ginzburg* theory of obscenity is a legal fiction premised upon a logical bait-and-switch; advertising a bareheaded dancer as "topless" might be deceptive, but it would not make her performance obscene.

As I explained in my dissent in *Splawn v. California,* 431 U.S. 595 (1977), *Ginzburg* was decided before the Court extended First Amendment protection to commercial speech, *Virginia Bd. of Pharmacy v. Virginia Citizens Consumer Council, Inc.,* 425 U.S. 748 (1976). JUSTICE SCALIA's proposal is thus not only anachronistic, it also overlooks a key premise upon which our commercial speech cases are based. The First Amendment assumes that, as a general matter, "information is not in itself harmful, that people will perceive their own best interests if only they are well enough informed, and that the best means to that end is to open the channels of communication rather than to close them." The very fact that the programs marketed by Playboy are offensive to many viewers provides a justification for protecting, not penalizing, truthful statements about their content.

JUSTICE THOMAS, concurring.

It would seem to me that, with respect to at least some of the cable programming affected by § 505 of the Telecommunications Act of 1996, the Government has ample constitutional and statutory authority to prohibit its broadcast entirely. A governmental restriction on the distribution of obscene materials receives no First Amendment scrutiny. *Roth.* Though perhaps not all of the programming at issue in the case is obscene as this Court defined the term in *Miller v. California*, one could fairly conclude that, under the standards applicable in many communities, some of the programming meets the *Miller* test. If this is so, the Government is empowered by statute to sanction these broadcasts with criminal penalties.[1]

However, as the Court points out, this case has been litigated on the assumption that the programming at issue is *not* obscene, but merely indecent. We have no factual finding that any of the materials at issue are, in fact, obscene. Indeed, the District Court described the materials as indecent but not obscene. The Government does not challenge that characterization in this Court, but instead asks this Court to ratify the statute on the assumption that this is protected speech. I am unwilling, in the absence of factual findings or advocacy of the position, to rely on the view that some of the relevant programming is obscene.

What remains then is the assumption that the programming restricted by § 505 is not obscene, but merely indecent. The Government, having declined to defend the statute as a regulation of obscenity, now asks us to dilute our stringent First Amendment standards to uphold § 505 as a proper regulation of protected (rather than unprotected) speech. I am unwilling to corrupt the First Amendment to reach this result. The "starch" in our constitutional standards cannot be sacrificed to accommodate the enforcement choices of the Government. Applying the First Amendment's exacting standards, the Court has correctly determined that § 505 cannot be upheld on the theory argued by the Government. Accordingly, I join the opinion of the Court.

JUSTICE SCALIA, dissenting.

I agree with the principal dissent in this case that § 505 of the Telecommunications Act of 1996 is supported by a compelling state interest and is narrowly tailored. I write separately to express my view that § 505 can be upheld in simpler fashion: by finding that it regulates the business of obscenity.

To be sure, § 505 and the Federal Communications Commission's implementing regulation, purport to capture programming that is indecent rather than merely that which is obscene. And I will assume for purposes of this discussion (though it is a highly fanciful assumption) that none of the transmissions at issue independently crosses the boundary we have established for obscenity, see *Miller*, so that the individual programs themselves

---

1. I am referring, here, to unscrambled programming on the Playboy and Spice channels, examples of which were lodged with the Court. The Government also lodged videotapes containing signal bleed from these channels. I assume that if the unscrambled programming on these channels is obscene, any scrambled but discernible images from the programs would be obscene as well. In fact, some of the examples of signal bleed contained in the record may fall within our definition of obscenity more easily than would the unscrambled programming because it is difficult to dispute that signal bleed "lacks serious literary, artistic, political, or scientific value."

would enjoy First Amendment protection. In my view, however, that assumption does not put an end to the inquiry.

We have recognized that commercial entities which engage in "the sordid business of pandering" by "deliberately emphasizing the sexually provocative aspects of [their nonobscene products], in order to catch the salaciously disposed," engage in constitutionally unprotected behavior. *Ginzburg*. We are more permissive of government regulation in these circumstances because it is clear from the context in which exchanges between such businesses and their customers occur that neither the merchant nor the buyer is interested in the work's literary, artistic, political, or scientific value. "The deliberate representation of petitioner's publications as erotically arousing ... stimulates the reader to accept them as prurient; he looks for titillation, not for saving intellectual content." Thus, a business that "(1) offers ... hardcore sexual material, (2) as a constant and intentional objective of [its] business, [and] (3) seeks to promote it as such" finds no sanctuary in the First Amendment.

Section 505 regulates just this sort of business. Its coverage is limited to programming that "describes or depicts sexual or excretory activities or organs *in a patently offensive manner* as measured by contemporary community standards [for cable television]" (emphasis added). It furthermore applies only to those channels that are *"primarily dedicated* to sexually-oriented programming."[1] (emphasis added). It is conceivable, I suppose, that a channel which is primarily dedicated to sex might not *hold itself forth* as primarily dedicated to sex—in which case its productions which contain "serious literary, artistic, political, or scientific value" (if any) would be as entitled to First Amendment protection as the statuary rooms of the National Gallery. But in the competitive world of cable programming, the possibility that a channel devoted to sex would not advertise itself as such is sufficiently remote, and the number of such channels sufficiently small (if not indeed nonexistent), as not to render the provision substantially overbroad.[2]

Playboy itself illustrates the type of business § 505 is designed to reach. Playboy provides, through its networks—Playboy Television, AdulTVision, Adam & Eve, and Spice—"virtually 100% sexually explicit adult programming." For example, on its Spice network, Playboy describes its own programming as depicting such activities as "female masturbation/external," "girl/girl sex," and "oral sex/cunnilingus." As one would expect, given this content,

---

1. Congress's attempt to limit the reach of § 505 is therefore, contrary to the Court's contention, a virtue rather than a vice.

2. JUSTICE STEVENS misapprehends in several respects the nature of the test I would apply. First, he mistakenly believes that the nature of the advertising controls the obscenity analysis, regardless of the nature of the material being advertised. I entirely agree with him that "advertising a bareheaded dancer as 'topless' might be deceptive, but it would not make her performance obscene." I believe, however, that *if* the material is "patently offensive" *and* it is being advertised as such, we have little reason to think it is being proffered for its socially redeeming value.

JUSTICE STEVENS' second misapprehension flows from the first: He sees the test I would apply as incompatible with the Court's com-

mercial-speech jurisprudence. There is no such conflict. Although the *Ginzburg* test, like most obscenity tests, has ordinarily been applied in a commercial context (most purveyors of obscenity are in the business for the money), its logic is not restricted to that context. The test applies equally to the improbable case in which a collector of indecent materials wishes to give them away, and takes out a classified ad in the local newspaper touting their salacious appeal. Commercial motive or not, the "'circumstances of ... dissemination are relevant to determining whether [the] social importance claimed for [the] material [is] ... pretense or reality.'" Perhaps this is why the Court in *Splawn* did not accept JUSTICE STEVENS' claim of incompatibility.

Playboy advertises accordingly, with calls to "Enjoy the sexiest, hottest adult movies in the privacy of your own home." An example of the promotion for a particular movie is as follows: "Little miss country girls are aching for a quick roll in the hay! Watch southern hospitality pull out all the stops as these ravin' nymphos tear down the barn and light up the big country sky." One may doubt whether—or marvel that—this sort of embarrassingly juvenile promotion really attracts what Playboy assures us is an "adult" audience. But it is certainly marketing sex.[3]

Thus, while I agree with JUSTICE BREYER's child-protection analysis, it leaves me with the same feeling of true-but-inadequate as the conclusion that Al Capone did not accurately report his income. It is not only children who can be protected from occasional uninvited exposure to what appellee calls "adult-oriented programming"; we can all be. Section 505 covers only businesses that engage in the "commercial exploitation of erotica solely for the sake of their prurient appeal,"which, as Playboy's own advertisements make plain, is what "adult" programming is all about. In most contexts, contemporary American society has chosen to permit such commercial exploitation. That may be a wise democratic choice, if only because of the difficulty in many contexts (though not this one) of identifying the panderer to sex. It is, however, not a course compelled by the Constitution. Since the Government is entirely free to *block* these transmissions, it may certainly take the less drastic step of dictating how, and during what times, they may occur.

JUSTICE BREYER, with whom THE CHIEF JUSTICE, JUSTICE O'CONNOR, and JUSTICE SCALIA join, dissenting.

This case involves the application, not the elucidation, of First Amendment principles. We apply established First Amendment law to a statute that focuses upon the broadcast of "sexually explicit adult programming" on AdulTVision, Adam & Eve, Spice, and Playboy cable channels. These channels are, as the statute requires, "primarily dedicated to sexually-oriented programming." Section 505 forbids cable operators from sending these adult channels into the homes of viewers who do not request them. In practice, it requires a significant number of cable operators either to upgrade their scrambling technology or to avoid broadcasting these channels during daylight and evening hours (6 a.m. to 10 p.m.). We must decide whether the First Amendment permits Congress to enact this statute.

The basic, applicable First Amendment principles are not at issue. The Court must examine the statute before us with great care to determine whether its speech-related restrictions are justified by a "compelling interest," namely an interest in limiting children's access to sexually explicit

---

3. Both the Court, and JUSTICE THOMAS, find great importance in the fact that "this case has been litigated on the assumption that the programming at issue is not obscene, but merely indecent." But as I noted in FW/PBS, Inc. v. Dallas, 493 U.S. 215 (1990) (opinion concurring in part and dissenting in part), we have not allowed the parties' litigating positions to place limits upon our development of obscenity law. See, *e.g.*, *Miller* (abandoning "utterly without redeeming social value" test *sua sponte*); *Ginzburg* (adopting pandering theory unargued by the Government); *Mishkin* (upholding convic-

tions on theory that obscenity could be defined by looking to the intent of the disseminator, despite respondent's express disavowal of that theory). As for JUSTICE THOMAS's concern that there has been no factual finding of obscenity in this case: This is not an as-applied challenge, in which the issue is whether a particular course of conduct constitutes obscenity; it is a facial challenge, in which the issue is whether the terms of this statute address obscenity. That is not for the factfinder below, but for this Court.

material. In doing so, it recognizes that the legislature must respect adults' viewing freedom by "narrowly tailoring" the statute so that it restricts no more speech than necessary, and choosing instead any alternative that would further the compelling interest in a "less restrictive" but "at least as effective" way.

Applying these principles, the majority invalidates § 505 for two reasons. It finds that (1) the "Government has failed to establish a pervasive, nation-wide problem justifying its nationwide daytime speech ban," and (2) the "Government ... failed to prove" the "ineffectiveness" of an alternative, namely, notified viewers requesting that the broadcaster of sexually explicit material stop sending it. In my view, the record supports neither reason.

I

At the outset, I would describe the statutory scheme somewhat differently than does the majority. I would emphasize three background points. First, the statutory scheme reflects more than a congressional effort to control incomplete scrambling. Previously, federal law had left cable operators free to decide whether, when, and how to transmit adult channels. Most channel operators on their own had decided not to send adult channels into a subscriber's home except on request. But the operators then implemented that decision with inexpensive technology. Through signal "bleeding," the scrambling technology (either inadvertently or by way of enticement) allowed non subscribers to see and hear what was going on. That is why Congress decided to act.

In 1995, Senator Dianne Feinstein, the present statute's legislative co-sponsor, pointed out that "numerous cable operators across the country are still automatically broadcasting sexually explicit programming into households across America, regardless of whether parents want this or subscribers want it." She complained that the "industry has only taken baby steps to address this problem through voluntary policies that simply recommend action," adding that the "problem is that there are no uniform laws or regulations that govern such sexually explicit adult programming on cable television." She consequently proposed, and Congress enacted, the present statute.

The statute is carefully tailored to respect viewer preferences. It regulates transmissions by creating two "default rules" applicable unless the subscriber decides otherwise. Section 504 requires a cable operator to "fully scramble" any channel (whether or not it broadcasts adult programming) *if* a subscriber asks *not* to receive it. Section 505 requires a cable operator to "fully scramble" every adult channel *unless* a subscriber asks to receive it. Taken together, the two provisions create a scheme that permits subscribers to choose to see what they want. But each law creates a different "default" assumption about silent subscribers. Section 504 assumes a silent subscriber wants to see the ordinary (non adult) channels that the cable operator includes in the paid-for bundle sent into the home. Section 505 assumes that a silent subscriber does not want to receive adult channels. Consequently, a subscriber wishing to view an adult channel must "opt in," and specifically request that channel. A subscriber wishing not to view any other channel (sent into the home) must "opt out."

The scheme addresses signal bleed but only indirectly. From the statute's perspective signal "bleeding"—*i.e.*, a failure to fully "rearrange the content of the signal ... so that the programming cannot be viewed or heard in an understandable manner,"—amounts to transmission into a home. Hence "bleeding" violates the statute whenever a clear transmission of an unrequested adult channel would violate the statute.

Second, the majority's characterization of this statutory scheme as "prohibiting ... speech" is an exaggeration. Rather, the statute places a *burden* on adult channel speech by requiring the relevant cable operator either to use better scrambling technology, or, if that technology is too expensive, to broadcast only between 10 p.m. and 6 a.m. Laws that burden speech, say, by making speech less profitable, may create serious First Amendment issues, but they are not the equivalent of an absolute ban on speech itself. Thus, this Court has upheld laws that do not ban the access of adults to sexually explicit speech, but burden that access through geographical or temporal zoning. See, *e.g.*, *Renton v. Playtime Theatres, Inc.; Pacifica; Young v. American Mini Theatres, Inc.* This Court has also recognized that material the First Amendment guarantees adults the right to see may not be suitable for children. And it has consequently held that legislatures maintain a limited power to protect children by restricting access to, but not banning, adult material. Compare *Ginsberg* with *Butler*. The difference—between imposing a burden and enacting a ban—can matter even when strict First Amendment rules are at issue.

Third, this case concerns only the regulation of commercial actors who broadcast "virtually 100% sexually explicit" material. The channels do not broadcast more than trivial amounts of more serious material such as birth control information, artistic images, or the visual equivalents of classical or serious literature. This case therefore does not present the kind of narrow tailoring concerns seen in other cases. See, *e.g.*, *Reno*.

With this background in mind, the reader will better understand my basic disagreement with each of the Court's two conclusions.

II

The majority first concludes that the Government failed to prove the seriousness of the problem—receipt of adult channels by children whose parents did not request their broadcast. This claim is flat-out wrong. For one thing, the parties concede that basic RF scrambling does not scramble the audio portion of the program. For another, Playboy itself conducted a survey of cable operators who were asked: "Is your system in full compliance with Section 505 (no discernible audio or video bleed)?" To this question, 75% of cable operators answered "no." Further, the Government's expert took the number of homes subscribing to Playboy or Spice, multiplied by the fraction of cable households with children and the average number of children per household, and found 29 million children are potentially exposed to audio and video bleed from adult programming. Even discounting by 25% for systems that might be considered in full compliance, this left 22 million children in homes with faulty scrambling systems. And, of course, the record contains additional anecdotal evidence and the concerns expressed by elected officials, probative of a larger problem.

I would add to this empirical evidence the majority's own statement that "*most* cable operators had 'no practical choice but to curtail' " adult programming by switching to nighttime only transmission of adult channels (emphasis added). *If signal bleed is not a significant empirical problem, then why, in light of the cost of its cure, must so many cable operators switch to night time hours?* There is no realistic answer to this question. I do not think it realistic to imagine that signal bleed occurs just enough to make cable operators skittish, without also significantly exposing children to these images.

If, as the majority suggests, the signal bleed problem is not significant, then there is also no significant burden on speech created by § 505. The majority cannot have this evidence both ways. And if, given this logical difficulty and the quantity of empirical evidence, the majority still believes that the Government has not proved its case, then it imposes a burden upon the Government beyond that suggested in any other First Amendment case of which I am aware.

III

The majority's second claim—that the Government failed to demonstrate the absence of a "less restrictive alternative"—presents a closer question. The specific question is whether § 504's "opt-out" amounts to a "less restrictive," but *similarly* practical and *effective*, way to accomplish § 505's child-protecting objective. As *Reno* tells us, a "less restrictive alternative" must be "at least as effective in achieving the legitimate purpose that the statute was enacted to serve."

The words I have just emphasized, "similarly" and "effective," are critical. In an appropriate case they ask a judge not to apply First Amendment rules mechanically, but to decide whether, in light of the benefits and potential alternatives, the statute works speech-related harm (here to adult speech) out of proportion to the benefits that the statute seeks to provide (here, child protection).

These words imply a degree of leeway, however small, for the legislature when it chooses among possible alternatives in light of predicted comparative effects. Without some such empirical leeway, the undoubted ability of lawyers and judges to imagine *some* kind of slightly less drastic or restrictive an approach would make it impossible to write laws that deal with the harm that called the statute into being. As Justice Blackmun pointed out, a "judge would be unimaginative indeed if he could not come up with something a little less 'drastic' or a little less 'restrictive' in almost any situation, and thereby enable himself to vote to strike legislation down." Used without a sense of the practical choices that face legislatures, "the test merely announces an inevitable [negative] result, and the test is no test at all."

The majority, in describing First Amendment jurisprudence, scarcely mentions the words "at least as effective"—a rather surprising omission since they happen to be what this case is all about. But the majority does refer to *Reno*'s understanding of less restrictive alternatives, and it addresses the Government's effectiveness arguments. I therefore assume it continues to recognize their role as part of the test that it enunciates.

I turn then to the major point of disagreement. Unlike the majority, I believe the record makes clear that § 504's opt-out is not a similarly effective alternative. Section 504 (opt-out) and § 505 (opt-in) work differently in order to achieve very different legislative objectives. Section 504 gives parents the power to tell cable operators to keep any channel out of their home. Section 505 does more. Unless parents explicitly consent, it inhibits the transmission of adult cable channels to children whose parents may be unaware of what they are watching, whose parents cannot easily supervise television viewing habits, whose parents do not know of their § 504 "opt-out" rights, or whose parents are simply unavailable at critical times. In this respect, § 505 serves the same interests as the laws that deny children access to adult cabarets or X-rated movies. These laws, and § 505, all act in the absence of direct parental supervision.

This legislative objective is perfectly legitimate. Where over 28 million school age children have both parents or their only parent in the work force, where at least 5 million children are left alone at home without supervision each week, and where children may spend afternoons and evenings watching television outside of the home with friends, § 505 offers independent protection for a large number of families. I could not disagree more when the majority implies that the Government's independent interest in offering such protection—preventing, say, an 8–year-old child from watching virulent pornography without parental consent—might not be "compelling." No previous case in which the protection of children was at issue has suggested any such thing. Indeed, they all say precisely the opposite. They make clear that Government has a compelling interest in helping parents by preventing minors from accessing sexually explicit materials in the absence of parental supervision.

By definition, § 504 does *nothing at all* to further the compelling interest I have just described. How then is it a similarly effective § 505 alternative?

The record, moreover, sets forth empirical evidence showing that the two laws are not equivalent with respect to the Government's objectives. As the majority observes, during the 14 months the Government was enjoined from enforcing § 505, "fewer than 0.5% of cable subscribers requested full blocking" under § 504. The majority describes this public reaction as "a collective yawn," adding that the Government failed to prove that the "yawn" reflected anything other than the lack of a serious signal bleed problem or a lack of notice which better information about § 504 might cure. The record excludes the first possibility—at least in respect to exposure. And I doubt that the public, though it may well consider the viewing habits of *adults* a matter of personal choice, would "yawn" when the exposure in question concerns young children, the absence of parental consent, and the sexually explicit material here at issue.

Neither is the record neutral in respect to the curative power of better notice. Section 504's opt-out right works only when parents (1) become aware of their § 504 rights, (2) discover that their children are watching sexually-explicit signal "bleed," (3) reach their cable operator and ask that it block the sending of its signal to their home, (4) await installation of an individual blocking device, and, perhaps (5) (where the block fails or the channel number changes) make a new request. Better notice of § 504 rights does little to help parents discover their children's viewing habits (step two). And it does nothing at all in respect to steps three through five. Yet the record contains considerable evidence that those problems matter, *i.e.,* evidence of endlessly delayed phone call responses, faulty installations, blocking failures, and other mishaps, leaving those steps as significant § 504 obstacles.

Further, the District Court's actual plan for "better notice"—the only plan that makes concrete the majority's "better notice" requirement—is fraught with difficulties. The District Court ordered Playboy to insist that cable operators place notice of § 504 "inserts in monthly billing statements, barker channels . . . and on-air advertising." But how can one say that placing one more insert in a monthly billing statement stuffed with others, or calling additional attention to adult channels through a "notice" on "barker" channels, will make more than a small difference? More importantly, why would doing so not interfere to some extent with the cable operators' own freedom to decide what to broadcast? And how is the District Court to supervise the contracts with thousands of cable operators that are to embody this requirement?

Even if better notice did adequately inform viewers of their § 504 rights, exercise of those rights by more than 6% of the subscriber base would itself raise Playboy's costs to the point that Playboy would be forced off the air entirely—a consequence that would not seem to further anyone's interest in free speech. The majority, resting on its own earlier conclusion that signal bleed is not widespread, denies any likelihood that more than 6% of viewers would need § 504. But that earlier conclusion is unsound. The majority also relies on the fact that Playboy, presumably aware of its own economic interests, "is willing to incur the costs of an effective § 504." Yet that denial, as the majority admits, may simply reflect Playboy's knowledge that § 504, even with better notice, will not work. Section 504 is not a similarly effective alternative to § 505 (in respect to the Government's interest in protecting children), unless more than a minimal number of viewers actually use it; yet the economic evidence shows that if more than 6% do so, Playboy's programming would be totally eliminated. The majority provides no answer to this argument in its opinion—and this evidence is sufficient in and of itself to dispose of this case.

Of course, it is logically *possible* that "better notice" will bring about near perfect parental knowledge (of what children watch and § 504 opt-out rights), that cable operators will respond rapidly to blocking requests, and that still 94% of all informed parents will decided not to have adult channels blocked for free. But the *probability* that this remote *possibility* will occur is neither a "draw" nor a "tie." And that fact is sufficient for the Government to have met its burden of proof.

All these considerations show that § 504's opt-out, even with the Court's plan for "better notice," is *not* similarly effective in achieving the legitimate goals that the statute was enacted to serve.

IV

Section 505 raises the cost of adult channel broadcasting. In doing so, it restricts, but does not ban adult speech. Adults may continue to watch adult channels, though less conveniently, by watching at night, recording programs with a VCR, or by subscribing to digital cable with better blocking systems. Cf. *Renton* (upholding zoning rules that force potential adult theatre patrons to travel to less convenient locations). The Government's justification for imposing this restriction—limiting the access of children to channels that broadcast virtually 100% "sexually explicit" material—is "compelling." The record shows no similarly effective, less restrictive alternative. Consequently § 505's restriction, viewed in light of the proposed alternative, is proportionate to need. That is to say, it restricts speech no more than necessary to further that compelling need. Taken together, these considerations lead to the conclusion that § 505 is lawful.

I repeat that my disagreement with the majority lies in the fact that, in my view, the Government has satisfied its burden of proof. In particular, it has proved both the existence of a serious problem and the comparative ineffectiveness of § 504 in resolving that problem. This disagreement is not about allocation of First Amendment burdens of proof, basic First Amendment principle nor the importance of that Amendment to our scheme of Government. First Amendment standards are rigorous. They safeguard speech. But they also permit Congress to enact a law that increases the costs associated with certain speech, where doing so serves a compelling interest that cannot be served through the adoption of a less restrictive, similarly effective alternative. Those standards at their strictest make it difficult for the Government to prevail. But they do not make it impossible for the Government to prevail.

The majority here, however, has applied those standards without making a realistic assessment of the alternatives. It thereby threatens to leave Congress without power to help the millions of parents who do not want to expose their children to commercial pornography—but will remain ill served by the Court's chosen remedy. Worse still, the logic of the majority's "505/504" comparison (but not its holding that the problem has not been established) would seem to apply whether "bleeding" or totally unscrambled transmission is at issue. If so, the public would have to depend solely upon the voluntary conduct of cable channel operators to avert considerably greater harm.

Case law does not mandate the Court's result. To the contrary, as I have pointed out, our prior cases recognize that, where the protection of children is at issue, the First Amendment poses a barrier that properly is high, but not insurmountable. It is difficult to reconcile today's decision with our foundational cases that have upheld similar laws, such as *Pacifica* and *Ginsberg*. It is not difficult to distinguish our cases striking down such laws—either because they applied far more broadly than the narrow regulation of adult channels here, see, *e.g.*, *Reno*, imposed a total ban on a form of adult speech, or because a less restrictive, similarly effective alternative was otherwise available, see, *e.g.*, *Denver Area* [infra].

Nor is it a satisfactory answer to say, as does JUSTICE THOMAS, that the Government remains free to prosecute under the obscenity laws. The obscenity exception permits censorship of communication even among *adults*. It must be kept narrow lest the Government improperly interfere with the communication choices that adults have freely made. To rely primarily upon law that bans speech for adults is to overlook the special need to protect children.

Congress has taken seriously the importance of maintaining adult access to the sexually explicit channels here at issue. It has tailored the restrictions to minimize their impact upon adults while offering parents help in keeping unwanted transmissions from their children. By finding "adequate alternatives" where there are none, the Court reduces Congress' protective power to the vanishing point. That is not what the First Amendment demands.

I respectfully dissent.

QUESTIONS AND NOTES

1. How, if at all, is *Pacifica* different from *Playboy*? Are Playboy's sexually explicit films less harmful to children than Carlin's seven dirty words?

2. How serious of a burden is it to Playboy to limit their telecasting to 10 PM to 6 AM? To its audience? Is the ready availability of VCRs relevant to these question?

3. Would a heightened awareness of 504 be *as effective* as 505? Should it be necessary that the alternative remedy be *as effective*?

4. In what sense is 504 less than a totally adequate remedy for parents? How much more can (should) government do than inform parents that they have the simple remedy of making a phone call and having their request honored?

5. Should Playboy be treated different from HBO and other cable stations that sometimes present sexually-explicit movies?

6. The Court makes much of this being a content based regulation. Aren't all rules limiting sexually-explicit speech (*e.g. Pacifica, Ginsberg*) content based regulations? Should this type of content regulation be invalid for that reason?

7. Are obscenity statutes content based classifications? Should they be constitutionally suspect for that reason?

8. Is Justice Scalia's view of sexually-explicit businesses sound? Should it be permissible to exclude such businesses even though their products would be lawful if marketed by a different source?

9. Is Justice Thomas advocating an all or nothing approach, *i.e.* the material is either obscene and nobody can see it, or it is not and therefore must be treated the same as any other speech? If so, is that the best way to construe the First Amendment?

Insert p. 349 after Question 2

ASHCROFT v. FREE SPEECH COALITION
122 S.Ct. 1389 (2002).

JUSTICE KENNEDY delivered the opinion of the Court.

We consider in this case whether the Child Pornography Prevention Act of 1996 (CPPA) abridges the freedom of speech. The CPPA extends the federal prohibition against child pornography to sexually explicit images that appear to depict minors but were produced without using any real children. The statute prohibits, in specific circumstances, possessing or distributing these images, which may be created by using adults who look like minors or by using computer imaging. The new technology, according to Congress, makes it possible to create realistic images of children who do not exist.

By prohibiting child pornography that does not depict an actual child, the statute goes beyond *New York v. Ferber,* which distinguished child pornography from other sexually explicit speech because of the State's interest in protecting the children exploited by the production process. As a general rule, pornography can be banned only if obscene, but under *Ferber*, pornography showing minors can be proscribed whether or not the images are obscene under the definition set forth in *Miller v. California. Ferber* recognized that "[t]he *Miller* standard, like all general definitions of what may be banned as obscene, does not reflect the State's particular and more compelling interest in prosecuting those who promote the sexual exploitation of children."

While we have not had occasion to consider the question, we may assume that the apparent age of persons engaged in sexual conduct is relevant to whether a depiction offends community standards. Pictures of young children engaged in certain acts might be obscene where similar depictions of adults, or perhaps even older adolescents, would not. The CPPA, however, is not directed at speech that is obscene; Congress has proscribed those materials through a separate statute. Like the law in *Ferber*, the CPPA seeks to reach beyond obscenity, and it makes no attempt to conform to the *Miller* standard. For instance, the statute would reach visual depictions, such as movies, even if they have redeeming social value.

The principal question to be resolved, then, is whether the CPPA is constitutional where it proscribes a significant universe of speech that is neither obscene under *Miller* nor child pornography under *Ferber*.

I

Before 1996, Congress defined child pornography as the type of depictions at issue in *Ferber*, images made using actual minors. The CPPA retains that prohibition and adds three other prohibited categories of speech, of which the first, and the third, are at issue in this case. Section 2256(8)(B) prohibits "any visual depiction, including any photograph, film, video, picture, or computer or computer-generated image or picture" that "is, or appears to be, of a minor engaging in sexually explicit conduct." The prohibition on "any visual depiction" does not depend at all on how the image is produced. The section captures a range of depictions, sometimes called "virtual child pornography," which include computer-generated images, as well as images produced by more traditional means. For instance, the literal terms of the statute embrace a Renaissance painting depicting a scene from classical mythology, a "picture" that "appears to be, of a minor engaging in sexually explicit conduct." The statute also prohibits Hollywood movies, filmed without any child actors, if a jury believes an actor "appears to be" a minor engaging in "actual or simulated . . . sexual intercourse."

These images do not involve, let alone harm, any children in the production process, but Congress decided the materials threaten children in other, less direct, ways. Pedophiles might use the materials to encourage children to participate in sexual activity. "[A] child who is reluctant to engage in sexual activity with an adult, or to pose for sexually explicit photographs, can sometimes be convinced by viewing depictions of other children 'having fun' participating in such activity." Furthermore, pedophiles might "whet their own sexual appetites" with the pornographic images, "thereby increasing the creation and distribution of child pornography and the sexual abuse and exploitation of actual children." Under these rationales, harm flows from the content of the images, not from the means of their production. In addition, Congress identified another problem created by computer-generated images: Their existence can make it harder to prosecute pornographers who do use real minors. As imaging technology improves, Congress found, it becomes more difficult to prove that a particular picture was produced using actual children. To ensure that defendants possessing child pornography using real minors cannot evade prosecution, Congress extended the ban to virtual child pornography.

Section 2256(8)(C) prohibits a more common and lower tech means of creating virtual images, known as computer morphing. Rather than creating original images, pornographers can alter innocent pictures of real children so that the children appear to be engaged in sexual activity. Although morphed images may fall within the definition of virtual child pornography, they implicate the interests of real children and are in that sense closer to the images in *Ferber*. Respondents do not challenge this provision, and we do not consider it.

Respondents do challenge § 2256(8)(D). Like the text of the "appears to be" provision, the sweep of this provision is quite broad. Section 2256(8)(D) defines child pornography to include any sexually explicit image that was "advertised, promoted, presented, described, or distributed in such a manner that conveys the impression" it depicts "a minor engaging in sexually explicit conduct." One Committee Report identified the provision as directed at sexually explicit images pandered as child pornography. See S. Rep. No. 104–358, p. 22 (1996) ("This provision prevents child pornographers and pedophiles from exploiting prurient interests in child sexuality and sexual activity through the production or distribution of pornographic material which is intentionally pandered as child pornography"). The statute is not so limited in its reach, however, as it punishes even those possessors who took no part in pandering. Once a work has been described as child pornography, the taint remains on the speech in the hands of subsequent possessors, making possession unlawful even though the content otherwise would not be objectionable.

II

The First Amendment commands, "Congress shall make no law ... abridging the freedom of speech." The government may violate this mandate in many ways, but a law imposing criminal penalties on protected speech is a stark example of speech suppression. The CPPA's penalties are indeed severe. A first offender may be imprisoned for 15 years. § 2252A(b)(1). A repeat offender faces a prison sentence of not less than 5 years and not more than 30 years in prison. While even minor punishments can chill protected speech, this case provides a textbook example of why we permit facial challenges to statutes that burden expression. With these severe penalties in force, few legitimate movie producers or book publishers, or few other speakers in any capacity, would risk distributing images in or near the uncertain reach of this law. The Constitution gives significant protection from overbroad laws that chill speech within the First Amendment's vast and privileged sphere. Under this principle, the CPPA is unconstitutional on its face if it prohibits a substantial amount of protected expression.

The sexual abuse of a child is a most serious crime and an act repugnant to the moral instincts of a decent people. In its legislative findings, Congress recognized that there are subcultures of persons who harbor illicit desires for children and commit criminal acts to gratify the impulses. Congress also found that surrounding the serious offenders are those who flirt with these impulses and trade pictures and written accounts of sexual activity with young children.

Congress may pass valid laws to protect children from abuse, and it has. The prospect of crime, however, by itself does not justify laws suppressing protected speech. It is also well established that speech may not be prohibited because it concerns subjects offending our sensibilities. See *Pacifica*, see also *Reno v. ACLU*. As a general principle, the First Amendment bars the government from dictating what we see or read or speak or hear. The freedom of speech has its limits; it does not embrace certain categories of speech, including defamation, incitement, obscenity, and pornography produced with real children. While these categories may be prohibited without violating the First Amendment, none of them includes the speech prohibited by the CPPA. In his dissent from the opinion of the Court of Appeals, Judge Ferguson recognized this to be the law and proposed that virtual child pornography should be regarded as an additional category of unprotected speech. It would be necessary for us to take this step to uphold the statute.

As we have noted, the CPPA is much more than a supplement to the existing federal prohibition on obscenity. Under *Miller v. California*, the Government must prove that the work, taken as a whole, appeals to the prurient interest, is patently offensive in light of community standards, and lacks serious literary, artistic, political, or scientific value. The CPPA, however, extends to images that appear to depict a minor engaging in sexually explicit activity without regard to the *Miller* requirements. The materials need not appeal to the prurient interest. Any depiction of sexually explicit activity, no matter how it is presented, is proscribed. The CPPA applies to a picture in a psychology manual, as well as a movie depicting the horrors of sexual abuse. It is not necessary, moreover, that the image be patently offensive. Pictures of what appear to be 17–year-olds engaging in sexually explicit activity do not in every case contravene community standards.

The CPPA prohibits speech despite its serious literary, artistic, political, or scientific value. The statute proscribes the visual depiction of an idea—that of teenagers engaging in sexual activity—that is a fact of modern society and has been a theme in art and literature throughout the ages. Under the CPPA, images are prohibited so long as the persons appear to be under 18 years of age. 18 U.S.C. § 2256(1). This is higher than the legal age for marriage in many States, as well as the age at which persons may consent to sexual relations. It is, of course, undeniable that some youths engage in sexual activity before the legal age, either on their own inclination or because they are victims of sexual abuse.

Both themes—teenage sexual activity and the sexual abuse of children—have inspired countless literary works. William Shakespeare created the most famous pair of teenage lovers, one of whom is just 13 years of age. See *Romeo and Juliet*, act I, sc. 2, l. 9 ("She hath not seen the change of fourteen years"). In the drama, Shakespeare portrays the relationship as something splendid and innocent, but not juvenile. The work has inspired no less than 40 motion pictures, some of which suggest that the teenagers consummated their relationship. Shakespeare may not have written sexually explicit scenes for the Elizabethean audience, but were modern directors to adopt a less conventional approach, that fact alone would not compel the conclusion that the work was obscene.

Contemporary movies pursue similar themes. Last year's Academy Awards featured the movie, *Traffic*, which was nominated for Best Picture. The film portrays a teenager, identified as a 16–year-old, who becomes addicted to drugs. The viewer sees the degradation of her addiction, which in the end leads her to a filthy room to trade sex for drugs. The year before, *American Beauty* won the Academy Award for Best Picture. In the course of the movie, a teenage girl engages in sexual relations with her teenage boyfriend, and another yields herself to the gratification of a middle-aged man. The film also contains a scene where, although the movie audience understands the act is not taking place, one character believes he is watching a teenage boy performing a sexual act on an older man.

Our society, like other cultures, has empathy and enduring fascination with the lives and destinies of the young. Art and literature express the vital interest we all have in the formative years we ourselves once knew, when wounds can be so grievous, disappointment so profound, and mistaken choices so tragic, but when moral acts and self-fulfillment are still in reach. Whether or not the films we mention violate the CPPA, they explore themes within the wide sweep of the statute's prohibitions. If these films, or hundreds of others of lesser note that explore those subjects, contain a single graphic depiction of sexual activity within the statutory definition, the possessor of the film would be subject to severe punishment without inquiry into the work's redeeming value. This is inconsistent with an essential First Amendment rule: The artistic merit of a work does not depend on the presence of a single explicit scene. See *Book Named "John Cleland's Memoirs of a Woman of Pleasure" v. Attorney General of Mass.*, (plurality opinion) ("[T]he social value of the book can neither be weighed against nor canceled by its prurient appeal or patent offensiveness"). Under *Miller*, the First Amendment requires that redeeming value be judged by considering the work as a whole. Where the scene is part of the narrative, the work itself does not for this reason become obscene, even though the scene in isolation might be offensive. For this reason, and the others we have noted, the CPPA cannot be read to prohibit obscenity, because it lacks the required link between its prohibitions and the affront to community standards prohibited by the definition of obscenity.

The Government seeks to address this deficiency by arguing that speech prohibited by the CPPA is virtually indistinguishable from child pornography, which may be banned without regard to whether it depicts works of value. Where the images are themselves the product of child sexual abuse, *Ferber* recognized that the State had an interest in stamping it out without regard to any judgment about its content. The production of the work, not its content, was the target of the statute. The fact that a work contained serious literary, artistic, or other value did not excuse the harm it caused to its child participants. It was simply "unrealistic to equate a community's toleration for sexually oriented materials with the permissible scope of legislation aimed at protecting children from sexual exploitation."

Ferber upheld a prohibition on the distribution and sale of child pornography, as well as its production, because these acts were "intrinsically related" to the sexual abuse of children in two ways. First, as a permanent record of a child's abuse, the continued circulation itself would harm the child who had participated. Like a defamatory statement, each new publication of the speech would cause new injury to the child's reputation and emotional well-being. Second, because the traffic in child pornography was an economic motive for its production, the State had an interest in closing the distribution network. "The most expeditious if not the only practical method of law enforcement may be to dry up the market for this material by imposing severe criminal penalties on persons selling, advertising, or otherwise promoting the product." Under either rationale, the speech had what the Court in effect held was a proximate link to the crime from which it came.

Later, in *Osborne v. Ohio*, the Court ruled that these same interests justified a ban on the possession of pornography produced by using children. "Given the importance of the State's interest in protecting the victims of child pornography," the State was justified in "attempting to stamp out this vice at all levels in the distribution chain." *Osborne* also noted the State's interest in preventing child pornography from being used as an aid in the solicitation of minors. The Court, however, anchored its holding in the concern for the participants, those whom it called the "victims of child pornography." It did not suggest that, absent this concern, other governmental interests would suffice.

In contrast to the speech in *Ferber*, speech that itself is the record of sexual abuse, the CPPA prohibits speech that records no crime and creates no victims by its production. Virtual child pornography is not "intrinsically related" to the sexual abuse of children, as were the materials in *Ferber*. While the Government asserts that the images can lead to actual instances of child abuse, the causal link is contingent and indirect. The harm does not necessarily follow from the speech, but depends upon some unquantified potential for subsequent criminal acts.

The Government says these indirect harms are sufficient because, as *Ferber* acknowledged, child pornography rarely can be valuable speech. ("The value of permitting live performances and photographic reproductions of children engaged in lewd sexual conduct is exceedingly modest, if not *de minimis*"). This argument, however, suffers from two flaws. First, *Ferber*'s judgment about child pornography was based upon how it was made, not on what it communicated. The case reaffirmed that where the speech is neither obscene nor the product of sexual abuse, it does not fall outside the protection of the First Amendment. ("[T]he distribution of descriptions or other depictions of sexual conduct, not otherwise obscene, which do not involve live performance or photographic or other visual reproduction of live performances, retains First Amendment protection").

The second flaw in the Government's position is that *Ferber* did not hold that child pornography is by definition without value. On the contrary, the Court recognized some works in this category might have significant value, but relied on virtual images—the very images prohibited by the CPPA—as an alternative and permissible means of expression: "[I]f it were necessary for literary or artistic value, a person over the statutory age who perhaps looked younger could be utilized. Simulation outside of the prohibition of the statute could provide another alternative." *Ferber*, then, not only referred to the distinction between actual and virtual child pornography, it relied on it as a reason supporting its holding. *Ferber* provides no support for a statute that eliminates the distinction and makes the alternative mode criminal as well.

III

The CPPA, for reasons we have explored, is inconsistent with *Miller* and finds no support in *Ferber*. The Government seeks to justify its prohibitions in other ways. It argues that the CPPA is necessary because pedophiles may use virtual child pornography to seduce children. There are many things innocent in themselves, however, such as cartoons, video games, and candy, that might be used for immoral purposes, yet we would not expect those to be prohibited because they can be misused. The Government, of course, may punish adults who provide unsuitable materials to children, see *Ginsberg v. New York*, and it may enforce criminal penalties for unlawful solicitation. The precedents establish, however, that speech within the rights of adults to hear may not be silenced completely in an attempt to shield children from it. In *Butler v. Michigan*, the Court invalidated a statute prohibiting distribution of an indecent publication because of its tendency to "incite minors to violent or depraved or immoral acts." A unanimous Court agreed upon the important First Amendment principle that the State could not "reduce the adult population . . . to reading only what is fit for children." We have reaffirmed this holding. See *Playboy, Reno, Sable*.

Here, the Government wants to keep speech from children not to protect them from its' content but to protect them from those who would commit other crimes. The principle, however, remains the same: The Government cannot ban speech fit for adults simply because it may fall into the hands of children. The evil in question depends upon the actor's unlawful conduct, conduct defined as criminal quite apart from any link to the speech in question. This establishes that the speech ban is not narrowly drawn. The objective is to prohibit illegal conduct, but this restriction goes well beyond that interest by restricting the speech available to law-abiding adults.

The Government submits further that virtual child pornography whets the appetites of pedophiles and encourages them to engage in illegal conduct. This rationale cannot sustain the provision in question. The mere tendency of speech to encourage unlawful acts is not a sufficient reason for banning it. The government "cannot constitutionally premise legislation on the desirability of controlling a person's private thoughts." *Stanley v. Georgia*. First Amendment freedoms are most in danger when the government seeks to control thought or to justify its laws for that impermissible end. The right to think is the beginning of freedom, and speech must be protected from the government because speech is the beginning of thought.

To preserve these freedoms, and to protect speech for its own sake, the Court's First Amendment cases draw vital distinctions between words and deeds, between ideas and conduct. The government may not prohibit speech because it increases the chance an unlawful act will be committed "at some indefinite future time." *Hess v. Indiana*. The government may suppress speech for advocating the use of force or a violation of law only if "such advocacy is directed to inciting or producing imminent lawless action and is likely to incite or produce such action." *Brandenburg v. Ohio*. There is here no attempt, incitement, solicitation, or conspiracy. The Government has shown no more than a remote connection between speech that might encourage thoughts or impulses and any resulting child abuse. Without a significantly stronger, more direct connection, the Government may not prohibit speech on the ground that it may encourage pedophiles to engage in illegal conduct.

The Government next argues that its objective of eliminating the market for pornography produced using real children necessitates a prohibition on virtual images as well. Virtual images, the Government contends, are indistinguishable from real ones; they are part of the same market and are often exchanged. In this way, it is said, virtual images promote the trafficking in works produced through the exploitation of real children. The hypothesis is somewhat implausible. If virtual images were identical to illegal child pornography, the illegal images would be driven from the market by the indistinguishable substitutes. Few pornographers would risk prosecution by abusing real children if fictional, computerized images would suffice.

In the case of the material covered by *Ferber*, the creation of the speech is itself the crime of child abuse; the prohibition deters the crime by removing the profit motive. Even where there is an underlying crime, however, the Court has not allowed the suppression of speech in all cases. E.g., *Bartnicki v. Vopper*, 532 U.S. 514 at 529 (2001) (market deterrence would not justify law prohibiting a radio commentator from distributing speech that had been unlawfully intercepted). We need not consider where to strike the balance in this case, because here, there is no underlying crime at all. Even if the Government's market deterrence theory were persuasive in some contexts, it would not justify this statute.

Finally, the Government says that the possibility of producing images by using computer imaging makes it very difficult for it to prosecute those who produce pornography by using real children. Experts, we are told, may have difficulty in saying whether the pictures were made by using real children or by using computer imaging. The necessary solution, the argument runs, is to prohibit both kinds of images. The argument, in essence, is that protected speech may be banned as a means to ban unprotected speech. This analysis turns the First Amendment upside down.

The Government may not suppress lawful speech as the means to suppress unlawful speech. Protected speech does not become unprotected merely because it resembles the latter. The Constitution requires the reverse. "[T]he possible harm to society in permitting some unprotected speech to go unpunished is outweighed by the possibility that protected speech of others may be muted. . . ." *Broadrick v. Oklahoma*, 413 U.S. at 612. The overbreadth doctrine prohibits the Government from banning unprotected speech if a substantial amount of protected speech is prohibited or chilled in the process.

To avoid the force of this objection, the Government would have us read the CPPA not as a measure suppressing speech but as a law shifting the burden to the accused to prove the speech is lawful. In this connection, the Government relies on an affirmative defense under the statute, which allows a defendant to avoid conviction for non-possession offenses by showing that the materials were produced using only adults and were not otherwise distributed in a manner conveying the impression that they depicted real children.

The Government raises serious constitutional difficulties by seeking to impose on the defendant the burden of proving his speech is not unlawful. An affirmative defense applies only after prosecution has begun, and the speaker must himself prove, on pain of a felony conviction, that his conduct falls within the affirmative defense. In cases under the CPPA, the evidentiary burden is not trivial. Where the defendant is not the producer of the work, he may have no way of establishing the identity, or even the existence, of the actors. If the evidentiary issue is a serious problem for the Government, as it asserts, it will be at least as difficult for the innocent possessor.

The statute, moreover, applies to work created before 1996, and the producers themselves may not have preserved the records necessary to meet the burden of proof. Failure to establish the defense can lead to a felony conviction.

We need not decide, however, whether the Government could impose this burden on a speaker. Even if an affirmative defense can save a statute from First Amendment challenge, here the defense is incomplete and insufficient, even on its own terms. It allows persons to be convicted in some instances where they can prove children were not exploited in the production. A defendant charged with possessing, as opposed to distributing, proscribed works may not defend on the ground that the film depicts only adult actors. So while the affirmative defense may protect a movie producer from prosecution for the act of distribution, that same producer, and all other persons in the subsequent distribution chain, could be liable for possessing the prohibited work. Furthermore, the affirmative defense provides no protection to persons who produce speech by using computer imaging, or through other means that do not involve the use of adult actors who appear to be minors. In these cases, the defendant can demonstrate no children were harmed in producing the images, yet the affirmative defense would not bar the prosecution. For this reason, the affirmative defense cannot save the statute, for it leaves unprotected a substantial amount of speech not tied to the Government's interest in distinguishing images produced using real children from virtual ones.

In sum, § 2256(8)(B) covers materials beyond the categories recognized in *Ferber* and *Miller*, and the reasons the Government offers in support of limiting the freedom of speech have no justification in our precedents or in the law of the First Amendment. The provision abridges the freedom to engage in a substantial amount of lawful speech. For this reason, it is overbroad and unconstitutional.

IV

Respondents challenge § 2256(8)(D) as well. This provision bans depictions of sexually explicit conduct that are "advertised, promoted, presented, described, or distributed in such a manner that conveys the impression that the material is or contains a visual depiction of a minor engaging in sexually explicit conduct." The parties treat the section as nearly identical to the provision prohibiting materials that appear to be child pornography. In the Government's view, the difference between the two is that "the 'conveys the impression' provision requires the jury to assess the material at issue in light of the manner in which it is promoted." The Government's assumption, however, is that the determination would still depend principally upon the content of the prohibited work.

We disagree with this view. The CPPA prohibits sexually explicit materials that conve[y] the impression" they depict minors. While that phrase may sound like the "appears to be" prohibition in § 2256(8)(B), it requires little judgment about the content of the image. Under § 2256(8)(D), the work must be sexually explicit, but otherwise the content is irrelevant. Even if a film contains no sexually explicit scenes involving minors, it could be treated as child pornography if the title and trailers convey the impression that the scenes would be found in the movie. The determination turns on how the speech is presented, not on what is depicted. While the legislative findings address at length the problems posed by materials that look like child pornography, they are silent on the evils posed by images simply pandered that way.

The Government does not offer a serious defense of this provision, and the other arguments it makes in support of the CPPA do not bear on § 2256(8)(D). The materials, for instance, are not likely to be confused for child pornography in a criminal trial. The Court has recognized that pandering may be relevant, as an evidentiary matter, to the question whether particular materials are obscene. See *Ginzburg v. United States* ("[I]n close cases evidence of pandering may be probative with respect to the nature of the material in question and thus satisfy the [obscenity] test"). Where a defendant engages in the "commercial exploitation of erotica solely for the sake of their prurient appeal," the context he or she creates may itself be relevant to the evaluation of the materials.

Section 2256(8)(D), however, prohibits a substantial amount of speech that falls outside *Ginzburg's* rationale. Materials falling within the proscription are tainted and unlawful in the hands of all who receive it, though they bear no responsibility for how it was marketed, sold, or described. The statute, furthermore, does not require that the context be part of an effort at "commercial exploitation." As a consequence, the CPPA does more than prohibit pandering. It prohibits possession of material described, or pandered, as child pornography by someone earlier in the distribution chain. The provision prohibits a sexually explicit film containing no youthful actors, just because it is placed in a box suggesting a prohibited movie. Possession is a crime even when the possessor knows the movie was mislabeled. The First Amendment requires a more precise restriction. For this reason, § 2256(8)(D) is substantially overbroad and in violation of the First Amendment.

V

For the reasons we have set forth, the prohibitions of §§ 2256(8)(B) and 2256(8)(D) are overbroad and unconstitutional. Having reached this conclusion, we need not address respondents' further contention that the provisions are unconstitutional because of vague statutory language.

The judgment of the Court of Appeals is affirmed.

JUSTICE THOMAS, concurring in the judgment.

In my view, the Government's most persuasive asserted interest in support of the Child Pornography Prevention Act is the prosecution rationale—that persons who possess and disseminate pornographic images of real children may escape conviction by claiming that the images are computer-generated, thereby raising a reasonable doubt as to their guilt. At this time, however, the Government asserts only that defendants raise such defenses, not that they have done so successfully. In fact, the Government points to no case in which a defendant has been acquitted based on a "computer-generated images" defense. While this speculative interest cannot support the broad reach of the CPPA, technology may evolve to the point where it becomes impossible to enforce actual child pornography laws because the Government cannot prove that certain pornographic images are of real children. In the event this occurs, the Government should not be foreclosed from enacting a regulation of virtual child pornography that contains an appropriate affirmative defense or some other narrowly drawn restriction. The Court suggests that the Government's interest in enforcing prohibitions against real child pornography cannot justify prohibitions on virtual child pornography, because "[t]his analysis turns the First Amendment upside down. The Government may not suppress lawful speech as the means to suppress unlawful speech." But if technological advances thwart prosecution of "unlawful speech," the Government may well have a compelling interest in barring or otherwise regulating some narrow category of "lawful speech" in order to enforce effectively laws against pornography made through the abuse of real children. The Court does leave open the possibility that a more complete affirmative defense could save a statute's constitutionality, implicitly accepting that some regulation of virtual child pornography might be constitutional. I would not prejudge, however, whether a more complete affirmative defense is the only way to narrowly tailor a criminal statute that prohibits the possession and dissemination of virtual child pornography. Thus, I concur in the judgment of the Court.

JUSTICE O'CONNOR, with whom THE CHIEF JUSTICE and JUSTICE SCALIA join as to Part II, concurring in the judgment in part and dissenting in part.

The Child Pornography Prevention Act of 1996 proscribes the "knowin[g]" reproduction, distribution, sale, reception, or possession of images that fall under the statute's definition of child pornography. Possession is punishable by up to 5 years in prison for a first offense, and all other transgressions are punishable by up to 15 years in prison for a first offense. The CPPA defines child pornography to include "any visual depiction ... of sexually explicit conduct" where "such visual depiction is, or appears to be, of a minor engaging in sexually explicit conduct," § 2256(8)(B) (emphasis added), or "such visual depiction is advertised, promoted, presented, described, or distributed in such a manner that *conveys the impression* that the material is or contains a visual depiction of a minor engaging in sexually explicit conduct," § 2256(8)(D) (emphasis added). The statute defines "sexually explicit conduct" as "actual or simulated ... sexual intercourse; ... bestiality; ... masturbation; ... sadistic or masochistic abuse; or ... lascivious exhibition of the genitals or pubic area of any person."

The CPPA provides for two affirmative defenses. First, a defendant is not liable for possession if the defendant possesses less than three proscribed images and promptly destroys such images or reports the matter to law enforcement. Second, a defendant is not liable for the remaining acts pro-scribed if the images involved were produced using only adult subjects and are not presented in such a manner as to "convey the impression" they contain depictions of minors engaging in sexually explicit conduct.

This litigation involves a facial challenge to the CPPA's prohibitions of pornographic images that "appea[r] to be . . . of a minor" and of material that "conveys the impression" that it contains pornographic images of minors. While I agree with the Court's judgment that the First Amendment requires that the latter prohibition be struck down, I disagree with its decision to strike down the former prohibition in its entirety. The "appears to be . . . of a minor" language in § 2256(8)(B) covers two categories of speech: pornographic images of adults that look like children ("youthful-adult pornography") and pornographic images of children created wholly on a computer, without using any actual children ("virtual-child pornography"). The Court concludes, correctly, that the CPPA's ban on youthful-adult pornography is overbroad. In my view, however, respondents fail to present sufficient evidence to demonstrate that the ban on virtual-child pornography is overbroad. Because invalidation due to overbreadth is such "strong medicine," *Broadrick v. Oklahoma*, 413 U.S. 601, 613 (1973), I would strike down the prohibition of pornography that "appears to be" of minors only insofar as it is applied to the class of youthful-adult pornography.

I

Respondents assert that the CPPA's prohibitions of youthful-adult pornography, virtual-child pornography, and material that "conveys the impression" that it contains actual-child pornography are overbroad, that the prohibitions are content-based regulations not narrowly tailored to serve a compelling Government interest, and that the prohibitions are unconstitutionally vague. The Government not only disagrees with these specific contentions, but also requests that the Court exclude youthful-adult and virtual-child pornography from the protection of the First Amendment.

I agree with the Court's decision not to grant this request. Because the Government may already prohibit obscenity without violating the First Amendment, what the Government asks this Court to rule is that it may also prohibit youthful-adult and virtual-adult pornography that is merely indecent without violating that Amendment.

Although such pornography looks like the material at issue in *New York v. Ferber*, no children are harmed in the process of creating such pornography. Therefore, *Ferber* does not support the Government's ban on youthful-adult and virtual-child pornography. The Government argues that, even if the production of such pornography does not directly harm children, this material aids and abets child abuse. The Court correctly concludes that the causal connection between pornographic images that "appear" to include minors and actual child abuse is not strong enough to justify withdrawing First Amendment protection for such speech.

I also agree with the Court's decision to strike down the CPPA's ban on material presented in a manner that "conveys the impression" that it contains pornographic depictions of actual children § 2256(8)(D). The Government fails to explain how this ban serves any compelling state interest. Any speech covered by § 2256(8)(D) that is obscene, actual-child pornography, or otherwise indecent is prohibited by other federal statutes. The Court concludes that § 2256(8)(D) is overbroad, but its reasoning also persuades me that the provision is not narrowly tailored. The provision therefore fails strict scrutiny. *Playboy.*

Finally, I agree with Court that that the CPPA's ban on youthful-adult pornography is overbroad. The Court provides several examples of movies that, although possessing serious literary, artistic or political value and employing only adult actors to perform simulated sexual conduct, fall under the CPPA's proscription on images that "appea[r] to be ... of a minor engaging in sexually explicit conduct," (citing *Romeo and Juliet*, *Traffic*, and *American Beauty*). Individuals or businesses found to possess just three such films have no defense to criminal liability under the CPPA.

II

I disagree with the Court, however, that the CPPA's prohibition of virtual-child pornography is overbroad. Before I reach that issue, there are two preliminary questions: whether the ban on virtual-child pornography fails strict scrutiny and whether that ban is unconstitutionally vague. I would answer both in the negative. The Court has long recognized that the Government has a compelling interest in protecting our Nation's children. This interest is promoted by efforts directed against sexual offenders and actual-child pornography. These efforts, in turn, are supported by the CPPA's ban on virtual-child pornography. Such images whet the appetites of child molesters, who may use the images to seduce young children. Of even more serious concern is the prospect that defendants indicted for the production, distribution, or possession of actual-child pornography may evade liability by claiming that the images attributed to them are in fact computer-generated. Respondents may be correct that no defendant has successfully employed this tactic. But, given the rapid pace of advances in computer-graphics technology, the Government's concern is reasonable. Computer-generated images lodged with the Court by *Amici Curiae* National Law Center for Children and Families et al. bear a remarkable likeness to actual human beings. Anyone who has seen, for example, the film *Final Fantasy: The Spirits Within* (H. Sakaguchi and M. Sakakibara directors, 2001) can understand the Government's concern. Moreover, this Court's cases do not require Congress to wait for harm to occur before it can legislate against it. See *Turner Broadcasting System, Inc. v. FCC*, 520 U.S. 180, 212 (1997).

Respondents argue that, even if the Government has a compelling interest to justify banning virtual-child pornography, the "appears to be ... of a minor" language is not narrowly tailored to serve that interest. They assert that the CPPA would capture even cartoon—sketches or statues of children that were sexually suggestive. Such images surely could not be used, for instance, to seduce children. I agree. A better interpretation of "appears to be ... of" is "virtually indistinguishable from"—an interpretation that would not cover the examples respondents provide. Not only does the text of the statute comfortably bear this narrowing interpretation, the interpretation comports with the language that Congress repeatedly used in its findings of fact.

Reading the statute only to bar images that are virtually indistinguishable from actual children would not only assure that the ban on virtual-child pornography is narrowly tailored, but would also assuage any fears that the "appears to be . . . of a minor" language is vague. The narrow reading greatly limits any risks from "discriminatory enforcement." Respondents maintain that the "virtually indistinguishable from" language is also vague because it begs the question: from whose perspective? This problem is exaggerated. This Court has never required "mathematical certainty" or "meticulous specificity" from the language of a statute.

The Court concludes that the CPPA's ban on virtual-child pornography is overbroad. The basis for this holding is unclear. Although a content-based regulation may serve a compelling state interest, and be as narrowly tailored as possible while substantially serving that interest, the regulation may unintentionally ensnare speech that has serious literary, artistic, political, or scientific value or that does not threaten the harms sought to be combated by the Government. If so, litigants may challenge the regulation on its face as overbroad, but in doing so they bear the heavy burden of demonstrating that the regulation forbids a substantial amount of valuable or harmless speech. See *Reno, supra*, at 896, (O'Connor, J., concurring in judgment in part and dissenting in part) (citing *Broadrick*, 413 U.S. at 615). Respondents have not made such a demonstration. Respondents provide no examples of films or other materials that are wholly computer-generated and contain images that "appea[r] to be . . . of minors" engaging in indecent conduct, but that have serious value or do not facilitate child abuse. Their overbreadth challenge therefore fails.

CHIEF JUSTICE REHNQUIST, with whom JUSTICE SCALIA joins in part, dissenting.

I agree with Part II of Justice O'Connor's opinion concurring in the judgment in part and dissenting in part. Congress has a compelling interest in ensuring the ability to enforce prohibitions of actual child pornography, and we should defer to its findings that rapidly advancing technology soon will make it all but impossible to do so.

I also agree with Justice O'Connor that serious First Amendment concerns would arise were the Government ever to prosecute someone for simple distribution or possession of a film with literary or artistic value, such as *"Traffic"* or *"American Beauty."* I write separately, however, because the Child Pornography Prevention Act of 1996 (CPPA) need not be construed to reach such materials.

We normally do not strike down a statute on First Amendment grounds "when a limiting instruction has been or could be placed on the challenged statute." This case should be treated no differently.

Other than computer generated images that are virtually indistinguishable from real children engaged in sexually explicitly conduct, the CPPA can be limited so as not to reach any material that was not already unprotected before the CPPA. The CPPA's definition of "sexually explicit conduct" is quite explicit in this regard. It makes clear that the statute only reaches "visual depictions" of:

"[A]ctual or simulated ... sexual intercourse, including genital-genital, oral-genital, anal-genital, or oral-anal, whether between persons of the same or opposite sex; ... bestiality; ... masturbation; ... sadistic or masochistic abuse; ... or lascivious exhibition of the genitals or pubic area of any person."

The Court and Justice O'Connor suggest that this very graphic definition reaches the depiction of youthful looking adult actors engaged in suggestive sexual activity, presumably because the definition extends to "simulated" intercourse. Read as a whole, however, I think the definition reaches only the sort of "hard core of child pornography" that we found without protection in *Ferber*. So construed, the CPPA bans visual depictions of youthful looking adult actors engaged in actual sexual activity; mere suggestions of sexual activity, such as youthful looking adult actors squirming under a blanket, are more akin to written descriptions than visual depictions, and thus fall outside the purview of the statute.[1]

The reference to "simulated" has been part of the definition of "sexually explicit conduct" since the statute was first passed. See Protection of Children Against Sexual Exploitation Act of 1977. But the inclusion of "simulated" conduct, alongside "actual" conduct, does not change the "hard core" nature of the image banned. The reference to "simulated" conduct simply brings within the statute's reach depictions of hard core pornography that are "made to look genuine," Webster's Ninth New Collegiate Dictionary 1099 (1983)— including the main target of the CPPA, computer generated images virtually indistinguishable from real children engaged in sexually explicit conduct. Neither actual conduct nor simulated conduct, however, is properly construed to reach depictions such as those in a film portrayal of *Romeo and Juliet*, which are far removed from the hard core pornographic depictions that Congress intended to reach.

Indeed, we should be loath to construe a statute as banning film portrayals of Shakespearian tragedies, without some indication—from text or legislative history—that such a result was intended. In fact, Congress explicitly instructed that such a reading of the CPPA would be wholly unwarranted. As the Court of Appeals for the First Circuit has observed:

"[T]he legislative record, which makes plain that the [CPPA] was intended to target only a narrow class of images—visual depictions 'which are virtually indistinguishable to unsuspecting viewers from unretouched photographs of actual children engaging in identical sexual conduct.' "

Judge Ferguson similarly observed in his dissent in the Court of Appeals in this case:

"From reading the legislative history, it becomes clear that the CPPA merely extends the existing prohibitions on 'real' child pornography to a narrow class of computer-generated pictures easily mistaken for real photographs of real children." *Free Speech Coalition v. Reno*, 198 F.3d 1083, 1102 (C.A.9 1999).

---

1. Of course, even the narrow class of youthful looking adult images prohibited under the CPPA is subject to an affirmative defense so long as materials containing such images are not advertised or promoted as child pornography. 18 U.S.C. § 2252A(c).

This narrow reading of "sexually explicit conduct" not only accords with the text of the CPPA and the intentions of Congress; it is exactly how the phrase was understood prior to the broadening gloss the Court gives it today. Indeed, had "sexually explicit conduct" been thought to reach the sort of material the Court says it does, then films such as *"Traffic"* and *"American Beauty"* would not have been made the way they were. *"Traffic"* won its Academy Award in 2001. *"American Beauty"* won its Academy Award in 2000. But the CPPA has been on the books, and has been enforced, since 1996. The chill felt by the Court ("[F]ew legitimate movie producers ... would risk distributing images in or near the uncertain reach of this law"), has apparently never been felt by those who actually make movies. To the extent the CPPA prohibits possession or distribution of materials that "convey the impression" of a child engaged in sexually explicit conduct, that prohibition can and should be limited to reach "the sordid business of pandering" which lies outside the bounds of First Amendment protection. *Ginzburg* (conduct that "deliberately emphasized the sexually provocative aspects of the work, in order to catch the salaciously disposed" may lose First Amendment protection); *Playboy* (SCALIA, J., dissenting) (collecting cases). This is how the Government asks us to construe the statute, and it is the most plausible reading of the text, which prohibits only materials *"advertised, promoted, presented, described, or distributed in such a manner* that conveys the impression that the material is or contains a visual depiction of a minor engaging in sexually explicit conduct." (emphasis added).

The First Amendment may protect the video shop owner or film distributor who promotes material as "entertaining" or "acclaimed" regardless of whether the material contains depictions of youthful looking adult actors engaged in nonobscene but sexually suggestive conduct. The First Amendment does not, however, protect the panderer. Thus, materials promoted as conveying the impression that they depict actual minors engaged in sexually explicit conduct do not escape regulation merely because they might warrant First Amendment protection if promoted in a different manner. I would construe "conveys the impression" as limited to the panderer, which makes the statute entirely consistent with *Ginzburg* and other cases.

The Court says that "conveys the impression" goes well beyond *Ginzburg* to "prohibi[t][the] possession of material described, or pandered, as child pornography by someone earlier in the distribution chain." The Court's concern is that an individual who merely possesses protected materials (such as videocassettes of *"Traffic"* or *"American Beauty"*) might offend the CPPA regardless of whether the individual actually intended to possess materials containing unprotected images.

This concern is a legitimate one, but there is, again, no need or reason to construe the statute this way. In *X-Citement Video* we faced a provision of the Protection of Children Against Sexual Exploitation Act of 1977, the precursor to the CPPA, which lent itself much less than the present statute to attributing a "knowingly" requirement to the contents of the possessed visual depictions. We held that such a requirement nonetheless applied, so that the Government would have to prove that a person charged with possessing child pornography actually knew that the materials contained depictions of real minors engaged in sexually explicit conduct. In light of this holding, and consistent with the narrow class of images the CPPA is intended to prohibit, the CPPA can be construed to prohibit only the knowing possession of materials actually containing visual depictions of real minors engaged in sexually explicit conduct, or computer generated images virtually indistinguishable from real minors engaged in sexually explicit conduct. The mere possession of materials containing only suggestive depictions of youthful looking adult actors need not be so included.

In sum, while potentially impermissible applications of the CPPA may exist, I doubt that they would be "substantial ... in relation to the statute's plainly legitimate sweep." The aim of ensuring the enforceability of our Nation's child pornography laws is a compelling one. The CPPA is targeted to this aim by extending the definition of child pornography to reach computer-generated images that are virtually indistinguishable from real children engaged in sexually explicit conduct. The statute need not be read to do any more than precisely this, which is not offensive to the First Amendment. For these reasons, I would construe the CPPA in a manner consistent with the First Amendment, reverse the Court of Appeals' judgment, and uphold the statute in its entirety.

QUESTIONS AND NOTES

1. Which opinion was truer to precedent? Explain.

2. Which opinion reached the best First Amendment policy? Explain.

3. Is there much true child pornography (*vis-a-vis* material other than movies like "American Beauty") that would not qualify as obscenity?

4. If your answer to question 3 is "no," is there any harm in compelling virtual child pornography cases to be prosecuted as obscenity? Would your answer be any different for real child pornography? Why? Why not?

5. If the Government had made a stronger case establishing that virtual child pornography was effective in seducing real children, would (should) the result have been different? Why? Why not?

6. If real and virtual child pornography become indistinguishable, what can the Government do? What should it be able to do?

C. PROTECTING COMMUNITY ENVIRONMENT

p. 417 after question 7

In *City of Erie v. Pap's A.M.*, the Court faced almost the same question as it faced in *Barnes*; and reached almost the same answer. As you read *Erie*, think about the similarities and differences between the two cases.

CITY OF ERIE v. PAP'S A.M.
529 U.S. 277, 120 S.Ct. 1382 (2000).

JUSTICE O'CONNOR announced the judgment of the Court and delivered the opinion of the Court with respect to Parts I and II, and an opinion with respect to Parts III and IV, in which THE CHIEF JUSTICE, JUSTICE KENNEDY, and JUSTICE BREYER join.

The city of Erie, Pennsylvania, enacted an ordinance banning public nudity. Respondent Pap's A.M. (hereinafter Pap's), which operated a nude dancing establishment in Erie, challenged the constitutionality of the ordinance and sought a permanent injunction against its enforcement. The Pennsylvania Supreme Court, although noting that this Court in *Barnes v. Glen Theatre* had upheld an Indiana ordinance that was "strikingly similar" to Erie's, found that the public nudity sections of the ordinance violated respondent's right to freedom of expression under the United States Constitution. This case raises the question whether the Pennsylvania Supreme Court properly evaluated the ordinance's constitutionality under the First Amendment. We hold that Erie's ordinance is a content-neutral regulation that satisfies the four-part test of *United States v. O'Brien*. Accordingly, we reverse the decision of the Pennsylvania Supreme Court and remand for the consideration of any remaining issues.

I

On September 28, 1994, the city council for the city of Erie, Pennsylvania, enacted Ordinance 75–1994, a public indecency ordinance that makes it a summary offense to knowingly or intentionally appear in public in a "state of nudity."[1] Respondent Pap's, a Pennsylvania corporation, operated an establishment in Erie known as "Kandyland" that featured totally nude erotic dancing performed by women. To comply with the ordinance, these dancers must wear, at a minimum, "pasties" and a "G-string." On October 14, 1994, two days after the ordinance went into effect, Pap's filed a complaint against the city of Erie, the mayor of the city, and members of the city council, seeking declaratory relief and a permanent injunction against the enforcement of the ordinance.

Although the Pennsylvania court noted that the Indiana statute at issue in *Barnes* "is strikingly similar to the Ordinance we are examining," it concluded that "unfortunately for our purposes, the *Barnes* Court splintered and produced four separate, non-harmonious opinions." After canvassing these separate opinions, the Pennsylvania court concluded that, although it is permissible to find precedential effect in a fragmented decision, to do so a majority of the Court must have been in agreement on the concept that is

---

1. Ordinance 75–1994, codified as Article 711 of the Codified Ordinances of the city of Erie, provides in relevant part:

"1. A person who knowingly or intentionally, in a public place:

"a. engages in sexual intercourse

"b. engages in deviate sexual intercourse as defined by the Pennsylvania Crimes Code

"c. appears in a state of nudity, or

"d. fondles the genitals of himself, herself or another person commits Public Indecency, a Summary Offense.

"2. 'Nudity' means the showing of the human male or female genital [sic], pubic hair or buttocks with less than a fully opaque covering; the showing of the female breast with less than a fully opaque covering of any part of the nipple; the exposure of any device, costume, or covering which gives the appearance of or simulates the genitals, pubic hair, natal cleft, perineum anal region or pubic hair region; or the exposure of any device worn as a cover over the nipples and/or areola of the female breast, which device simulates and gives the realistic appearance of nipples and/or areola.

"3. 'Public Place' includes all outdoor places owned by or open to the general public, and all buildings and enclosed places owned by or open to the general public, including such places of entertainment, taverns, restaurants, clubs, theaters, dance halls, banquet halls, party rooms or halls limited to specific members, restricted to adults or to patrons invited to attend, whether or not an admission charge is levied.

"4. The prohibition set forth in subsection 1(c) shall not apply to:

"a. Any child under ten (10) years of age; or

"b. Any individual exposing a breast in the process of breastfeeding an infant under two (2) years of age."

deemed to be the holding. See *Marks v. United States,* 430 U.S. 188 (1977). The Pennsylvania court noted that "aside from the agreement by a majority of the *Barnes* Court that nude dancing is entitled to some First Amendment protection, we can find no point on which a majority of the *Barnes* Court agreed." Accordingly, the court concluded that "no clear precedent arises out of *Barnes* on the issue of whether the [Erie] ordinance ... passes muster under the First Amendment."

Having determined that there was no United States Supreme Court precedent on point, the Pennsylvania court conducted an independent examination of the ordinance to ascertain whether it was related to the suppression of expression. The court concluded that although one of the purposes of the ordinance was to combat negative secondary effects, "inextricably bound up with this stated purpose is an unmentioned purpose ... to impact negatively on the erotic message of the dance." As such, the court determined the ordinance was content based and subject to strict scrutiny. The ordinance failed the narrow tailoring requirement of strict scrutiny because the court found that imposing criminal and civil sanctions on those who commit sex crimes would be a far narrower means of combating secondary effects than the requirement that dancers wear pasties and G-strings.

Because the court determined that the public nudity provisions of the ordinance violated Pap's right to freedom of expression under the United States Constitution, it did not address the constitutionality of the ordinance under the Pennsylvania Constitution or the claim that the ordinance is unconstitutionally overbroad.

In a separate concurrence, two justices of the Pennsylvania court noted that, because this Court upheld a virtually identical statute in *Barnes,* the ordinance should have been upheld under the United States Constitution. They reached the same result as the majority, however, because they would have held that the public nudity sections of the ordinance violate the Pennsylvania Constitution.

The city of Erie petitioned for a writ of certiorari, which we granted. Shortly thereafter, Pap's filed a motion to dismiss the case as moot, noting that Kandyland was no longer operating as a nude dancing club, and Pap's was not operating a nude dancing club at any other location. We denied the motion.

II

As a preliminary matter, we must address the justiciability question. Here, Pap's submitted an affidavit stating that it had "ceased to operate a nude dancing establishment in Erie." Pap's asserts that the case is therefore moot because "the outcome of this case will have no effect upon Respondent." Simply closing Kandyland is not sufficient to render this case moot, however. Pap's is still incorporated under Pennsylvania law, and it could again decide to operate a nude dancing establishment in Erie. JUSTICE SCALIA differs with our assessment as to the likelihood that Pap's may resume its nude dancing operation. Several Members of this Court can attest, however, that the "advanced age" of Pap's owner (72) does not make it "absolutely clear" that a life of quiet retirement is his only reasonable expectation. Moreover, our appraisal of Pap's affidavit is influenced by Pap's failure, despite its obligation to the Court, to mention a word about the potential mootness issue in its brief in opposition to the petition for writ of certiorari, which was filed in April 1999, even though, as JUSTICE SCALIA points out, Kandyland was closed and that property sold in 1998.

In any event, this is not a run of the mill voluntary cessation case. Here it is the plaintiff who, having prevailed below, now seeks to have the case declared moot. And it is the city of Erie that seeks to invoke the federal judicial power to obtain this Court's review of the Pennsylvania Supreme Court decision. The city has an ongoing injury because it is barred from enforcing the public nudity provisions of its ordinance. If the challenged ordinance is found constitutional, then Erie can enforce it, and the availability of such relief is sufficient to prevent the case from being moot. And Pap's still has a concrete stake in the outcome of this case because, to the extent Pap's has an interest in resuming operations, it has an interest in preserving the judgment of the Pennsylvania Supreme Court. Our interest in preventing litigants from attempting to manipulate the Court's jurisdiction to insulate a favorable decision from review further counsels against a finding of mootness here. Although the issue is close, we conclude that the case is not moot, and we turn to the merits.

III

Being "in a state of nudity" is not an inherently expressive condition. As we explained in *Barnes*, however, nude dancing of the type at issue here is expressive conduct, although we think that it falls only within the outer ambit of the First Amendment's protection.

To determine what level of scrutiny applies to the ordinance at issue here, we must decide "whether the State's regulation is related to the suppression of expression." *Texas v. Johnson; O'Brien*. If the governmental purpose in enacting the regulation is unrelated to the suppression of expression, then the regulation need only satisfy the "less stringent" standard from *O'Brien* for evaluating restrictions on symbolic speech. If the government interest is related to the content of the expression, however, then the regulation falls outside the scope of the *O'Brien* test and must be justified under a more demanding standard.

In *Barnes*, we analyzed an almost identical statute, holding that Indiana's public nudity ban did not violate the First Amendment, although no five Members of the Court agreed on a single rationale for that conclusion. We now clarify that government restrictions on public nudity such as the ordinance at issue here should be evaluated under the framework set forth in *O'Brien* for content-neutral restrictions on symbolic speech.

The city of Erie argues that the ordinance is a content-neutral restriction that is reviewable under *O'Brien* because the ordinance bans conduct, not speech; specifically, public nudity. Respondent counters that the ordinance targets nude dancing and, as such, is aimed specifically at suppressing expression, making the ordinance a content-based restriction that must be subjected to strict scrutiny.

The ordinance here, like the statute in *Barnes*, is on its face a general prohibition on public nudity. By its terms, the ordinance regulates conduct alone. It does not target nudity that contains an erotic message; rather, it bans all public nudity, regardless of whether that nudity is accompanied by expressive activity. And like the statute in *Barnes*, the Erie ordinance replaces and updates provisions of an "Indecency and Immorality" ordinance that has been on the books since 1866, predating the prevalence of nude dancing establishments such as Kandyland.

Respondent and JUSTICE STEVENS contend nonetheless that the ordinance is related to the suppression of expression because language in the ordinance's preamble suggests that its actual purpose is to prohibit erotic dancing of the type performed at Kandyland. That is not how the Pennsylvania Supreme Court interpreted that language, however. In the preamble to the ordinance, the city council stated that it was adopting the regulation

> " 'for the purpose of limiting a recent increase in nude live entertainment within the City, which activity adversely impacts and threatens to impact on the public health, safety and welfare by providing an atmosphere conducive to violence, sexual harassment, public intoxication, prostitution, the spread of sexually transmitted diseases and other deleterious effects.' "

The Pennsylvania Supreme Court construed this language to mean that one purpose of the ordinance was "to combat negative secondary effects."

As JUSTICE SOUTER noted in *Barnes*, "on its face, the governmental interest in combating prostitution and other criminal activity is not at all inherently related to expression." In that sense, this case is similar to *O'Brien*. O'Brien burned his draft registration card as a public statement of his antiwar views, and he was convicted under a statute making it a crime to knowingly mutilate or destroy such a card. This Court rejected his claim that the statute violated his First Amendment rights, reasoning that the law punished him for the "noncommunicative impact of his conduct, and for nothing else." In other words, the Government regulation prohibiting the destruction of draft cards was aimed at maintaining the integrity of the Selective Service System and not at suppressing the message of draft resistance that O'Brien sought to convey by burning his draft card. So too here, the ordinance prohibiting public nudity is aimed at combating crime and other negative secondary effects caused by the presence of adult entertainment establishments like Kandyland and not at suppressing the erotic message conveyed by this type of nude dancing. Put another way, the ordinance does not attempt to regulate the primary effects of the expression, *i.e.*, the effect on the audience of watching nude erotic dancing, but rather the secondary effects, such as the impacts on public health, safety, and welfare, which we have previously recognized are "caused by the presence of even one such" establishment.

Although the Pennsylvania Supreme Court acknowledged that one goal of the ordinance was to combat the negative secondary effects associated with nude dancing establishments, the court concluded that the ordinance was nevertheless content based, relying on Justice White's position in dissent in *Barnes* for the proposition that a ban of this type *necessarily* has the purpose of suppressing the erotic message of the dance. Because the Pennsylvania court agreed with Justice White's approach, it concluded that the ordinance must have another, "unmentioned" purpose related to the suppression of expression. That is, the Pennsylvania court adopted the dissent's view in

Barnes that "since the State permits the dancers to perform if they wear pasties and G-strings but forbids nude dancing, it is precisely because of the distinctive, expressive content of the nude dancing performances at issue in this case that the State seeks to apply the statutory prohibition." A majority of the Court rejected that view in *Barnes*, and we do so again here.

Respondent's argument that the ordinance is "aimed" at suppressing expression through a ban on nude dancing—an argument that respondent supports by pointing to statements by the city attorney that the public nudity ban was not intended to apply to "legitimate" theater productions—is really an argument that the city council also had an illicit motive in enacting the ordinance. As we have said before, however, this Court will not strike down an otherwise constitutional statute on the basis of an alleged illicit motive. *O'Brien; Renton v. Playtime Theatres.* In light of the Pennsylvania court's determination that one purpose of the ordinance is to combat harmful secondary effects, the ban on public nudity here is no different from the ban on burning draft registration cards in *O'Brien*, where the Government sought to prevent the means of the expression and not the expression of antiwar sentiment itself.

JUSTICE STEVENS argues that the ordinance enacts a complete ban on expression. We respectfully disagree with that characterization. The public nudity ban certainly has the effect of limiting one particular means of expressing the kind of erotic message being disseminated at Kandyland. But simply to define what is being banned as the "message" is to assume the conclusion. We did not analyze the regulation in *O'Brien* as having enacted a total ban on expression. Instead, the Court recognized that the regulation against destroying one's draft card was justified by the Government's interest in preventing the harmful "secondary effects" of that conduct (disruption to the Selective Service System), even though that regulation may have some incidental effect on the expressive element of the conduct. Because this justification was unrelated to the suppression of O'Brien's antiwar message, the regulation was content neutral. Although there may be cases in which banning the means of expression so interferes with the message that it essentially bans the message, that is not the case here.

Even if we had not already rejected the view that a ban on public nudity is necessarily related to the suppression of the erotic message of nude dancing, we would do so now because the premise of such a view is flawed. The State's interest in preventing harmful secondary effects is not related to the suppression of expression. In trying to control the secondary effects of nude dancing, the ordinance seeks to deter crime and the other deleterious effects caused by the presence of such an establishment in the neighborhood. In *Clark v. Community for Creative Non–Violence,* we held that a National Park Service regulation prohibiting camping in certain parks did not violate the First Amendment when applied to prohibit demonstrators from sleeping in Lafayette Park and the Mall in Washington, D. C., in connection with a demonstration intended to call attention to the plight of the homeless. Assuming, *arguendo,* that sleeping can be expressive conduct, the Court concluded that the Government interest in conserving park property was unrelated to the demonstrators' message about homelessness. So, while the demonstrators were allowed to erect "symbolic tent cities," they were not allowed to sleep overnight in those tents. Even though the regulation may have directly limited the expressive element involved in actually sleeping in the park, the regulation was nonetheless content neutral.

Similarly, even if Erie's public nudity ban has some minimal effect on the erotic message by muting that portion of the expression that occurs when the last stitch is dropped, the dancers at Kandyland and other such establishments are free to perform wearing pasties and G-strings. Any effect on the overall expression is *de minimis*. And as JUSTICE STEVENS eloquently stated for the plurality in *Young v. American Mini Theatres*, "even though we recognize that the First Amendment will not tolerate the total suppression of erotic materials that have some arguably artistic value, it is manifest that society's interest in protecting this type of expression is of a wholly different, and lesser, magnitude than the interest in untrammeled political debate," and "few of us would march our sons or daughters off to war to preserve the citizen's right to see" specified anatomical areas exhibited at establishments like Kandyland. If States are to be able to regulate secondary effects, then *de minimis* intrusions on expression such as those at issue here cannot be sufficient to render the ordinance content based.

This case is, in fact, similar to *O'Brien, Community for Creative Non–Violence,* and *Ward v. Rock Against Racism.* The justification for the government regulation in each case prevents harmful "secondary" effects that are unrelated to the suppression of expression. While the doctrinal theories behind "incidental burdens" and "secondary effects" are, of course, not identical, there is nothing objectionable about a city passing a general ordinance to ban public nudity (even though such a ban may place incidental burdens on some protected speech) and at the same time recognizing that one specific occurrence of public nudity—nude erotic dancing—is particularly problematic because it produces harmful secondary effects.

JUSTICE STEVENS claims that today we "[f]or the first time" extend *Renton*'s secondary effects doctrine to justify restrictions other than the location of a commercial enterprise. Our reliance on *Renton* to justify other restrictions is not new, however. In *Ward,* the Court relied on *Renton* to evaluate restrictions on sound amplification at an outdoor bandshell, rejecting the dissent's contention that *Renton* was inapplicable. See *Ward v. Rock Against Racism* ("Today, for the first time, a majority of the Court applies *Renton* analysis to a category of speech far afield from that decision's original limited focus"). Moreover, Erie's ordinance does not effect a "total ban" on protected expression.

In *Renton,* the regulation explicitly treated "adult" movie theaters differently from other theaters, and defined "adult" theaters solely by reference to the content of their movies. We nonetheless treated the zoning regulation as content neutral because the ordinance was aimed at the secondary effects of adult theaters, a justification unrelated to the content of the adult movies themselves. Here, Erie's ordinance is on its face a content-neutral restriction on conduct. Even if the city thought that nude dancing at clubs like Kandyland constituted a particularly problematic instance of public nudity, the regulation is still properly evaluated as a content-neutral restriction because the interest in combating the secondary effects associated with those clubs is unrelated to the suppression of the erotic message conveyed by nude dancing.

We conclude that Erie's asserted interest in combating the negative secondary effects associated with adult entertainment establishments like Kandyland is unrelated to the suppression of the erotic message conveyed by nude dancing. The ordinance prohibiting public nudity is therefore valid if it satisfies the four-factor test from *O'Brien* for evaluating restrictions on symbolic speech.

IV

Applying that standard here, we conclude that Erie's ordinance is justified under *O'Brien*. The first factor of the *O'Brien* test is whether the government regulation is within the constitutional power of the government to enact. Here, Erie's efforts to protect public health and safety are clearly within the city's police powers. The second factor is whether the regulation furthers an important or substantial government interest. The asserted interests of regulating conduct through a public nudity ban and of combating the harmful secondary effects associated with nude dancing are undeniably important. And in terms of demonstrating that such secondary effects pose a threat, the city need not "conduct new studies or produce evidence independent of that already generated by other cities" to demonstrate the problem of secondary effects, "so long as whatever evidence the city relies upon is reasonably believed to be relevant to the problem that the city addresses." *Renton*. Because the nude dancing at Kandyland is of the same character as the adult entertainment at issue in *Renton*, *American Mini Theatres*, and *California v. LaRue*, 409 U.S. 109 (1972), it was reasonable for Erie to conclude that such nude dancing was likely to produce the same secondary effects. And Erie could reasonably rely on the evidentiary foundation set forth in *Renton* and *American Mini Theatres* to the effect that secondary effects are caused by the presence of even one adult entertainment establishment in a given neighborhood. See *Renton* (indicating that reliance on a judicial opinion that describes the evidentiary basis is sufficient). In fact, Erie expressly relied on *Barnes* and its discussion of secondary effects, including its reference to *Renton* and *American Mini Theatres*. Even in cases addressing regulations that strike closer to the core of First Amendment values, we have accepted a state or local government's reasonable belief that the experience of other jurisdictions is relevant to the problem it is addressing. Regardless of whether JUSTICE SOUTER now wishes to disavow his opinion in *Barnes* on this point, evidentiary standard described in *Renton* controls here, and Erie meets that standard.

In any event, Erie also relied on its own findings. The preamble to the ordinance states that "the Council of the City of Erie *has, at various times over more than a century, expressed its findings* that certain lewd, immoral activities carried on in public places for profit are highly detrimental to the public health, safety and welfare, and lead to the debasement of both women and men, promote violence, public intoxication, prostitution and other serious criminal activity." (emphasis added). The city council members, familiar with commercial downtown Erie, are the individuals who would likely have had first-hand knowledge of what took place at and around nude dancing establishments in Erie, and can make particularized, expert judgments about the resulting harmful secondary effects. Kandyland has had ample opportunity to contest the council's findings about secondary effects—before the council itself, throughout the state proceedings, and before this Court. Yet to this day, Kandyland has never challenged the city council's findings or cast any specific doubt on the validity of those findings. Instead, it has simply asserted that the council's evidentiary proof was lacking. In the absence of any reason to doubt it, the city's expert judgment should be credited.

Finally, it is worth repeating that Erie's ordinance is on its face a content neutral restriction that regulates conduct, not First Amendment expression. And the government should have sufficient leeway to justify such a law based on secondary effects. On this point, *O'Brien* is especially instructive. The Court there did not require evidence that the integrity of the Selective Service System would be jeopardized by the knowing destruction or mutilation of draft cards. It simply reviewed the Government's various administrative interests in issuing the cards, and then concluded that "Congress has a legitimate and substantial interest in preventing their wanton and unrestrained destruction and assuring their continuing availability by punishing people who knowingly and willfully destroy or mutilate them." There was no study documenting instances of draft card mutilation or the actual effect of such mutilation on the Government's asserted efficiency interests. But the Court permitted Congress to take official notice, as it were, that draft card destruction would jeopardize the system. The fact that this sort of leeway is appropriate in a case involving conduct says nothing whatsoever about its appropriateness in a case involving actual regulation of First Amendment expression. As we have said, so long as the regulation is unrelated to the suppression of expression, "the government generally has a freer hand in restricting expressive conduct than it has in restricting the written or spoken word."

JUSTICE SOUTER, however, would require Erie to develop a specific evidentiary record supporting its ordinance. JUSTICE SOUTER agrees that Erie's interest in combating the negative secondary effects associated with nude dancing establishments is a legitimate government interest unrelated to the suppression of expression, and he agrees that the ordinance should therefore be evaluated under *O'Brien*. *O'Brien*, of course, required no evidentiary showing at all that the threatened harm was real. But that case is different, JUSTICE SOUTER contends, because in *O'Brien* "there could be no doubt" that a regulation prohibiting the destruction of draft cards would alleviate the harmful secondary effects flowing from the destruction of those cards.

But whether the harm is evident to our "intuition" is not the proper inquiry. If it were, we would simply say there is no doubt that a regulation prohibiting public nudity would alleviate the harmful secondary effects associated with nude dancing. In any event, JUSTICE SOUTER conflates two distinct concepts under *O'Brien*: whether there is a substantial government interest and whether the regulation furthers that interest. As to the government interest, *i.e.*, whether the threatened harm is real, the city council relied on this Court's opinions detailing the harmful secondary effects caused by establishments like Kandyland, as well as on its own experiences in Erie. JUSTICE SOUTER attempts to denigrate the city council's conclusion that the threatened harm was real, arguing that we cannot accept Erie's findings because the subject of nude dancing is "fraught with some emotionalism." Yet surely the subject of drafting our citizens into the military is "fraught" with more emotionalism than the subject of regulating nude dancing. JUSTICE

SOUTER next hypothesizes that the reason we cannot accept Erie's conclusion is that, since the question whether these secondary effects occur is "amenable to empirical treatment," we should ignore Erie's actual experience and instead require such an empirical analysis.

As to the second point—whether the regulation furthers the government interest—it is evident that, since crime and other public health and safety problems are caused by the presence of nude dancing establishments like Kandyland, a ban on such nude dancing would further Erie's interest in preventing such secondary effects. To be sure, requiring dancers to wear pasties and G-strings may not greatly reduce these secondary effects, but *O'Brien* requires only that the regulation further the interest in combating such effects. Even though the dissent questions the wisdom of Erie's chosen remedy, the " 'city must be allowed a reasonable opportunity to experiment with solutions to admittedly serious problems.' " *Renton* (quoting *American Mini Theatres,* (plurality opinion)). It also may be true that a pasties and G-string requirement would not be as effective as, for example, a requirement that the dancers be fully clothed, but the city must balance its efforts to address the problem with the requirement that the restriction be no greater than necessary to further the city's interest.

The fourth and final *O'Brien* factor—that the restriction is no greater than is essential to the furtherance of the government interest—is satisfied as well. The ordinance regulates conduct, and any incidental impact on the expressive element of nude dancing is *de minimis*. The requirement that dancers wear pasties and G-strings is a minimal restriction in furtherance of the asserted government interests, and the restriction leaves ample capacity to convey the dancer's erotic message. JUSTICE SOUTER points out that zoning is an alternative means of addressing this problem. It is far from clear, however, that zoning imposes less of a burden on expression than the minimal requirement implemented here. In any event, since this is a content-neutral restriction, least restrictive means analysis is not required. See *Ward* [infra].

We hold, therefore, that Erie's ordinance is a content-neutral regulation that is valid under *O'Brien*. Accordingly, the judgment of the Pennsylvania Supreme Court is reversed, and the case is remanded for further proceedings not inconsistent with this opinion.

It is so ordered.

JUSTICE SCALIA, with whom JUSTICE THOMAS joins, concurring in the judgment.

I

In my view, the case before us here is moot. The Court concludes that it is not because respondent could resume its nude dancing operations in the future, and because petitioners have suffered an ongoing, redressable harm consisting of the state court's invalidation of their public nudity ordinance.

As to the first point: Petitioners do not dispute that Kandyland no longer exists; the building in which it was located has been sold to a real estate developer, and the premises are currently being used as a comedy club. We have a sworn affidavit from respondent's sole shareholder, Nick Panos, to the effect that Pap's "operates no active business," and is "a 'shell' corporation."

More to the point, Panos swears that neither Pap's nor Panos "employs any individuals involved in the nude dancing business," "maintains any contacts in the adult entertainment business," "has any current interest in any establishment providing nude dancing," or "has any intention to own or operate a nude dancing establishment in the future."[1]

It strains credulity to suppose that the 72–year-old Mr. Panos shut down his going business *after* securing his victory in the Pennsylvania Supreme Court, and before the city's petition for certiorari was even filed, in order to increase his chances of preserving his judgment in the statistically unlikely event that a (not yet filed) petition might be granted. Given the timing of these events, given the fact that respondent has no existing interest in nude dancing (or in any other business), given Panos' sworn representation that he does not intend to invest—through Pap's or otherwise—in any nude dancing business, and given Panos' advanced age,[2] it seems to me that there is "no reasonable *expectation*," even if there remains a theoretical possibility, that Pap's will resume nude dancing operations in the future.

II

Because the Court resolves the threshold mootness question differently and proceeds to address the merits, I will do so briefly as well. I agree that the decision of the Pennsylvania Supreme Court must be reversed, but disagree with the mode of analysis the Court has applied.

The city of Erie self-consciously modeled its ordinance on the public nudity statute we upheld against constitutional challenge in *Barnes*, calculating (one would have supposed reasonably) that the courts of Pennsylvania would consider themselves bound by our judgment on a question of federal constitutional law. In *Barnes*, I voted to uphold the challenged Indiana statute "not because it survives some lower level of First Amendment scrutiny, but because, as a general law regulating conduct and not specifically directed at expression, it is not subject to First Amendment scrutiny at all." Erie's ordinance, too, by its terms prohibits not merely nude dancing, but the act—irrespective of whether it is engaged in for expressive purposes—of going nude in public. The facts that a preamble to the ordinance explains that its purpose, in part, is to "limit a recent increase in nude live entertainment,"

1. Curiously, the Court makes no mention of Panos' averment of no intention to operate a nude dancing establishment in the future, but discusses the issue as though the only factor suggesting mootness is the closing of Kandyland. I see no basis for ignoring this averment. The only fact mentioned by the Court to justify regarding it as perjurious is that respondent failed to raise mootness in its brief in opposition to the petition for certiorari. That may be good basis for censure, but it is scant basis for suspicion of perjury—particularly since respondent, far from seeking to "insulate a favorable decision from review," asks us in light of the mootness to vacate the judgment below.

2. The Court asserts that "several Members of this Court can attest ... that the 'advanced age' " of 72 "does not make it 'absolutely clear' that a life of quiet retirement is [one's] only reasonable expectation." That is

tres gallant, but it misses the point. Now as heretofore, Justices in their seventies continue to do their work competently—indeed, perhaps better than their youthful colleagues because of the wisdom that age imparts. But to respond to my point what the Court requires is citation of an instance in which a Member of this Court (or of any other court, for that matter) resigned at the age of 72 to begin a new career—or more remarkable still (for this is what the Court suspects the young Mr. Panos is up to) resigned at the age of 72 to go judge on a different court, of no greater stature, and located in Erie, Pennsylvania rather than Palm Springs. I base my assessment of reasonable expectations not upon Mr. Panos' age alone, but upon that combined with his sale of the business and his assertion, under oath, that he does not intend to enter another.

that city councilmembers in supporting the ordinance commented to that effect, and that the ordinance includes in the definition of nudity the exposure of devices simulating that condition, neither make the law any less general in its reach nor demonstrate that what the municipal authorities *really* find objectionable is expression rather than public nakedness. As far as appears (and as seems overwhelmingly likely), the preamble, the councilmembers' comments, and the chosen definition of the prohibited conduct simply reflect the fact that Erie had recently been having a public nudity problem not with streakers, sunbathers or hot-dog vendors, but with lap dancers.

There is no basis for the contention that the ordinance does not apply to nudity in theatrical productions such as Equus or Hair. Its text contains no such limitation. It was stipulated in the trial court that no effort was made to enforce the ordinance against a production of Equus involving nudity that was being staged in Erie at the time the ordinance became effective. Notwithstanding JUSTICE STEVENS' assertion to the contrary, however, neither in the stipulation, nor elsewhere in the record, does it appear that the city was aware of the nudity—and before this Court counsel for the city attributed nonenforcement not to a general exception for theatrical productions, but to the fact that no one had complained. One instance of nonenforcement— against a play already in production that prosecutorial discretion might reasonably have "grandfathered"—does not render this ordinance discriminatory on its face. To be sure, in the trial court counsel for the city said that "to the extent that the expressive activity that is contained in [such] productions rises to a higher level of protected expression, they would not be [covered],"— but he rested this assertion upon the provision in the preamble that expressed respect for "fundamental Constitutional guarantees of free speech and free expression," and the provision of Paragraph 6 of the ordinance that provided for severability of unconstitutional provisions.[5] What he was saying there (in order to fend off the overbreadth challenge of respondent, who was in no doubt that the ordinance *did* cover theatrical productions) was essentially what he said at oral argument before this Court: that the ordinance would not be enforceable against theatrical productions if the Constitution forbade it. Surely that limitation does not cause the ordinance to be not generally applicable, in the relevant sense of being *targeted* against expressive conduct.[6]

Moreover, even were I to conclude that the city of Erie had specifically singled out the activity of nude dancing, I still would not find that this regulation violated the First Amendment unless I could be persuaded (as on this record I cannot) that it was the communicative character of nude dancing

5. This follow-up explanation rendered what JUSTICE STEVENS calls counsel's "categorical" assertion that such productions would be exempt, notably *un*categorical. Rather than accept counsel's explanation—in the trial court and here—that is compatible with the text of the ordinance, JUSTICE STEVENS rushes to assign the ordinance a meaning that its words cannot bear, on the basis of counsel's initial foot-fault. That is not what constitutional adjudication ought to be.

6. To correct JUSTICE STEVENS' characterization of my present point: I do not argue that Erie "carved out an exception" for Equus and Hair. Rather, it is my contention that the city

attorney assured the trial court that the ordinance was susceptible of an interpretation that would carve out such exceptions to the extent the Constitution required them. Contrary to JUSTICE STEVENS' view, I do not believe that a law directed against all public nudity ceases to be a "general law" (rather than one directed at expression) if it makes exceptions for nudity protected by decisions of this Court. To put it another way, I do not think a law contains the vice of being directed against expression if it bans all public nudity, except that public nudity which the Supreme Court has held cannot be banned because of its expressive content.

that prompted the ban. When conduct other than speech itself is regulated, it is my view that the First Amendment is violated only "where the government prohibits conduct precisely because of its communicative attributes." Here, even if one hypothesizes that the city's object was to suppress only nude dancing, that would not establish an intent to suppress what (if anything) nude dancing communicates. I do not feel the need, as the Court does, to identify some "secondary effects" associated with nude dancing that the city could properly seek to eliminate. (I am highly skeptical, to tell the truth, that the addition of pasties and G-strings will at all reduce the tendency of establishments such as Kandyland to attract crime and prostitution, and hence to foster sexually transmitted disease.) The traditional power of government to foster good morals (*bonos mores*), and the acceptability of the traditional judgment (if Erie wishes to endorse it) that nude public dancing *itself* is immoral, have not been repealed by the First Amendment.

JUSTICE SOUTER, concurring in part and dissenting in part.

I join Parts I and II of the Court's opinion and agree with the analytical approach that the plurality employs in deciding this case. Erie's stated interest in combating the secondary effects associated with nude dancing establishments is an interest unrelated to the suppression of expression under *O'Brien*, and the city's regulation is thus properly considered under the *O'Brien* standards. I do not believe, however, that the current record allows us to say that the city has made a sufficient evidentiary showing to sustain its regulation, and I would therefore vacate the decision of the Pennsylvania Supreme Court and remand the case for further proceedings.

I

In several recent cases, we have confronted the need for factual justifications to satisfy intermediate scrutiny under the First Amendment. See, *e.g.*, *Nixon* v. *Shrink Missouri Government PAC; Turner Broadcasting System, Inc. v. FCC*. Those cases do not identify with any specificity a particular quantum of evidence, nor do I seek to do so in this brief concurrence. What the cases do make plain, however, is that application of an intermediate scrutiny test to a government's asserted rationale for regulation of expressive activity demands some factual justification to connect that rationale with the regulation in issue.

In *Turner I*, for example, we stated that

"[w]hen the Government defends a regulation on speech as a means to address past harms or prevent anticipated harms, it must do more than simply 'posit the existence of the disease sought to be cured.' It must demonstrate that the recited harms are real, not merely conjectural, and that the regulation will in fact alleviate these harms in a direct and material way."

The plurality concluded there, of course, that the record, though swollen by three years of hearings on the Cable Television Consumer Protection and Competition Act of 1992, was insufficient to permit the necessary determinations and remanded for a more thorough factual development. When the case came back to us, in *Turner II*, a majority of the Court reiterated those requirements, characterizing the enquiry into the acceptability of the Government's regulations as one that turned on whether they "were designed to address a real harm, and whether those provisions will alleviate it in a material way." Most recently, in *Nixon*, we repeated that "we have never accepted mere conjecture as adequate to carry a First Amendment burden," and we examined the "evidence introduced into the record by respondents or cited by the lower courts in this action."

The focus on evidence appearing in the record is consistent with the approach earlier applied in *American Mini Theatres* and *Renton*. In *American Mini Theatres*, Detroit adopted a zoning ordinance requiring dispersal of adult theaters through the city and prohibiting them within 500 feet of a residential area. Urban planners and real estate experts attested to the harms created by clusters of such theaters, and we found that "the record discloses a factual basis" supporting the efficacy of Detroit's chosen remedy. In *Renton*, the city similarly enacted a zoning ordinance requiring specified distances between adult theaters and residential zones, churches, parks, or schools. The city "held public hearings, reviewed the experiences of Seattle and other cities, and received a report from the City Attorney's Office advising as to developments in other cities." We found that Renton's failure to conduct its own studies before enacting the ordinance was not fatal; "the First Amendment does not require a city ... to conduct new studies or produce evidence independent of that already generated by other cities, so long as whatever evidence the city relies upon is reasonably believed to be relevant to the problem that the city addresses."

The upshot of these cases is that intermediate scrutiny requires a regulating government to make some demonstration of an evidentiary basis for the harm it claims to flow from the expressive activity, and for the alleviation expected from the restriction imposed.[2] That evidentiary basis may be borrowed from the records made by other governments if the experience elsewhere is germane to the measure under consideration and actually relied upon. I will assume, further, that the reliance may be shown by legislative invocation of a judicial opinion that accepted an evidentiary foundation as sufficient for a similar regulation. What is clear is that the evidence of reliance must be a matter of demonstrated fact, not speculative supposition.

By these standards, the record before us today is deficient in its failure to reveal any evidence on which Erie may have relied, either for the seriousness of the threatened harm or for the efficacy of its chosen remedy. The plurality does the best it can with the materials to hand, but the pickings are slim. The plurality quotes the ordinance's preamble asserting that over the course of more than a century the city council had expressed "findings" of detrimental secondary effects flowing from lewd and immoral profitmaking activity in public places. But however accurate the recital may be and however honestly the councilors may have held those conclusions to be true over the years, the recitation does not get beyond conclusions on a subject usually fraught with some emotionalism.[3] As to current fact, the city council's closest approach to

2. The plurality excuses Erie from this requirement with the simple observation that "it is evident" that the regulation will have the required efficacy. The *ipse dixit* is unconvincing. While I do agree that evidentiary demands need not ignore an obvious fit between means and ends, it is not obvious that this is such a case. It is not apparent to me as a matter of common sense that establishments featuring dancers with pasties and G-strings will differ markedly in their effects on neighborhoods from those whose dancers are nude. If the plurality does find it apparent, we may have to agree to disagree.

3. The proposition that the presence of nude dancing establishments increases the in-an evidentiary record on secondary effects and their causes was the statement of one councilor, during the debate over the ordinance, who spoke of increases in sex crimes in a way that might be construed as a reference to secondary effects. But that reference came at the end of a litany of concerns ("free condoms in schools, drive-by shootings, abortions, suicide machines" and declining student achievement test scores) that do not seem to be secondary effects of nude dancing. Nor does the invocation of *Barnes* in one paragraph of the preamble to Erie's ordinance suffice. The plurality opinion in *Barnes* made no mention of evidentiary showings at all, and though my separate opinion did make a pass at the issue, I did not demand reliance on germane evidentiary demonstrations, whether specific to the statute in question or developed elsewhere. To invoke *Barnes*, therefore, does not indicate that the issue of evidence has been addressed.

There is one point, however, on which an evidentiary record is not quite so hard to find, but it hurts, not helps, the city. The final *O'Brien* requirement is that the incidental speech restriction be shown to be no greater than essential to achieve the government's legitimate purpose. To deal with this issue, we have to ask what basis there is to think that the city would be unsuccessful in countering any secondary effects by the significantly lesser restriction of zoning to control the location of nude dancing, thus allowing for efficient law enforcement, restricting effects on property values, and limiting exposure of the public. The record shows that for 23 years there has been a zoning ordinance on the books to regulate the location of establishments like Kandyland, but the city has not enforced it. One councilor remarked that "I think there's one of the problems. The ordinances are on the books and not enforced. Now this takes place. You really didn't need any other ordinances." Another commented, "I felt very, very strongly, and I feel just as strongly right now, that this is a zoning matter." Even on the plurality's view of the evidentiary burden, this hurdle to the application of *O'Brien* requires an evidentiary response.

The record suggests that Erie simply did not try to create a record of the sort we have held necessary in other cases, and the suggestion is confirmed by the course of this litigation. The evidentiary question was never decided (or, apparently, argued) below, nor was the issue fairly joined before this Court. While respondent did claim that the evidence before the city council was insufficient to support the ordinance, Erie's reply urged us not to consider the question, apparently assuming that *Barnes* authorized us to disregard it. The question has not been addressed, and in that respect this case has come unmoored from the general standards of our First Amendment jurisprudence.

Careful readers, and not just those on the Erie City Council, will of course realize that my partial dissent rests on a demand for an evidentiary basis that I failed to make when I concurred in *Barnes*. I should have demanded the evidence then, too, and my mistake calls to mind Justice Jackson's foolproof explanation of a lapse of his own, when he quoted Samuel Johnson, " 'Ignorance, sir, ignorance.' " I may not be less ignorant of nude dancing than I was

cidence of prostitution and violence is amenable to empirical treatment, and the city councilors who enacted Erie's ordinance are in a position to look to the facts of their own community's experience as well as to experiences elsewhere. Their failure to do so is made all the clearer by one of the *amicus* briefs, largely devoted to the argument that scientifically sound studies show no such correlation.

nine years ago, but after many subsequent occasions to think further about the needs of the First Amendment, I have come to believe that a government must toe the mark more carefully than I first insisted. I hope it is enlightenment on my part, and acceptable even if a little late.

II

The record before us now does not permit the conclusion that Erie's ordinance is reasonably designed to mitigate real harms. This does not mean that the required showing cannot be made, only that, on this record, Erie has not made it. I would remand to give it the opportunity to do so.[5] Accordingly, although I join with the plurality in adopting the *O'Brien* test, I respectfully dissent from the Court's disposition of the case.

JUSTICE STEVENS, with whom JUSTICE GINSBURG joins, dissenting.

Far more important than the question whether nude dancing is entitled to the protection of the First Amendment are the dramatic changes in legal doctrine that the Court endorses today. Until now, the "secondary effects" of commercial enterprises featuring indecent entertainment have justified only the regulation of their location. For the first time, the Court has not held that such effects may justify total suppression of protected speech. Indeed, the plurality opinion concludes that admittedly trivial advancements of a State's interest may provide the basis for censorship. The Court's commendable attempt to replace the fractured decision in *Barnes* with a single coherent rationale is strikingly unsuccessful; it is supported neither by precedent nor by persuasive reasoning.

I

As the preamble to Ordinance No. 75–1994 candidly acknowledges, the council of the city of Erie enacted the restriction at issue "for the purpose of limiting a recent increase in nude live entertainment within the City." Prior to the enactment of the ordinance, the dancers at Kandyland performed in the nude. As the Court recognizes, after its enactment they can perform precisely the same dances if they wear "pasties and G-strings." In both instances, the erotic messages conveyed by the dancers to a willing audience are a form of expression protected by the First Amendment.[1] Despite the similarity between the messages conveyed by the two form of dance, they are not identical.

If we accept Chief Judge Posner's evaluation of this art form from *Miller v. South Bend,* 904 F.2d 1081 (7th 1990)(en banc), the difference between the two messages is significant. The plurality assumes, however, that the difference in the content of the message resulting from the mandated costume change is *"de minimis."* Although I suspect that the patrons of Kandyland are more likely to share Chief Judge Posner's view than the plurality's, for

---

5. This suggestion does not, of course, bar the Pennsylvania Supreme Court from choosing simpler routes to disposition of the case if they exist. Respondent mounted a federal overbreadth challenge to the ordinance; it also asserted a violation of the Pennsylvania Constitution. Either one of these arguments, if successful, would obviate the need for the factual development that is a prerequisite to *O'Brien* analysis.

1. Respondent does not contend that there is a constitutional right to engage in conduct such as lap dancing. The message of eroticism conveyed by the nudity aspect of the dance is quite different from the issue of the proximity between dancer and audience. Respondent's contention is not that Erie has focused on lap dancers, but that it has focused on the message conveyed by nude dancing.

present purposes I shall accept the assumption that the difference in the message is small. The crucial point to remember, however, is that whether one views the difference as large or small, nude dancing still receives First Amendment protection, even if that protection lies only in the "outer ambit" of that Amendment. Erie's ordinance, therefore, burdens a message protected by the First Amendment. If one assumes that the same erotic message is conveyed by nude dancers as by those wearing miniscule costumes, one means of expressing that message is banned;[2] if one assumes that the messages are different, one of those messages is banned. In either event, the ordinance is a total ban.

The Court relies on the so-called "secondary effects" test to defend the ordinance. The present use of that rationale, however, finds no support whatsoever in our precedents. Never before have we approved the use of that doctrine to justify a total ban on protected First Amendment expression. On the contrary, we have been quite clear that the doctrine would not support that end.

In *American Mini Theatres*, we upheld a Detroit zoning ordinance that placed special restrictions on the location of motion picture theaters that exhibited "adult" movies. The "secondary effects" of the adult theaters on the neighborhoods where they were located—lower property values and increases in crime (especially prostitution) to name a few—justified the burden imposed by the ordinance. Essential to our holding, however, was the fact that the ordinance was "nothing more than a limitation on the place where adult films may be exhibited" and did not limit the size of the market in such speech. As Justice Powell emphasized in his concurrence:

> "At most the impact of the ordinance on [the First Amendment] interests is incidental and minimal. Detroit has silenced no message, has invoked no censorship, and has imposed no limitation upon those who wish to view them. The ordinance is addressed only to the places at which this type of expression may be presented, a restriction that does not interfere with content. Nor is there any significant overall curtailment of adult movie presentations, or the opportunity for a message to reach an audience."

("[A] zoning ordinance that merely specifies where a theater may locate, and that does not reduce significantly the number or accessibility of theaters presenting particular films, stifles no expression").

In *Renton*, we upheld a similar ordinance, again finding that the "secondary effects of such theaters on the surrounding community" justified a restrictive zoning law. We noted, however, that "the Renton ordinance, like the one in *American Mini Theatres*, does not ban adult theaters altogether," but merely "circumscribes their choice as to location." ("In our view, the First Amendment requires ... that Renton refrain from effectively denying respondents a reasonable opportunity to open and operate an adult theater within the city ..."). Indeed, in both *Renton* and *American Mini Theatres*,

---

2. Although nude dancing might be described as one protected "means" of conveying an erotic message, it does not follow that a protected message has not been totally banned simply because there are other, similar ways to convey erotic messages. A State's prohibition of a particular book, for example, does not fail to be a total ban simply because other books conveying a similar message are available.

the zoning ordinances were analyzed as mere "time, place, and manner" regulations.[3] Because time, place, and manner regulations must "leave open ample alternative channels for communication of information," a total ban would necessarily fail that test.[4]

And we so held in *Schad v. Mount Ephraim*. There, we addressed a zoning ordinance that did not merely require the dispersal of adult theaters, but prohibited them altogether. In striking down that law, we focused precisely on that distinction, holding that the secondary effects analysis endorsed in the past did not apply to an ordinance that totally banned nude dancing: "The restriction [in *American Mini Theatres*] did not affect the number of adult movie theaters that could operate in the city; it merely dispersed them. The Court did not imply that a municipality could ban all adult theaters—much less all live entertainment or all nude dancing—from its commercial districts citywide." (plurality opinion); see also (Blackmun, J., concurring) (joining plurality); (Powell, J., concurring) (same).

The reason we have limited our secondary effects cases to zoning and declined to extend their reasoning to total bans is clear and straightforward: A dispersal that simply limits the places where speech may occur is a minimal imposition whereas a total ban is the most exacting of restrictions. The State's interest in fighting presumed secondary effects is sufficiently strong to justify the former, but far too weak to support the latter, more severe burden.[5] Yet it is perfectly clear that in the present case—to use Justice Powell's metaphor in *American Mini Theatres*—the city of Erie has totally silenced a message the dancers at Kandyland want to convey. The fact that this censorship may have a laudable ulterior purpose cannot mean that censorship is not censorship. For these reasons, the Court's holding rejects the explicit reasoning in *American Mini Theatres* and *Renton* and the express holding in *Schad*.

3. The Court contends, that *Ward v. Rock Against Racism*, 491 U.S. 781 (1989), shows that we have used the secondary effects rationale to justify more burdensome restrictions than those approved in *Renton* and *American Mini Theatres*. That argument is unpersuasive for two reasons. First, as in the two cases just mentioned, the regulation in *Ward* was as a time, place, and manner restriction. Second, as discussed below, *Ward* is not a secondary effects case.

4. We also held in *Renton* that in enacting its adult theater zoning ordinance, the city of Renton was permitted to rely on a detailed study conducted by the city of Seattle that examined the relationship between zoning controls and the secondary effects of adult theaters. (It was permitted to rely as well on "the 'detailed findings' summarized" in an opinion of the Washington Supreme Court to the same effect.). Renton, having identified the same problem in its own city as that experienced in Seattle, quite logically drew on Seattle's experience and adopted a similar solution. But if Erie is relying on the Seattle study as well (as the

Court suggests), its use of that study is most peculiar. After identifying a problem in its own city similar to that in Seattle, Erie has implemented a solution (pasties and G-strings) bearing no relationship to the efficacious remedy identified by the Seattle study (dispersal through zoning).

But the city of Erie, of course, has not in fact pointed to any study by anyone suggesting that the adverse secondary effects of commercial enterprises featuring erotic dancing depends in the slightest on the precise costume warn by the performers—it merely assumes it to be so. If the city is permitted simply to assume that a slight addition to the dancers' costumes will sufficiently decrease secondary effects, then presumably the city can require more and more clothing as long as any danger of adverse effects remains.

5. As the Court recognizes by quoting my opinion in *American Mini Theatres, Inc.*, "the First Amendment will not tolerate the total suppression of erotic materials that have some artistic value," though it will permit zoning regulations.

The Court's use of the secondary effects rationale to permit a total ban has grave implications for basic free speech principles. Ordinarily, laws regulating the primary effects of speech, *i.e.,* the intended persuasive effects caused by the speech, are presumptively invalid. Under today's opinion, a State may totally ban speech based on its secondary effects—which are defined as those effects that "happen to be associated" with speech,—yet the regulation is not presumptively invalid. Because the category of effects that "happen to be associated" with speech includes the narrower subset of effects caused by speech, today's holding has the effect of swallowing whole a most fundamental principle of First Amendment jurisprudence.

II

The Court's mishandling of our secondary effects cases is not limited to its approval of a total ban. It compounds that error by dramatically reducing the degree to which the State's interest must be furthered by the restriction imposed on speech, and by ignoring the critical difference between secondary effects caused by speech and the incidental effects on speech that may be caused by a regulation of conduct.

In what can most delicately be characterized as an enormous understatement, the plurality concedes that "requiring dancers to wear pasties and G-strings may not greatly reduce these secondary effects." To believe that the mandatory addition of pasties and a G-string will have *any* kind of noticeable impact on secondary effects requires nothing short of a titanic surrender to the implausible. It would be more accurate to acknowledge, as JUSTICE SCALIA does, that there is no reason to believe that such a requirement "will at all reduce the tendency of establishments such as Kandyland to attract crime and prostitution, and hence to foster sexually transmitted disease." Nevertheless, the plurality concludes that the "less stringent" test announced in *United States v. O'Brien*, 391 U.S. 367 (1968), "requires only that the regulation further the interest in combating such effects." It is one thing to say, however, that *O'Brien* is more lenient than the "more demanding standard" we have imposed in cases such as *Texas v. Johnson*. It is quite another to say that the test can be satisfied by nothing more than the mere possibility of *de minimis* effects on the neighborhood.

The Court is also mistaken in equating our secondary effects cases with the "incidental burdens" doctrine applied in cases such as *O'Brien*; and it aggravates the error by invoking the latter line of cases to support its assertion that Erie's ordinance is unrelated to speech. The incidental burdens doctrine applies when " 'speech' and 'nonspeech' elements are combined in the same course of conduct," and the government's interest in regulating the latter justifies incidental burdens on the former. Secondary effects, on the other hand, are indirect consequences of protected speech and may justify regulation of the places where that speech may occur. See *American Mini Theatres* ("[A] concentration of 'adult' movie theaters causes the area to deteriorate and become a focus of crime").[6] When a State enacts a regulation, it might focus on the secondary effects of speech as its aim, or it might concentrate on nonspeech related concerns, having no thoughts at all with

6. A secondary effect on the neighborhood that "happens to be associated with" a form of speech is, of course, critically different from "the direct impact of speech on its audience." The primary effect of speech is the persuasive effect of the message itself.

respect to how its regulation will affect speech—and only later, when the regulation is found to burden speech, justify the imposition as an unintended incidental consequence.[7] But those interests are not the same, and the Court cannot ignore their differences and insist that both aims are equally unrelated to speech simply because Erie might have "recognized" that it could possibly have had either aim in mind.[8] One can think of an apple and an orange at the same time; that does not turn them into the same fruit.

Of course, the line between governmental interests aimed at conduct and unrelated to speech, on the one hand, and interests arising out of the effects of the speech, on the other, may be somewhat imprecise in some cases. In this case, however, we need not wrestle with any such difficulty because Erie has expressly justified its ordinance with reference to secondary effects. Indeed, if Erie's concern with the effects of the message were unrelated to the message itself, it is strange that the only means used to combat those effects is the suppression of the message.[9] For these reasons, the Court's argument that "this case is similar to *O'Brien*," is quite wrong, as are its citations to *Clark v. Community for Creative Non–Violence*, 468 U.S. 288 (1984), and *Ward*, neither of which involved secondary effects. The Court cannot have its cake and eat it too—either Erie's ordinance was not aimed at speech and the Court may attempt to justify the regulation under the incidental burdens test, or Erie has aimed its law at the secondary effects of speech, and the Court can try to justify the law under that doctrine. But it cannot conflate the two with the expectation that Erie's interests aimed at secondary effects will be rendered unrelated to speech by virtue of this doctrinal polyglot.

Correct analysis of the issue in this case should begin with the proposition that nude dancing is a species of expressive conduct that is protected by the First Amendment. As Chief Judge Posner has observed, nude dancing fits well within a broad, cultural tradition recognized as expressive in nature and entitled to First Amendment protection. The nudity of the dancer is both a component of the protected expression and the specific target of the ordinance. It is pure sophistry to reason from the premise that the regulation of the nudity component of nude dancing is unrelated to the message conveyed by nude dancers. Indeed, both the text of the ordinance and the reasoning in the Court's opinion make it pellucidly clear that the city of Erie has prohibited nude dancing *"precisely because of its communicative attributes."* Barnes

---

7. In fact, the very notion of focusing in on incidental burdens at the time of enactment appears to be a contradiction in terms. And if it were not the case that there is a difference between laws aimed at secondary effects and general bans incidentally burdening speech, then one wonders why JUSTICES SCALIA and SOUTER adopted such strikingly different approaches in *Barnes*.

8. I frankly do not understand the Court's declaration that a State's interest in the secondary effects of speech that "happen to be associated" with the speech are not "related" to the speech. See, *e.g.*, Webster's Third International Dictionary 132 (1966) (defining "associate" as "closely related"). Sometimes, though, the Court says that the secondary effects are "caused" by the speech, rather than

merely "associated with" the speech. If that is the definition of secondary effects the Court adopts, then it is even more obvious that an interest in secondary effects is related to the speech at issue. See *Barnes*, 501 U.S. at 585–586 (SOUTER, J., concurring) (secondary effects are not related to speech because their connection to speech is only one of correlation, not causation).

9. As Justice Powell said in his concurrence in *American Mini Theatres*, "Had [Detroit] been concerned with restricting the message purveyed by adult theaters, it would have tried to close them or restrict their number rather than circumscribe their choice as to location." Quite plainly, Erie's total ban evinces its concern with the message being regulated.

(SCALIA, J., concurring in judgment)(emphasis in original); (White, J., dissenting).

III

The censorial purpose of Erie's ordinance precludes reliance on the judgment in *Barnes* as sufficient support for the Court's holding today. Several differences between the Erie ordinance and the statute at issue in *Barnes* belie the Court's assertion that the two laws are "almost identical." To begin with, the preamble to Erie's ordinance candidly articulates its agenda, declaring:

> "Council specifically wishes to adopt the concept of Public Indecency prohibited by the laws of the State of Indiana, which was approved by the U.S. Supreme Court in *Barnes vs. Glen Theatre Inc.*, ... *for the purpose of limiting a recent increase in nude live entertainment within the City*" (emphasis added).[10]

As its preamble forthrightly admits, the ordinance's "purpose" is to "limit" a protected form of speech; its invocation of *Barnes* cannot obliterate that professed aim.[11]

Erie's ordinance differs from the statute in *Barnes* in another respect. In *Barnes*, the Court expressly observed that the Indiana statute had not been given a limiting construction by the Indiana Supreme Court. As presented to this Court, there was nothing about the law itself that would confine its application to nude dancing in adult entertainment establishments. Erie's ordinance, however, comes to us in a much different posture. In an earlier proceeding in this case, the Court of Common Pleas asked Erie's counsel "what effect would this ordinance have on theater ... productions such as Equus, Hair, O[h!] Calcutta[!]? Under your ordinance would these things be prevented ...?" Counsel responded: "No, they wouldn't, Your Honor."[12] Indeed, as *stipulated* in the record, the city permitted a production of Equus to proceed without prosecution, even after the ordinance was in effect, and despite its awareness of the nudity involved in the production.[13] Even if, in

---

10. The preamble also states: "The Council of the City of Erie has [found] ... that certain lewd, immoral activities carried on in public places for profit ... lead to the debasement of both women and men...."

11. Relying on five words quoted from the Supreme Court of Pennsylvania, the Court suggests that I have misinterpreted that Court's reading of the preamble. What follows, however, is a more complete statement of what that Court said on this point:

> "We acknowledge that one of the purposes of the Ordinance is to combat negative secondary effects. That, however, is not its only goal. Inextricably bound up with this stated purpose is an unmentioned purpose that directly impacts on the freedom of expression: that purpose is to impact negatively on the erotic message of the dance.... We believe ... that the stated purpose for promulgating the Ordinance is inextricably linked with the content-based motivation to suppress the expressive nature of nude dancing."

12. In my view, Erie's categorical response forecloses JUSTICE SCALIA's assertion that the city's position on Equus and Hair was limited to "one instance," where "the city was [not] aware of the nudity," and "no one had complained." Nor could it be contended that selective applicability by stipulated enforcement should be treated differently from selective applicability by statutory text (SCALIA, J., concurring) (selective enforcement may affect a law's generality). Were it otherwise, constitutional prohibitions could be circumvented with impunity.

13. The stipulation read: "The play, 'Equus' featured frontal nudity and was performed for several weeks in October/November 1994 at the Roadhouse Theater in downtown Erie with no efforts to enforce the nudity prohibition which became effective during the run of the play."

light of its broad applicability, the statute in *Barnes* was not aimed at a particular form of speech, Erie's ordinance is quite different. As presented to us, the ordinance is deliberately targeted at Kandyland's type of nude dancing (to the exclusion of plays like Equus), in terms of both its applicable scope and the city's enforcement.[14]

This narrow aim is confirmed by the expressed views of the Erie City Councilmembers who voted for the ordinance. The four city councilmembers who approved the measure (of the six total councilmembers) each stated his or her view that the ordinance was aimed specifically at nude adult entertainment, and not at more mainstream forms of entertainment that include total nudity, nor even at nudity in general. One lawmaker observed: "We're not talking about nudity. We're not talking about the theater or art.... We're talking about what is indecent and immoral.... We're not prohibiting nudity, we're prohibiting nudity when it's used in a lewd and immoral fashion." Though not quite as succinct, the other councilmembers expressed similar convictions. For example, one member illustrated his understanding of the aim of the law by contrasting it with his recollection about high school students swimming in the nude in the school's pool. The ordinance was not intended to cover those incidents of nudity: "But what I'm getting at is [the swimming] wasn't indecent, it wasn't an immoral thing, and yet there was nudity." The same lawmaker then disfavorably compared the nude swimming incident to the activities that occur in "some of these clubs" that exist in Erie—clubs that would be covered by the law.[15] Though such comments could be consistent with an interest in a general prohibition of nudity, the complete absence of commentary on that broader interest, and the councilmembers' exclusive focus on adult entertainment, is evidence of the ordinance's aim. In my view, we need not strain to find consistency with more general purposes when the most natural reading of the record reflects a near obsessive preoccupation with a single target of the law.[16]

14. JUSTICE SCALIA argues that Erie might have carved out an exception for Equus and Hair because it guessed that this Court would consider them protected forms of expression, see *Southeastern Promotions, Ltd. v. Conrad,* 420 U.S. 546 (1975) (holding that Hair, including the "group nudity and simulated sex" involved in the production, is protected speech); in his view, that makes the distinction unobjectionable and renders the ordinance no less of a general law. This argument appears to contradict his earlier definition of a general law: "A law is 'general' ... if it regulates conduct without regard to whether that conduct is expressive." If the ordinance regulates conduct (public nudity), it does not do so without regard to whether the nudity is expressive if it exempts the public nudity in Hair *precisely* "because of its expressive content." Moreover, if Erie exempts Hair because it wants to avoid a conflict with the First Amendment (rather than simply to exempt instances of nudity it finds inoffensive), that rationale still does not explain why Hair is exempted but Kandyland is not, since *Barnes* held that both are constitutionally protected.

JUSTICE SCALIA also states that even if the ordinance singled out nude dancing, he would not strike down the law unless the dancing was singled out because of its message. He opines that here, the basis for singling out Kandyland is morality. But since the "morality" of the public nudity in Hair is left untouched by the ordinance, while the "immorality" of the public nudity in Kandyland is singled out, the distinction cannot be that "nude public dancing *itself* is immoral." (emphasis in original). Rather, the only arguable difference between the two is that one's message is more immoral than the other's.

15. Other members said their focus was on "bottle clubs," and the like, and attempted to downplay the effect of the ordinance by acknowledging that "the girls can wear thongs or a G-string and little pasties that are smaller than a diamond." Echoing that focus, another member stated that "there still will be adult entertainment in this town, only it will be in a little different form."

16. The Court dismisses this evidence, declaring that it "will not strike down an otherwise constitutional statute on the basis of an alleged illicit motive." First, it is worth pointing out that this doctrinaire formulation of

The text of Erie's ordinance is also significantly different from the law upheld in *Barnes*. In *Barnes*, the statute defined "nudity" as "the showing of the human male or female genitals" (and certain other regions of the body) "with less than fully opaque covering." The Erie ordinance duplicates that definition in all material respects, but adds the following to its definition of "nudity":

> "[T]he exposure of any device, costume, or covering *which gives the appearance of or simulates* the genitals, pubic hair, natal cleft, perineum anal region or pubic hair region; or the exposure of any device worn as a cover over the nipples and/or areola of the female breast, *which device simulates and gives the realistic appearance* of nipples and/or areola." (emphasis added).

Can it be doubted that this out-of-the-ordinary definition of "nudity" is aimed directly at the dancers in establishments such as Kandyland? Who else is likely to don such garments?[17] We should not stretch to embrace fanciful explanations when the most natural reading of the ordinance unmistakably identifies its intended target.

It is clear beyond a shadow of a doubt that the Erie ordinance was a response to a more specific concern than nudity in general, namely, nude dancing of the sort found in Kandyland.[18] Given that the Court has not even tried to defend the ordinance's total ban on the ground that its censorship of

O'Brien's cautionary statement is overbroad. See generally L. Tribe, American Constitutional Law § 12–5, pp. 819–820 (2d ed. 1988). Moreover, *O'Brien* itself said only that we would not strike down a law "on the *assumption* that a wrongful purpose or motive has caused the power to be exerted," (emphasis added; internal quotation marks omitted), and that statement was due to our recognition that it is a "hazardous matter" to determine the actual intent of a body as large as Congress "on the basis of what fewer than a handful of Congressmen said about [a law]." Yet neither consideration is present here. We need not base our inquiry on an "assumption," nor must we infer the collective intent of a large body based on the statements of a few, for we have in the record the actual statements of all the city councilmembers who voted in favor of the ordinance.

17. Is it seriously contended (as would be necessary to sustain the ordinance as a general prohibition) that, when crafting this bizarre definition of "nudity," Erie's concern was with the use of simulated nipple covers on "nude beaches and [by otherwise] unclothed purveyors of hot dogs and machine tools"? *Barnes* (SCALIA, J., concurring in judgment). It is true that one might *conceivably* imagine that is Erie's aim. But it is far more likely that this novel definition was written with the Kandyland dancers and the like in mind, since they are the only ones covered by the law (recall that plays like Equus are exempted from coverage) who are likely to utilize such unconventional clothing.

18. The Court states that Erie's ordinance merely "replaces and updates provisions of an 'Indecency and Immorality' ordinance" from the mid–19th century, just as the statute in *Barnes* did. First of all, it is not clear that this is correct. The record does indicate that Erie's Ordinance No. 75–1994 updates an older ordinance of similar import. Unfortunately, that old regulation is not in the record. Consequently, whether the new ordinance merely "replaces" the old one is a matter of debate. From statements of one councilmember, it can reasonably be inferred that the old ordinance was merely a residential zoning restriction, not a total ban. If that is so, it leads to the further question why Erie felt it necessary to shift to a total ban in 1994.

But even if the Court's factual contention is correct, it does not undermine the points I have made in the text. In *Barnes*, the point of noting the ancient pedigree of the Indiana statute was to demonstrate that its passage antedated the appearance of adult entertainment venues, and therefore could not have been motivated by the presence of those establishments. The inference supposedly rebutted in *Barnes* stemmed from the *timing* of the enactment. Here, however, the inferences I draw depend on the text of the ordinance, its preamble, its scope and enforcement, and the comments of the councilmembers. These do not depend on the timing of the ordinance's enactment.

protected speech might be justified by an overriding state interest, it should conclude that the ordinance is patently invalid. For these reasons, as well as the reasons set forth in Justice White's dissent in *Barnes,* I respectfully dissent.

QUESTIONS AND NOTES

1. How is the *PAP's* ordinance like the *Barnes'* statute? How is it different?

2. Why didn't the Pennsylvania Court follow *Barnes*? Was there anything to follow?

3. Is the precedential value of *PAP's* any clearer than the precedential value of *Barnes*? Explain.

4. Had you been on the Court, with which of the four opinions would you have aligned yourself? Why?

5. Should *O'Brien* have been relevant? Determinative? Why? Why not? Explain.

6. Does the Court treat nude dancing as low value speech? Should it? On that score, is Justice Stevens' dissent consistent with his earlier opinions in *Pacifica* and *Young*?

6. Does *Young* support the Court's result*?* Does *Renton?*

7. Are erotic dancing and nude dancing the same thing? Are either constitutionally protected? Are both constitutionally protected? After *PAP's*?

8. If Justice Scalia is correct, should *Erznoznik* be overruled? Explain.

CITY OF LOS ANGELES v. ALAMEDA BOOKS, INC.

122 S.Ct. 1728 (2002).

JUSTICE O'CONNOR announced the judgment of the Court and delivered an opinion, in which THE CHIEF JUSTICE, JUSTICE SCALIA, and JUSTICE THOMAS join.

Los Angeles Municipal Code § 12.70(C) (1983), as amended, prohibits "the establishment or maintenance of more than one adult entertainment business in the same building, structure or portion thereof." Respondents, two adult establishments that each operated an adult bookstore and an adult video arcade in the same building, filed a suit, alleging that § 12.70(C) violates the First Amendment and seeking declaratory and injunctive relief. The Court of Appeals found that the city failed to present evidence upon which it could reasonably rely to demonstrate a link between multiple-use adult establishments and negative secondary effects. Therefore, the Court of Appeals held the Los Angeles prohibition on such establishments invalid under *Renton* and its precedents interpreting that case. We reverse and remand. The city of Los Angeles may reasonably rely on a study it conducted some years before enacting the present version of § 12.70(C) to demonstrate that its ban on multiple-use adult establishments serves its interest in reducing crime.

I

In 1977, the city of Los Angeles conducted a comprehensive study of adult establishments and concluded that concentrations of adult businesses are associated with higher rates of prostitution, robbery, assaults, and thefts in surrounding communities. Accordingly, the city enacted an ordinance prohibiting the establishment, substantial enlargement, or transfer of ownership of an adult arcade, bookstore, cabaret, motel, theater, or massage parlor or a place for sexual encounters within 1,000 feet of another such enterprise or within 500 feet of any religious institution, school, or public park.

There is evidence that the intent of the city council when enacting this prohibition was not only to disperse distinct adult establishments housed in separate buildings, but also to disperse distinct adult businesses operated under common ownership and housed in a single structure. The ordinance the city enacted, however, directed that "[t]he distance between any two adult entertainment businesses shall be measured in a straight line ... from the closest exterior structural wall of each business." Subsequent to enactment, the city realized that this method of calculating distances created a loophole permitting the concentration of multiple adult enterprises in a single structure.

Concerned that allowing an adult-oriented department store to replace a strip of adult establishments could defeat the goal of the original ordinance, the city council amended § 12.70(C) by adding a prohibition on "the establishment or maintenance of more than one adult entertainment business in the same building, structure or portion thereof." The amended ordinance defines an "Adult Entertainment Business" as an adult arcade, bookstore, cabaret, motel, theater, or massage parlor or a place for sexual encounters, and notes that each of these enterprises "shall constitute a separate adult entertainment business even if operated in conjunction with another adult entertainment business at the same establishment. The ordinance uses the term "business" to refer to certain types of goods or services sold in adult establishments, rather than the establishment itself. Relevant for purposes of this case are also the ordinance's definitions of adult bookstores and arcades. An "Adult Bookstore" is an operation that "has as a substantial portion of its stock-in-trade and offers for sale" printed matter and videocassettes that emphasize the depiction of specified sexual activities. An adult arcade is an operation where, "for any form of consideration," five or fewer patrons together may view films or videocassettes that emphasize the depiction of specified sexual activities.

Respondents, Alameda Books, Inc., and Highland Books, Inc., are two adult establishments operating in Los Angeles. Neither is located within 1,000 feet of another adult establishment or 500 feet of any religious institution, public park, or school. Each establishment occupies less than 3,000 square feet. Both respondents rent and sell sexually oriented products, including videocassettes. Additionally, both provide booths where patrons can view videocassettes for a fee. Although respondents are located in different buildings, each operates its retail sales and rental operations in the same commercial space in which its video booths are located. There are no physical distinctions between the different operations within each establishment and each establishment has only one entrance. Respondents concede they are openly operating in violation of § 12.70(C) of the city's Code, as amended.

II

In *Renton*, this Court considered the validity of a municipal ordinance that prohibited any adult movie theater from locating within 1,000 feet of any residential zone, family dwelling, church, park, or school. Our analysis of the ordinance proceeded in three steps. First, we found that the ordinance did not ban adult theaters altogether, but merely required that they be distanced from certain sensitive locations. The ordinance was properly analyzed, therefore, as a time, place, and manner regulation. We next considered whether the ordinance was content neutral or content based. We held that the *Renton* ordinance was aimed not at the content of the films shown at adult theaters, but rather at the secondary effects of such theaters on the surrounding community, namely at crime rates, property values, and the quality of the city's neighborhoods. Therefore, the ordinance was deemed content neutral. Finally, given this finding, we stated that the ordinance would be upheld so long as the city of Renton showed that its ordinance was designed to serve a substantial government interest and that reasonable alternative avenues of communication remained available.

The Court of Appeals did not draw any conclusions about whether the Los Angeles ordinance was content based. It explained that, even if the Los Angeles ordinance were content neutral, the city had failed to demonstrate that its prohibition on multiple-use adult establishments was designed to serve its substantial interest in reducing crime. The Court of Appeals noted that the primary evidence relied upon by Los Angeles to demonstrate a link between combination adult businesses and harmful secondary effects was the 1977 study conducted by the city's planning department. The Court of Appeals found, however, that the city could not rely on that study because it did not " 'suppor[t] a reasonable belief that [the] combination [of] businesses . . . produced harmful secondary effects of the type asserted.' " For similar reasons, the Court of Appeals also rejected the city's attempt to rely on a report on health conditions inside adult video arcades described in *Hart Book Stores*, a case that upheld a North Carolina statute similar to the Los Angeles ordinance challenged in this case. 612 F.2d 821.

The central component of the 1977 study is a report on city crime patterns provided by the Los Angeles Police Department. That report indicated that, during the period from 1965 to 1975, certain crime rates grew much faster in Hollywood, which had the largest concentration of adult establishments in the city, than in the city of Los Angeles as a whole. For example, robberies increased 3 times faster and prostitution 15 times faster in Hollywood than citywide.

The 1977 study also contains reports conducted directly by the staff of the Los Angeles Planning Department that examine the relationship between adult establishments and property values. These staff reports, however, are inconclusive. Not surprisingly, the parties focus their dispute before this Court on the report by the Los Angeles Police Department. Because we find that reducing crime is a substantial government interest and that the police department report's conclusions regarding crime patterns may reasonably be relied upon to overcome summary judgment against the city, we also focus on the portion of the 1977 study drawn from the police department report. The Court of Appeals found that the 1977 study did not reasonably support the inference that a concentration of adult operations within a single adult establishment produced greater levels of criminal activity because the study focused on the effect that a concentration of establishments—not a concentration of operations within a single establishment—had on crime rates. The

Court of Appeals pointed out that the study treated combination adult bookstore/arcades as single establishments and did not study the effect of any separate-standing adult bookstore or arcade.

The Court of Appeals misunderstood the implications of the 1977 study. While the study reveals that areas with high concentrations of adult establishments are associated with high crime rates, areas with high concentrations of adult establishments are also areas with high concentrations of adult operations, albeit each in separate establishments. It was therefore consistent with the findings of the 1977 study, and thus reasonable, for Los Angeles to suppose that a concentration of adult establishments is correlated with high crime rates because a concentration of operations in one locale draws, for example, a greater concentration of adult consumers to the neighborhood, and a high density of such consumers either attracts or generates criminal activity. The assumption behind this theory is that having a number of adult operations in one single adult establishment draws the same dense foot traffic as having a number of distinct adult establishments in close proximity, much as minimalls and department stores similarly attract the crowds of consumers. Under this view, it is rational for the city to infer that reducing the concentration of adult operations in a neighborhood, whether within separate establishments or in one large establishment, will reduce crime rates.

Neither the Court of Appeals, nor respondents, nor the dissent provides any reason to question the city's theory. In particular, they do not offer a competing theory, let alone data, that explains why the elevated crime rates in neighborhoods with a concentration of adult establishments can be attributed entirely to the presence of permanent walls between, and separate entrances to, each individual adult operation. While the city certainly bears the burden of providing evidence that supports a link between concentrations of adult operations and asserted secondary effects, it does not bear the burden of providing evidence that rules out every theory for the link between concentrations of adult establishments that is inconsistent with its own.

The error that the Court of Appeals made is that it required the city to prove that its theory about a concentration of adult operations attracting crowds of customers, much like a minimall or department store does, is a necessary consequence of the 1977 study. For example, the Court of Appeals refused to allow the city to draw the inference that "the expansion of an adult bookstore to include an adult arcade would increase" business activity and "produce the harmful secondary effects identified in the Study." It reasoned that such an inference would justify limits on the inventory of an adult bookstore, not a ban on the combination of an adult bookstore and an adult arcade. The Court of Appeals simply replaced the city's theory—that having many different operations in close proximity attracts crowds—with its own— that the size of an operation attracts crowds. If the Court of Appeals' theory is correct, then inventory limits make more sense. If the city's theory is correct, then a prohibition on the combination of businesses makes more sense.

Both theories are consistent with the data in the 1977 study. The Court of Appeals' analysis, however, implicitly requires the city to prove that its theory is the only one that can plausibly explain the data because only in this manner can the city refute the Court of Appeals' logic.

Respondents make the same logical error as the Court of Appeals when they suggest that the city's prohibition on multiuse establishments will raise crime rates in certain neighborhoods because it will force certain adult businesses to relocate to areas without any other adult businesses. Respondents' claim assumes that the 1977 study proves that all adult businesses, whether or not they are located near other adult businesses, generate crime. This is a plausible reading of the results from the 1977 study, but respondents do not demonstrate that it is a compelled reading. Nor do they provide evidence that refutes the city's interpretation of the study, under which the city's prohibition should on balance reduce crime. If this Court were nevertheless to accept respondents' speculation, it would effectively require that the city provide evidence that not only supports the claim that its ordinance serves an important government interest, but also does not provide support for any other approach to serve that interest.

This case is at a very early stage in this process. It arrives on a summary judgment motion by respondents defended only by complaints that the 1977 study fails to prove that the city's justification for its ordinance is necessarily correct. Therefore, we conclude that the city, at this stage of the litigation, has complied with the evidentiary requirement in *Renton*.

Justice SOUTER faults the city for relying on the 1977 study not because the study fails to support the city's theory that adult department stores, like adult minimalls, attract customers and thus crime, but because the city does not demonstrate that free-standing single-use adult establishments reduce crime. In effect, Justice SOUTER asks the city to demonstrate, not merely by appeal to common sense, but also with empirical data, that its ordinance will successfully lower crime. Our cases have never required that municipalities make such a showing, certainly not without actual and convincing evidence from plaintiffs to the contrary. See, e.g., *Barnes*, (SOUTER, J., concurring in judgment). Such a requirement would go too far in undermining our settled position that municipalities must be given a " 'reasonable opportunity to experiment with solutions' " to address the secondary effects of protected speech. *Renton* (plurality opinion)). A municipality considering an innovative solution may not have data that could demonstrate the efficacy of its proposal because the solution would, by definition, not have been implemented previously. The city's ordinance banning multiple-use adult establishments is such a solution. Respondents contend that there are no adult video arcades in Los Angeles County that operate independently of adult bookstores. But without such arcades, the city does not have a treatment group to compare with the control group of multiple-use adult establishments, and without such a comparison Justice SOUTER would strike down the city's ordinance. This leaves the city with no means to address the secondary effects with which it is concerned.

Justice SOUTER would have us rethink this balance, and indeed the entire *Renton* framework. We think this proposal unwise. First, none of the parties request the Court to depart from the *Renton* framework. Nor is the proposal fairly encompassed in the question presented, which focuses on the sorts of evidence upon which the city may rely to demonstrate that its ordinance is designed to serve a substantial governmental interest. Second, there is no evidence suggesting that courts have difficulty determining whether municipal ordinances are motivated primarily by the content of adult speech or by its secondary effects without looking to evidence connecting such speech to the asserted secondary effects. In this case, the Court of Appeals has not yet had an opportunity to address the issue, having assumed for the sake of argument that the city's ordinance is content neutral. It would be inappropriate for this Court to reach the question of content neutrality before permitting the lower court to pass upon it. Finally, Justice SOUTER does not clarify the sort of evidence upon which municipalities may rely to meet the evidentiary burden he would require. It is easy to say that courts must demand evidence when "common experiences" or "common assumptions" are incorrect but it is difficult for courts to know ahead of time whether that condition is met. Municipalities will, in general, have greater experience with and understanding of the secondary effects that follow certain protected speech than will the courts. See *Pap's A.M.* (plurality opinion). For this reason our cases require only that municipalities rely upon evidence that is "reasonably believed to be relevant" to the secondary effects that they seek to address.

III

The city of Los Angeles argues that its prohibition on multiuse establishments draws further support from a study of the poor health conditions in adult video arcades described in *Hart Book Stores*, a case that upheld a North Carolina ordinance similar to that challenged here. See 612 F.2d, at 828, n. 9. Respondents argue that the city cannot rely on evidence from *Hart Book Stores* because the city cannot prove it examined that evidence before it enacted the current version of § 12.70(C). Respondents note, moreover, that unsanitary conditions in adult video arcades would persist regardless of whether arcades were operated in the same buildings as, say, adult bookstores. We do not, however, need to resolve the parties' dispute over evidence cited in *Hart Book Stores*. Unlike the city of Renton, the city of Los Angeles conducted its own study of adult businesses. We have concluded that the Los Angeles study provides evidence to support the city's theory that a concentration of adult operations in one locale attracts crime, and can be reasonably relied upon to demonstrate that Los Angeles Municipal Code § 12.70(C) (1983) is designed to promote the city's interest in reducing crime. Therefore, the city need not present foreign studies to overcome the summary judgment against it.

Before concluding, it should be noted that respondents argue, as an alternative basis to sustain the Court of Appeals' judgment, that the Los Angeles ordinance is not a typical zoning regulation. Rather, respondents explain, the prohibition on multiuse adult establishments is effectively a ban on adult video arcades because no such business exists independently of an adult bookstore. Respondents request that the Court hold that the Los Angeles ordinance is not a time, place, and manner regulation, and that the Court subject the ordinance to strict scrutiny. This also appears to be the theme of Justice KENNEDY's concurrence. He contends that "[a] city may not assert that it will reduce secondary effects by reducing speech in the same proportion." We consider that unobjectionable proposition as simply a reformulation of the requirement that an ordinance warrants intermediate scrutiny only if it is a time, place, and manner regulation and not a ban. The Court of Appeals held, however, that the city's prohibition on the combination of adult bookstores and arcades is not a ban and respondents did not petition for review of that determination.

Accordingly, we reverse the Court of Appeals' judgment granting summary judgment to respondents and remand the case for further proceedings.

JUSTICE SCALIA, concurring.

I join the plurality opinion because I think it represents a correct application of our jurisprudence concerning regulation of the "secondary effects" of pornographic speech. As I have said elsewhere, however, in a case such as this our First Amendment traditions make "secondary effects" analysis quite unnecessary. The Constitution does not prevent those communities that wish to do so from regulating, or indeed entirely suppressing, the business of pandering sex. See, e.g., *Erie* (SCALIA, J., concurring in judgment); *FW/PBS, Inc. v. Dallas*, 493 U.S. 215, 256–261 (1990) (SCALIA, J., concurring in part and dissenting in part).

JUSTICE KENNEDY, concurring in the judgment.

Speech can produce tangible consequences. It can change minds. It can prompt actions. These primary effects signify the power and the necessity of free speech. Speech can also cause secondary effects, however, unrelated to the impact of the speech on its audience. A newspaper factory may cause pollution, and a billboard may obstruct a view. These secondary consequences are not always immune from regulation by zoning laws even though they are produced by speech.

Municipal governments know that high concentrations of adult businesses can damage the value and the integrity of a neighborhood. The damage is measurable; it is all too real. The law does not require a city to ignore these consequences if it uses its zoning power in a reasonable way to ameliorate them without suppressing speech. A city's "interest in attempting to preserve the quality of urban life is one that must be accorded high respect." *Young v. American Mini Theatres, Inc.* (plurality opinion).

The question in this case is whether Los Angeles can seek to reduce these tangible, adverse consequences by separating adult speech businesses from one another—even two businesses that have always been under the same roof. In my view our precedents may allow the city to impose its regulation in the exercise of the zoning authority. The city is not, at least, to be foreclosed by summary judgment, so I concur in the judgment.

This separate statement seems to me necessary, however, for two reasons. First, *Renton* described a similar ordinance as "content neutral," and I agree with the dissent that the designation is imprecise. Second, in my view, the plurality's application of *Renton* might constitute a subtle expansion, with which I do not concur.

I

In *Renton*, the Court determined that while the material inside adult bookstores and movie theaters is speech, the consequent sordidness outside is not. The challenge is to correct the latter while leaving the former, as far as possible, untouched. If a city can decrease the crime and blight associated with certain speech by the traditional exercise of its zoning power, and at the same time leave the quantity and accessibility of the speech substantially undiminished, there is no First Amendment objection. This is so even if the measure identifies the problem outside by reference to the speech inside—that is, even if the measure is in that sense content based. On the other hand, a city may not regulate the secondary effects of speech by suppressing the speech itself. A city may not, for example, impose a content-based fee or tax. See *Arkansas Writers' Project, Inc. v. Ragland*, 481 U.S. 221, 230 (1987) ("[O]fficial scrutiny of the content of publications as the basis for imposing a tax is entirely incompatible with the First Amendment's guarantee of freedom of the press"). This is true even if the government purports to justify the fee by reference to secondary effects. See *Forsyth County v. Nationalist Movement*, 505 U.S. 123, 134–135 (1992). Though the inference may be inexorable that a city could reduce secondary effects by reducing speech, this is not a permissible strategy. The purpose and effect of a zoning ordinance must be to reduce secondary effects and not to reduce speech.

A zoning measure can be consistent with the First Amendment if it is likely to cause a significant decrease in secondary effects and a trivial decrease in the quantity of speech. It is well documented that multiple adult businesses in close proximity may change the character of a neighborhood for the worse. Those same businesses spread across the city may not have the same deleterious effects. At least in theory, a dispersal ordinance causes these businesses to separate rather than to close, so negative externalities are diminished but speech is not.

The calculus is a familiar one to city planners, for many enterprises other than adult businesses also cause undesirable externalities. Factories, for example, may cause pollution, so a city may seek to reduce the cost of that externality by restricting factories to areas far from residential neighborhoods. With careful urban planning a city in this way may reduce the costs of pollution for communities, while at the same time allowing the productive work of the factories to continue. The challenge is to protect the activity inside while controlling side effects outside.

Such an ordinance might, like a speech restriction, be "content based." It might, for example, single out slaughterhouses for specific zoning treatment, restricting them to a particularly remote part of town. Without knowing more, however, one would hardly presume that because the ordinance is specific to that business, the city seeks to discriminate against it or help a favored group. One would presume, rather, that the ordinance targets not the business but its particular noxious side effects. But cf. *Slaughter-House Cases*, 16 Wall. 36, 21 L. Ed. 394 (1872). The business might well be the city's most valued enterprise; nevertheless, because of the pollution it causes, it may warrant special zoning treatment. This sort of singling out is not impermissible content discrimination; it is sensible urban planning. Cf. *Village of Euclid v. Ambler Realty Co.*, 272 U.S. 365, 388 (1926) ("A nuisance may be merely a right thing in the wrong place,—like a pig in the parlor instead of the barnyard. If the validity of the legislative classification for zoning purposes be fairly debatable, the legislative judgment must be allowed to control").

True, the First Amendment protects speech and not slaughterhouses. But in both contexts, the inference of impermissible discrimination is not strong. An equally strong inference is that the ordinance is targeted not at the activity, but at its side effects. If a zoning ordinance is directed to the secondary effects of adult speech, the ordinance does not necessarily constitute impermissible content discrimination. A zoning law need not be blind to the secondary effects of adult speech, so long as the purpose of the law is not to suppress it.

The ordinance at issue in this case is not limited to expressive activities. It also extends, for example, to massage parlors, which the city has found to cause similar secondary effects. This ordinance, moreover, is just one part of an elaborate web of land-use regulations in Los Angeles, all of which are intended to promote the social value of the land as a whole without suppressing some activities or favoring others. All this further suggests that the ordinance is more in the nature of a typical land-use restriction and less in the nature of a law suppressing speech.

For these reasons, the ordinance is not so suspect that we must employ the usual rigorous analysis that content-based laws demand in other instances. The ordinance may be a covert attack on speech, but we should not presume it to be so. In the language of our First Amendment doctrine it calls for intermediate and not strict scrutiny, as we held in *Renton*.

II

In *Renton*, the Court began by noting that a zoning ordinance is a time, place, or manner restriction. The Court then proceeded to consider the question whether the ordinance was "content based." The ordinance "by its terms [was] designed to prevent crime, protect the city's retail trade, maintain property values, and generally protec[t] and preserv[e] the quality of [the city's] neighborhoods, commercial districts, and the quality of urban life, not to suppress the expression of unpopular views." On this premise, the Court designated the restriction "content neutral."

The Court appeared to recognize, however, that the designation was something of a fiction, which, perhaps, is why it kept the phrase in quotes. After all, whether a statute is content neutral or content based is something that can be determined on the face of it; if the statute describes speech by content then it is content based. And the ordinance in *Renton* "treat[ed] theaters that specialize in adult films differently from other kinds of theaters." The fiction that this sort of ordinance is content neutral—or "content neutral"—is perhaps more confusing than helpful, as Justice SOUTER demonstrates. It is also not a fiction that has commanded our consistent adherence. See *Thomas v. Chicago Park Dist.*, 534 U.S. 316, 322, and n. 2, (2002) (suggesting that a licensing scheme targeting only those businesses purveying sexually explicit speech is not content neutral). These ordinances are content based and we should call them so.

Nevertheless, for the reasons discussed above, the central holding of *Renton* is sound: A zoning restriction that is designed to decrease secondary effects and not speech should be subject to intermediate rather than strict scrutiny. Generally, the government has no power to restrict speech based on content, but there are exceptions to the rule. And zoning regulations do not automatically raise the specter of impermissible content discrimination, even if they are content based, because they have a *prima facie* legitimate purpose: to limit the negative externalities of land use. As a matter of common experience, these sorts of ordinances are more like a zoning restriction on slaughterhouses and less like a tax on unpopular newspapers. The zoning context provides a built-in legitimate rationale, which rebuts the usual presumption that content-based restrictions are unconstitutional. For this reason, we apply intermediate rather than strict scrutiny.

III

The narrow question presented in this case is whether the ordinance at issue is invalid "because the city did not study the negative effects of such combinations of adult businesses, but rather relied on judicially approved statutory precedent from other jurisdictions." This question is actually two questions. First, what proposition does a city need to advance in order to sustain a secondary-effects ordinance? Second, how much evidence is required to support the proposition? The plurality skips to the second question and gives the correct answer; but in my view more attention must be given to the first.

At the outset, we must identify the claim a city must make in order to justify a content-based zoning ordinance. As discussed above, a city must advance some basis to show that its regulation has the purpose and effect of suppressing secondary effects, while leaving the quantity and accessibility of speech substantially intact. The ordinance may identify the speech based on content, but only as a shorthand for identifying the secondary effects outside. A city may not assert that it will reduce secondary effects by reducing speech in the same proportion. On this point, I agree with Justice SOUTER. The rationale of the ordinance must be that it will suppress secondary effects—and not by suppressing speech.

The plurality's statement of the proposition to be supported is somewhat different. It suggests that Los Angeles could reason as follows: (1) "a concentration of operations in one locale draws ... a greater concentration of adult consumers to the neighborhood, and a high density of such consumers either attracts or generates criminal activity"; (2) "having a number of adult operations in one single adult establishment draws the same dense foot traffic as having a number of distinct adult establishments in close proximity"; (3) "reducing the concentration of adult operations in a neighborhood, whether within separate establishments or in one large establishment, will reduce crime rates."

These propositions all seem reasonable, and the inferences required to get from one to the next are sensible. Nevertheless, this syllogism fails to capture an important part of the inquiry. The plurality's analysis does not address how speech will fare under the city's ordinance. As discussed, the necessary rationale for applying intermediate scrutiny is the promise that zoning ordinances like this one may reduce the costs of secondary effects without substantially reducing speech. For this reason, it does not suffice to say that inconvenience will reduce demand and fewer patrons will lead to fewer secondary effects. This reasoning would as easily justify a content-based tax: Increased prices will reduce demand, and fewer customers will mean fewer secondary effects. But a content-based tax may not be justified in this manner. It is no trick to reduce secondary effects by reducing speech or its audience; but a city may not attack secondary effects indirectly by attacking speech.

The analysis requires a few more steps. If two adult businesses are under the same roof, an ordinance requiring them to separate will have one of two results: One business will either move elsewhere or close. The city's premise cannot be the latter. It is true that cutting adult speech in half would probably reduce secondary effects proportionately. But again, a promised proportional reduction does not suffice. Content-based taxes could achieve that, yet these are impermissible.

The premise, therefore, must be that businesses—even those that have always been under one roof—will for the most part disperse rather than shut down. True, this premise has its own conundrum. As Justice SOUTER writes, "[t]he city . . . claims no interest in the proliferation of adult businesses." The claim, therefore, must be that this ordinance will cause two businesses to split rather than one to close, that the quantity of speech will be substantially undiminished, and that total secondary effects will be significantly reduced. This must be the rationale of a dispersal statute.

Only after identifying the proposition to be proved can we ask the second part of the question presented: is there sufficient evidence to support the proposition? As to this, we have consistently held that a city must have latitude to experiment, at least at the outset, and that very little evidence is required.

In this case the proposition to be shown is supported by a single study and common experience. The city's study shows a correlation between the concentration of adult establishments and crime. Two or more adult businesses in close proximity seem to attract a critical mass of unsavory characters and the crime rate may increase as a result. The city, therefore, sought to disperse these businesses. This original ordinance is not challenged here, and we may assume that it is constitutional.

If we assume that the study supports the original ordinance, then most of the necessary analysis follows. We may posit that two adult stores next door to each other attract 100 patrons per day. The two businesses split apart might attract 49 patrons each. (Two patrons, perhaps, will be discouraged by the inconvenience of the separation—a relatively small cost to speech.) On the other hand, the reduction in secondary effects might be dramatic, because secondary effects may require a critical mass. Depending on the economics of vice, 100 potential customers/victims might attract a coterie of thieves, prostitutes, and other ne'er-do-wells; yet 49 might attract none at all. If so, a dispersal ordinance would cause a great reduction in secondary effects at very small cost to speech. Indeed, the very absence of secondary effects might increase the audience for the speech; perhaps for every two people who are discouraged by the inconvenience of two-stop shopping, another two are encouraged by hospitable surroundings. In that case, secondary effects might be eliminated at no cost to speech whatsoever, and both the city and the speaker will have their interests well served.

Only one small step remains to justify the ordinance at issue in this case. The city may next infer—from its study and from its own experience—that two adult businesses under the same roof are no better than two next door. The city could reach the reasonable conclusion that knocking down the wall between two adult businesses does not ameliorate any undesirable secondary effects of their proximity to one another. If the city's first ordinance was justified, therefore, then the second is too. Dispersing two adult businesses under one roof is reasonably likely to cause a substantial reduction in secondary effects while reducing speech very little.

IV

These propositions are well established in common experience and in zoning policies that we have already examined, and for these reasons this ordinance is not invalid on its face. If these assumptions can be proved unsound at trial, then the ordinance might not withstand intermediate scrutiny. The ordinance does, however, survive the summary judgment motion that the Court of Appeals ordered granted in this case.

JUSTICE SOUTER, with whom JUSTICE STEVENS and JUSTICE GINSBURG join, and with whom JUSTICE BREYER joins as to Part II, dissenting.

In 1977, the city of Los Angeles studied sections of the city with high and low concentrations of adult business establishments catering to the market for the erotic. The city found no certain correlation between the location of those establishments and depressed property values, but it did find some correlation between areas of higher concentrations of such business and higher crime rates. On that basis, Los Angeles followed the examples of other cities in adopting a zoning ordinance requiring dispersion of adult establishments. I assume that the ordinance was constitutional when adopted, see, e.g., *Young v. American Mini Theatres, Inc.*, and assume for purposes of this case that the original ordinance remains valid today.[1]

The city subsequently amended its ordinance to forbid clusters of such businesses at one address, as in a mall. The city has, in turn, taken a third step to apply this amendment to prohibit even a single proprietor from doing business in a traditional way that combines an adult bookstore, selling books, magazines, and videos, with an adult arcade, consisting of open viewing booths, where potential purchasers of videos can view them for a fee. From a policy of dispersing adult establishments, the city has thus moved to a policy of dividing them in two. The justification claimed for this application of the new policy remains, however, the 1977 survey, as supplemented by the authority of one decided case on regulating adult arcades in another State. The case authority is not on point and the 1977 survey provides no support for the breakup policy. Its evidentiary insufficiency bears emphasis and is the principal reason that I respectfully dissent from the Court's judgment today.

I

This ordinance stands or falls on the results of what our cases speak of as intermediate scrutiny, generally contrasted with the demanding standard applied under the First Amendment to a content-based regulation of expression. The variants of middle-tier tests cover a grab-bag of restrictive statutes, with a corresponding variety of justifications. While spoken of as content neutral, these regulations are not uniformly distinct from the content-based regulations calling for scrutiny that is strict, and zoning of businesses based

---

1. Although amicus First Amendment Lawyers Association argues that recent studies refute the findings of adult business correlations with secondary effects sufficient to justify such an ordinance, Brief for First Amendment Lawyers Association as Amicus Curiae 21–23, the issue is one I do not reach.

on their sales of expressive adult material receives mid-level scrutiny, even though it raises a risk of content-based restriction. It is worth being clear, then, on how close to a content basis adult business zoning can get, and why the application of a middle-tier standard to zoning regulation of adult bookstores calls for particular care.

Because content-based regulation applies to expression by very reason of what is said, it carries a high risk that expressive limits are imposed for the sake of suppressing a message that is disagreeable to listeners or readers, or the government.

The comparatively softer intermediate scrutiny is reserved for regulations justified by something other than content of the message, such as a straightforward restriction going only to the time, place, or manner of speech or other expression. It is easy to see why review of such a regulation may be relatively relaxed. No one has to disagree with any message to find something wrong with a loudspeaker at three in the morning, see *Kovacs v. Cooper*, 336 U.S. 77 (1949); the sentiment may not provoke, but being blasted out of a sound sleep does. In such a case, we ask simply whether the regulation is "narrowly tailored to serve a significant governmental interest, and . . . leave[s] open ample alternative channels for communication of the information." As mentioned already, yet another middle-tier variety is zoning restriction as a means of responding to the "secondary effects" of adult businesses, principally crime and declining property values in the neighborhood. *Renton*.

Although this type of land-use restriction has even been called a variety of time, place, or manner regulation, equating a secondary-effects zoning regulation with a mere regulation of time, place, or manner jumps over an important difference between them. A restriction on loudspeakers has no obvious relationship to the substance of what is broadcast, while a zoning regulation of businesses in adult expression just as obviously does. And while it may be true that an adult business is burdened only because of its secondary effects, it is clearly burdened only if its expressive products have adult content. Thus, the Court has recognized that this kind of regulation, though called content neutral, occupies a kind of limbo between full-blown, content-based restrictions and regulations that apply without any reference to the substance of what is said.

It would in fact make sense to give this kind of zoning regulation a First Amendment label of its own, and if we called it content correlated, we would not only describe it for what it is, but keep alert to a risk of content-based regulation that it poses. The risk lies in the fact that when a law applies selectively only to speech of particular content, the more precisely the content is identified, the greater is the opportunity for government censorship. Adult speech refers not merely to sexually explicit content, but to speech reflecting a favorable view of being explicit about sex and a favorable view of the practices it depicts; a restriction on adult content is thus also a restriction turning on a particular viewpoint, of which the government may disapprove.

This risk of viewpoint discrimination is subject to a relatively simple safeguard, however. If combating secondary effects of property devaluation and crime is truly the reason for the regulation, it is possible to show by empirical evidence that the effects exist, that they are caused by the expressive activity subject to the zoning, and that the zoning can be expected either to ameliorate them or to enhance the capacity of the government to combat them (say, by concentrating them in one area), without suppressing the expressive activity itself. This capacity of zoning regulation to address the practical problems without eliminating the speech is, after all, the only possible excuse for speaking of secondary-effects zoning as akin to time, place, or manner regulations.

In examining claims that there are causal relationships between adult businesses and an increase in secondary effects (distinct from disagreement), and between zoning and the mitigation of the effects, stress needs to be placed on the empirical character of the demonstration available. The weaker the demonstration of facts distinct from disapproval of the "adult" viewpoint, the greater the likelihood that nothing more than condemnation of the viewpoint drives the regulation.[2]

Equal stress should be placed on the point that requiring empirical justification of claims about property value or crime is not demanding anything Herculean. Increased crime, like prostitution and muggings, and declining property values in areas surrounding adult businesses, are all readily observable, often to the untrained eye and certainly to the police officer and urban planner. These harms can be shown by police reports, crime statistics, and studies of market value, all of which are within a municipality's capacity or available from the distilled experiences of comparable communities.

And precisely because this sort of evidence is readily available, reviewing courts need to be wary when the government appeals, not to evidence, but to an uncritical common sense in an effort to justify such a zoning restriction. It is not that common sense is always illegitimate in First Amendment demonstration. The need for independent proof varies with the point that has to be established, and zoning can be supported by common experience when there is no reason to question it. We have appealed to common sense in analogous cases, even if we have disagreed about how far it took us. See *Erie v. Pap's A.M.* (plurality opinion) and n. 2, (SOUTER, J., concurring in part and dissenting in part). But we must be careful about substituting common assumptions for evidence, when the evidence is as readily available as public statistics and municipal property valuations, lest we find out when the evidence is gathered that the assumptions are highly debatable. The record in this very case makes the point. It has become a commonplace, based on our own cases, that concentrating adult establishments drives down the value of neighboring property used for other purposes. In fact, however, the city found that general assumption unjustified by its 1977 study.

The lesson is that the lesser scrutiny applied to content-correlated zoning restrictions is no excuse for a government's failure to provide a factual

---

2. Regulation of commercial speech, which is like secondary-effects zoning in being subject to an intermediate level of First Amendment scrutiny, see Central Hudson Gas & Elec. Corp. v. Public Serv. Comm'n of N. Y., 447 U.S. 557, 569 (1980), provides an instructive parallel in the cases enforcing an evidentiary requirement to ensure that an asserted rationale does not cloak an illegitimate governmental motive. See, e.g., Rubin v. Coors Brewing Co., 514 U.S. 476, 487 (1995); Edenfield v. Fane, 507 U.S. 761 (1993). The government's "burden is not satisfied by mere speculation or conjecture," but only by "demonstrat[ing] that the harms [the government] recites are real and that its restriction will in fact alleviate them to a material degree." For unless this "critical" requirement is met, *Rubin, supra,* at 487 "a State could with ease restrict commercial speech in the service of other objectives that could not themselves justify a burden on commercial expression."

demonstration for claims it makes about secondary effects; on the contrary, this is what demands the demonstration. In this case, however, the government has not shown that bookstores containing viewing booths, isolated from other adult establishments, increase crime or produce other negative secondary effects in surrounding neighborhoods, and we are thus left without substantial justification for viewing the city's First Amendment restriction as content correlated but not simply content based. By the same token, the city has failed to show any causal relationship between the breakup policy and elimination or regulation of secondary effects.

II

Our cases on the subject have referred to studies, undertaken with varying degrees of formality, showing the geographical correlations between the presence or concentration of adult business establishments and enhanced crime rates or depressed property values. Although we have held that intermediate scrutiny of secondary-effects legislation does not demand a fresh evidentiary study of its factual basis if the published results of investigations elsewhere are "reasonably" thought to be applicable in a different municipal setting, *Renton*, the city here took responsibility to make its own enquiry. As already mentioned, the study was inconclusive as to any correlation between adult business and lower property values, and it reported no association between higher crime rates and any isolated adult establishments. But it did find a geographical correlation of higher concentrations of adult establishments with higher crime rates, and with this study in hand, Los Angeles enacted its 1978 ordinance requiring dispersion of adult stores and theaters. This original position of the ordinance is not challenged today, and I will assume its justification on the theory accepted in *Young*, that eliminating concentrations of adult establishments will spread out the documented secondary effects and render them more manageable that way.

The application of the 1983 amendment now before us is, however, a different matter. My concern is not with the assumption behind the amendment itself, that a conglomeration of adult businesses under one roof, as in a minimall or adult department store, will produce undesirable secondary effects comparable to what a cluster of separate adult establishments brings about. That may or may not be so. The assumption that is clearly unsupported, however, goes to the city's supposed interest in applying the amendment to the book and video stores in question, and in applying it to break them up. The city, of course, claims no interest in the proliferation of adult establishments, the ostensible consequence of splitting the sales and viewing activities so as to produce two stores where once there was one. Nor does the city assert any interest in limiting the sale of adult expressive material as such, or reducing the number of adult video booths in the city, for that would be clear content-based regulation, and the city was careful in its 1977 report to disclaim any such intent.[3]

---

3. Finally, the city does not assert an interest in curbing any secondary effects within the combined bookstore-arcades. In Hart Book Stores, Inc. v. Edmisten, 612 F.2d 821 (1979), the Fourth Circuit upheld a similar ban in North Carolina, relying in part on a county health department report on the results of an inspection of several of the combined adult bookstore-video arcades in Wake County, North Carolina. Id., at 828–829, n. 9. The inspection revealed unsanitary conditions and evidence of salacious activities taking place

Rather, the city apparently assumes that a bookstore selling videos and providing viewing booths produces secondary effects of crime, and more crime than would result from having a single store without booths in one part of town and a video arcade in another. But the city neither says this in so many words nor proffers any evidence to support even the simple proposition that an otherwise lawfully located adult bookstore combined with video booths will produce any criminal effects. The Los Angeles study treats such combined stores as one, and draws no general conclusion that individual stores spread apart from other adult establishments (as under the basic Los Angeles ordinance) are associated with any degree of criminal activity above the general norm; nor has the city called the Court's attention to any other empirical study, or even anecdotal police evidence, that supports the city's assumption. In fact, if the Los Angeles study sheds any light whatever on the city's position, it is the light of skepticism, for we may fairly suspect that the study said nothing about the secondary effects of freestanding stores because no effects were observed. The reasonable supposition, then, is that splitting some of them up will have no consequence for secondary effects whatever.

The inescapable point is that the city does not even claim that the 1977 study provides any support for its assumption. We have previously accepted studies, like the city's own study here, as showing a causal connection between concentrations of adult business and identified secondary effects. Since that is an acceptable basis for requiring adult businesses to disperse when they are housed in separate premises, there is certainly a relevant argument to be made that restricting their concentration at one spacious address should have some effect on sales, traffic, and effects in the neighborhood. But even if that argument may justify a ban on adult "minimalls," it provides no support for what the city proposes to do here. The bookstores involved here are not concentrations of traditionally separate adult businesses that have been studied and shown to have an association with secondary effects, and they exemplify no new form of concentration like a mall under one roof. They are combinations of selling and viewing activities that have commonly been combined, and the plurality itself recognizes, that no study conducted by the city has reported that this type of traditional business, any more than any other adult business, has a correlation with secondary effects in the absence of concentration with other adult establishments in the neighborhood. And even if splitting viewing booths from the bookstores that continue to sell videos were to turn some customers away (or send them in search of video arcades in other neighborhoods), it is nothing but speculation to think that marginally lower traffic to one store would have any measurable

within the video cubicles. The city introduces this case to defend its breakup policy although it is not clear from the opinion how separating these video arcades from the adult bookstores would deter the activities that took place within them. In any event, while *Renton* allowed a city to rely on the experiences and studies of other cities, it did not dispense with the requirement that "whatever evidence the city relies upon [be] reasonably believed to be relevant to the problem that the city addresses," and the evidence relied upon by the Fourth Circuit is certainly not necessarily relevant to the Los Angeles ordinance. Since November 1977, five years before the enactment of the ordinance at issue, Los Angeles has regulated adult video booths, prohibiting doors, setting minimum levels of lighting, and requiring that their interiors be fully visible from the entrance to the premises. Los Angeles Municipal Code §§ 103.101(i), (j). Thus, it seems less likely that the unsanitary conditions identified in Hart Book Stores would exist in video arcades in Los Angeles, and the city has suggested no evidence that they do. For that reason, *Hart Book Stores* gives no indication of a substantial governmental interest that the ban on multiuse adult establishments would further.

effect on the neighborhood, let alone an effect on associated crime that has never been shown to exist in the first place.[4]

Nor is the plurality's position bolstered, as it seems to think, by relying on the statement in *Renton*, that courts should allow cities a " 'reasonable opportunity to experiment with solutions to admittedly serious problems.' " The plurality overlooks a key distinction between the zoning regulations at issue in *Renton* and *Young* (and in Los Angeles as of 1978), and this new Los Angeles breakup requirement. In those two cases, the municipalities' substantial interest for purposes of intermediate scrutiny was an interest in choosing between two strategies to deal with crime or property value, each strategy tied to the businesses' location, which had been shown to have a causal connection with the secondary effects: the municipality could either concentrate businesses for a concentrated regulatory strategy, or disperse them in order to spread out its regulatory efforts. The limitations on location required no further support than the factual basis tying location to secondary effects; the zoning approved in those two cases had no effect on the way the owners of the stores carried on their adult businesses beyond controlling location, and no heavier burden than the location limit was approved by this Court.

The Los Angeles ordinance, however, does impose a heavier burden, and one lacking any demonstrable connection to the interest in crime control. The city no longer accepts businesses as their owners choose to conduct them within their own four walls, but bars a video arcade in a bookstore, a combination shown by the record to be commercially natural, if not universal. Whereas *Young* and *Renton* gave cities the choice between two strategies when each was causally related to the city's interest, the plurality today gives Los Angeles a right to "experiment" with a First Amendment restriction in response to a problem of increased crime that the city has never even shown to be associated with combined bookstore-arcades standing alone. But the government's freedom of experimentation cannot displace its burden under the intermediate scrutiny standard to show that the restriction on speech is no greater than essential to realizing an important objective, in this case policing crime. Since we cannot make even a best guess that the city's breakup policy will have any effect on crime or law enforcement, we are a very far cry from any assurance against covert content-based regulation.[5]

4. Justice KENNEDY would indulge the city in this speculation, so long as it could show that the ordinance will "leav[e] the quantity and accessibility of speech substantially intact." But the suggestion that the speculated consequences may justify content-correlated regulation if speech is only slightly burdened turns intermediate scrutiny on its head. Although the goal of intermediate scrutiny is to filter out laws that unduly burden speech, this is achieved by examining the asserted governmental interest, not the burden on speech, which must simply be no greater than necessary to further that interest. Nor has Justice Kennedy even shown that this ordinance leaves speech "substantially intact." He posits an example in which two adult stores draw 100 customers, and each business operating separately draws 49. It does not follow, however, that a combined bookstore-arcade that draws

100 customers, when split, will yield a bookstore and arcade that together draw nearly that many customers. Given the now double outlays required to operate the businesses at different locations, the far more likely outcome is that the stand-alone video store will go out of business. (Of course, the bookstore owner could, consistently with the ordinance, continue to operate video booths at no charge, but if this were always commercially feasible then the city would face the separate problem that under no theory could a rule simply requiring that video booths be operated for free be said to reduce secondary effects.)

5. The plurality's assumption that the city's "motive" in applying secondary-effects zoning can be entirely compartmentalized from the proffer of evidence required to justify the zoning scheme, is indulgent to an unrealistic

And concern with content-based regulation targeting a viewpoint is right to the point here, as witness a fact that involves no guesswork. If we take the city's breakup policy at its face, enforcing it will mean that in every case two establishments will operate instead of the traditional one. Since the city presumably does not wish merely to multiply adult establishments, it makes sense to ask what offsetting gain the city may obtain from its new breakup policy. The answer may lie in the fact that two establishments in place of one will entail two business overheads in place of one: two monthly rents, two electricity bills, two payrolls. Every month business will be more expensive than it used to be, perhaps even twice as much. That sounds like a good strategy for driving out expressive adult businesses. It sounds, in other words, like a policy of content-based regulation.

I respectfully dissent.

QUESTIONS AND NOTES

1. Given *Barnes* and *Pap's*, which totally outlawed a type of adult entertainment, why is *Alameda* a close case?

2. After *Alameda* will cases like *Young* and *Renton* be analyzed as content-based cases, content-neutral cases, or something else? Explain.

3. Should the *Hart Bookstore* evidence of sanitary problems have been relevant to the resolution of this case? Why? Why not?

4. Detroit attempted to disperse bookstores. Renton attempted to consolidate them by not letting them be too close to a residential neighborhood, church, or school. North Carolina attempted to eliminate the sex supermarket atmosphere of multi-sex businesses in the same store. Los Angeles seems to be trying all three, plus others (no enlargement or transfer of ownership). Even if none of these alone unduly trammels free speech, is it clear that the composite of all of them doesn't create a problem?

5. What will the City try to prove on remand? What will the bookstore try to prove? Who is likely to win? Why?

degree, as the record in this case shows. When the original dispersion ordinance was enacted in 1978, the city's study showing a correlation between concentrations of adult business and higher crime rates showed that the dispersal of adult businesses was causally related to the city's law enforcement interest, and that in turn was a fair indication that the city's concern was with the secondary effect of higher crime rates. When, however, the city takes the further step of breaking up businesses with no showing that a traditionally combined business has any association with a higher crime rate that could be affected by the breakup, there is no indication that the breakup policy addresses a secondary effect, but there is reason to doubt that secondary effects are the city's concern. The plurality seems to ask us to shut our eyes to the city's failings by emphasizing that this case is merely at the stage of summary judgment, but ignores the fact that at this summary judgment stage the city has made it plain that it relies on no evidence beyond the 1977 study, which provides no support for the city's action.

D. DOES FORUM STATUS REALLY AFFECT TIME, PLACE, AND MANNER ANALYSIS?

Insert p. 504 after Question 5

WATCHTOWER BIBLE AND TRACT SOCIETY OF NEW YORK, INC. v. VILLAGE OF STRATTON

122 S.Ct. 2080 (2002).

JUSTICE STEVENS delivered the opinion of the Court:

Petitioners contend that a village ordinance making it a misdemeanor to engage in door-to-door advocacy without first registering with the mayor and receiving a permit violates the First Amendment. Through this facial challenge, we consider the door-to-door canvassing regulation not only as it applies to religious proselytizing, but also to anonymous political speech and the distribution of handbills.

Petitioner Watchtower Bible and Tract Society of New York, Inc., coordinates the preaching activities of Jehovah's Witnesses throughout the United States and publishes Bibles and religious periodicals that are widely distributed. Petitioner Wellsville, Ohio, Congregation of Jehovah's Witnesses, Inc., supervises the activities of approximately 59 members in a part of Ohio that includes the Village of Stratton (Village). Petitioners offer religious literature without cost to anyone interested in reading it. They allege that they do not solicit contributions or orders for the sale of merchandise or services, but they do accept donations.

Section 116.01 prohibits "canvassers" and others from "going in and upon" private residential property for the purpose of promoting any "cause" without first having obtained a permit pursuant to § 116.03.[1] That section provides that any canvasser who intends to go on private property to promote a cause, must obtain a "Solicitation Permit" from the office of the mayor; there is no charge for the permit, and apparently one is issued routinely after an applicant fills out a fairly detailed "Solicitor's Registration Form." The canvasser is then authorized to go upon premises that he listed on the registration form, but he must carry the permit upon his person and exhibit it whenever requested to do so by a police officer or by a resident. The ordinance sets forth grounds for the denial or revocation of a permit, but the record

---

1. Section 116.01 provides: The practice of going in and upon private property and/or the private residence of Village residents in the Village by canvassers, solicitors, peddlers, hawkers, itinerant merchants or transient vendors of merchandise or services, not having been invited to do so by the owners or occupants of such private property or residences, and not having first obtained a permit pursuant to Section 116.03 of this Chapter, for the purpose of advertising, promoting, selling and/or explaining any product, service, organization or cause, or for the purpose of soliciting orders for the sale of goods, wares, merchandise or services, is hereby declared to be a nuisance and is prohibited. App. to Brief for Respondents 2a. The Village has interpreted the term canvassers to include Jehovah's Witnesses and the term cause to include their ministry. The ordinance does not appear to require a permit for a surveyor since such an individual would not be entering private property for the purpose of advertising, promoting, selling and/or explaining any product, service, organization or cause, or for the purpose of soliciting orders for the sale of goods, wares, merchandise or services. Thus, contrary to the assumption of the dissent in its heavy reliance on the example from Dartmouth, *post*, at 2, 7, 9, the Villages ordinance would have done nothing to prevent that tragic crime.

before us does not show that any application has been denied or that any permit has been revoked. Petitioners did not apply for a permit.

A section of the ordinance that petitioners do not challenge establishes a procedure by which a resident may prohibit solicitation even by holders of permits. If the resident files a "No Solicitation Registration Form" with the mayor, and also posts a "No Solicitation" sign on his property, no uninvited canvassers may enter his property, unless they are specifically authorized to do so in the "No Solicitation Registration Form" itself. Only 32 of the Village's 278 residents filed such forms. Each of the forms in the record contains a list of 19 suggested exceptions;[2] on one form, a resident checked 17 exceptions, thereby excluding only "Jehovah's Witnesses" and "Political Candidates" from the list of invited canvassers. Although Jehovah's Witnesses do not consider themselves to be "solicitors" because they make no charge for their literature or their teaching, leaders of the church testified at trial that they would honor "no solicitation" signs in the Village. They also explained at trial that they did not apply for a permit because they derive their authority to preach from Scripture. "For us to seek a permit from a municipality to preach we feel would almost be an insult to God."

II

For over 50 years, the Court has invalidated restrictions on door-to-door canvassing and pamphleteering. It is more than historical accident that most of these cases involved First Amendment challenges brought by Jehovah's Witnesses, because door-to-door canvassing is mandated by their religion. As we noted in *Murdock v. Pennsylvania*, 319 U.S. 105, 108, (1943), the Jehovah's Witnesses "claim to follow the example of Paul, teaching 'publicly, and from house to house.' Acts 20:20. They take literally the mandate of the Scriptures, 'Go ye into all the world, and preach the gospel to every creature.' Mark 16:15. In doing so they believe that they are obeying a commandment of God." Moreover, because they lack significant financial resources, the ability of the Witnesses to proselytize is seriously diminished by regulations that burden their efforts to canvass door-to-door.

Although our past cases involving Jehovah's Witnesses, most of which were decided shortly before and during World War II, do not directly control the question we confront today, they provide both a historical and analytical backdrop for consideration of petitioners' First Amendment claim that the breadth of the Village's ordinance offends the First Amendment.[3] Those cases involved petty offenses that raised constitutional questions of the most serious magnitude—questions that implicated the free exercise of religion, the freedom of speech, and the freedom of the press. From these decisions, several themes emerge that guide our consideration of the ordinance at issue here.

---

2. The suggested exceptions listed on the form are: 1. Scouting Organizations 2. Camp Fire Girls 3. Children's Sports Organizations 4. Children's Solicitation for supporting School Activities 5. Volunteer Fire Dept. 6. Jehovah's Witnesses 7. Political Candidates 8. Beauty Products Sales People 9. Watkins Sales 10. Christmas Carolers 11. Parcel Delivery 12. Little League 13. Trick or Treaters during Halloween Season 14. Police 15. Campaigners 16. Newspaper Carriers 17. Persons Affiliated with Stratton Church 18. Food Salesmen 19. Salespersons. Apparently the ordinance would prohibit each of these 19 categories from canvassing unless expressly exempted.

3. The question presented is similar to one raised, but not decided in *Hynes*. The ordinance that we held invalid in that case on vagueness grounds required advance notice to the police before "casually soliciting the votes of neighbors." 425 U.S., at 620, n. 4.

First, the cases emphasize the value of the speech involved. For example, in *Murdock v. Pennsylvania*, the Court noted that "hand distribution of religious tracts is an age-old form of missionary evangelism—as old as the history of printing presses. It has been a potent force in various religious movements down through the years.... This form of religious activity occupies the same high estate under the First Amendment as do worship in the churches and preaching from the pulpits. It has the same claim to protection as the more orthodox and conventional exercises of religion. It also has the same claim as the others to the guarantees of freedom of speech and freedom of the press."

In addition, the cases discuss extensively the historical importance of door-to-door canvassing and pamphleteering as vehicles for the dissemination of ideas. In *Schneider v. State (Town of Irvington)*, the petitioner was a Jehovah's Witness who had been convicted of canvassing without a permit based on evidence that she had gone from house to house offering to leave books or booklets. Writing for the Court, Justice Roberts stated that "pamphlets have proved most effective instruments in the dissemination of opinion. And perhaps the most effective way of bringing them to the notice of individuals is their distribution at the homes of the people. On this method of communication the ordinance imposes censorship, abuse of which engendered the struggle in England which eventuated in the establishment of the doctrine of the freedom of the press embodied in our Constitution. To require a censorship through license which makes impossible the *free and unhampered* distribution of pamphlets strikes at the very heart of the constitutional guarantees." (emphasis added).

Despite the emphasis on the important role that door-to-door canvassing and pamphleteering has played in our constitutional tradition of free and open discussion, these early cases also recognized the interests a town may have in some form of regulation, particularly when the solicitation of money is involved. In *Cantwell v. Connecticut*, 310 U.S. 296 (1940), the Court held that an ordinance requiring Jehovah's Witnesses to obtain a license before soliciting door to door was invalid because the issuance of the license depended on the exercise of discretion by a city official. Our opinion recognized that "a State may protect its citizens from fraudulent solicitation by requiring a stranger in the community, before permitting him publicly to solicit funds for any purpose, to establish his identity and his authority to act for the cause which he purports to represent." Similarly, in *Martin v. City of Struthers*, the Court recognized crime prevention as a legitimate interest served by these ordinances and noted that "burglars frequently pose as canvassers, either in order that they may have a pretense to discover whether a house is empty and hence ripe for burglary, or for the purpose of spying out the premises in order that they may return later." Despite recognition of these interests as legitimate, our precedent is clear that there must be a balance between these interests and the effect of the regulations on First Amendment rights. We "must 'be astute to examine the effect of the challenged legislation' and must 'weigh the circumstances and ... appraise the substantiality of the reasons advanced in support of the regulation.' "

Finally, the cases demonstrate that efforts of the Jehovah's Witnesses to resist speech regulation have not been a struggle for their rights alone. In *Martin*, after cataloging the many groups that rely extensively upon this method of communication, the Court summarized that "[d]oor to door distribution of circulars is essential to the poorly financed causes of little people."

That the Jehovah's Witnesses are not the only "little people" who face the risk of silencing by regulations like the Village's is exemplified by our cases involving nonreligious speech. See, e.g., *Schaumburg v. Citizens for a Better Environment*, 444 U.S. 620 (1980); *Hynes v. Mayor and Council of Oradell*, 425 U.S. 610 (1976); *Thomas v. Collins*, 323 U.S. 516 (1945). In *Thomas*, the issue was whether a labor leader could be required to obtain a permit before delivering a speech to prospective union members. After reviewing the Jehovah's Witnesses cases discussed above, the Court observed:

> "As a matter of principle a requirement of registration in order to make a public speech would seem generally incompatible with an exercise of the rights of free speech and free assembly. . . .

> "If the exercise of the rights of free speech and free assembly cannot be made a crime, we do not think this can be accomplished by the device of requiring previous registration as a condition for exercising them and making such a condition the foundation for restraining in advance their exercise and for imposing a penalty for violating such a restraining order. So long as no more is involved than exercise of the rights of free speech and free assembly, it is immune to such a restriction. If one who solicits support for the cause of labor may be required to register as a condition to the exercise of his right to make a public speech, so may he who seeks to rally support for any social, business, religious or political cause. We think a requirement that one must register before he undertakes to make a public speech to enlist support for a lawful movement is quite incompatible with the requirements of the First Amendment."

Although these World War II-era cases provide guidance for our consideration of the question presented, they do not answer one preliminary issue that the parties adamantly dispute. That is, what standard of review ought we use in assessing the constitutionality of this ordinance. We find it unnecessary, however, to resolve that dispute because the breadth of speech affected by the ordinance and the nature of the regulation make it clear that the Court of Appeals erred in upholding it.

III

The Village argues that three interests are served by its ordinance: the prevention of fraud, the prevention of crime, and the protection of residents' privacy. We have no difficulty concluding, in light of our precedent, that these are important interests that the Village may seek to safeguard through some form of regulation of solicitation activity. We must also look, however, to the amount of speech covered by the ordinance and whether there is an appropriate balance between the affected speech and the governmental interests that the ordinance purports to serve.

The text of the Village's ordinance prohibits "canvassers" from going on private property for the purpose of explaining or promoting any "cause," unless they receive a permit and the residents visited have not opted for a "no solicitation" sign. Had this provision been construed to apply only to commercial activities and the solicitation of funds, arguably the ordinance would have been tailored to the Village's interest in protecting the privacy of its residents and preventing fraud. Yet, even though the Village has explained that the ordinance was adopted to serve those interests, it has never contended that it should be so narrowly interpreted. To the contrary, the Village's administration of its ordinance unquestionably demonstrates that the provisions apply to a significant number of noncommercial "canvassers" promoting a wide variety of "causes." Indeed, on the "No Solicitation Forms" provided to the residents, the canvassers include "Camp Fire Girls," "Jehovah's Witnesses," "Political Candidates," "Trick or Treaters during Halloween Season," and "Persons Affiliated with Stratton Church." The ordinance unquestionably applies, not only to religious causes, but to political activity as well. It would seem to extend to "residents casually soliciting the votes of neighbors," or ringing doorbells to enlist support for employing a more efficient garbage collector.

The mere fact that the ordinance covers so much speech raises constitutional concerns. It is offensive—not only to the values protected by the First Amendment, but to the very notion of a free society—that in the context of everyday public discourse a citizen must first inform the government of her desire to speak to her neighbors and then obtain a permit to do so. Even if the issuance of permits by the mayor's office is a ministerial task that is performed promptly and at no cost to the applicant, a law requiring a permit to engage in such speech constitutes a dramatic departure from our national heritage and constitutional tradition. Three obvious examples illustrate the pernicious effect of such a permit requirement.

First, as our cases involving distribution of unsigned handbills demonstrate,[4] there are a significant number of persons who support causes anonymously.[5] "The decision to favor anonymity may be motivated by fear of economic or official retaliation, by concern about social ostracism, or merely by a desire to preserve as much of one's privacy as possible." *McIntyre v. Ohio Elections Comm'n*, 514 U.S. at 341–342. The requirement that a canvasser must be identified in a permit application filed in the mayor's office and available for public inspection necessarily results in a surrender of that anonymity. Although it is true, as the Court of Appeals suggested, that persons who are known to the resident reveal their allegiance to a group or cause when they present themselves at the front door to advocate an issue or to deliver a handbill, the Court of Appeals erred in concluding that the ordinance does not implicate anonymity interests. The Sixth Circuit's reasoning is undermined by our decision in *Buckley v. American Constitutional Law Foundation, Inc.*, 525 U.S. 182 (1999). The badge requirement that we invalidated in *Buckley* applied to petition circulators seeking signatures in face-to-face interactions. The fact that circulators revealed their physical identities did not foreclose our consideration of the circulators' interest in maintaining their anonymity. In the Village, strangers to the resident certainly maintain their anonymity, and the ordinance may preclude such persons from canvassing for unpopular causes. Such preclusion may well be justified

4. Talley v. California, 362 U.S. 60, (1960); McIntyre v. Ohio Elections Comm'n, 514 U.S. 334 (1995).

5. Although the Jehovah's Witnesses do not themselves object to a loss of anonymity, they bring this facial challenge in part on the basis of overbreadth. We may, therefore, consider the impact of this ordinance on the free speech rights of individuals who are deterred from speaking because the registration provision would require them to forgo their right to speak anonymously. See Broadrick v. Oklahoma, 413 U.S. 601, 612, (1973).

in some situations—for example, by the special state interest in protecting the integrity of a ballot-initiative process, or by the interest in preventing fraudulent commercial transactions. The Village ordinance, however, sweeps more broadly, covering unpopular causes unrelated to commercial transactions or to any special interest in protecting the electoral process.

Second, requiring a permit as a prior condition on the exercise of the right to speak imposes an objective burden on some speech of citizens holding religious or patriotic views. As our World War II-era cases dramatically demonstrate, there are a significant number of persons whose religious scruples will prevent them from applying for such a license. There are no doubt other patriotic citizens, who have such firm convictions about their constitutional right to engage in uninhibited debate in the context of door-to-door advocacy, that they would prefer silence to speech licensed by a petty official.

Third, there is a significant amount of spontaneous speech that is effectively banned by the ordinance. A person who made a decision on a holiday or a weekend to take an active part in a political campaign could not begin to pass out handbills until after he or she obtained the required permit. Even a spontaneous decision to go across the street and urge a neighbor to vote against the mayor could not lawfully be implemented without first obtaining the mayor's permission. In this respect, the regulation is analogous to the circulation licensing tax the Court invalidated in *Grosjean v. American Press Co.*, 297 U.S. 233 (1936). In *Grosjean*, while discussing the history of the Free Press Clause of the First Amendment, the Court stated that " '[t]he evils to be prevented were not the censorship of the press merely, but any action of the government by means of which it might prevent such free and general discussion of public matters as seems absolutely essential to prepare the people for an intelligent exercise of their rights as citizens.' "

The breadth and unprecedented nature of this regulation does not alone render the ordinance invalid. Also central to our conclusion that the ordinance does not pass First Amendment scrutiny is that it is not tailored to the Village's stated interests. Even if the interest in preventing fraud could adequately support the ordinance insofar as it applies to commercial transactions and the solicitation of funds, that interest provides no support for its application to petitioners, to political campaigns, or to enlisting support for unpopular causes. The Village, however, argues that the ordinance is nonetheless valid because it serves the two additional interests of protecting the privacy of the resident and the prevention of crime.

With respect to the former, it seems clear that § 107 of the ordinance, which provides for the posting of "No Solicitation" signs and which is not challenged in this case, coupled with the resident's unquestioned right to refuse to engage in conversation with unwelcome visitors, provides ample protection for the unwilling listener. *Schaumburg*, 444 U.S. at 639 ("[T]he provision permitting homeowners to bar solicitors from their property by posting [no solicitation] signs ... suggest[s] the availability of less intrusive and more effective measures to protect privacy"). The annoyance caused by an uninvited knock on the front door is the same whether or not the visitor is armed with a permit.

With respect to the latter, it seems unlikely that the absence of a permit would preclude criminals from knocking on doors and engaging in conversations not covered by the ordinance. They might, for example, ask for directions or permission to use the telephone, or pose as surveyors or census takers. See n. 1, *supra*. Or they might register under a false name with impunity because the ordinance contains no provision for verifying an applicant's identity or organizational credentials. Moreover, the Village did not assert an interest in crime prevention below, and there is an absence of any evidence of a special crime problem related to door-to-door solicitation in the record before us.

The rhetoric used in the World War II-era opinions that repeatedly saved petitioners' coreligionists from petty prosecutions reflected the Court's evaluation of the First Amendment freedoms that are implicated in this case. The value judgment that then motivated a united democratic people fighting to defend those very freedoms from totalitarian attack is unchanged. It motivates our decision today.

The judgment of the Court of Appeals is reversed, and the case is remanded for further proceedings consistent with this opinion.

JUSTICE BREYER, with whom JUSTICE SOUTER and JUSTICE GINSBURG join, concurring.

While joining the Court's opinion, I write separately to note that the dissent's "crime prevention" justification for this ordinance is not a strong one. For one thing, there is no indication that the legislative body that passed the ordinance considered this justification. Stratton did not rely on the rationale in the courts below, and its general references to "deter[ing] crime" in its brief to this Court cannot fairly be construed to include anything other than the fraud it discusses specifically. In the intermediate scrutiny context, the Court ordinarily does not supply reasons the legislative body has not given. That does not mean, as THE CHIEF JUSTICE suggests, that only a government with a "battery of constitutional lawyers," could satisfy this burden. It does mean that we expect a government to give its real reasons for passing an ordinance. Legislators, in even the smallest town, are perfectly able to do so—sometimes better on their own than with too many lawyers, e.g., a "battery," trying to offer their advice. I can only conclude that if the village of Stratton thought preventing burglaries and violent crimes was an important justification for this ordinance, it would have said so.

But it is not just that. It is also intuitively implausible to think that Stratton's ordinance serves any governmental interest in preventing such crimes. As the Court notes, several categories of potential criminals will remain entirely untouched by the ordinance. n. 1, *supra*. And as to those who might be affected by it, "[w]e have never accepted mere conjecture as adequate to carry a First Amendment burden." Even less readily should we accept such implausible conjecture offered not by the party itself but only by an amicus, see Brief for Ohio et al. as *Amici Curiae*.

Because Stratton did not rely on the crime prevention justification, because Stratton has not now "present[ed] more than anecdote and supposition," and because the relationship between the interest and the ordinance is doubtful, I am unwilling to assume that these conjectured benefits outweigh the cost of abridging the speech covered by the ordinance.

JUSTICE SCALIA, with whom JUSTICE THOMAS joins, concurring in the judgment.

I concur in the judgment, for many but not all of the reasons set forth in the opinion for the Court. I do not agree, for example, that one of the causes of the invalidity of Stratton's ordinance is that some people have a religious objection to applying for a permit, and others (posited by the Court) "have such firm convictions about their constitutional right to engage in uninhibited debate in the context of door-to-door advocacy, that they would prefer silence to speech licensed by a petty official."

If a licensing requirement is otherwise lawful, it is in my view not invalidated by the fact that some people will choose, for religious reasons, to forgo speech rather than observe it. That would convert an invalid free-exercise claim, see *Employment Div., Dept. of Human Resources of Ore. v. Smith*, 494 U.S. 872, (1990), into a valid free-speech claim—and a more destructive one at that. Whereas the free-exercise claim, if acknowledged, would merely exempt Jehovah's Witnesses from the licensing requirement, the free-speech claim exempts everybody, thanks to Jehovah's Witnesses.

As for the Court's fairy-tale category of "patriotic citizens," who would rather be silenced than licensed in a manner that the Constitution (but for their "patriotic" objection) would permit: If our free-speech jurisprudence is to be determined by the predicted behavior of such crackpots, we are in a sorry state indeed.

CHIEF JUSTICE REHNQUIST, dissenting.

Stratton is a village of 278 people located along the Ohio River where the borders of Ohio, West Virginia, and Pennsylvania converge. It is strung out along a multilane highway connecting it with the cities of East Liverpool to the north and Steubenville and Weirton, West Virginia, to the south. One may doubt how much legal help a village of this size has available in drafting an ordinance such as the present one, but even if it had availed itself of a battery of constitutional lawyers, they would have been of little use in the town's effort. For the Court today ignores the cases on which those lawyers would have relied, and comes up with newly fashioned doctrine. This doctrine contravenes well-established precedent, renders local governments largely impotent to address the very real safety threat that canvassers pose, and may actually result in less of the door-to-door communication that it seeks to protect.

More than half a century ago we recognized that canvassers, "whether selling pots or distributing leaflets, may lessen the peaceful enjoyment of a home," and that "burglars frequently pose as canvassers, either in order that they may have a pretense to discover whether a house is empty and hence ripe for burglary, or for the purpose of spying out the premises in order that they may return later." *Martin v. City of Struthers*, 319 U.S. 141 (1943). These problems continue to be associated with door-to-door canvassing, as are even graver ones.

A recent double murder in Hanover, New Hampshire, a town of approximately 7,500 that would appear tranquil to most Americans but would probably seem like a bustling town of Dartmouth College students to Stratton residents, illustrates these dangers. Two teenagers murdered a married couple of Dartmouth College professors, Half and Susanne Zantop, in the Zantop's home. Investigators have concluded, based on the confession of one of the teenagers, that the teenagers went door-to-door intent on stealing access numbers to bank debit cards and then killing their owners. Their *modus operandi* was to tell residents that they were conducting an environmental survey for school. They canvassed a few homes where no one answered. At another, the resident did not allow them in to conduct the "survey." They were allowed into the Zantop home. After conducting the phony environmental survey, they stabbed the Zantops to death.

In order to reduce these very grave risks associated with canvassing, the 278 " 'little people,' " of Stratton, who, unlike petitioners, do not have a team of attorneys at their ready disposal, enacted the ordinance at issue here. The residents did not prohibit door-to-door communication, they simply required that canvassers obtain a permit before going door-to-door. And the village does not have the discretion to reject an applicant who completes the application.

The town had little reason to suspect that the negligible burden of having to obtain a permit runs afoul of the First Amendment. For over 60 years, we have categorically stated that a permit requirement for door-to-door canvassers, which gives no discretion to the issuing authority, is constitutional. The District Court and Court of Appeals, relying on our cases, upheld the ordinance. The Court today, however, abruptly changes course and invalidates the ordinance.

The Court speaks of the "historical and analytical backdrop for consideration of petitioners' First Amendment claim." But this "backdrop" is one of longstanding and unwavering approval of a permit requirement like Stratton's. Our early decisions in this area expressly sanction a law that merely requires a canvasser to register. In *Cantwell v. Connecticut*, 310 U.S. 296, 306 (1940), we stated that "[w]ithout doubt a State may protect its citizens from fraudulent solicitation by requiring a stranger in the community, before permitting him publicly to solicit funds for any purpose, to establish his identity and his authority to act for the cause which he purports to represent." In *Murdock v. Pennsylvania*, 319 U.S. 105 (1943), we contrasted the license tax struck down in that case with "merely a registration ordinance calling for an identification of the solicitors so as to give the authorities some basis for investigating strangers coming into the community." And *Martin* states that a "city can punish those who call at a home in defiance of the previously expressed will of the occupant and, in addition, can by identification devices control the abuse of the privilege by criminals posing as canvassers."

It is telling that Justices Douglas and Black, perhaps the two Justices in this Court's history most identified with an expansive view of the First Amendment, authored, respectively, *Murdock* and *Martin*. Their belief in the constitutionality of the permit requirement that the Court strikes down today demonstrates just how far the Court's present jurisprudence has strayed from the core concerns of the First Amendment.

We reaffirmed our view that a discretionless permit requirement is constitutional in *Hynes v. Mayor and Council of Oradell*, 425 U.S. 610, (1976). *Hynes*, though striking down a registration ordinance on vagueness grounds, noted that "the Court has consistently recognized a municipality's power to protect its citizens from crime and undue annoyance by regulating soliciting and canvassing. A narrowly drawn ordinance, that does not vest in municipal officials the undefined power to determine what messages residents will hear, may serve these important interests without running afoul of the First Amendment."

The Stratton ordinance suffers from none of the defects deemed fatal in these earlier decisions. The ordinance does not prohibit door-to-door canvassing; it merely requires that canvassers fill out a form and receive a permit. The mayor does not exercise any discretion in deciding who receives a permit; approval of the permit is automatic upon proper completion of the form. And petitioners do not contend in this Court that the ordinance is vague.

Just as troubling as the Court's ignoring over 60 years of precedent is the difficulty of discerning from the Court's opinion what exactly it is about the Stratton ordinance that renders it unconstitutional. It is not clear what test the Court is applying, or under which part of that indeterminate test the ordinance fails. We are instead told that the "breadth of speech affected" and "the nature of the regulation" render the permit requirement unconstitutional. Under a straightforward application of the applicable First Amendment framework, however, the ordinance easily passes muster.

There is no support in our case law for applying anything more stringent than intermediate scrutiny to the ordinance. The ordinance is content neutral and does not bar anyone from going door-to-door in Stratton. It merely regulates the manner in which one must canvass: A canvasser must first obtain a permit. It is, or perhaps I should say was, settled that the "government may impose reasonable restrictions on the time, place, or manner of protected speech, provided the restrictions 'are justified without reference to the content of the regulated speech, that they are narrowly tailored to serve a significant governmental interest, and that they leave open ample alternative channels for communication of the information.'" Earlier this Term, the Court reaffirmed that this test applies to content-neutral time, place, or manner restrictions on speech in public forums. See *Thomas v. Chicago Park Dist.*, 534 U.S. 316 (2002).

The Court suggests that Stratton's regulation of speech warrants greater scrutiny. But it would be puzzling if regulations of speech taking place on another citizen's private property warranted greater scrutiny than regulations of speech taking place in public forums. Common sense and our precedent say just the opposite. In *Hynes*, the Court explained: "'Of all the methods of spreading unpopular ideas, [house-to-house canvassing] seems the least entitled to extensive protection. The possibilities of persuasion are slight compared with the certainties of annoyance. Great as is the value of exposing citizens to novel views, home is one place where a man ought to be able to shut himself up in his own ideas if he desires.' In *Ward*, the Court held that intermediate scrutiny was appropriate "*even* in a public forum," (emphasis added), appropriately recognizing that speech enjoys greater protection in a public forum that has been opened to all citizens. Indeed, we have held that the mere proximity of private residential property to a public forum permits more extensive regulation of speech taking place at the public forum than would otherwise be allowed. See *Frisby v. Schultz.* Surely then, intermediate scrutiny applies to a content-neutral regulation of speech that occurs not just near, but at, another citizen's private residence.

The Stratton regulation is aimed at three significant governmental interests: the prevention of fraud, the prevention of crime, and the protection of privacy.[6] The Court concedes that "in light of our precedent, ... these are important interests that [Stratton] may seek to safeguard through some form of regulation of solicitation activity." Although initially recognizing the important interest in preventing crime, the Court later indicates that the "absence of any evidence of a special crime problem related to door-to-door solicitation in the record before us" lessens this interest. But the village is entitled to rely on our assertion in *Martin* that door-to-door canvassing poses a risk of crime, and the experience of other jurisdictions with crime stemming from door-to-door canvassing,

The double murder in Hanover described above is but one tragic example of the crime threat posed by door-to-door canvassing. Other recent examples include a man soliciting gardening jobs door-to-door who tied up and robbed elderly residents, a door-to-door vacuum cleaner salesman who raped a woman, and a man going door-to-door purportedly on behalf of a church group who committed multiple sexual assaults. The Constitution does not require that Stratton first endure its own crime wave before it takes measures to prevent crime.

What is more, the Court soon forgets both the privacy and crime interests. It finds the ordinance too broad because it applies to a "significant number of non-commercial 'canvassers.' "But noncommercial canvassers, for example, those purporting to conduct environmental surveys for school, can violate no trespassing signs and engage in burglaries and violent crimes just as easily as commercial canvassers can. Stratton's ordinance is thus narrowly tailored. It applies to everyone who poses the risks associated with door-to-door canvassing, i.e., it applies to everyone who canvasses door-to-door. The Court takes what should be a virtue of the ordinance-that it is content neutral, and turns it into a vice.

The next question is whether the ordinance serves the important interests of protecting privacy and preventing fraud and crime. With respect to the interest in protecting privacy, the Court concludes that "[t]he annoyance caused by an uninvited knock on the front door is the same whether or not the visitor is armed with a permit." True, but that misses the key point: the permit requirement results in fewer uninvited knocks. Those who have complied with the permit requirement are less likely to visit residences with no trespassing signs, as it is much easier for the authorities to track them down.

The Court also fails to grasp how the permit requirement serves Stratton's interest in preventing crime.[7] We have approved of permit requirements for those engaging in protected First Amendment activity because of a

---

6. Of course, fraud itself may be a crime. I assume, as does the majority, that the interest in preventing "crime" refers to a separate interest in preventing burglaries and violent crimes.

7. It is sufficient that the ordinance serves the important interest of protecting residents'

privacy. A law need only serve a governmental interest. Because the Court's treatment of Stratton's interest in preventing crime gives short shrift to Stratton's attempt to deal with a very serious problem, I address that issue as well.

common-sense recognition that their existence both deters and helps detect wrongdoing. See, e.g., *Thomas v. Chicago Park Dist.*, 534 U.S. 316 (2002) (upholding a permit requirement aimed, in part, at preventing unlawful uses of a park and assuring financial accountability for damage caused by the event). And while some people, intent on committing burglaries or violent crimes, are not likely to be deterred by the prospect of a misdemeanor for violating the permit ordinance, the ordinance's effectiveness does not depend on criminals registering.

The ordinance prevents and detects serious crime by making it a crime not to register. Take the Hanover double murder discussed earlier. The murderers did not achieve their objective until they visited their fifth home over a period of seven months. If Hanover had a permit requirement, the teens may have been stopped before they achieved their objective. One of the residents they visited may have informed the police that there were two canvassers who lacked a permit. Such neighborly vigilance, though perhaps foreign to those residing in modern day cities, is not uncommon in small towns. Or the police on their own may have discovered that two canvassers were violating the ordinance. Apprehension for violating the permit requirement may well have frustrated the teenagers' objectives; it certainly would have assisted in solving the murders had the teenagers gone ahead with their plan.[8]

Of course, the Stratton ordinance does not guarantee that no canvasser will ever commit a burglary or violent crime. The Court seems to think this dooms the ordinance, erecting an insurmountable hurdle that a law must provide a fool-proof method of preventing crime. In order to survive intermediate scrutiny, however, a law need not solve the crime problem, it need only further the interest in preventing crime. Some deterrence of serious criminal activity is more than enough to survive intermediate scrutiny.

The final requirement of intermediate scrutiny is that a regulation leave open ample alternatives for expression. Undoubtedly, ample alternatives exist here. Most obviously, canvassers are free to go door-to-door after filling out the permit application. And those without permits may communicate on public sidewalks, on street corners, through the mail, or through the telephone.

Intermediate scrutiny analysis thus confirms what our cases have long said: A discretionless permit requirement for canvassers does not violate the First Amendment. Today, the Court elevates its concern with what is, at most, a negligible burden on door-to-door communication above this established proposition. Ironically, however, today's decision may result in less of the door-to-door communication that the Court extols. As the Court recognizes, any homeowner may place a "No Solicitation" sign on his or her property, and it is a crime to violate that sign. In light of today's decision depriving Stratton residents of the degree of accountability and safety that the permit requirement provides, more and more residents may decide to

---

8. Indeed, an increased focus on apprehending criminals for "petty" offenses, such as not paying subway fares, is credited with the dramatic reduction in violent crimes in New York City during the last decade. See, e.g., M. Gladwell, The Tipping Point: How Little Things Can Make a Big Difference (2000). If this works in New York City, surely it can work in a small village like Stratton.

place these signs in their yards and cut off door-to-door communication altogether.

QUESTIONS AND NOTES

1. Is there any way that Stratton could have narrowed its ordinance in a manner that would have satisfied the Court?

2. What (if anything) is wrong with Chief Justice Rehnquist's contention that the ordinance passes intermediate scrutiny?

3. What's the harm (if any) of requiring a nondiscretionary permit? Realistically is there such a thing? *Cf. Poulos v. New Hampshire.*

4. Given what Justice Scalia does not think supports the majority's result, what would he think does support it?

5. Is (should) the size and financial wherewithal (be) relevant to the result? Why? Why not? The Court emphasizes Jehovah's Witnesses' financial limitation while Justice Rehnquist emphasizes Stratton's size limitations.

6. Should the possibility of crime (*e.g.* the Dartmouth murders) have been relevant to the resolution of this case? Why? Why not?

Chapter VI

NON-CONTENT LIMITATIONS ON SPEECH

E. DOES IT MATTER IF SOMETHING IS A PUBLIC FORUM?

Insert p. 569 after Question 3

REPUBLICAN PARTY OF MINNESOTA v. WHITE
122 S.Ct. 2528 (2002).

JUSTICE SCALIA delivered the opinion of the Court.

The question presented in this case is whether the First Amendment permits the Minnesota Supreme Court to prohibit candidates for judicial election in that State from announcing their views on disputed legal and political issues.

I

Since Minnesota's admission to the Union in 1858, the State's Constitution has provided for the selection of all state judges by popular election. Since 1912, those elections have been nonpartisan. Since 1974, they have been subject to a legal restriction which states that a "candidate for a judicial office, including an incumbent judge," shall not "announce his or her views on disputed legal or political issues." This prohibition, promulgated by the Minnesota Supreme Court and based on Canon 7(B) of the 1972 American Bar Association (ABA) Model Code of Judicial Conduct, is known as the "announce clause." Incumbent judges who violate it are subject to discipline, including removal, censure, civil penalties, and suspension without pay. Lawyers who run for judicial office also must comply with the announce clause. Those who violate it are subject to, *inter alia*, disbarment, suspension, and probation.

In 1996, one of the petitioners, Gregory Wersal, ran for associate justice of the Minnesota Supreme Court. In the course of the campaign, he distributed literature criticizing several Minnesota Supreme Court decisions on issues such as crime, welfare, and abortion. A complaint against Wersal challenging, among other things, the propriety of this literature was filed with the Office of Lawyers Professional Responsibility, the agency which, under the direction of the Minnesota Lawyers Professional Responsibility Board, investigates and prosecutes ethical violations of lawyer candidates for judicial office. The Lawyers Board dismissed the complaint; with regard to the charges that his campaign materials violated the announce clause, it expressed doubt whether the clause could constitutionally be enforced. Nonetheless, fearing that further ethical complaints would jeopardize his ability to practice law, Wersal withdrew from the election. In 1998, Wersal ran again for the same office. Early in that race, he sought an advisory opinion from the Lawyers Board with regard to whether it planned to enforce the announce clause. The Lawyers Board responded equivocally, stating that, although it had significant doubts about the constitutionality of the provision, it was unable to answer his question because he had not submitted a list of the announcements he wished to make.

Shortly thereafter, Wersal filed this lawsuit in Federal District Court against respondents, seeking, *inter alia*, a declaration that the announce clause violates the First Amendment and an injunction against its enforcement. Wersal alleged that he was forced to refrain from announcing his views on disputed issues during the 1998 campaign, to the point where he declined response to questions put to him by the press and public, out of concern that he might run afoul of the announce clause. Other plaintiffs in the suit, including the Minnesota Republican Party, alleged that, because the clause kept Wersal from announcing his views, they were unable to learn those views and support or oppose his candidacy accordingly. The parties filed cross-motions for summary judgment, and the District Court found in favor of respondents, holding that the announce clause did not violate the First Amendment. We granted certiorari.

II

Before considering the constitutionality of the announce clause, we must be clear about its meaning. Its text says that a candidate for judicial office shall not "announce his or her views on disputed legal or political issues." We know that "announc[ing] ... views" on an issue covers much more than *promising* to decide an issue a particular way. The prohibition extends to the candidate's mere statement of his current position, even if he does not bind himself to maintain that position after election. All the parties agree this is the case, because the Minnesota Code contains a so-called "pledges or promises" clause, which *separately* prohibits judicial candidates from making "pledges or promises of conduct in office other than the faithful and impartial performance of the duties of the office,"—a prohibition that is not challenged here and on which we express no view.

There are, however, some limitations that the Minnesota Supreme Court has placed upon the scope of the announce clause that are not (to put it politely) immediately apparent from its text. The statements that formed the basis of the complaint against Wersal in 1996 included criticism of past decisions of the Minnesota Supreme Court. One piece of campaign literature stated that "[t]he Minnesota Supreme Court has issued decisions which are marked by their disregard for the Legislature and a lack of common sense." It went on to criticize a decision excluding from evidence confessions by criminal defendants that were not tape-recorded, asking "[s]hould we conclude that because the Supreme Court does not trust police, it allows confessed criminals to go free?" It criticized a decision striking down a state law restricting welfare benefits, asserting that "[i]t's the Legislature which should set our spending policies." And it criticized a decision requiring public financing of abortions for poor women as "unprecedented" and a "pro-abortion stance." Although one would think that all of these statements touched on disputed legal or political issues, they did not (or at least do not now) fall within the scope of the announce clause. The Judicial Board issued an opinion stating that judicial candidates may criticize past decisions, and the Lawyers Board refused to discipline Wersal for the foregoing statements because, in part, it thought they did not violate the announce clause. The Eighth Circuit relied on the Judicial Board's opinion in upholding the announce clause and the Minnesota Supreme Court recently embraced the Eighth Circuit's interpretation, *In re Code of Judicial Conduct*, 639 N.W.2d 55 (Minn.2002).

There are yet further limitations upon the apparent plain meaning of the announce clause: In light of the constitutional concerns, the District Court construed the clause to reach only disputed issues that are likely to come before the candidate if he is elected judge. The Eighth Circuit accepted this limiting interpretation by the District Court, and in addition construed the clause to allow general discussions of case law and judicial philosophy. The Supreme Court of Minnesota adopted these interpretations as well when it ordered enforcement of the announce clause in accordance with the Eighth Circuit's opinion.

It seems to us, however, that—like the text of the announce clause itself—these limitations upon the text of the announce clause are not all that they appear to be. First, respondents acknowledged at oral argument that statements critical of past judicial decisions are *not* permissible if the candidate also states that he is against *stare decisis*.[1] Thus, candidates must choose between stating their views critical of past decisions and stating their views in opposition to *stare decisis*. Or, to look at it more concretely, they may state their view that prior decisions were erroneous only if they do not assert that they, if elected, have any power to eliminate erroneous decisions. Second, limiting the scope of the clause to issues likely to come before a court is not much of a limitation at all. One would hardly expect the "disputed legal or political issues" raised in the course of a state judicial election to include such matters as whether the Federal Government should end the embargo of Cuba. Quite obviously, they will be those legal or political disputes that are the proper (or by past decisions have been made the improper) business of the state courts. And within that relevant category, "[t]here is almost no legal or political issue that is unlikely to come before a judge of an American court, state or federal, of general jurisdiction." Third, construing the clause to allow "general" discussions of case law and judicial philosophy turns out to be of little help in an election campaign. At oral argument, respondents gave, as an example of this exception, that a candidate is free to assert that he is a " 'strict constructionist.' "But that, like most other philosophical generalities, has little meaningful content for the electorate unless it is exemplified by

---

1. Justice GINSBURG argues that we should ignore this concession at oral argument because it is inconsistent with the Eighth Circuit's interpretation of the announce clause. As she appears to acknowledge, however, the Eighth Circuit was merely silent on this particular question. Silence is hardly inconsistent with what respondents conceded at oral argument.

application to a particular issue of construction likely to come before a court— for example, whether a particular statute runs afoul of any provision of the Constitution. Respondents conceded that the announce clause would prohibit the candidate from exemplifying his philosophy in this fashion. Without such application to real-life issues, all candidates can claim to be "strict constructionists" with equal (and unhelpful) plausibility.

In any event, it is clear that the announce clause prohibits a judicial candidate from stating his views on any specific nonfanciful legal question within the province of the court for which he is running, except in the context of discussing past decisions—and in the latter context as well, if he expresses the view that he is not bound by *stare decisis*.

Respondents contend that this still leaves plenty of topics for discussion on the campaign trail. These include a candidate's "character," "education," "work habits," and "how [he] would handle administrative duties if elected." Indeed, the Judicial Board has printed a list of preapproved questions which judicial candidates are allowed to answer. These include how the candidate feels about cameras in the courtroom, how he would go about reducing the caseload, how the costs of judicial administration can be reduced, and how he proposes to ensure that minorities and women are treated more fairly by the court system. Whether this list of preapproved subjects, and other topics not prohibited by the announce clause, adequately fulfill the First Amendment's guarantee of freedom of speech is the question to which we now turn.

III

As the Court of Appeals recognized, the announce clause both prohibits speech on the basis of its content and burdens a category of speech that is "at the core of our First Amendment freedoms"—speech about the qualifications of candidates for public office.

The Court of Appeals concluded that the proper test to be applied to determine the constitutionality of such a restriction is what our cases have called strict scrutiny, the parties do not dispute that this is correct. Under the strict-scrutiny test, respondents have the burden to prove that the announce clause is (1) narrowly tailored, to serve (2) a compelling state interest. In order for respondents to show that the announce clause is narrowly tailored, they must demonstrate that it does not "unnecessarily circumscrib[e] protected expression." The Court of Appeals concluded that respondents had established two interests as sufficiently compelling to justify the announce clause: preserving the impartiality of the state judiciary and preserving the appearance of the impartiality of the state judiciary. Respondents reassert these two interests before us, arguing that the first is compelling because it protects the due process rights of litigants, and that the second is compelling because it preserves public confidence in the judiciary. Respondents are rather vague, however, about what they mean by "impartiality." Indeed, although the term is used throughout the Eighth Circuit's opinion, the briefs, the Minnesota Code of Judicial Conduct, and the ABA Codes of Judicial Conduct, none of these sources bothers to define it. Clarity on this point is essential before we can decide whether impartiality is indeed a compelling state interest, and, if so, whether the announce clause is narrowly tailored to achieve it.

A

One meaning of "impartiality" in the judicial context—and of course its root meaning—is the lack of bias for or against either *party* to the proceeding. Impartiality in this sense assures equal application of the law. That is, it guarantees a party that the judge who hears his case will apply the law to him in the same way he applies it to any other party. This is the traditional sense in which the term is used. See Webster's New International Dictionary 1247 (2d ed.1950) (defining "impartial" as "[n]ot partial; esp., not favoring one more than another; treating all alike; unbiased; equitable; fair; just"). It is also the sense in which it is used in the cases cited by respondents and *amici* for the proposition that an impartial judge is essential to due process. *Tumey v. Ohio*, 273 U.S. 510, 523, 531–534 (1927) (judge violated due process by sitting in a case in which it would be in his financial interest to find against one of the parties); *Aetna Life Ins. Co. v. Lavoie*, 475 U.S. 813, 822–825 (1986) (same); *Ward v. Monroeville*, 409 U.S. 57, 58–62 (1972) (same); Johnson v. Mississippi, 403 U.S. 212, 215–216 (1971) (*per curiam*) (judge violated due process by sitting in a case in which one of the parties was a previously successful litigant against him); *Bracy v. Gramley*, 520 U.S. 899, 905 (1997) (would violate due process if a judge was disposed to rule against defendants who did not bribe him in order to cover up the fact that he regularly ruled in favor of defendants who did bribe him); *In re Murchison*, 349 U.S. 133, 137–139 (1955) (judge violated due process by sitting in the criminal trial of defendant whom he had indicted).

We think it plain that the announce clause is not narrowly tailored to serve impartiality (or the appearance of impartiality) in this sense. Indeed, the clause is barely tailored to serve that interest *at all*, inasmuch as it does not restrict speech for or against particular *parties*, but rather speech for or against particular *issues*. To be sure, when a case arises that turns on a legal issue on which the judge (as a candidate) had taken a particular stand, the party taking the opposite stand is likely to lose. But not because of any bias against that party, or favoritism toward the other party. *Any* party taking that position is just as likely to lose. The judge is applying the law (as he sees it) evenhandedly.[2]

B

It is perhaps possible to use the term "impartiality" in the judicial context (though this is certainly not a common usage) to mean lack of preconception in favor of or against a particular *legal view*. This sort of impartiality would be concerned, not with guaranteeing litigants equal application of the law, but rather with guaranteeing them an equal chance to persuade the court on the legal points in their case. Impartiality in this sense may well be an interest served by the announce clause, but it is not a

---

2. Justice STEVENS asserts that the announce clause "serves the State's interest in maintaining both the appearance of this form of impartiality and its actuality." We do not disagree. Some of the speech prohibited by the announce clause may well exhibit a bias against parties—including Justice STEVENS' example of an election speech stressing the candidate's unbroken record of affirming con-victions for rape. That is why we are careful to say that the announce clause is "barely tailored to serve that interest," (emphasis added). The question under our strict scrutiny test, however, is not whether the announce clause serves this interest at all, but whether it is narrowly tailored to serve this interest. It is not

compelling state interest, as strict scrutiny requires. A judge's lack of predisposition regarding the relevant legal issues in a case has never been thought a necessary component of equal justice, and with good reason. For one thing, it is virtually impossible to find a judge who does not have preconceptions about the law. As then-Justice REHNQUIST observed of our own Court: "Since most Justices come to this bench no earlier than their middle years, it would be unusual if they had not by that time formulated at least some tentative notions that would influence them in their interpretation of the sweeping clauses of the Constitution and their interaction with one another. It would be not merely unusual, but extraordinary, if they had not at least given opinions as to constitutional issues in their previous legal careers." *Laird v. Tatum*, 409 U.S. 824, 835 (1972) (memorandum opinion). Indeed, even if it were possible to select judges who did not have preconceived views on legal issues, it would hardly be desirable to do so. "Proof that a Justice's mind at the time he joined the Court was a complete *tabula rasa* in the area of constitutional adjudication would be evidence of lack of qualification, not lack of bias." The Minnesota Constitution positively forbids the selection to courts of general jurisdiction of judges who are impartial in the sense of having no views on the law. Minn. Const., Art. VI, § 5 ("Judges of the supreme court, the court of appeals and the district court shall be learned in the law"). And since avoiding judicial preconceptions on legal issues is neither possible nor desirable, pretending otherwise by attempting to preserve the "appearance" of that type of impartiality can hardly be a compelling state interest either.

C

A third possible meaning of "impartiality" (again not a common one) might be described as open-mindedness. This quality in a judge demands, not that he have no preconceptions on legal issues, but that he be willing to consider views that oppose his preconceptions, and remain open to persuasion, when the issues arise in a pending case. This sort of impartiality seeks to guarantee each litigant, not an *equal* chance to win the legal points in the case, but at least *some* chance of doing so. It may well be that impartiality in this sense, and the appearance of it, are desirable in the judiciary, but we need not pursue that inquiry, since we do not believe the Minnesota Supreme Court adopted the announce clause for that purpose.

Respondents argue that the announce clause serves the interest in open-mindedness, or at least in the appearance of open-mindedness, because it relieves a judge from pressure to rule a certain way in order to maintain consistency with statements the judge has previously made. The problem is, however, that statements in election campaigns are such an infinitesimal portion of the public commitments to legal positions that judges (or judges-to-be) undertake, that this object of the prohibition is implausible. Before they arrive on the bench (whether by election or otherwise) judges have often committed themselves on legal issues that they must later rule upon. See, *e.g.*, *Laird*, supra, at 831–833 (describing Justice Black's participation in several cases construing and deciding the constitutionality of the Fair Labor Standards Act, even though as a Senator he had been one of its principal authors; and Chief Justice Hughes's authorship of the opinion overruling *Adkins v. Children's Hospital of D. C.*, 261 U.S. 525 (1923), a case he had criticized in a book written before his appointment to the Court). More common still is a judge's confronting a legal issue on which he has expressed an opinion while on the bench. Most frequently, of course, that prior expression will have occurred in ruling on an earlier case. But judges often state their views on disputed legal issues outside the context of adjudication—in classes that they conduct, and in books and speeches.

The short of the matter is this: In Minnesota, a candidate for judicial office may not say "I think it is constitutional for the legislature to prohibit same-sex marriages." He may say the very same thing, however, up until the very day before he declares himself a candidate, and may say it repeatedly (until litigation is pending) after he is elected. As a means of pursuing the objective of open-mindedness that respondents now articulate, the announce clause is so woefully underinclusive as to render belief in that purpose a challenge to the credulous.

Justice STEVENS asserts that statements made in an election campaign pose a special threat to open-mindedness because the candidate, when elected judge, will have a *particular* reluctance to contradict them. That might be plausible, perhaps, with regard to campaign *promises*. A candidate who says "If elected, I will vote to uphold the legislature's power to prohibit same-sex marriages" will positively be breaking his word if he does not do so (although one would be naïve not to recognize that campaign promises are—by long democratic tradition—the least binding form of human commitment). But, as noted earlier, the Minnesota Supreme Court has adopted a separate prohibition on campaign "pledges or promises," which is not challenged here. The proposition that judges feel significantly greater compulsion, or appear to feel significantly greater compulsion, to maintain consistency with *nonpromissory* statements made during a judicial campaign than with such statements made before or after the campaign is not self-evidently true. It seems to us quite likely, in fact, that in many cases the opposite is true. We doubt, for example, that a mere statement of position enunciated during the pendency of an election will be regarded by a judge as more binding—or as more likely to subject him to popular disfavor if reconsidered—than a carefully considered holding that the judge set forth in an earlier opinion denying some individual's claim to justice. In any event, it suffices to say that respondents have not carried the burden imposed by our strict-scrutiny test to establish this proposition (that campaign statements are uniquely destructive of open-mindedness) on which the validity of the announce clause rests.[3]

Moreover, the notion that the special context of electioneering justifies an *abridgment* of the right to speak out on disputed issues sets our First Amendment jurisprudence on its head. "[D]ebate on the qualifications of candidates" is "at the core of our electoral process and of the First Amendment freedoms," not at the edges. "The role that elected officials play in our

---

3. We do not agree with Justice STEVENS' broad assertion that "to the extent that [statements on legal issues] seek to enhance the popularity of the candidate by indicating how he would rule in specific cases if elected, they evidence *a lack of fitness for office*." (emphasis added). Of course all statements on real-world legal issues "indicate" how the speaker would rule "in specific cases." And if making such statements (*of honestly held views*) with the hope of enhancing one's chances with the electorate displayed a lack of fitness for office, so would similarly motivated honest statements of judicial candidates made with the hope of enhancing their chances of confirmation by the Senate, or indeed of appointment by the President. Since such statements are made, we think, in every confirmation hearing, Justice STEVENS must contemplate a federal bench filled with the unfit.

society makes it all the more imperative that they be allowed freely to express themselves on matters of current public importance." "It is simply not the function of government to select which issues are worth discussing or debating in the course of a political campaign." We have never allowed the government to prohibit candidates from communicating relevant information to voters during an election.

Justice GINSBURG would do so—and much of her dissent confirms rather than refutes our conclusion that the purpose behind the announce clause is not openmindedness in the judiciary, but the undermining of judicial elections. She contends that the announce clause must be constitutional because due process would be denied if an elected judge sat in a case involving an issue on which he had previously announced his view. She reaches this conclusion because, she says, such a judge would have a "direct, personal, substantial, and pecuniary interest" in ruling consistently with his previously announced view, in order to reduce the risk that he will be "voted off the bench and thereby lose [his] salary and emoluments." But elected judges—regardless of whether they have announced any views beforehand—always face the pressure of an electorate who might disagree with their rulings and therefore vote them off the bench. Surely the judge who frees Timothy McVeigh places his job much more at risk than the judge who (horror of horrors!) reconsiders his previously announced view on a disputed legal issue. So if, as Justice GINSBURG claims, it violates due process for a judge to sit in a case in which ruling one way rather than another increases his prospects for reelection, then—quite simply—the practice of electing judges is itself a violation of due process. It is not difficult to understand how one with these views would approve the election-nullifying effect of the announce clause.[4] They are not, however, the views reflected in the Due Process Clause of the Fourteenth Amendment, which has coexisted with the election of judges ever since it was adopted.

Justice GINSBURG devotes the rest of her dissent to attacking arguments we do not make. For example, despite the number of pages she dedicates to disproving this proposition, we neither assert nor imply that the First Amendment requires campaigns for judicial office to sound the same as those for legislative office.[5] What we do assert, and what Justice GINSBURG ignores, is that, even if the First Amendment allows greater regulation of judicial election campaigns than legislative election campaigns, the announce clause still fails strict scrutiny because it is woefully underinclusive, prohibiting announcements by judges(and would-be judges) only at certain times and in certain forms. We rely on the cases involving speech during elections, only to make the obvious point that this underinclusiveness cannot be explained by resort to the notion that the First Amendment provides less protection during an election campaign than at other times.[6]

4. Justice GINSBURG argues that the announce clause is not election nullifying because Wersal criticized past decisions of the Minnesota Supreme Court in his campaign literature and the Lawyers Board decided not to discipline him for doing so. As we have explained, however, had Wersal additionally stated during his campaign that he did not feel bound to follow those erroneous decisions, he would not have been so lucky. This predicament hardly reflects "the robust communication of ideas and views from judicial candidate to voter."

5. Justice STEVENS devotes most of his dissent to this same argument that we do not make.

6. Nor do we assert that candidates for judicial office should be compelled to announce their views on disputed legal issues. Thus, Jus-

But in any case, Justice GINSBURG greatly exaggerates the difference between judicial and legislative elections. She asserts that "the rationale underlying unconstrained speech in elections for political office—that representative government depends on the public's ability to choose agents who will act at its behest—does not carry over to campaigns for the bench." This complete separation of the judiciary from the enterprise of "representative government" might have some truth in those countries where judges neither make law themselves nor set aside the laws enacted by the legislature. It is not a true picture of the American system. Not only do state-court judges possess the power to "make" common law, but they have the immense power to shape the States' constitutions as well. Which is precisely why the election of state judges became popular.

IV

To sustain the announce clause, the Eighth Circuit relied heavily on the fact that a pervasive practice of prohibiting judicial candidates from discussing disputed legal and political issues developed during the last half of the 20th century. It is true that a "universal and long-established" tradition of prohibiting certain conduct creates "a strong presumption" that the prohibition is constitutional: "Principles of liberty fundamental enough to have been embodied within constitutional guarantees are not readily erased from the Nation's consciousness." *McIntyre v. Ohio Elections Comm'n*, 514 U.S. 334, 375–377 (1995) (SCALIA, J., dissenting). The practice of prohibiting speech by judicial candidates on disputed issues, however, is neither long nor universal. At the time of the founding, only Vermont (before it became a State) selected any of its judges by election. Starting with Georgia in 1812, States began to provide for judicial election, a development rapidly accelerated by Jacksonian democracy. By the time of the Civil War, the great majority of States elected their judges. We know of no restrictions upon statements that could be made by judicial candidates (including judges) throughout the 19th and the first quarter of the 20th century. Indeed, judicial elections were generally partisan during this period, the movement toward nonpartisan judicial elections not even beginning until the 1870's. Thus, not only were judicial candidates (including judges) discussing disputed legal and political issues on the campaign trail, but they were touting party affiliations and angling for party nominations all the while.

The first code regulating judicial conduct was adopted by the ABA in 1924. It contained a provision akin to the announce clause: "A candidate for judicial position ... should not announce in advance his conclusions of law on disputed issues to secure class support...." The States were slow to adopt the canons, however. "By the end of World War II, the canons ... were binding by the bar associations or supreme courts of only eleven states." Even today, although a majority of States have adopted either the announce clause

tice GINSBURG's repeated invocation of instances in which nominees to this Court declined to announce such views during Senate confirmation hearings is pointless. That the practice of voluntarily demurring does not establish the legitimacy of legal compulsion to demur is amply demonstrated by the unredacted text of the sentence she quotes in part, from

Laird v. Tatum, 409 U.S. 824, 836, n. 5, (1972): "*In terms of propriety, rather than disqualification*, I would distinguish quite sharply between a public statement made prior to nomination for the bench, on the one hand, and a public statement made by a nominee to the bench." (Emphasis added.)

or its 1990 ABA successor, adoption is not unanimous. Of the 31 States that select some or all of their appellate and general-jurisdiction judges by election, see American Judicature Society, Judicial Selection in the States: Appellate and General Jurisdiction Courts (Apr.2002), 4 have adopted no candidate-speech restriction comparable to the announce clause, and 1 prohibits only the discussion of "pending litigation." This practice, relatively new to judicial elections and still not universally adopted, does not compare well with the traditions deemed worthy of our attention in prior cases. *E.g., Burson v. Freeman,* 504 U.S. 191, 205–206 (1992) (crediting tradition of prohibiting speech around polling places that began with the very adoption of the secret ballot in the late 19th century, and in which every State participated); *id.,* at 214–216, (SCALIA, J., concurring in judgment) (same); *McIntyre, supra,* at 375–377 (SCALIA, J., dissenting) (crediting tradition of prohibiting anonymous election literature, which again began in 1890 and was universally adopted).

* * *

There is an obvious tension between the article of Minnesota's popularly approved Constitution which provides that judges shall be elected, and the Minnesota Supreme Court's announce clause which places most subjects of interest to the voters off limits. (The candidate-speech restrictions of all the other States that have them are also the product of judicial fiat.) The disparity is perhaps unsurprising, since the ABA, which originated the announce clause, has long been an opponent of judicial elections. That opposition may be well taken (it certainly had the support of the Founders of the Federal Government), but the First Amendment does not permit it to achieve its goal by leaving the principle of elections in place while preventing candidates from discussing what the elections are about. "[T]he greater power to dispense with elections altogether does not include the lesser power to conduct elections under conditions of state-imposed voter ignorance. If the State chooses to tap the energy and the legitimizing power of the democratic process, it must accord the participants in that process ... the First Amendment rights that attach to their roles."

The Minnesota Supreme Court's canon of judicial conduct prohibiting candidates for judicial election from announcing their views on disputed legal and political issues violates the First Amendment. Accordingly, we reverse the grant of summary judgment to respondents and remand the case for proceedings consistent with this opinion.

JUSTICE O'CONNOR, concurring.

I join the opinion of the Court but write separately to express my concerns about judicial elections generally. Respondents claim that "[t]he Announce Clause is necessary ... to protect the State's compelling governmental interes [t] in an actual and perceived ... impartial judiciary." I am concerned that, even aside from what judicial candidates may say while campaigning, the very practice of electing judges undermines this interest.

We of course want judges to be impartial, in the sense of being free from any personal stake in the outcome of the cases to which they are assigned. But if judges are subject to regular elections they are likely to feel that they have at least some personal stake in the outcome of every publicized case. Elected judges cannot help being aware that if the public is not satisfied with the outcome of a particular case, it could hurt their reelection prospects. See Eule, Crocodiles in the Bathtub: State Courts, Voter Initiatives and the Threat of Electoral Reprisal, 65 U. Colo. L. Rev. 733, 739 (1994) (quoting former California Supreme Court Justice Otto Kaus' statement that ignoring the political consequences of visible decisions is " 'like ignoring a crocodile in your bathtub' "); Bright & Keenan, Judges and the Politics of Death: Deciding Between the Bill of Rights and the Next Election in Capital Cases, 75 B. U. L. Rev. 759, 793–794 (1995) (citing statistics indicating that judges who face elections are far more likely to override jury sentences of life without parole and impose the death penalty than are judges who do not run for election). Even if judges were able to suppress their awareness of the potential electoral consequences of their decisions and refrain from acting on it, the public's confidence in the judiciary could be undermined simply by the possibility that judges would be unable to do so. Moreover, contested elections generally entail campaigning. And campaigning for a judicial post today can require substantial funds.

Unless the pool of judicial candidates is limited to those wealthy enough to independently fund their campaigns, a limitation unrelated to judicial skill, the cost of campaigning requires judicial candidates to engage in fundraising. Yet relying on campaign donations may leave judges feeling indebted to certain parties or interest groups. Even if judges were able to refrain from favoring donors, the mere possibility that judges' decisions may be motivated by the desire to repay campaign contributors is likely to undermine the public's confidence in the judiciary.

Despite these significant problems, 39 States currently employ some form of judicial elections for their appellate courts, general jurisdiction trial courts, or both. Judicial elections were not always so prevalent. The first 29 States of the Union adopted methods for selecting judges that did not involve popular elections. As the Court explains, however, beginning with Georgia in 1812, States began adopting systems for judicial elections. From the 1830's until the 1850's, as part of the Jacksonian movement toward greater popular control of public office, this trend accelerated, and by the Civil War, 22 of the 34 States elected their judges. By the beginning of the 20th century, however, elected judiciaries increasingly came to be viewed as incompetent and corrupt, and criticism of partisan judicial elections mounted. In 1906, Roscoe Pound gave a speech to the American Bar Association in which he claimed that "compelling judges to become politicians, in many jurisdictions has almost destroyed the traditional respect for the bench."

In response to such concerns, some States adopted a modified system of judicial selection that became known as the Missouri Plan (because Missouri was the first State to adopt it for most of its judicial posts). Under the Missouri Plan, judges are appointed by a high elected official, generally from a list of nominees put together by a nonpartisan nominating commission, and then subsequently stand for unopposed retention elections in which voters are asked whether the judges should be recalled. If a judge is recalled, the vacancy is filled through a new nomination and appointment. This system obviously reduces threats to judicial impartiality, even if it does not eliminate all popular pressure on judges.

Minnesota has chosen to select its judges through contested popular elections instead of through an appointment system or a combined appointment and retention election system along the lines of the Missouri Plan. In doing so the State has voluntarily taken on the risks to judicial bias described above. As a result, the State's claim that it needs to significantly restrict judges' speech in order to protect judicial impartiality is particularly troubling. If the State has a problem with judicial impartiality, it is largely one the State brought upon itself by continuing the practice of popularly electing judges.

JUSTICE KENNEDY, concurring.

I agree with the Court that Minnesota's prohibition on judicial candidates' announcing their legal views is an unconstitutional abridgment of the freedom of speech. There is authority for the Court to apply strict scrutiny analysis to resolve some First Amendment cases and the Court explains in clear and forceful terms why the Minnesota regulatory scheme fails that test. So I join its opinion.

I adhere to my view, however, that content-based speech restrictions that do not fall within any traditional exception should be invalidated without inquiry into narrow tailoring or compelling government interests. The speech at issue here does not come within any of the exceptions to the First Amendment recognized by the Court. "Here, a law is directed to speech alone where the speech in question is not obscene, not defamatory, not words tantamount to an act otherwise criminal, not an impairment of some other constitutional right, not an incitement to lawless action, and not calculated or likely to bring about imminent harm the State has the substantive power to prevent. No further inquiry is necessary to reject the State's argument that the statute should be upheld." The political speech of candidates is at the heart of the First Amendment, and direct restrictions on the content of candidate speech are simply beyond the power of government to impose.

Here, Minnesota has sought to justify its speech restriction as one necessary to maintain the integrity of its judiciary. Nothing in the Court's opinion should be read to cast doubt on the vital importance of this state interest. Courts, in our system, elaborate principles of law in the course of resolving disputes. The power and the prerogative of a court to perform this function rest, in the end, upon the respect accorded to its judgments. The citizen's respect for judgments depends in turn upon the issuing court's absolute probity. Judicial integrity is, in consequence, a state interest of the highest order.

Articulated standards of judicial conduct may advance this interest. To comprehend, then to codify, the essence of judicial integrity is a hard task, however. "The work of deciding cases goes on every day in hundreds of courts throughout the land. Any judge, one might suppose, would find it easy to describe the process which he had followed a thousand times and more. Nothing could be farther from the truth." B. Cardozo, The Nature of the Judicial Process 9 (1921). Much the same can be said of explicit standards to ensure judicial integrity. To strive for judicial integrity is the work of a lifetime. That should not dissuade the profession. The difficulty of the undertaking does not mean we should refrain from the attempt. Explicit standards of judicial conduct provide essential guidance for judges in the proper discharge of their duties and the honorable conduct of their office. The legislative bodies, judicial committees, and professional associations that promulgate those standards perform a vital public service. Yet these standards may not be used by the State to abridge the speech of aspiring judges in a judicial campaign. Minnesota may choose to have an elected judiciary. It may strive to define those characteristics that exemplify judicial excellence. It may enshrine its definitions in a code of judicial conduct. It may adopt recusal standards more rigorous than due process requires, and censure judges who violate these standards. What Minnesota may not do, however, is censor what the people hear as they undertake to decide for themselves which candidate is most likely to be an exemplary judicial officer. Deciding the relevance of candidate speech is the right of the voters, not the State. See *Brown v. Hartlage*, 456 U.S. 45, 60 (1982). The law in question here contradicts the principle that unabridged speech is the foundation of political freedom.

The State of Minnesota no doubt was concerned, as many citizens and thoughtful commentators are concerned, that judicial campaigns in an age of frenetic fundraising and mass media may foster disrespect for the legal system. Indeed, from the beginning there have been those who believed that the rough-and-tumble of politics would bring our governmental institutions into ill repute. And some have sought to cure this tendency with governmental restrictions on political speech. See Sedition Act of 1798, ch. 74, 1 Stat. 596. Cooler heads have always recognized, however, that these measures abridge the freedom of speech—not because the state interest is insufficiently compelling, but simply because content-based restrictions on political speech are " 'expressly and positively forbidden by' " the First Amendment. The State cannot opt for an elected judiciary and then assert that its democracy, in order to work as desired, compels the abridgment of speech.

If Minnesota believes that certain sorts of candidate speech disclose flaws in the candidate's credentials, democracy and free speech are their own correctives. The legal profession, the legal academy, the press, voluntary groups, political and civic leaders, and all interested citizens can use their own First Amendment freedoms to protest statements inconsistent with standards of judicial neutrality and judicial excellence. Indeed, if democracy is to fulfill its promise, they must do so. They must reach voters who are uninterested or uninformed or blinded by partisanship, and they must urge upon the voters a higher and better understanding of the judicial function and a stronger commitment to preserving its finest traditions. Free elections and free speech are a powerful combination: Together they may advance our understanding of the rule of law and further a commitment to its precepts.

There is general consensus that the design of the Federal Constitution, including lifetime tenure and appointment by nomination and confirmation, has preserved the independence of the federal judiciary. In resolving this case, however, we should refrain from criticism of the State's choice to use open elections to select those persons most likely to achieve judicial excellence. States are free to choose this mechanism rather than, say, appointment and confirmation. By condemning judicial elections across the board, we implicitly condemn countless elected state judges and without warrant. Many of them, despite the difficulties imposed by the election system, have discovered in the law the enlightenment, instruction, and inspiration that make them independent-minded and faithful jurists of real integrity. We should not, even by inadvertence, "impute to judges a lack of firmness, wisdom, or honor."

These considerations serve but to reinforce the conclusion that Minnesota's regulatory scheme is flawed. By abridging speech based on its content, Minnesota impeaches its own system of free and open elections. The State may not regulate the content of candidate speech merely because the speakers are candidates. This case does not present the question whether a State may restrict the speech of judges because they are judges—for example, as part of a code of judicial conduct; the law at issue here regulates judges only when and because they are candidates. Whether the rationale of *Pickering v. Board of Ed. of Township High School Dist. 205, Will Cty.*, 391 U.S. 563, 568 (1968), and *Connick v. Myers*, 461 U.S. 138 (1983), could be extended to allow a general speech restriction on sitting judges—regardless of whether they are campaigning—in order to promote the efficient administration of justice, is not an issue raised here.

Petitioner Gregory Wersal was not a sitting judge but a challenger; he had not voluntarily entered into an employment relationship with the State or surrendered any First Amendment rights. His speech may not be controlled or abridged in this manner. Even the undoubted interest of the State in the excellence of its judiciary does not allow it to restrain candidate speech by reason of its content. Minnesota's attempt to regulate campaign speech is impermissible.

JUSTICE STEVENS, with whom JUSTICE SOUTER, JUSTICE GINSBURG, and JUSTICE BREYER join, dissenting.

In her dissenting opinion, Justice GINSBURG has cogently explained why the Court's holding is unsound. I therefore join her opinion without reservation. I add these comments to emphasize the force of her arguments and to explain why I find the Court's reasoning even more troubling than its holding. The limits of the Court's holding are evident: Even if the Minnesota Lawyers Professional Responsibility Board (Board) may not sanction a judicial candidate for announcing his views on issues likely to come before him, it may surely advise the electorate that such announcements demonstrate the speaker's unfitness for judicial office. If the solution to harmful speech must be more speech, so be it. The Court's reasoning, however, will unfortunately endure beyond the next election cycle. By obscuring the fundamental distinction between campaigns for the judiciary and the political branches, and by failing to recognize the difference between statements made in articles or opinions and those made on the campaign trail, the Court defies any sensible notion of the judicial office and the importance of impartiality in that context.

The Court's disposition rests on two seriously flawed premises—an inaccurate appraisal of the importance of judicial independence and impartiality, and an assumption that judicial candidates should have the same freedom " 'to express themselves on matters of current public importance' "as do all other elected officials. Elected judges, no less than appointed judges, occupy an office of trust that is fundamentally different from that occupied by policymaking officials. Although the fact that they must stand for election makes their job more difficult than that of the tenured judge, that fact does not lessen their duty to respect essential attributes of the judicial office that have been embedded in Anglo–American law for centuries.

There is a critical difference between the work of the judge and the work of other public officials. In a democracy, issues of policy are properly decided by majority vote; it is the business of legislators and executives to be popular. But in litigation, issues of law or fact should not be determined by popular vote; it is the business of judges to be indifferent to unpopularity. Sir Matthew Hale pointedly described this essential attribute of the judicial office in words which have retained their integrity for centuries:

> " '11. That popular or court applause or distaste have no influence in anything I do, in point of distribution of justice.
>
> " '12. Not to be solicitous what men will say or think, so long as I keep myself exactly according to the rule of justice.' "

Consistent with that fundamental attribute of the office, countless judges in countless cases routinely make rulings that are unpopular and surely disliked by at least 50 percent of the litigants who appear before them. It is equally common for them to enforce rules that they think unwise, or that are contrary to their personal predilections. For this reason, opinions that a lawyer may have expressed before becoming a judge, or a judicial candidate, do not disqualify anyone for judicial service because every good judge is fully aware of the distinction between the law and a personal point of view. It is equally clear, however, that such expressions after a lawyer has been nominated to judicial office shed little, if any, light on his capacity for judicial service. Indeed, to the extent that such statements seek to enhance the popularity of the candidate by indicating how he would rule in specific cases if elected, they evidence a lack of fitness for the office.

Of course, any judge who faces reelection may believe that he retains his office only so long as his decisions are popular. Nevertheless, the elected judge, like the lifetime appointee, does not serve a constituency while holding that office. He has a duty to uphold the law and to follow the dictates of the Constitution. If he is not a judge on the highest court in the State, he has an obligation to follow the precedent of that court, not his personal views or public opinion polls.[7] He may make common law, but judged on the merits of individual cases, not as a mandate from the voters.

---

7. The Court largely ignores the fact that judicial elections are not limited to races for the highest court in the State. Even if announcing one's views in the context of a campaign for the State Supreme Court might be permissible, the same statements are surely less appropriate when one is running for an intermediate or trial court judgeship. Such statements not only display a misunderstanding of the judicial role, but they also mislead the voters by giving them the false impression that a candidate for the trial court will be able to and should decide cases based on his personal views rather than precedent.

Indeed, the Court's entire analysis has a hypothetical quality to it that stems, in part, from the fact that no candidate has yet been sanctioned for violating the announce clause. The one complaint filed against petitioner George Wersal for campaign materials during his 1996 election run was dismissed by the Board. Moreover, when Wersal sought an advisory opinion during his 1998 campaign, the Board could not evaluate his request because he had "not specified what statement[he] would make that may or may not be a view on a disputed, legal or political issue." Since Wersal failed to provide examples of statements he wished to make, and because the Board had its own doubts about the constitutionality of the announce clause, it advised Wersal that "unless the speech at issue violates other prohibitions listed in Canon 5 or other portions of the Code of Judicial Conduct, it is our belief that this section is not, as written, constitutionally enforceable." Consequently, the Court is left to decide a question of great constitutional importance in a case in which the petitioner's statements were either not subject to the prohibition in question, or he neglected to supply any concrete examples of statements he wished to make, and the Board refused to enforce the prohibition because of its own constitutional concerns.

By recognizing a conflict between the demands of electoral politics and the distinct characteristics of the judiciary, we do not have to put States to an all or nothing choice of abandoning judicial elections or having elections in which anything goes. As a practical matter, we cannot know for sure whether an elected judge's decisions are based on his interpretation of the law or political expediency. In the absence of reliable evidence one way or the other, a State may reasonably presume that elected judges are motivated by the highest aspirations of their office. But we do know that a judicial candidate, who announces his views in the context of a campaign, is effectively telling the electorate: "Vote for me because I believe X, and I will judge cases accordingly." Once elected, he may feel free to disregard his campaign statements, but that does not change the fact that the judge announced his position on an issue likely to come before him *as a reason to vote for him.* Minnesota has a compelling interest in sanctioning such statements.

A candidate for judicial office who goes beyond the expression of "general observation about the law ... in order to obtain favorable consideration" of his candidacy, demonstrates either a lack of impartiality or a lack of understanding of the importance of maintaining public confidence in the impartiality of the judiciary. It is only by failing to recognize the distinction, clearly stated by then-Justice REHNQUIST, between statements made during a campaign or confirmation hearing and those made before announcing one's candidacy, that the Court is able to conclude: "[S]ince avoiding judicial preconceptions on legal issues is neither possible nor desirable, pretending otherwise by attempting to preserve the 'appearance' of that type of impartiality can hardly be a compelling state interest either."

Even when "impartiality" is defined in its narrowest sense to embrace only "the lack of bias for or against either party to the proceeding," the announce clause serves that interest. Expressions that stress a candidate's unbroken record of affirming convictions for rape, for example, imply a bias in favor of a particular litigant (the prosecutor) and against a class of litigants (defendants in rape cases). Contrary to the Court's reasoning in its first attempt to define impartiality, an interpretation of the announce clause that prohibits such statements serves the State's interest in maintaining both the appearance of this form of impartiality and its actuality.

When the Court evaluates the importance of impartiality in its broadest sense, which it describes as "the interest in open-mindedness, or at least in the appearance of, open-mindedness" it concludes that the announce clause is "so woefully underinclusive as to render belief in that purpose a challenge to the credulous." It is underinclusive, in the Court's view, because campaign statements are an infinitesimal portion of the public commitments to legal positions that candidates make during their professional careers. It is not, however, the number of legal views that a candidate may have formed or discussed in his prior career that is significant. Rather, it is the ability both to reevaluate them in the light of an adversarial presentation, and to apply the governing rule of law even when inconsistent with those views, that characterize judicial open-mindedness.

The Court boldly asserts that respondents have failed to carry their burden of demonstrating "that campaign statements are uniquely destructive of open-mindedness." But the very purpose of most statements prohibited by the announce clause is to convey the message that the candidate's mind is not open on a particular issue. The lawyer who writes an article advocating harsher penalties for polluters surely does not commit to that position to the same degree as the candidate who says "vote for me because I believe all polluters deserve harsher penalties." At the very least, such statements obscure the appearance of open-mindedness. More importantly, like the reasoning in the Court's opinion, they create the false impression that the standards for the election of political candidates apply equally to candidates for judicial office.[8]

The judicial reputation for impartiality and open-mindedness is compromised by electioneering that emphasizes the candidate's personal predilections rather than his qualifications for judicial office. As an elected judge recently noted:

> "Informed criticism of court rulings, or of the professional or personal conduct of judges, should play an important role in maintaining judicial accountability. However, attacking courts and judges—not because they are wrong on the law or the facts of a case, but because the decision is considered wrong simply as a matter of political judgment—maligns one of the basic tenets of judicial independence—intellectual honesty and dedication to enforcement of the rule of law regardless of popular sentiment. Dedication to the rule of law requires judges to rise above the political moment in making judicial decisions. What is so troubling about criticism of court rulings and individual judges based solely on political disagreement with the outcome is that it evidences a fundamentally misguided belief that the judicial branch should operate and be treated just like another constituency-driven political arm of government. Judges should not have 'political constituencies.' Rather, a judge's fidelity must be to enforcement of the rule of law regardless of perceived popular will."
> De Muniz, Politicizing State Judicial Elections: A Threat to Judicial Independence, 38 Willamette L. Rev. 367, 387 (2002).

The disposition of this case on the flawed premise that the criteria for the election to judicial office should mirror the rules applicable to political elections is profoundly misguided. I therefore respectfully dissent.

JUSTICE GINSBURG, with whom JUSTICE STEVENS, JUSTICE JOUTER, and JUSTICE BREYER join, dissenting.

Whether state or federal, elected or appointed, judges perform a function fundamentally different from that of the people's elected representatives. Legislative and executive officials act on behalf of the voters who placed them in office; "judge[s] represen[t] the Law." *Chisom v. Roemer*, 501 U.S. 380, 411 (1991) (SCALIA, J., dissenting). Unlike their counterparts in the political branches, judges are expected to refrain from catering to particular constituencies or committing themselves on controversial issues in advance of adversarial presentation. Their mission is to decide "individual cases and controver-

---

8. Justice KENNEDY would go even further and hold that no content-based restriction of a judicial candidate's speech is permitted under the First Amendment. While he does not say so explicitly, this extreme position would preclude even Minnesota's prohibition against "pledges or promises" by a candidate for judi-cial office. A candidate could say "vote for me because I promise to never reverse a rape conviction," and the Board could do nothing to formally sanction that candidate. The unwisdom of this proposal illustrates why the same standards should not apply to speech in campaigns for judicial and legislative office.

sies" on individual records, neutrally applying legal principles, and, when necessary, "stand[ing] up to what is generally supreme in a democracy: the popular will," Scalia, The Rule of Law as a Law of Rules, 56 U. Chi. L. Rev. 1175, 1180 (1989).

A judiciary capable of performing this function, owing fidelity to no person or party, is a "longstanding Anglo–American tradition," an essential bulwark of constitutional government, a constant guardian of the rule of law. The guarantee of an independent, impartial judiciary enables society to "withdraw certain subjects from the vicissitudes of political controversy, to place them beyond the reach of majorities and officials and to establish them as legal principles to be applied by the courts." *West Virginia Bd. of Ed. v. Barnette*, 319 U.S. 624, 638 (1943). "Without this, all the reservations of particular rights or privileges would amount to nothing."

The ability of the judiciary to discharge its unique role rests to a large degree on the manner in which judges are selected. The Framers of the Federal Constitution sought to advance the judicial function through the structural protections of Article III, which provide for the selection of judges by the President on the advice and consent of the Senate, generally for lifetime terms. Through its own Constitution, Minnesota, in common with most other States, has decided to allow its citizens to choose judges directly in periodic elections. But Minnesota has not thereby opted to install a corps of political actors on the bench; rather, it has endeavored to preserve the integrity of its judiciary by other means. Recognizing that the influence of political parties is incompatible with the judge's role, for example, Minnesota has designated all judicial elections nonpartisan. And it has adopted a provision, here called the Announce Clause, designed to prevent candidates for judicial office from "publicly making known how they would decide issues likely to come before them as judges."

The question this case presents is whether the First Amendment stops Minnesota from furthering its interest in judicial integrity through this precisely targeted speech restriction.

I

The speech restriction must fail, in the Court's view, because an electoral process is at stake; if Minnesota opts to elect its judges, the Court asserts, the State may not rein in what candidates may say.

I do not agree with this unilocular, "an election is an election," approach. Instead, I would differentiate elections for political offices, in which the First Amendment holds full sway, from elections designed to select those whose office it is to administer justice without respect to persons. Minnesota's choice to elect its judges, I am persuaded, does not preclude the State from installing an election process geared to the judicial office.

Legislative and executive officials serve in representative capacities. They are agents of the people; their primary function is to advance the interests of their constituencies. Candidates for political offices, in keeping with their representative role, must be left free to inform the electorate of their positions on specific issues. Armed with such information, the individual voter will be equipped to cast her ballot intelligently, to vote for the candidate committed to positions the voter approves. Campaign statements committing the candidate to take sides on contentious issues are therefore not only appropriate in political elections, they are "at the core of our electoral process," for they "enhance the accountability of government officials to the people whom they represent," *Brown v. Hartlage*, 456 U.S. 45, 55 (1982).

Judges, however, are not political actors. They do not sit as representatives of particular persons, communities, or parties; they serve no faction or constituency. "[I]t is the business of judges to be indifferent to popularity." They must strive to do what is legally right, all the more so when the result is not the one "the home crowd" wants. Rehnquist, Dedicatory Address: Act Well Your Part: Therein All Honor Lies, 7 Pepperdine L. Rev. 227, 229–300 (1980). Even when they develop common law or give concrete meaning to constitutional text, judges act only in the context of individual cases, the outcome of which cannot depend on the will of the public.

Thus, the rationale underlying unconstrained speech in elections for political office—that representative government depends on the public's ability to choose agents who will act at its behest—does not carry over to campaigns for the bench. As to persons aiming to occupy the seat of judgment, the Court's unrelenting reliance on decisions involving contests for legislative and executive posts is manifestly out of place.

The Court sees in this conclusion, and in the Announce Clause that embraces it, "an obvious tension": The Minnesota electorate is permitted to select its judges by popular vote, but is not provided information on "subjects of interest to the voters,"—in particular, the voters are not told how the candidate would decide controversial cases or issues if elected. This supposed tension, however, rests on the false premise that by departing from the federal model with respect to who chooses judges, Minnesota necessarily departed from the federal position on the *criteria* relevant to the exercise of that choice.[9]

The Minnesota Supreme Court thought otherwise:

"The methods by which the federal system and other states initially select and then elect or retain judges are varied, yet the explicit or implicit goal of the constitutional provisions and enabling legislation is the same: to create and maintain an independent judiciary as free from political, economic and social pressure as possible so judges can decide cases without those influences."

9. In the context of the federal system, how a prospective nominee for the bench would resolve particular contentious issues would certainly be "of interest" to the President and the Senate in the exercise of their respective nomination and confirmation powers, just as information of that type would "interest" a Minnesota voter. But in accord with a longstanding norm, every Member of this Court declined to furnish such information to the Senate, and presumably to the President as well. See Brief for Respondents 17–42 (collecting statements at Senate confirmation hearings).

Surely the Court perceives no tension here; the line each of us drew in response to preconfirmation questioning, the Court would no doubt agree, is crucial to the health of the Federal Judiciary. But by the Court's reasoning, the reticence of prospective and current federal judicial nominees dishonors Article II, for it deprives the President and the Senate of information that might aid or advance the decision to nominate or confirm. The point is not, of course, that this "practice of voluntarily demurring" by itself "establish[es] the legitimacy of legal compulsion to demur." The federal norm simply illustrates that, contrary to the Court's suggestion, there is nothing inherently incongruous in depriving those charged with choosing judges of certain information they might desire during the selection process.

Nothing in the Court's opinion convincingly explains why Minnesota may not pursue that goal in the manner it did.

Minnesota did not choose a judicial selection system with all the trappings of legislative and executive races. While providing for public participation, it tailored judicial selection to fit the character of third branch office holding.

II

Proper resolution of this case requires correction of the Court's distorted construction of the provision before us for review. According to the Court, the Announce Clause "prohibits a judicial candidate from stating his views on any specific nonfanciful legal question within the province of the court for which he is running, except in the context of discussing past decisions—and in the latter context as well, if he expresses the view that he is not bound by *stare decisis*." In two key respects, that construction misrepresents the meaning of the Announce Clause as interpreted by the Eighth Circuit and embraced by the Minnesota Supreme Court.

First and most important, the Court ignores a crucial limiting construction placed on the Announce Clause by the courts below. The provision does not bar a candidate from generally "stating [her] views" on legal questions it prevents her from "publicly making known how [she] would decide" disputed issues, 247 F.3d, at 881–882 (emphasis added). That limitation places beyond the scope of the Announce Clause a wide range of comments that may be highly informative to voters. Consistent with the Eighth Circuit's construction, such comments may include, for example, statements of historical fact ("As a prosecutor, I obtained 15 drunk driving convictions"); qualified statements ("Judges should use sparingly their discretion to grant lenient sentences to drunk drivers"); and statements framed at a sufficient level of generality ("Drunk drivers are a threat to the safety of every driver"). What remains within the Announce Clause is the category of statements that essentially commit the candidate to a position on a specific issue, such as "I think all drunk drivers should receive the maximum sentence permitted by law." (candidate may not say " 'I'm going to decide this particular issue this way in the future' ").

Second, the Court misportrays the scope of the Clause as applied to a candidate's discussion of past decisions. Citing an apparent concession by respondents at argument, the Court concludes that "statements critical of past judicial decisions are not permissible if the candidate also states that he is against *stare decisis*." That conclusion, however, draws no force from the meaning attributed to the Announce Clause by the Eighth Circuit. In line with the Minnesota Board on Judicial Standards, the Court of Appeals stated without qualification that the Clause "does not prohibit candidates from discussing appellate court decisions." The Eighth Circuit's controlling construction should not be modified by respondents' on the spot answers to fast-paced hypothetical questions at oral argument.

The Announce Clause is thus more tightly bounded, and campaigns conducted under that provision more robust, than the Court acknowledges. Judicial candidates in Minnesota may not only convey general information about themselves they may also describe their conception of the role of a judge and their views on a wide range of subjects of interest to the voters. (e.g., the criteria for deciding whether to depart from sentencing guidelines, the remedies for racial and gender bias, and the balance between "free speech rights [and] the need to control [hate crimes]"). Further, they may discuss, criticize, or defend past decisions of interest to voters. What candidates may not do—simply or with sophistication—is remove themselves from the constraints characteristic of the judicial office and declare how they would decide an issue, without regard to the particular context in which it is presented, sans briefs, oral argument, and, as to an appellate bench, the benefit of one's colleagues' analyses. Properly construed, the Announce Clause prohibits only a discrete subcategory of the statements the Court's misinterpretation encompasses.

The Court's characterization of the Announce Clause as "election-nullifying," "plac[ing] most subjects of interest to the voters off limits," is further belied by the facts of this case. In his 1996 bid for office, petitioner Gregory Wersal distributed literature sharply criticizing three Minnesota Supreme Court decisions. Of the court's holding in the first case—that certain unrecorded confessions must be suppressed—Wersal asked, "Should we conclude that because the Supreme Court does not trust police, it allows confessed criminals to go free?" App. 37. Of the second case, invalidating a state welfare law, Wersal stated: "The Court should have deferred to the Legislature. It's the Legislature which should set our spending policies." And of the third case, a decision involving abortion rights, Wersal charged that the court's holding was "directly contrary to the opinion of the U.S. Supreme Court," "unprecedented," and a "pro-abortion stance."

When a complaint was filed against Wersal on the basis of those statements the Lawyers Professional Responsibility Board concluded that no discipline was warranted, in part because it thought the disputed campaign materials did not violate the Announce Clause. And when, at the outset of his 1998 campaign, Wersal sought to avoid the possibility of sanction for future statements, he pursued the option, available to all Minnesota judicial candidates, of requesting an advisory opinion concerning the application of the Announce Clause. In response to that request, the Board indicated that it did not anticipate any adverse action against him.[10] Wersal has thus never been sanctioned under the Announce Clause for any campaign statement he made. On the facts before us, in sum, the Announce Clause has hardly stifled the robust communication of ideas and views from judicial candidate to voter.

III

Even as it exaggerates the reach of the Announce Clause, the Court ignores the significance of that provision to the integrated system of judicial campaign regulation Minnesota has developed. Coupled with the Announce Clause in Minnesota's Code of Judicial Conduct is a provision that prohibits candidates from "mak[ing] pledges or promises of conduct in office other than the faithful and impartial performance of the duties of the office." Although

---

10. In deciding not to sanction Wersal for his campaign statements, and again in responding to his inquiry about the application of the Announce Clause, the Board expressed "doubts about the constitutionality of the current Minnesota Canon." Those doubts, however, concerned the meaning of the Announce Clause before the Eighth Circuit applied, and the Minnesota Supreme Court adopted, the limiting constructions that now define that provision's scope.

the Court is correct that this "pledges or promises" provision is not directly at issue in this case the Court errs in overlooking the interdependence of that prohibition and the one before us. In my view, the constitutionality of the Announce Clause cannot be resolved without an examination of that interaction in light of the interests the pledges or promises provision serves.

A

All parties to this case agree that, whatever the validity of the Announce Clause, the State may constitutionally prohibit judicial candidates from pledging or promising certain results.

The reasons for this agreement are apparent. Pledges or promises of conduct in office, however commonplace in races for the political branches, are inconsistent "with the judge's obligation to decide cases in accordance with his or her role." This judicial obligation to avoid prejudgment corresponds to the litigant's right, protected by the Due Process Clause of the Fourteenth Amendment, to "an impartial and disinterested tribunal in both civil and criminal cases." The proscription against pledges or promises thus represents an accommodation of "constitutionally protected interests [that] lie on both sides of the legal equation." Balanced against the candidate's interest in free expression is the litigant's "powerful and independent constitutional interest in fair adjudicative procedure."

The impartiality guaranteed to litigants through the Due Process Clause adheres to a core principle: "[N]o man is permitted to try cases where he has an interest in the outcome." Our cases have "jealously guarded" that basic concept, for it "ensur[es] that no person will be deprived of his interests in the absence of a proceeding in which he may present his case with assurance that the arbiter is not predisposed to find against him."

These cases establish three propositions important to this dispute. First, a litigant is deprived of due process where the judge who hears his case has a "direct, personal, substantial, and pecuniary" interest in ruling against him. Second, this interest need not be as direct as it was in *Tumey*, where the judge was essentially compensated for each conviction he obtained; the interest may stem, as in *Ward*, from the judge's knowledge that his success and tenure in office depend on certain outcomes. "[T]he test," we have said, "is whether the ... situation is one 'which would offer a possible temptation to the average man as a judge [that] might lead him not to hold the balance nice, clear, and true.'"Ward, 409 U.S., at 60 (quoting *Tumey*, 273 U.S. at 532). And third, due process does not require a showing that the judge is actually biased as a result of his self-interest. Rather, our cases have "always endeavored to prevent even the probability of unfairness." "[T]he requirement of due process of law in judicial procedure is not satisfied by the argument that men of the highest honor and the greatest self-sacrifice could carry it on without danger of injustice." *Tumey*, 273 U.S. at 532.[11]

---

11. To avoid the import of our due process decisions, the Court dissects the concept of judicial "impartiality," concluding that only one variant of that concept—lack of prejudice against a party—is secured by the Fourteenth Amendment. Our Due Process Clause cases do not focus solely on bias against a particular party, but rather inquire more broadly into whether the surrounding circumstances and incentives compromise the judge's ability faithfully to discharge her assigned duties. To be sure, due process violations may arise where a judge has been so personally "enmeshed in matters" concerning one party that he is bi-

The justification for the pledges or promises prohibition follows from these principles. When a judicial candidate promises to rule a certain way on an issue that may later reach the courts, the potential for due process violations is grave and manifest. If successful in her bid for office, the judicial candidate will become a judge, and in that capacity she will be under pressure to resist the pleas of litigants who advance positions contrary to her pledges on the campaign trail. If the judge fails to honor her campaign promises, she will not only face abandonment by supporters of her professed views, she will also "ris[k] being assailed as a dissembler" willing to say one thing to win an election and to do the opposite once in office. A judge in this position therefore may be thought to have a "direct, personal, substantial, [and] pecuniary interest" in ruling against certain litigants, for she may be voted off the bench and thereby lose her salary and emoluments unless she honors the pledge that secured her election.

Given this grave danger to litigants from judicial campaign promises, States are justified in barring expression of such commitments, for they typify the "situatio[n] ... in which experience teaches that the probability of actual bias on the part of the judge ... is too high to be constitutionally tolerable."

In addition to protecting litigants' due process rights, the parties in this case further agree, the pledges or promises clause advances another compelling state interest: preserving the public's confidence in the integrity and impartiality of its judiciary. As the Minnesota Supreme Court has recognized, all legal systems—regardless of their method of judicial selection—"can function only so long as the public, having confidence in the integrity of its judges, accepts and abides by judicial decisions."

Prohibiting a judicial candidate from pledging or promising certain results if elected directly promotes the State's interest in preserving public faith in the bench. When a candidate makes such a promise during a campaign, the public will no doubt perceive that she is doing so in the hope of garnering votes. And the public will in turn likely conclude that when the candidate decides an issue in accord with that promise, she does so at least in part to discharge her undertaking to the voters in the previous election and to prevent voter abandonment in the next. The perception of that unseemly *quid pro quo*—a judicial candidate's promises on issues in return for the electorate's votes at the polls—inevitably diminishes the public's faith in the ability of judges to administer the law without regard to personal or political self-interest.[12] Then–Justice REHNQUIST's observations about the federal system

ased against him. They may also arise, however, not because of any predisposition toward a party, but rather because of the judge's personal interest in resolving an issue a certain way. See Aetna Life Ins. Co. v. Lavoie, 475 U.S. 813 (1986). Due process will not countenance the latter situation, even though the self-interested judge "will apply the law to [the losing party] in the same way he [would apply] it to any other party" advancing the same position.

12. The author of the Court's opinion declined on precisely these grounds to tell the Senate whether he would overrule a particular case:

"Let us assume that I have people arguing before me to do it or not to do it. I think it is quite a thing to be arguing to somebody who you know has made a representation in the course of his confirmation hearings, and that is, by way of condition to his being confirmed, that he will do this or do that. I think I would be in a very bad position to adjudicate the case without being accused of having a less than impartial view of the matter." (hearings before the Senate Judiciary Committee on the nomination of then-Judge Scalia).

apply with equal if not greater force in the context of Minnesota's elective judiciary: Regarding the appearance of judicial integrity,

> "[one must] distinguish quite sharply between a public statement made prior to nomination for the bench, on the one hand, and a public statement made by a nominee to the bench. For the latter to express any but the most general observation about the law would suggest that, in order to obtain favorable consideration of his nomination, he deliberately was announcing in advance, without benefit of judicial oath, briefs, or argument, how he would decide a particular question that might come before him as a judge." *Laird v. Tatum*, 409 U.S. 824, 836, n. 5 (1972) (memorandum opinion).

B

The constitutionality of the pledges or promises clause is thus amply supported; the provision not only advances due process of law for litigants in Minnesota courts, it also reinforces the authority of the Minnesota judiciary by promoting public confidence in the State's judges. The Announce Clause, however, is equally vital to achieving these compelling ends, for without it, the pledges or promises provision would be feeble, an arid form, a matter of no real importance.

Uncoupled from the Announce Clause, the ban on pledges or promises is easily circumvented. By prefacing a campaign commitment with the caveat, "although I cannot promise anything," or by simply avoiding the language of promises or pledges altogether, a candidate could declare with impunity how she would decide specific issues. Semantic sanitizing of the candidate's commitment would not, however, diminish its pernicious effects on actual and perceived judicial impartiality. To use the Court's example, a candidate who campaigns by saying, "If elected, I will vote to uphold the legislature's power to prohibit same-sex marriages," will feel scarcely more pressure to honor that statement than the candidate who stands behind a podium and tells a throng of cheering supporters: "I think it is constitutional for the legislature to prohibit same-sex marriages." Made during a campaign, both statements contemplate a *quid pro quo* between candidate and voter. Both effectively "bind [the candidate] to maintain that position after election." And both convey the impression of a candidate prejudging an issue to win votes. Contrary to the Court's assertion, the "nonpromissory" statement averts none of the dangers posed by the "promissory" one. (Emphasis omitted).

By targeting statements that do not technically constitute pledges or promises but nevertheless "publicly mak[e] known how [the candidate] would decide" legal issues, the Announce Clause prevents this end run around the letter and spirit of its companion provision. No less than the pledges or promises clause itself, the Announce Clause is an indispensable part of Minnesota's effort to maintain the health of its judiciary, and is therefore constitutional for the same reasons.

* * *

This Court has recognized in the past, as Justice O'CONNOR does today a "fundamental tension between the ideal character of the judicial office and the real world of electoral politics." We have no warrant to resolve that tension, however, by forcing States to choose one pole or the other. Judges are not politicians, and the First Amendment does not require that they be treated as politicians simply because they are chosen by popular vote. Nor does the First Amendment command States who wish to promote the integrity of their judges in fact and appearance to abandon systems of judicial selection that the people, in the exercise of their sovereign prerogatives, have devised. For more than three-quarters of a century, States like Minnesota have endeavored, through experiment tested by experience, to balance the constitutional interests in judicial integrity and free expression within the unique setting of an elected judiciary. The Announce Clause, borne of this long effort, "comes to this Court bearing a weighty title of respect." I would uphold it as an essential component in Minnesota's accommodation of the complex and competing concerns in this sensitive area. Accordingly, I would affirm the judgment of the Court of Appeals for the Eighth Circuit.

QUESTIONS AND NOTES

1. Which side takes the more "liberal" position? Explain.

2. Is the disagreement among the Justices primarily about constitutional doctrine or the scope of the prohibition? Explain.

3. With which Justice would you have agreed, if any? Why?

4. To what extent are elections a threat to judicial independence?

5. Is there any good reason for judges to be less responsive to the people than other elected officials?

6. Taking *Burson* and *White* together is it fair to say that the advent of an election is cause for decreasing First Amendment rights, increasing First Amendment rights, or neither? What should the interrelationship between elections and the First Amendment be?

HILL v. COLORADO

530 U.S. 703 (2000).

JUSTICE STEVENS delivered the opinion of the Court.

At issue is the constitutionality of a 1993 Colorado statute that regulates speech-related conduct within 100 feet of the entrance to any health care facility. The specific section of the statute that is challenged, Colo. Rev. Stat. § 18–9–122(3) (1999), makes it unlawful within the regulated areas for any person to "knowingly approach" within eight feet of another person, without that person's consent, "for the purpose of passing a leaflet or handbill to, displaying a sign to, or engaging in oral protest, education, or counseling with such other person...."[1] Although the statute prohibits speakers from ap-

---

1. Section 18–9–122 reads as follows:

"(1) The general assembly recognizes that access to health care facilities for the purpose of obtaining medical counseling and treatment is imperative for the citizens of this state; that the exercise of a person's right to protest or counsel against certain medical procedures must be balanced against another person's right to obtain medical counseling and treatment in an unobstructed manner; and that preventing the willful obstruction of a person's access to medical counseling and treatment at a health care facility is a matter of statewide concern. The general assembly therefore declares that it is appropriate to enact legislation that prohib-

proaching unwilling listeners, it does not require a standing speaker to move away from anyone passing by. Nor does it place any restriction on the content of any message that anyone may wish to communicate to anyone else, either inside or outside the regulated areas. It does, however, make it more difficult to give unwanted advice, particularly in the form of a handbill or leaflet, to persons entering or leaving medical facilities.

The question is whether the First Amendment rights of the speaker are abridged by the protection the statute provides for the unwilling listener.

II

Before confronting the question whether the Colorado statute reflects an acceptable balance between the constitutionally protected rights of law-abiding speakers and the interests of unwilling listeners, it is appropriate to examine the competing interests at stake. A brief review of both sides of the dispute reveals that each has legitimate and important concerns.

The First Amendment interests of petitioners are clear and undisputed. As a preface to their legal challenge, petitioners emphasize three propositions. First, they accurately explain that the areas protected by the statute encompass all the public ways within 100 feet of every entrance to every health care facility everywhere in the State of Colorado. There is no disagreement on this point, even though the legislative history makes it clear that its enactment was primarily motivated by activities in the vicinity of abortion clinics. Second, they correctly state that their leafletting, sign displays, and oral communications are protected by the First Amendment. The fact that the messages conveyed by those communications may be offensive to their recipients does not deprive them of constitutional protection. Third, the public sidewalks, streets, and ways affected by the statute are "quintessential" public forums for free speech. Finally, although there is debate about the magnitude of the statutory impediment to their ability to communicate effectively with persons in the regulated zones, that ability, particularly the ability to distribute leaflets, is unquestionably lessened by this statute.

On the other hand, petitioners do not challenge the legitimacy of the state interests that the statute is intended to serve. It is a traditional exercise of the States' "police powers to protect the health and safety of their citizens." That interest may justify a special focus on unimpeded access to health care facilities and the avoidance of potential trauma to patients associated with confrontational protests. Moreover, as with every exercise of a State's police powers, rules that provide specific guidance to enforcement authorities serve the interest in even-handed application of the law. Whether

its a person from knowingly obstructing another person's entry to or exit from a health care facility.

"(2) A person commits a class 3 misdemeanor if such person knowingly obstructs, detains, hinders, impedes, or blocks another person's entry to or exit from a health care facility.

"(3) No person shall knowingly approach another person within eight feet of such person, unless such other person consents, for the purpose of passing a leaflet or hand-

bill to, displaying a sign to, or engaging in oral protest, education, or counseling with such other person in the public way or sidewalk area within a radius of one hundred feet from any entrance door to a health care facility. Any person who violates this subsection (3) commits a class 3 misdemeanor.

"(4) For the purposes of this section, 'health care facility' means any entity that is licensed, certified, or otherwise authorized or permitted by law to administer medical treatment in this state . . .

or not those interests justify the particular regulation at issue, they are unquestionably legitimate.

It is also important when conducting this interest analysis to recognize the significant difference between state restrictions on a speaker's right to address a willing audience and those that protect listeners from unwanted communication. This statute deals only with the latter.

The right to free speech, of course, includes the right to attempt to persuade others to change their views, and may not be curtailed simply because the speaker's message may be offensive to his audience. But the protection afforded to offensive messages does not always embrace offensive speech that is so intrusive that the unwilling audience cannot avoid it. *Frisby v. Schultz*. Indeed, "it may not be the content of the speech, as much as the deliberate 'verbal or visual assault,' that justifies proscription." *Erznoznik v. Jacksonville*. Even in a public forum, one of the reasons we tolerate a protester's right to wear a jacket expressing his opposition to government policy in vulgar language is because offended viewers can "effectively avoid further bombardment of their sensibilities simply by averting their eyes." *Cohen v. California*.

The recognizable privacy interest in avoiding unwanted communication varies widely in different settings. It is far less important when "strolling through Central Park" than when "in the confines of one's own home," or when persons are "powerless to avoid" it. But even the interest in preserving tranquility in "the Sheep Meadow" portion of Central Park may at times justify official restraints on offensive musical expression. *Ward v. Rock Against Racism*. More specific to the facts of this case, we have recognized that "the First Amendment does not demand that patients at a medical facility undertake Herculean efforts to escape the cacophony of political protests." *Madsen v. Women's Health Center*, 512 U.S. 753, 772–773 (1979).

The unwilling listener's interest in avoiding unwanted communication has been repeatedly identified in our cases. It is an aspect of the broader "right to be let alone" that one of our wisest Justices characterized as "the most comprehensive of rights and the right most valued by civilized men." *Olmstead v. United States*, 277 U.S. 438, 478 (1928) (Brandeis, J., dissenting). The right to avoid unwelcome speech has special force in the privacy of the home, *Rowan v. Post Office Dept.*, 397 U.S. 728 (1970), and its immediate surroundings, but can also be protected in confrontational settings. Thus, this comment on the right to free passage in going to and from work applies equally—or perhaps with greater force—to access to a medical facility:

"How far may men go in persuasion and communication, and still not violate the right of those whom they would influence? In going to and from work, men have a right to as free a passage without obstruction as the streets afford, consistent with the right of others to enjoy the same privilege. We are a social people, and the accosting by one of another in an inoffensive way and an offer by one to communicate and discuss information with a view to influencing the other's action, are not regarded as aggression or a violation of that other's rights. If, however, the offer is declined, as it may rightfully be, then persistence, importunity, following and dogging, become unjustifiable annoyance and obstruction which is likely soon to savor of intimidation. From all of this the person sought to be influenced has a right to be free, and his employer has a right to have him free." *American Steel Foundries v. Tri–City Central Trades Council*, 257 U.S. 184, 204 (1921).

None of our decisions has minimized the enduring importance of "the right to be free" from persistent "importunity, following and dogging" after an offer to communicate has been declined. While the freedom to communicate is substantial, "the right of every person 'to be let alone' must be placed in the scales with the right of others to communicate." It is that right, as well as the right of "passage without obstruction," that the Colorado statute legitimately seeks to protect. The restrictions imposed by the Colorado statute only apply to communications that interfere with these rights rather than those that involve willing listeners.

The dissenters argue that we depart from precedent by recognizing a "right to avoid unpopular speech in a public forum." We, of course, are not addressing whether there is such a "right." Rather, we are merely noting that our cases have repeatedly recognized the interests of unwilling listeners in situations where "the degree of captivity makes it impractical for the unwilling viewer or auditor to avoid exposure. See *Lehman* v. [*Shaker Heights*, 418 U.S. 298 (1974)]." We explained in *Erznoznik* that "this Court has considered analogous issues—pitting the First Amendment rights of speakers against the privacy rights of those who may be unwilling viewers or auditors—in a variety of contexts. Such cases demand delicate balancing." The dissenters, however, appear to consider recognizing any of the interests of unwilling listeners—let alone balancing those interests against the rights of speakers—to be unconstitutional. Our cases do not support this view.[25]

III

All four of the state court opinions upholding the validity of this statute concluded that it is a content-neutral time, place, and manner regulation. Moreover, they all found support for their analysis in *Ward v. Rock Against Racism*. It is therefore appropriate to comment on the "content neutrality" of the statute. As we explained in *Ward*:

"The principal inquiry in determining content neutrality, in speech cases generally and in time, place, or manner cases in particular, is whether the government has adopted a regulation of speech because of disagreement with the message it conveys."

The Colorado statute passes that test for three independent reasons. First, it is not a "regulation of speech." Rather, it is a regulation of the places where some speech may occur. Second, it was not adopted "because of disagreement with the message it conveys." This conclusion is supported not just by the Colorado courts' interpretation of legislative history, but more importantly by the State Supreme Court's unequivocal holding that the statute's "restric-

---

25. Furthermore, whether there is a "right" to avoid unwelcome expression is not before us in this case. The purpose of the Colorado statute is not to protect a potential listener from hearing a particular message. It is to protect those who seek medical treatment from the potential physical and emotional harm suffered when an unwelcome individual delivers a message (whatever its content) by physically approaching an individual at close range, *i.e.*, within eight feet. In offering protection from that harm, while maintaining free access to health clinics, the State pursues interests constitutionally distinct from the freedom from unpopular speech to which JUSTICE KENNEDY refers.

tions apply equally to all demonstrators, regardless of viewpoint, and the statutory language makes no reference to the content of the speech." Third, the State's interests in protecting access and privacy, and providing the police with clear guidelines, are unrelated to the content of the demonstrators' speech. As we have repeatedly explained, government regulation of expressive activity is "content neutral" if it is justified without reference to the content of regulated speech.

Petitioners nevertheless argue that the statute is not content neutral insofar as it applies to some oral communication. The statute applies to all persons who "knowingly approach" within eight feet of another for the purpose of leafletting or displaying signs; for such persons, the content of their oral statements is irrelevant. With respect to persons who are neither leafletters nor sign carriers, however, the statute does not apply unless their approach is "for the purpose of ... engaging in oral protest, education, or counseling." Petitioners contend that an individual near a health care facility who knowingly approaches a pedestrian to say "good morning" or to random- ly recite lines from a novel would not be subject to the statute's restrictions. Because the content of the oral statements made by an approaching speaker must sometimes be examined to determine whether the knowing approach is covered by the statute, petitioners argue that the law is "content-based" under our reasoning in *Carey v. Brown*.

The Colorado statute's regulation of the location of protests, education, and counseling is easily distinguishable from *Carey*. It places no restrictions on—and clearly does not prohibit—either a particular viewpoint or any subject matter that may be discussed by a speaker. Rather, it simply estab- lishes a minor place restriction on an extremely broad category of communica- tions with unwilling listeners. Instead of drawing distinctions based on the subject that the approaching speaker may wish to address, the statute applies equally to used car salesmen, animal rights activists, fundraisers, environmen- talists, and missionaries. Each can attempt to educate unwilling listeners on any subject, but without consent may not approach within eight feet to do so.

The dissenters, nonetheless, contend that the statute is not "content neutral." As JUSTICE SCALIA points out, the vice of content-based legislation in this context is that "it lends itself" to being "used for invidious thought- control purposes." But a statute that restricts certain categories of speech only lends itself to invidious use if there is a significant number of communi- cations, raising the same problem that the statute was enacted to solve, that fall outside the statute's scope, while others fall inside. *E.g., Police Dept. of Chicago v. Mosley.* Here, the statute's restriction seeks to protect those who enter a health care facility from the harassment, the nuisance, the persistent importuning, the following, the dogging, and the implied threat of physical touching that can accompany an unwelcome approach within eight feet of a patient by a person wishing to argue vociferously face-to-face and perhaps thrust an undesired handbill upon her. The statutory phrases, "oral protest, education, or counseling," distinguish speech activities likely to have those consequences from speech activities (such as JUSTICE SCALIA'S "happy speech") that are most unlikely to have those consequences. The statute does not distinguish among speech instances that are similarly likely to raise the legitimate concerns to which it responds. Hence, the statute cannot be struck down for failure to maintain "content neutrality," or for "underbreadth."

Also flawed is JUSTICE KENNEDY's theory that a statute restricting speech becomes unconstitutionally content based because of its application "to the specific locations where that discourse occurs." A statute prohibiting solicitation in airports that was motivated by the aggressive approaches of Hari-Krishnas does not become content based solely because its application is confined to airports—"the specific location where that discourse occurs." A statute making it a misdemeanor to sit at a lunch counter for an hour without ordering any food would also not be "content based" even if it were enacted by a racist legislature that hated civil rights protesters (although it might raise separate questions about the State's legitimate interest at issue).

Similarly, the contention that a statute is "viewpoint based" simply because its enactment was motivated by the conduct of the partisans on one side of a debate is without support. The antipicketing ordinance upheld in *Frisby v. Schultz*, a decision in which both of today's dissenters joined, was obviously enacted in response to the activities of antiabortion protesters who wanted to protest at the home of a particular doctor to persuade him and others that they viewed his practice of performing abortions to be murder. We nonetheless summarily concluded that the statute was content neutral.

JUSTICE KENNEDY further suggests that a speaker who approaches a patient and "chants in praise of the Supreme Court and its abortion decisions, or hands out a simple leaflet saying, 'We are for abortion rights,'" would not be subject to the statute. But what reason is there to believe the statute would not apply to that individual? She would be engaged in "oral protest" and "education," just as the abortion opponent who expresses her view that the Supreme Court decisions were incorrect would be "protesting" the decisions and "educating" the patient on the issue. The close approach of the latter, more hostile, demonstrator may be more likely to risk being perceived as a form of physical harassment; but the relevant First Amendment point is that the statute would prevent both speakers, unless welcome, from entering the 8–foot zone. The statute is not limited to those who oppose abortion. It applies to the demonstrator in JUSTICE KENNEDY's example. It applies to all "protest," to all "counseling," and to all demonstrators whether or not the demonstration concerns abortion, and whether they oppose or support the woman who has made an abortion decision. That is the level of neutrality that the Constitution demands.

IV

We also agree with the state courts' conclusion that § 18–9–122(3) is a valid time, place, and manner regulation under the test applied in *Ward* because it is "narrowly tailored." We already have noted that the statute serves governmental interests that are significant and legitimate and that the restrictions are content neutral. We are likewise persuaded that the statute is "narrowly tailored" to serve those interests and that it leaves open ample alternative channels for communication. As we have emphasized on more than one occasion, when a content-neutral regulation does not entirely foreclose any means of communication, it may satisfy the tailoring requirement even though it is not the least restrictive or least intrusive means of serving the statutory goal.[32]

---

32. "Lest any confusion on the point re-   main, we reaffirm today that a regulation of

The three types of communication regulated by § 18–9–122(3) are the display of signs, leafletting, and oral speech. The 8–foot separation between the speaker and the audience should not have any adverse impact on the readers' ability to read signs displayed by demonstrators. In fact, the separation might actually aid the pedestrians' ability to see the signs by preventing others from surrounding them and impeding their view. Furthermore, the statute places no limitations on the number, size, text, or images of the placards. And, as with all of the restrictions, the 8–foot zone does not affect demonstrators with signs who remain in place.

With respect to oral statements, the distance certainly can make it more difficult for a speaker to be heard, particularly if the level of background noise is high and other speakers are competing for the pedestrian's attention. Notably, the statute places no limitation on the number of speakers or the noise level, including the use of amplification equipment, although we have upheld such restrictions in past cases. More significantly, this statute does not suffer from the failings that compelled us to reject the "floating buffer zone" in *Schenck v. Pro–Choice Network of Western New York*, 519 U.S., 357, 377 (1997). Unlike the 15–foot zone in *Schenck*, this 8–foot zone allows the speaker to communicate at a "normal conversational distance." Additionally, the statute allows the speaker to remain in one place, and other individuals can pass within eight feet of the protester without causing the protester to violate the statute. Finally, here there is a "knowing" requirement that protects speakers "who thought they were keeping pace with the targeted individual" at the proscribed distance from inadvertently violating the statute.

It is also not clear that the statute's restrictions will necessarily impede, rather than assist, the speakers' efforts to communicate their messages. The statute might encourage the most aggressive and vociferous protesters to moderate their confrontational and harassing conduct, and thereby make it easier for thoughtful and law-abiding sidewalk counselors like petitioners to make themselves heard. But whether or not the 8–foot interval is the best possible accommodation of the competing interests at stake, we must accord a measure of deference to the judgment of the Colorado Legislature. Once again, it is worth reiterating that only attempts to address unwilling listeners are affected.

The burden on the ability to distribute handbills is more serious because it seems possible that an 8–foot interval could hinder the ability of a leafletter to deliver handbills to some unwilling recipients. The statute does not, however, prevent a leafletter from simply standing near the path of oncoming pedestrians and proffering his or her material, which the pedestrians can easily accept.[33] And, as in all leafletting situations, pedestrians continue to be free to decline the tender.

the time, place, or manner of protected speech must be narrowly tailored to serve the government's legitimate, content-neutral interests but that it need not be the least restrictive or least intrusive means of doing so." *Ward v. Rock Against Racism.*

33. JUSTICE KENNEDY states that the statute "forecloses peaceful leafletting." This is not correct. All of the cases he cites in support of his argument involve a total ban on a medium of expression to both willing and unwilling recipients. Nothing in this statute, however, prevents persons from proffering their literature, they simply cannot approach within eight feet of an unwilling recipient.

Finally, in determining whether a statute is narrowly tailored, we have noted that "we must, of course, take account of the place to which the regulations apply in determining whether these restrictions burden more speech than necessary." States and municipalities plainly have a substantial interest in controlling the activity around certain public and private places. For example, we have recognized the special governmental interests surrounding schools, courthouses, polling places, and private homes. Additionally, we previously have noted the unique concerns that surround health care facilities:

> " 'Hospitals, after all, are not factories or mines or assembly plants. They are hospitals, where human ailments are treated, where patients and relatives alike often are under emotional strain and worry, where pleasing and comforting patients are principal facets of the day's activity, and where the patient and [her] family ... need a restful, uncluttered, relaxing, and helpful atmosphere.' " (quoting *NLRB v. Baptist Hospital, Inc.*, 442 U.S., 773, 783–784, n. 12 (1979)).

Persons who are attempting to enter health care facilities—for any purpose—are often in particularly vulnerable physical and emotional conditions. The State of Colorado has responded to its substantial and legitimate interest in protecting these persons from unwanted encounters, confrontations, and even assaults by enacting an exceedingly modest restriction on the speakers' ability to approach.

JUSTICE KENNEDY, however, argues that the statute leaves petitioners without adequate means of communication. This is a considerable overstatement. The statute seeks to protect those who wish to enter health care facilities, many of whom may be under special physical or emotional stress, from close physical approaches by demonstrators. In doing so, the statute takes a prophylactic approach; it forbids all unwelcome demonstrators to come closer than eight feet. We recognize that by doing so, it will sometimes inhibit a demonstrator whose approach in fact would have proved harmless. But the statute's prophylactic aspect is justified by the great difficulty of protecting, say, a pregnant woman from physical harassment with legal rules that focus exclusively on the individual impact of each instance of behavior, demanding in each case an accurate characterization (as harassing or not harassing) of each individual movement within the 8–foot boundary. Such individualized characterization of each individual movement is often difficult to make accurately. A bright-line prophylactic rule may be the best way to provide protection, and, at the same time, by offering clear guidance and avoiding subjectivity, to protect speech itself.

As we explained above, the 8–foot restriction on an unwanted physical approach leaves ample room to communicate a message through speech. Signs, pictures, and voice itself can cross an 8–foot gap with ease. If the clinics in Colorado resemble those in *Schenck*, demonstrators with leaflets might easily stand on the sidewalk at entrances (without blocking the entrance) and, without physically approaching those who are entering the clinic, peacefully hand them leaflets as they pass by.

Finally, the 8–foot restriction occurs only within 100 feet of a health care facility—the place where the restriction is most needed. The restriction interferes far less with a speaker's ability to communicate than did the total ban on picketing on the sidewalk outside a residence (upheld in *Frisby v. Schultz*)), the restriction of leafletting at a fairground to a booth (upheld in *Heffron v. International Society for Krishna Consciousness, Inc.*, 452 U.S. 640 (1981)), or the "silence" often required outside a hospital. Special problems that may arise where clinics have particularly wide entrances or are situated within multipurpose office buildings may be worked out as the statute is applied.

This restriction is thus reasonable and narrowly tailored.

V

Petitioners argue that § 18–9–122(3) is invalid because it is "overbroad." There are two parts to petitioners' "overbreadth" argument. On the one hand, they argue that the statute is too broad because it protects too many people in too many places, rather than just the patients at the facilities where confrontational speech had occurred. Similarly, it burdens all speakers, rather than just persons with a history of bad conduct. On the other hand, petitioners also contend that the statute is overbroad because it "bans virtually the universe of protected expression, including displays of signs, distribution of literature, and mere verbal statements."

The first part of the argument does not identify a constitutional defect. The fact that the coverage of a statute is broader than the specific concern that led to its enactment is of no constitutional significance. What is important is that all persons entering or leaving health care facilities share the interests served by the statute. It is precisely because the Colorado Legislature made a general policy choice that the statute is assessed under the constitutional standard set forth in *Ward*, rather than a more strict standard. The cases cited by petitioners are distinguishable from this statute. In those cases, the government attempted to regulate nonprotected activity, yet because the statute was overbroad, protected speech was also implicated. See *Houston v. Hill*, 482 U.S. 451 (1987); *Secretary of State of Md. v. Joseph H. Munson Co.*, 467 U.S. 947 (1984). In this case, it is not disputed that the regulation affects protected speech activity, the question is thus whether it is a "reasonable restriction on the time, place, or manner of protected speech." Here, the comprehensiveness of the statute is a virtue, not a vice, because it is evidence against there being a discriminatory governmental motive. As we have observed, "there is no more effective practical guaranty against arbitrary and unreasonable government than to require that the principles of law which officials would impose upon a minority must be imposed generally." *Railway Express Agency, Inc. v. New York*, 336 U.S. 106, 112 (1949) (Jackson, J., concurring).

The second part of the argument is based on a misreading of the statute and an incorrect understanding of the overbreadth doctrine. As we have already noted, § 18–9–122(3) simply does not "ban" any messages, and likewise it does not "ban" any signs, literature, or oral statements. It merely regulates the places where communications may occur. Petitioners have not persuaded us that the impact of the statute on the conduct of other speakers will differ from its impact on their own sidewalk counseling. Like petitioners' own activities, the conduct of other protesters and counselors at all health care facilities are encompassed within the statute's "legitimate sweep." Therefore, the statute is not overly broad.

VI

Petitioners also claim that § 18–9–122(3) is unconstitutionally vague. They find a lack of clarity in three parts of the section: the meaning of "protest, education, or counseling"; the "consent" requirement; and the determination of whether one is "approaching" within eight feet of another.

A statute can be impermissibly vague for either of two independent reasons. First, if it fails to provide people of ordinary intelligence a reasonable opportunity to understand what conduct it prohibits. Second, if it authorizes or even encourages arbitrary and discriminatory enforcement.

In this case, the first concern is ameliorated by the fact that § 18–9–122(3) contains a scienter requirement. The statute only applies to a person who "knowingly" approaches within eight feet of another, without that person's consent, for the purpose of engaging in oral protest, education, or counseling. The likelihood that anyone would not understand any of those common words seems quite remote.

Petitioners proffer hypertechnical theories as to what the statute covers, such as whether an outstretched arm constitutes "approaching." And while "there is little doubt that imagination can conjure up hypothetical cases in which the meaning of these terms will be in nice question," because we are "condemned to the use of words, we can never expect mathematical certainty from our language," *Grayned v. City of Rockford*, 408 U.S. 104, 110 (1972). For these reasons, we rejected similar vagueness challenges to the injunctions at issue in *Schenck* and *Madsen*. We thus conclude that "it is clear what the ordinance as a whole prohibits." More importantly, speculation about possible vagueness in hypothetical situations not before the Court will not support a facial attack on a statute when it is surely valid "in the vast majority of its intended applications."

For the same reason, we are similarly unpersuaded by the suggestion that § 18–9–122(3) fails to give adequate guidance to law enforcement authorities. Indeed, it seems to us that one of the section's virtues is the specificity of the definitions of the zones described in the statute. "As always, enforcement requires the exercise of some degree of police judgment," and the degree of judgment involved here is acceptable.

The judgment of the Colorado Supreme Court is affirmed.

It is so ordered.

JUSTICE SOUTER, with whom JUSTICE O'CONNOR, JUSTICE GINSBURG, and JUSTICE BREYER join, concurring.

I join the opinion of the Court and add this further word. The key to determining whether Colo. Rev. Stat. § 18–9–122(3) (1999), makes a content-based distinction between varieties of speech lies in understanding that content-based discriminations are subject to strict scrutiny because they place the weight of government behind the disparagement or suppression of some messages, whether or not with the effect of approving or promoting others. Thus the government is held to a very exacting and rarely satisfied standard when it disfavors the discussion of particular subjects, or particular viewpoints within a given subject matter.

Concern about employing the power of the State to suppress discussion of a subject or a point of view is not, however, raised in the same way when a law addresses not the content of speech but the circumstances of its delivery. The right to express unpopular views does not necessarily immunize a speaker from liability for resorting to otherwise impermissible behavior meant to shock members of the speaker's audience, see *United States v. O'Brien*, or to guarantee their attention, see *Kovacs v. Cooper*. Unless regulation limited to the details of a speaker's delivery results in removing a subject or viewpoint from effective discourse (or otherwise fails to advance a significant public interest in a way narrowly fitted to that objective), a reasonable restriction intended to affect only the time, place, or manner of speaking is perfectly valid. See *Ward*.

It is important to recognize that the validity of punishing some expressive conduct, and the permissibility of a time, place, or manner restriction, does not depend on showing that the particular behavior or mode of delivery has no association with a particular subject or opinion. Draft card burners disapprove of the draft, and abortion protesters believe abortion is morally wrong. There is always a correlation with subject and viewpoint when the law regulates conduct that has become the signature of one side of a controversy. But that does not mean that every regulation of such distinctive behavior is content based as First Amendment doctrine employs that term. The correct rule, rather, is captured in the formulation that a restriction is content based only if it is imposed because of the content of the speech, and not because of offensive behavior identified with its delivery.

Since this point is as elementary as anything in traditional speech doctrine, it would only be natural to suppose that today's disagreement between the Court and the dissenting Justices must turn on unusual difficulty in evaluating the facts of this case. But it does not. The facts overwhelmingly demonstrate the validity of subsection (3) as a content-neutral regulation imposed solely to regulate the manner in which speakers may conduct themselves within 100 feet of the entrance of a health care facility.

No one disputes the substantiality of the government's interest in protecting people already tense or distressed in anticipation of medical attention (whether an abortion or some other procedure) from the unwanted intrusion of close personal importunity by strangers. The issues dividing the Court, then, go to the content neutrality of the regulation, its fit with the interest to be served by it, and the availability of other means of expressing the desired message (however offensive it may be even without physically close communication).

Each of these issues is addressed principally by the fact that subsection (3) simply does not forbid the statement of any position on any subject. It does not declare any view as unfit for expression within the 100–foot zone or beyond it. What it forbids, and all it forbids, is approaching another person closer than eight feet (absent permission) to deliver the message. Anyone (let him be called protester, counselor, or educator) may take a stationary position within the regulated area and address any message to any person within sight or hearing. The stationary protester may be quiet and ingratiating, or loud and offensive; the law does not touch him, even though in some ways it could.

This is not to say that enforcement of the approach restriction will have no effect on speech; of course it will make some difference. The effect of speech is a product of ideas and circumstances, and time, place, and manner are circumstances. The question is simply whether the ostensible reason for regulating the circumstances is really something about the ideas. Here, the evidence indicates that the ostensible reason is the true reason. The fact that speech by a stationary speaker is untouched by this statute shows that the reason for its restriction on approaches goes to the approaches, not to the content of the speech of those approaching. What is prohibited is a close encounter when the person addressed does not want to get close. So, the intended recipient can stay far enough away to prevent the whispered argument, mitigate some of the physical shock of the shouted denunciation, and avoid the unwanted handbill. But the content of the message will survive on any sign readable at eight feet and in any statement audible from that slight distance. Hence the implausibility of any claim that an anti-abortion message, not the behavior of protesters, is what is being singled out.

The matter of proper tailoring to limit no more speech than necessary to vindicate the public interest deserves a few specific comments, some on matters raised by JUSTICE KENNEDY's dissent. Subsection (3) could possibly be applied to speakers unlike the present petitioners, who might not know that the entrance to the facility was within 100 feet, or who might try to engage people within 100 feet of a health facility other than a physician's office or hospital, or people having no business with the facility. These objections do not, however, weigh very heavily on a facial challenge like this. The specter of liability on the part of those who importune while oblivious of the facility is laid to rest by the requirement that a defendant act "knowingly." While it is true that subsection (3) was not enacted to protect dental patients, I cannot say it goes beyond the State's interest to do so; someone facing an hour with a drill in his tooth may reasonably be protected from the intrusive behavior of strangers who are otherwise free to speak. While some mere passersby may be protected needlessly, I am skeptical about the number of health care facilities with substantial pedestrian traffic within 100 feet of their doors but unrelated to the business conducted inside. Hence, I fail to see danger of the substantial overbreadth required to be shown before a statute is struck down out of concern for the speech rights of those not before the Court.

As for the claim of vagueness, at first blush there is something objectionable. Those who do not choose to remain stationary may not approach within eight feet with a purpose, among others, of "engaging in oral protest, education, or counseling." While that formula excludes liability for enquiring about the time or the bus schedule within eight feet, "education" does not convey much else by way of limitation. But that is not fatal here. What is significant is not that the word fails to limit clearly, but that it pretty clearly fails to limit very much at all. It succeeds in naturally covering any likely address by one person approaching another on a street or parking lot outside a building entrance (aside from common social greetings, protests, or requests for assistance). Someone planning to spread a message by accosting strangers is likely to understand the statute's application to "education." And just because the coverage is so obviously broad, the discretion given to the police in deciding whether to charge an offense seems no greater than the prosecutorial discretion inherent in any generally applicable criminal statute.

Although petitioners have not argued that the "floating bubble" feature of the 8–foot zone around a pedestrian is itself a failure of narrow tailoring, I would note the contrast between the operation of subsection (3) and that of the comparable portion of the injunction struck down in *Schenck v. Pro-Choice Network of Western N. Y.*, 519 U.S. 357 (1997), where we observed that the difficulty of administering a floating bubble zone threatened to burden more speech than necessary. In *Schenck*, the floating bubble was larger (15 feet) and was associated with near-absolute prohibitions on speech. Since subsection (3) prohibits only 8–foot approaches, however, with the stationary speaker free to speak, the risk is less. Whether floating bubble zones are so inherently difficult to administer that only fixed, no-speech zones (or prohibitions on ambulatory counseling within a fixed zone) should pass muster is an issue neither before us nor well suited to consideration on a facial challenge.

JUSTICE SCALIA, with whom JUSTICE THOMAS joins, dissenting.

I

Colorado's statute makes it a criminal act knowingly to approach within 8 feet of another person on the public way or sidewalk area within 100 feet of the entrance door of a health care facility for the purpose of passing a leaflet to, displaying a sign to, or engaging in oral protest, education, or counseling with such person. Whatever may be said about the restrictions on the other types of expressive activity, the regulation as it applies to oral communications is obviously and undeniably content-based. A speaker wishing to approach another for the purpose of communicating *any* message except one of protest, education, or counseling may do so without first securing the other's consent. Whether a speaker must obtain permission before approaching within eight feet—and whether he will be sent to prison for failing to do so—depends entirely on *what he intends to say* when he gets there. I have no doubt that this regulation would be deemed content-based *in an instant* if the case before us involved antiwar protesters, or union members seeking to "educate" the public about the reasons for their strike. "It is," we would say, "the content of the speech that determines whether it is within or without the statute's blunt prohibition." *Carey v. Brown*. But the jurisprudence of this Court has a way of changing when abortion is involved.

The Court asserts that this statute is not content-based for purposes of our First Amendment analysis because it neither (1) discriminates among viewpoints nor (2) places restrictions on "any subject matter that may be discussed by a speaker." But we have never held that the universe of content-based regulations is limited to those two categories, and such a holding would be absurd. Imagine, for instance, special place-and-manner restrictions on all speech except that which "conveys a sense of contentment or happiness." This "happy speech" limitation would not be "viewpoint-based"—citizens would be able to express their joy in equal measure at either the rise or fall of the NASDAQ, at either the success or the failure of the Republican Party—and would not discriminate on the basis of subject matter, since gratification could be expressed about anything at all. Or consider a law restricting the writing or recitation of poetry—neither viewpoint-based nor limited to any particular subject matter. Surely this Court would consider such regulations to be "content-based" and deserving of the most exacting scrutiny.[1]

"The vice of content-based legislation—what renders it deserving of the high standard of strict scrutiny—is not that it is always used for invidious, thought-control purposes, but that it lends itself to use for those purposes." A restriction that operates only on speech that communicates a message of protest, education, or counseling presents exactly this risk. When applied, as it is here, at the entrance to medical facilities, it is a means of impeding speech against abortion. The Court's confident assurance that the statute poses no special threat to First Amendment freedoms because it applies alike to "used car salesmen, animal rights activists, fundraisers, environmentalists, and missionaries," is a wonderful replication (except for its lack of sarcasm) of Anatole France's observation that "the law, in its majestic equality, forbids the rich as well as the poor to sleep under bridges...." This Colorado law is no more targeted at used car salesmen, animal rights activists, fund raisers, environmentalists, and missionaries than French vagrancy law was targeted at the rich. We know what the Colorado legislators, by their careful selection of content ("protest, education, and counseling"), were taking aim at, for they set it forth in the statute itself: the "right to protest or counsel *against* certain medical procedures" on the sidewalks and streets surrounding health care facilities. Col. Rev. Stat. § 18–9–122(1) (1999) (emphasis added).

But in any event, if one accepts the Court's description of the interest served by this regulation, it is clear that the regulation is *both* based on content *and* justified by reference to content. Constitutionally proscribable "secondary effects" of speech are directly addressed in subsection (2) of the statute, which makes it unlawful to obstruct, hinder, impede, or block access to a health care facility—a prohibition broad enough to include all physical threats and all physically threatening approaches. The purpose of subsection (3), however (according to the Court), is to protect "the unwilling listener's interest in avoiding unwanted communication." On this analysis, Colorado has restricted certain categories of speech—protest, counseling, and education—out of an apparent belief that only speech with this content is sufficiently likely to be annoying or upsetting as to require consent before it may be engaged in at close range. It is reasonable enough to conclude that even the most gentle and peaceful close approach by a so-called "sidewalk counselor"—who wishes to "educate" the woman entering an abortion clinic about the nature of the procedure, to "counsel" against it and in favor of

---

1. The Court responds that statutes which restrict categories of speech—as opposed to subject matter or viewpoint—are constitutionally worrisome only if a "significant number of communications, raising the same problem that the statute was enacted to solve, ... fall outside the statute's scope, while others fall inside." I am not sure that is correct, but let us assume, for the sake of argument, that it is. The Court then proceeds to assert that "the statutory phrases, 'oral protest, education, or counseling,' distinguish speech activities likely to" present the problem of "harassment, ... nuisance, ... persistent importuning, ... following, ... dogging, and ... implied threat of physical touching," from "speech activities [such as my example of 'happy speech'] that are most unlikely to have those consequences." Well, that may work for "oral protest"; but it is beyond imagining why "education" and "counseling" are especially *likely*, rather than especially *unlikely*, to involve such conduct. (Socrates *was* something of a *noodge*, but even he did not go *that* far.) *Unless*, of course, "education" and "counseling" are code words for efforts to dissuade women from abortion—in which event the statute would not be viewpoint neutral, which the Court concedes makes it invalid.

other alternatives, and perhaps even (though less likely if the approach is to be successful) to "protest" her taking of a human life—will often, indeed usually, have what might be termed the "secondary effect" of annoying or deeply upsetting the woman who is planning the abortion. *But that is not an effect which occurs "without reference to the content" of the speech.* This singling out of presumptively "unwelcome" communications fits precisely the description of prohibited regulation set forth in *Boos v. Barry*, 485 U.S. 312, 321 (1988): It "targets the *direct impact* of a particular category of speech, not a secondary feature that happens to be associated with that type of speech." (emphasis added).[2]

In sum, it blinks reality to regard this statute, in its application to oral communications, as anything other than a content-based restriction upon speech in the public forum. As such, it must survive that stringent mode of constitutional analysis our cases refer to as "strict scrutiny," which requires that the restriction be narrowly tailored to serve a compelling state interest. Since the Court does not even attempt to support the regulation under this standard, I shall discuss it only briefly. Suffice it to say that if protecting people from unwelcome communications (the governmental interest the Court posits) is a compelling state interest, the First Amendment is a dead letter. And if (as I shall discuss at greater length below) forbidding peaceful, nonthreatening, but uninvited speech from a distance closer than eight feet is a "narrowly tailored" means of preventing the obstruction of entrance to medical facilities (the governmental interest the State asserts) narrow tailoring must refer not to the standards of Versace, but to those of Omar the tentmaker. In the last analysis all of this does not matter, however, since as I proceed to discuss neither the restrictions upon oral communications nor those upon handbilling can withstand a proper application of even the less demanding scrutiny we apply to truly content-neutral regulations of speech in a traditional public forum.

II

As the Court explains, under our precedents even a content-neutral, time, place, and manner restriction must be narrowly tailored to advance a significant state interest, and must leave open ample alternative means of communication. It cannot be sustained if it "burdens substantially more speech than is necessary to further the government's legitimate interests."

This requires us to determine, first, what *is* the significant interest the State seeks to advance? Here there appears to be a bit of a disagreement between the State of Colorado (which should know) and the Court (which is eager to speculate). Colorado has identified in the text of the statute itself the interest it sought to advance: to ensure that the State's citizens may "obtain medical counseling and treatment in an unobstructed manner" by "preventing the willful obstruction of a person's access to medical counseling and

---

2. The Court's contention that the statute is content-neutral because it is not a " 'regulation of speech' " but a "regulation of the places where some speech may occur," is simply baffling. First, because the proposition that a restriction upon the places where speech may occur is not a restriction upon speech is both absurd and contradicted by innumerable cases. And second, because the fact that a restriction is framed as a "regulation of the places where some speech may occur" has nothing whatever to do with whether the restriction is content-neutral—which is why *Boos* held to be content-based the ban on displaying, within 500 feet of foreign embassies, banners designed to ' "bring into public odium any foreign government.' "

treatment at a health care facility." In its brief here, the State repeatedly confirms the interest squarely identified in the statute under review. The Court nevertheless concludes that the Colorado provision is narrowly tailored to serve ... *the State's interest in protecting its citizens' rights to be let alone from unwanted speech.*

Indeed, the situation is even more bizarre than that. The interest that the Court makes the linchpin of its analysis was not only unasserted by the State; it is not only completely *different* from the interest that the statute specifically sets forth; it was explicitly *disclaimed* by the State in its brief before this Court, and characterized as a "straw interest" *petitioners* served up in the hope of discrediting the State's case. We may thus add to the lengthening list of "firsts" generated by this Court's relentlessly proabortion jurisprudence, the first case in which, in order to sustain a statute, the Court has relied upon a governmental interest not only unasserted by the State, but positively repudiated.

I shall discuss below the obvious invalidity of this statute assuming, first (in Part A), the fictitious state interest that the Court has invented, and then (in Part B), the interest actually recited in the statute and asserted by counsel for Colorado.

A

To support the legitimacy of its self-invented state interest, the Court relies upon a bon mot in a 1928 dissent (which we evidently overlooked in *Schenck*). It characterizes the "unwilling listener's interest in avoiding unwanted communication" as an "aspect of the broader 'right to be let alone'" Justice Brandeis coined in his dissent in *Olmstead v. United States*, 277 U.S. 438, 478 (1928). The amusing feature is that even this slim reed contradicts rather than supports the Court's position. The right to be let alone that Justice Brandeis identified was a right the Constitution "conferred, *as against the government*"; it was *that* right, not some generalized "common-law right" or "interest" to be free from hearing the unwanted opinions of one's fellow citizens, which he called the "most comprehensive" and "most valued by civilized men." (emphasis added). To the extent that there can be gleaned from our cases a "right to be let alone" in the sense that Justice Brandeis intended, it is the right of the *speaker* in the public forum to be free from government interference of the sort Colorado has imposed here.

In any event, the Court's attempt to disguise the "right to be let alone" as a "governmental interest in protecting the right to be let alone" is unavailing for the simple reason that this is not an interest that may be legitimately weighed against the speakers' First Amendment rights. We have consistently held that "the Constitution does not *permit* the government to decide which types of otherwise protected speech are sufficiently offensive to require protection *for the unwilling listener or viewer*." *Erznoznik v. Jacksonville* (emphasis added). And as recently as in *Schenck*, the Court reiterated that "as a general matter, we have indicated that in public debate our own citizens must tolerate insulting, and even outrageous, speech in order to provide adequate breathing space to the freedoms protected by the First Amendment."

The limitation on a speaker's right to bombard the home with unwanted messages which we approved in *Frisby*—and in *Rowan v. Post Office Dept.*, 397 U.S. 728 (1970), upon which the Court also relies—was predicated on the fact that " 'we are often 'captives' *outside* the sanctuary of the home and subject to objectionable speech.' '' (emphasis added). As the universally understood state of First Amendment law is described in a leading treatise: "Outside the home, the burden is generally on the observer or listener to avert his eyes or plug his ears against the verbal assaults, lurid advertisements, tawdry books and magazines, and other 'offensive' intrusions which increasingly attend urban life." L. Tribe, American Constitutional Law § 12–19, p. 948 (2d ed. 1988). The Court today elevates the abortion clinic to the status of the home.

There is apparently no end to the distortion of our First Amendment law that the Court is willing to endure in order to sustain this restriction upon the free speech of abortion opponents. The labor movement, in particular, has good cause for alarm in the Court's extensive reliance upon *American Steel Foundries v. Tri–City Central Trades Council*, 257 U.S. 184 (1921), an opinion in which the Court held that the Clayton Act's prohibition of injunctions against lawful and peaceful labor picketing did not forbid the injunction in that particular case. The First Amendment was not at issue, and was not so much as mentioned in the opinion, so the case is scant authority for the point the Court wishes to make. The case is also irrelevant because it was "clear from the evidence that from the outset, violent methods were pursued from time to time in such a way as to characterize the attitude of the picketers as continuously threatening." No such finding was made, or could be made, here. More importantly, however, as far as our future labor cases are concerned: If a "right to be free" from "persistence, importunity, following and dogging" short of actual intimidation was part of our infant First Amendment law in 1921, I am shocked to think that it is there today. The Court's assertion that "none of our decisions has minimized the enduring importance of 'the right to be free' from persistent 'importunity, following and dogging' after an offer to communicate has been declined" is belied by the fact that this passage from *American Steel Foundries* has never—not once—found its way into any of the many First Amendment cases this Court has decided since 1921. We will have cause to regret today's injection of this irrelevant anachronism into the mainstream of our First Amendment jurisprudence.

Of course even if one accepted the *American Steel Foundries* dictum as an accurate expression of First Amendment law, the statute here is plainly not narrowly tailored to protect the interest that dictum describes. Preserving the "right to be free" from "persistent importunity, following and dogging" does not remotely require imposing upon all speakers who wish to protest, educate, or counsel a duty to request permission to approach closer than eight feet. The only way the narrow-tailoring objection can be eliminated is to posit a state-created, First–Amendment-trumping "right to be let alone" as broad and undefined as Brandeis's *Olmstead* dictum, which may well (why not, if the Court wishes it?) embrace a right not to be spoken to without permission from a distance closer than eight feet. Nothing stands in the way of *that* solution to the narrow-tailoring problem—except, of course, its utter absurdity, which is no obstacle in abortion cases.

B

I turn now to the real state interest at issue here—the one set forth in the statute and asserted in Colorado's brief: the preservation of unimpeded access to health care facilities. We need look no further than subsection (2) of the statute to see what a provision would look like that is narrowly tailored to serve *that* interest. Under the terms of that subsection, any person who "knowingly obstructs, detains, hinders, impedes, or blocks another person's entry to or exit from a health care facility" is subject to criminal and civil liability. It is possible, I suppose, that subsection (2) of the Colorado statute will leave unrestricted some expressive activity that, if engaged in from within eight feet, may be sufficiently harassing as to have the effect of impeding access to health care facilities. In subsection (3), however, the State of Colorado has prohibited a vast amount of speech that cannot possibly be thought to correspond to that evil.

To begin with, the 8–foot buffer zone attaches to *every* person on the public way or sidewalk within 100 feet of the entrance of a medical facility, regardless of whether that person is seeking to enter or exit the facility. In fact, the State acknowledged at oral argument that the buffer zone would attach to any person within 100 feet of the entrance door of a skyscraper in which a single doctor occupied an office on the 18th floor. And even with respect to those who *are* seeking to enter or exit the facilities, the statute does not protect them only from speech that is so intimidating or threatening as to impede access. Rather, it covers *all* unconsented-to approaches for the purpose of oral protest, education, or counseling (including those made for the purpose of the most peaceful appeals) and, perhaps even more significantly, *every* approach made for the purposes of leafletting or handbilling, which we have never considered, standing alone, obstructive or unduly intrusive. The sweep of this prohibition is breathtaking.

The Court makes no attempt to justify on the facts this blatant violation of the narrow-tailoring principle. Instead, it flirts with the creation of yet a new constitutional "first" designed for abortion cases: "[W]hen," it says, "a content-neutral regulation does not entirely foreclose any means of communication, it may satisfy the tailoring requirement even though it is not the least restrictive or least intrusive means of serving the statutory goal." The implication is that the availability of alternative means of communication permits the imposition of the speech restriction upon more individuals, or more types of communication, than narrow tailoring would otherwise demand. The Court assures us that "we have emphasized" this proposition "on more than one occasion." The only citation the Court provides, however, says no such thing. *Ward v. Rock Against Racism*, says only that narrow tailoring is not synonymous with "least restrictive alternative." It does not at all suggest—and to my knowledge no other case does either—that narrow tailoring can be relaxed when there are other speech alternatives.

The burdens this law imposes upon the right to speak are substantial. I have certainly held conversations at a distance of eight feet seated in the quiet of my chambers, but I have never walked along the public sidewalk—and have not seen others do so—"conversing" at an 8–foot remove. The suggestion is absurd. So is the suggestion that the opponents of abortion can take comfort in the fact that the statute "places no limitation on the number of speakers or the noise level, including the use of amplification equipment." That is good enough, I suppose, for "protesting"; but the Court must know that most of the "counseling" and "educating" likely to take place outside a health care facility cannot be done at a distance and at a high-decibel level. The availability of a powerful amplification system will be of little help to the woman who hopes to forge, in the last moments before another of her sex is to have an abortion, a bond of concern and intimacy that might enable her to persuade the woman to change her mind and heart. The counselor may wish to walk alongside and to say, sympathetically and as softly as the circumstances allow, something like: "My dear, I know what you are going through. I've been through it myself. You're not alone and you do not have to do this. There are other alternatives. Will you let me help you? May I show you a picture of what your child looks like at this stage of her human development?" The Court would have us believe that this can be done effectively—yea, perhaps even *more* effectively—by shouting through a bullhorn at a distance of eight feet.

The Court seems prepared, if only for a moment, to take seriously the magnitude of the burden the statute imposes on simple handbilling and leafletting. That concern is fleeting, however, since it is promptly assuaged by the realization that a leafletter may, without violating the statute, stand "near the path" of oncoming pedestrians and make his "proffe[r] . . ., which the pedestrians can easily accept." It does not take a veteran labor organizer to recognize—although surely any would—that leafletting will be rendered utterly ineffectual by a requirement that the leafletter obtain from each subject permission to approach, or else man a stationary post (one that does not obstruct access to the facility, lest he violate subsection (2) of statute) and wait for passersby voluntarily to approach an outstretched hand. That simply is not how it is done, and the Court knows it—or should. A leafletter, whether he is working on behalf of Operation Rescue, Local 109, or Bubba's Bar–B–Que, stakes out the best piece of real estate he can, and then walks a few steps toward individuals passing in his vicinity, extending his arm and making it *as easy as possible* for the passerby, whose natural inclination is generally not to seek out such distributions, to simply accept the offering. Few pedestrians are likely to give their "consent" to the approach of a handbiller (indeed, by the time he requested it they would likely have passed by), and even fewer are likely to walk over in order to pick up a leaflet. In the abortion context, therefore, ordinary handbilling, which we have in other contexts recognized to be a "classic form of speech that lies at the heart of the First Amendment," will in its most effective locations be rendered futile, the Court's implausible assertions to the contrary notwithstanding.

The Colorado provision differs in one fundamental respect from the "content-neutral" time, place, and manner restrictions the Court has previously upheld. Each of them rested upon a necessary connection between the regulated expression and the evil the challenged regulation sought to eliminate. So, for instance, in *Ward*, the Court approved the city's control over sound amplification because every occasion of amplified sound presented the evil of excessive noise and distortion disturbing the areas surrounding the public forum. The regulation we upheld in *Ward*, rather than "bann[ing] all concerts, or even all rock concerts, . . . instead focus[ed] on the source of the evils the city seeks to eliminate . . . and eliminates them without at the same time banning or significantly restricting a substantial quantity of speech that does not create the same evils."

In contrast, the law before us here enacts a broad prophylactic restriction which does not "respond precisely to the substantive problem which legitimately concerned" the State. In *United States v. Grace*, we declined to uphold a ban on certain expressive activity on the sidewalks surrounding the Supreme Court. The purpose of the restriction was the perfectly valid interest in security, just as the purpose of the restriction here is the perfectly valid interest in unobstructed access; and there, as here, the restriction furthered that interest—but it furthered it with insufficient precision and hence at excessive cost to the freedom of speech. There was, we said, "an insufficient nexus" between security and all the expressive activity that was banned—just as here there is an insufficient nexus between the assurance of access and forbidding unconsented communications within eight feet.[4]

Compare with these venerable and consistent descriptions of our First Amendment law the defenses that the Court makes to the contention that the present statute is overbroad. (To be sure, the Court is assuming its own invented state interest—protection of the "right to be let alone"—rather than the interest that the statute describes, but even so the statements are extraordinary.) "The fact," the Court says, "that the coverage of a statute is broader than the specific concern that led to its enactment is of no constitutional significance." That is true enough ordinarily, but it is *not* true with respect to restraints upon speech, which is what the doctrine of overbreadth is all about. (Of course it is also not true, thanks to one of the other proabortion "firsts" announced by the current Court, with respect to restrictions upon abortion, which—as our decision in *Stenberg* v. *Carhart,* exemplifies—has been raised to First Amendment status, even as speech opposing abortion has been demoted from First Amendment status.)

The foregoing discussion of overbreadth was written before the Court, in responding to JUSTICE KENNEDY, abandoned any pretense at compliance with that doctrine, and acknowledged—indeed, boasted—that the statute it approves "takes a prophylactic approach" and adopts "[a] bright-line prophylactic rule."[5] I scarcely know how to respond to such an unabashed repudiation of our First Amendment doctrine. Prophylaxis is the antithesis of narrow tailoring. If the Court were going to make this concession, it could simply

---

4. The Court's suggestion that the restrictions imposed by the Colorado ban are unobjectionable because they "interfere far less with a speaker's ability to communicate," than did the regulations involved in *Frisby* and *Heffron*, and in cases requiring "silence" outside of a hospital misses the point of narrow-tailoring analysis. We do not compare restrictions on speech to some Platonic ideal of speech restrictiveness, or to each other. Rather, our First Amendment doctrine requires us to consider whether the regulation in question burdens substantially more speech than necessary to achieve *the particular interest* the government has identified and asserted. *Ward*. In each of the instances the Court cites, we concluded that the challenged regulation contained the precision that our cases require and that Colorado's statute (which the Court itself calls "prophylactic") manifestly lacks.

5. Of course the Court greatly understates the scope of the prophylaxis, saying that "the statute's prophylactic aspect is justified by the great difficulty of protecting, say, a pregnant woman from physical harassment with legal rules that focus exclusively on the individual impact of each instance of behavior." But the statute prevents the "physically harassing" act of (shudder!) approaching within closer than eight feet not only when it is directed against pregnant women, but also (just to be safe) when it is directed against 300–pound, male, and unpregnant truck drivers—surely a distinction that is not "difficult to make accurately."

have dispensed with its earlier (unpersuasive) attempt to show that the statute *was* narrowly tailored. So one can add to the casualties of our whatever-it-takes proabortion jurisprudence the First Amendment doctrine of narrow tailoring and overbreadth.

Does the deck seem stacked? You bet. As I have suggested throughout this opinion, today's decision is not an isolated distortion of our traditional constitutional principles, but is one of many aggressively proabortion novelties announced by the Court in recent years. Today's distortions, however, are particularly blatant. Restrictive views of the First Amendment that have been in dissent since the 1930's suddenly find themselves in the majority. "Uninhibited, robust, and wide open" debate is replaced by the power of the state to protect an unheard-of "right to be let alone" on the public streets. I dissent.

JUSTICE KENNEDY, dissenting.

The Court's holding contradicts more than a half century of well-established First Amendment principles. For the first time, the Court approves a law which bars a private citizen from passing a message, in a peaceful manner and on a profound moral issue, to a fellow citizen on a public sidewalk. If from this time forward the Court repeats its grave errors of analysis, we shall have no longer the proud tradition of free and open discourse in a public forum. In my view, JUSTICE SCALIA's First Amendment analysis is correct and mandates outright reversal. In addition to undermining established First Amendment principles, the Court's decision conflicts with the essence of the joint opinion in *Planned Parenthood of Southeastern Pa. v. Casey*, 505 U.S. 833 (1992). It seems appropriate in these circumstances to reinforce JUSTICE SCALIA's correct First Amendment conclusions and to set forth my own views.

I

The Court wields the categories of *Ward* so that what once were rules to protect speech now become rules to restrict it. This is twice unfortunate. The rules of *Ward* are diminished in value for later cases; and the *Ward* analysis ought not have been undertaken at all. To employ *Ward*'s complete framework is a mistake at the outset, for *Ward* applies only if a statute is content neutral. Colorado's statute is a textbook example of a law which is content based.

A

Under the Colorado enactment, the State must review content to determine whether a person has engaged in criminal "protest, education, or counseling." When a citizen approaches another on the sidewalk in a disfavored-speech zone, an officer of the State must listen to what the speaker says. If, in the officer's judgment, the speaker's words stray too far toward "protest, education, or counseling"—the boundaries of which are far from clear—the officer may decide the speech has moved from the permissible to the criminal. The First Amendment does not give the government such power.

If, just a few decades ago, a State with a history of enforcing racial discrimination had enacted a statute like this one, regulating "oral protest, education, or counseling" within 100 feet of the entrance to any lunch counter, our predecessors would not have hesitated to hold it was content based or viewpoint based. It should be a profound disappointment to defenders of the First Amendment that the Court today refuses to apply the same structural analysis when the speech involved is less palatable to it.

The Court, in error and irony, validates the Colorado statute because it purports to restrict all of the proscribed expressive activity regardless of the subject. The evenhandedness the Court finds so satisfying, however, is but a disguise for a glaring First Amendment violation. The Court, by citing the breadth of the statute, cannot escape the conclusion that its categories are nonetheless content based. The liberty of a society is measured in part by what its citizens are free to discuss among themselves. Colorado's scheme of disfavored-speech zones on public streets and sidewalks, and the Court's opinion validating them, are antithetical to our entire First Amendment tradition. To say that one citizen can approach another to ask the time or the weather forecast or the directions to Main Street but not to initiate discussion on one of the most basic moral and political issues in all of contemporary discourse, a question touching profound ideas in philosophy and theology, is an astonishing view of the First Amendment. For the majority to examine the statute under rules applicable to content-neutral regulations is an affront to First Amendment teachings.

The statute's operation reflects its objective. Under the most reasonable interpretation of Colorado's law, if a speaker approaches a fellow citizen within any one of Colorado's thousands of disfavored-speech zones and chants in praise of the Supreme Court and its abortion decisions, I should think there is neither protest, nor education, nor counseling. If the opposite message is communicated, however, a prosecution to punish protest is warranted. The antispeech distinction also pertains if a citizen approaches a public official visiting a health care facility to make a point in favor of abortion rights. If she says, "Good job, Governor," there is no violation; if she says, "Shame on you, Governor," there is. Furthermore, if the speaker addresses a woman who is considering an abortion and says, "Please take just a moment to read these brochures and call our support line to talk with women who have been in your situation," the speaker would face criminal penalties for counseling. Yet if the speaker simply says, "We are for abortion rights," I should think this is neither education or counseling. Thus does the Court today ensure its own decisions can be praised but not condemned. Thus does it restrict speech designed to teach that the exercise of a constitutional right is not necessarily concomitant with making a sound moral choice. Nothing in our law or our enviable free speech tradition sustains this self-serving rule. Colorado is now allowed to punish speech because of its content and viewpoint.

The State has failed to sustain its burden of proving that its statute is content and viewpoint neutral. See *United States* v. *Playboy Entertainment Group, Inc.* ("When the Government restricts speech, the Government bears the burden of proving the constitutionality of its actions"). The *Ward* time, place, and manner analysis is simply inapplicable to this law. I would hold the statute invalid from the very start.

B

In a further glaring departure from precedent we learn today that citizens have a right to avoid unpopular speech in a public forum.

In *Erznoznik*, the Court struck down a municipal ordinance prohibiting drive-in movie theaters visible from either a public street or a public place from showing films containing nudity. The ordinance, the Court concluded, imposed a content-based restriction upon speech and was both too broad and too narrow to serve the interests asserted by the municipality. The law, moreover, was not analogous to the rare, "selective restrictions" on speech previously upheld to protect individual privacy. The Court did not, contrary to the majority's assertions, suggest that government is free to enact categorical measures restricting traditional, peaceful communications among citizens in a public forum. Instead, the Court admonished that citizens usually bear the burden of disregarding unwelcome messages (citing *Cohen v. California*).

Today's decision is an unprecedented departure from this Court's teachings respecting unpopular speech in public fora.

II

The Colorado statute offends settled First Amendment principles in another fundamental respect. It violates the constitutional prohibitions against vague or overly broad criminal statutes regulating speech. The enactment's fatal ambiguities are multiple and interact to create further imprecisions. The result is a law more vague and overly broad than any criminal statute the Court has sustained as a permissible regulation of speech. The statute's imprecisions are so evident that this, too, ought to have ended the case without further discussion.

In the context of a law imposing criminal penalties for pure speech, "protest" is an imprecise word; "counseling" is an imprecise word; "education" is an imprecise word. No custom, tradition, or legal authority gives these terms the specificity required to sustain a criminal prohibition on speech. I simply disagree with the majority's estimation that it is "quite remote" that "anyone would not understand any of those common words." The criminal statute is subject to manipulation by police, prosecutors, and juries. Its substantial imprecisions will chill speech, so the statute violates the First Amendment.

In operation the statute's inevitable arbitrary effects create vagueness problems of their own. The 8–foot no-approach zone is so unworkable it will chill speech. Assume persons are about to enter a building from different points and a protestor is walking back and forth with a sign or attempting to hand out leaflets. If she stops to create the 8–foot zone for one pedestrian, she cannot reach other persons with her message; yet if she moves to maintain the 8–foot zone while trying to talk to one patron she may move knowingly closer to a patron attempting to enter the facility from a different direction. In addition, the statute requires a citizen to give affirmative consent before the exhibitor of a sign or the bearer of a leaflet can approach. When dealing with strangers walking fast toward a building's entrance, there is a middle ground of ambiguous answers and mixed signals in which misinterpretation can subject a good-faith speaker to criminal liability. The mere failure to give a reaction, for instance, is a failure to give consent. These elements of ambiguity compound the others. Finally, as we all know, the identity or enterprise of the occupants of a building which fronts on a public street are not always known to the public. Health care providers may occupy but a single office in a large building. The Colorado citizen may walk from a disfavored-speech zone to a free zone with little or no ability to discern when one ends and the other begins. The statute's vagueness thus becomes as well one source of its overbreadth. The only sure way to avoid violating the law is to refrain from picketing, leafleting, or oral advocacy altogether. Scienter cannot save so vague a statute as this.

In *Carlson v. California*, 310 U.S. 106 (1940), a unanimous Court invalidated an ordinance prohibiting individuals from carrying or displaying any sign or banner or from picketing near a place of business "for the purpose of inducing or influencing, or attempting to induce or influence, any person to refrain from entering any such works, or factory, or place of business, or employment." The statute employed imprecise language, providing citizens with no guidance as to whether particular expressive activities fell within its reach. The Court found that the "sweeping and inexact terms of the ordinance disclose the threat to freedom of speech inherent in its existence," a result at odds with the guarantees of the First Amendment.

Rather than adhere to this rule, the Court turns it on its head, stating the statute's overbreadth is "a virtue, not a vice." The Court goes even further, praising the statute's "prophylactic approach; it forbids all unwelcome demonstrators to come closer than eight feet." Indeed, in the Court's view, "bright-line prophylactic rules may be the best way to provide protection" to those individuals unwilling to hear a fellow citizen's message in a public forum. The Court is quite wrong. Overbreadth is a constitutional flaw, not a saving feature. Sweeping within its ambit even more protected speech does not save a criminal statute invalid in its essential reach and design. The Court, moreover, cannot meet the concern that the statute is vague; for neither the Colorado courts nor established legal principles offer satisfactory guidance in interpreting the statute's imprecisions.

III

Even aside from the erroneous, most disturbing assumptions that the statute is content neutral, viewpoint neutral, and neither vague nor overbroad, the Court falls into further serious error when it turns to the time, place, and manner rules set forth in *Ward*.

An essential requirement under *Ward* is that the regulation in question not "burden substantially more speech than necessary to further the government's legitimate interests." As we have seen, however, Colorado and the Court attempt to justify the law on just the opposite assumption.

Our precedents do not permit content censoring to be cured by taking even more protected speech within a statute's reach. The statute before us, as construed by the majority, would do just that. If it indeed proscribes "oral protest, education, or counseling" on all subjects across the board, it by definition becomes "substantially broader than necessary to achieve the government's interest."

The whimsical, arbitrary nature of the statute's operation is further demonstration of a restriction upon more speech than necessary. The happenstance of a dental office being located in a building brings the restricted-speech zone into play. If the same building also houses an organization dedicated, say, to environmental issues, a protest against the group's policies would be barred. Yet if, on the next block there were a public interest enterprise in a building with no health care facility, the speech would be unrestricted. The statute is a classic example of a proscription not narrowly tailored and resulting in restrictions of far more speech than necessary to achieve the legislature's object. The first time, place, and manner requirement of *Ward* cannot be satisfied.

Assuming Colorado enacted the statute to respond to incidents of disorderly and unlawful conduct near abortion clinics, there were alternatives to restricting speech. It is beyond dispute that pinching or shoving or hitting is a battery actionable under the criminal law and punishable as a crime. State courts have also found an actionable tort when there is a touching, done in an offensive manner, of an object closely identified with the body, even if it is not clothing or the body itself. The very statute before us, in its other parts, includes a provision aimed at ensuring access to health care facilities. The law imposes criminal sanctions upon any person who "knowingly obstructs, detains, hinders, impedes, or blocks another person's entry to or exit from a health care facility." With these means available to ensure access, the statute's overreaching in the regulation of speech becomes again apparent.

The majority insists the statute aims to protect distraught women who are embarrassed, vexed, or harassed as they attempt to enter abortion clinics. If these are punishable acts, they should be prohibited in those terms. In the course of praising Colorado's approach, the majority does not pause to tell us why, in its view, substantially less restrictive means cannot be employed to ensure citizens access to health care facilities or to prevent physical contact between citizens. The Court's approach is at odds with the rigor demanded by *Ward*.

There are further errors in the Court's novel, prophylactic analysis. The prophylactic theory seems to be based on a supposition that most citizens approaching a health care facility are unwilling to listen to a fellow citizen's message and that face-to-face communications will lead to lawless behavior within the power of the State to punish. These premises have no support in law or in fact. The Court places our free speech traditions in grave jeopardy by licensing legislatures to adopt "bright-line prophylactic rules . . . to provide protection" to unwilling listeners in a quintessential public forum.

The statute fails a further test under *Ward*, for it does not " 'leave open ample alternative channels for communication of the information.' " *Frisby* again instructs us. A second reason we sustained the ordinance banning targeted residential picketing was because "ample alternative" avenues for communication remained open:

> " 'Protestors have not been barred from the residential neighborhoods. They may enter such neighborhoods, alone or in groups, even marching. . . . They may go door-to-door to proselytize their views. They may distribute literature in this manner . . . or through the mails. They may contact residents by telephone, short of harassment.' "

The residential picketing ordinance, the Court concluded, "permitted the more general dissemination of a message" to the targeted audience.

The same conclusion cannot be reached here. Door-to-door distributions or mass mailing or telephone campaigns are not effective alternative avenues of communication for petitioners. They want to engage in peaceful face-to-face communication with individuals the petitioners believe are about to commit a profound moral wrong. Without the ability to interact in person, however momentarily, with a clinic patron near the very place where a woman might elect to receive an abortion, the statute strips petitioners of using speech in the time, place, and manner most vital to the protected expression.

In addition to leaving petitioners without adequate means of communication, the law forecloses peaceful leafleting, a mode of speech with deep roots in our Nation's history and traditions. In an age when vast resources and talents are commanded by a sophisticated media to shape opinions on limitless subjects and ideas, the distribution of leaflets on a sidewalk may seem a bit antiquated. This case proves the necessity for the traditional mode of speech. It must be remembered that the whole course of our free speech jurisprudence, sustaining the idea of open public discourse which is the hallmark of the American constitutional system, rests to a significant extent on cases involving picketing and leafleting. Our foundational First Amendment cases are based on the recognition that citizens, subject to rare exceptions, must be able to discuss issues, great or small, through the means of expression they deem best suited to their purpose. It is for the speaker, not the government, to choose the best means of expressing a message. "The First Amendment," our cases illustrate, "protects [citizens'] right not only to advocate their cause but also to select what they believe to be the most effective means for so doing." The Court's conclusion that Colorado's 8–foot no-approach zone protects citizens' ability to leaflet or otherwise engage in peaceful protest is untenable.

The Court's more recent precedents honor the same principles: Government cannot foreclose a traditional medium of expression. In *City of Ladue v. Gilleo*, we considered a challenge to a municipal ordinance prohibiting, *inter alia*, "such absolutely pivotal speech as [the display of] a sign protesting an imminent governmental decision to go to war." Respondent had placed a sign in a window of her home calling "For Peace in the Gulf." We invalidated the ordinance, finding that the local government "had almost completely foreclosed a venerable means of communication that is both unique and important." The opinion, which drew upon *Schneider v. State (Town of Irvington)*, was also careful to note the importance of the restriction on place imposed by the ordinance in question: "Displaying a sign from one's own residence often carries a message quite distinct from placing the same sign someplace else, or conveying the same text or picture by other means." So, too, did we stress the importance of preserving the means citizens use to express messages bearing on important public debates. ("Residential signs are an unusually cheap and convenient form of communication[,] [e]specially for persons of modest means or limited mobility . . .").

A year later in *McIntyre v. Ohio Elections Comm'n*, 514 U.S. 334 (1995), we once more confirmed the privileged status peaceful leafleting enjoys in our free speech tradition. Ohio prohibited anonymous leafleting in connection with election campaigns. Invalidating the law, we observed as follows: " 'Anonymous pamphlets, leaflets, brochures and even books have played an important role in the progress of mankind.' " We rejected the State's claim that the restriction was needed to prevent fraud and libel in its election processes. Ohio had other laws in place to achieve these objectives. The case, we concluded, rested upon fundamental free speech principles:

> "Indeed, the speech in which Mrs. McIntyre engaged—handing out leaflets in the advocacy of a politically controversial viewpoint—is the essence of First Amendment expression. That this advocacy occurred in the heat of a controversial referendum vote only strengthens the protection afforded to Mrs. McIntyre's expression: Urgent, important, and effective speech can be no less protected than impotent speech, lest the right to speak be relegated to those instances when it is least needed. No form of speech is entitled to greater constitutional protection than Mrs. McIntyre's."

Petitioners commenced the present suit to challenge a statute preventing them from expressing their views on abortion through the same peaceful and vital methods approved in [our prior cases]. Laws punishing speech which protests the lawfulness or morality of the government's own policy are the essence of the tyrannical power the First Amendment guards against. We must remember that, by decree of this Court in discharging our duty to interpret the Constitution, any plea to the government to outlaw some abortions will be to no effect. See *Planned Parenthood of Southeastern Pa. v. Casey*, 505 U.S. 833 (1992). Absent the ability to ask the government to intervene, citizens who oppose abortion must seek to convince their fellow citizens of the moral imperative of their cause. In a free society protest serves to produce stability, not to undermine it. "The right to speak freely and to promote diversity of ideas and programs is therefore one of the chief distinctions that sets us apart from totalitarian regimes." *Terminiello v. Chicago*. As Justice Brandeis observed: "[The framers] recognized the risks to which all human institutions are subject. But they knew that order cannot be secured merely through fear of punishment for its infraction; that it is hazardous to discourage thought, hope and imagination; that fear breeds repression; that repression breeds hate; that hate menaces stable government; that the path of safety lies in the opportunity to discuss freely supposed grievances and proposed remedies; and that the fitting remedy for evil counsels is good ones. Believing in the power of reason as applied through public discussion, they eschewed silence coerced by law—the argument of force in its worst form." *Whitney v. California* (concurring opinion).

The means of expression at stake here are of controlling importance. Citizens desiring to impart messages to women considering abortions likely do not have resources to use the mainstream media for their message, much less resources to locate women contemplating the option of abortion. Lacking the aid of the government or the media, they seek to resort to the time honored method of leafleting and the display of signs. Nowhere is the speech more important than at the time and place where the act is about to occur. As the named plaintiff, Leila Jeanne Hill, explained, "I engage in a variety of activities designed to impart information to abortion-bound women and their friends and families...." "In my many years of sidewalk counseling I have seen a number of [these] women change their minds about aborting their unborn children as a result of my sidewalk counseling, and God's grace."

When a person is walking at a hurried pace to enter a building, a solicitor who must stand still eight feet away cannot know whether the person can be persuaded to accept the leaflet or not. Merely viewing a picture or brief message on the outside of the leaflet might be critical in the choice to receive it. To solicit by pamphlet is to tender it to the person. The statute ignores this fact. What the statute restricts is one person trying to communicate to another, which ought to be the heart of civilized discourse.

Colorado's excuse, and the Court's excuse, for the serious burden imposed upon the right to leaflet or to discuss is that it occurs at the wrong place. Again, Colorado and the Court have it just backwards. For these protestors the 100–foot zone in which young women enter a building is not just the last place where the message can be communicated. It likely is the only place. It is the location where the Court should expend its utmost effort to vindicate free speech, not to burden or suppress it.

Perhaps the leaflet will contain a picture of an unborn child, a picture the speaker thinks vital to the message. One of the arguments by the proponents of abortion, I had thought, was that a young woman might have been so uninformed that she did not know how to avoid pregnancy. The speakers in this case seek to ask the same uninformed woman, or indeed any woman who is considering an abortion, to understand and to contemplate the nature of the life she carries within her. To restrict the right of the speaker to hand her a leaflet, to hold a sign, or to speak quietly is for the Court to deny the neutrality that must be the first principle of the First Amendment. In this respect I am in full agreement with JUSTICE SCALIA's explanation of the insult the Court gives when it tells us these grave moral matters can be discussed just as well through a bullhorn. It would be remiss, moreover, not to observe the profound difference a leaflet can have in a woman's decisionmaking process. Consider the account of one young woman who testified before the Colorado Senate:

> "Abortion is a major decision. Unfortunately, most women have to make this decision alone. I did and I know that I am not the only one. As soon as I said the word 'pregnant,' he was history, never to be heard of, from again. I was scared and all alone. I was too embarrassed to ask for help. If this law had been in effect then, I would not have got any information at all and gone through with my abortion because the only people that were on my side were the people at the abortion clinic. They knew exactly how I was feeling and what to say to make it all better. In my heart, I knew abortion was wrong, but it didn't matter. I had never taken responsibility for my actions so why start then. One of the major reasons I did not go through with my scheduled abortion was the picture I was given while I was pregnant. This was the first time I had ever seen the other side of the story. I think I speak for a lot of women, myself included, when I say abortion is the only way out because of *[sic]* it's all I knew. In Sex Education, I was not taught about adoption or the fetus or anything like that. All I learned about was venereal diseases and abortion. The people supplying the pamphlet helped me make my choice. I got an informed decision, I got information from both sides, and I made an informed decision that my son and I could both live with. Because of this picture I was given, right there, this little boy got a chance at life that he would never have had."

There are, no doubt, women who would testify that abortion was necessary and unregretted. The point here is simply that speech makes a difference, as it must when acts of lasting significance and profound moral consequence are being contemplated. The majority reaches a contrary conclusion only by disregarding settled free speech principles. In doing so it delivers a grave wound to the First Amendment as well as to the essential reasoning in the joint opinion in *Casey*, a concern to which I now turn.

IV

In *Planned Parenthood of Southeastern Pa.* v. *Casey*, the Court reaffirmed its prior holding that the Constitution protects a woman's right to terminate her pregnancy in its early stages. The joint opinion in *Casey* considered the woman's liberty interest and principles of *stare decisis*, but took care to recognize the gravity of the personal decision: "[Abortion] is an act fraught with consequences for others: for the woman who must live with the implications of her decision; for the persons who perform and assist in the procedure; for the spouse, family, and society which must confront the knowledge that these procedures exist, procedures some deem nothing short of an act of violence against innocent human life; and, depending on one's beliefs, for the life or potential life that is aborted."

The Court now strikes at the heart of the reasoned, careful balance I had believed was the basis for the joint opinion in *Casey*. The vital principle of the opinion was that in defined instances the woman's decision whether to abort her child was in its essence a moral one, a choice the State could not dictate. Foreclosed from using the machinery of government to ban abortions in early term, those who oppose it are remitted to debate the issue in its moral dimensions. In a cruel way, the Court today turns its back on that balance. It in effect tells us the moral debate is not so important after all and can be conducted just as well through a bullhorn from an 8–foot distance as it can through a peaceful, face-to-face exchange of a leaflet. The lack of care with which the Court sustains the Colorado statute reflects a most troubling abdication of our responsibility to enforce the First Amendment.

There runs through our First Amendment theory a concept of immediacy, the idea that thoughts and pleas and petitions must not be lost with the passage of time. In a fleeting existence we have but little time to find truth through discourse. No better illustration of the immediacy of speech, of the urgency of persuasion, of the preciousness of time, is presented than in this case. Here the citizens who claim First Amendment protection seek it for speech which, if it is to be effective, must take place at the very time and place a grievous moral wrong, in their view, is about to occur. The Court tears away from the protesters the guarantees of the First Amendment when they most need it. So committed is the Court to its course that it denies these protesters, in the face of what they consider to be one of life's gravest moral crises, even the opportunity to try to offer a fellow citizen a little pamphlet, a handheld paper seeking to reach a higher law.

I dissent.

QUESTIONS AND NOTES

1.   Does *Hill* involve speech in a public forum?
2.   Do you agree with the Court's categorization of Colorado's statute as "content neutral"? Why? Why not?

3. Is the Colorado statute narrowly tailored? Why? Why not?

4. Is the concept of a prophylactic rule limiting speech inherently overbroad?

5. What is the State's interest? Safe access to medical facilities? Avoidance of unpalatable speech? Is the latter a legitimate interest?

6. Is this decision good for abortion and abortion only?

7. Is the problem raised by *Hill* similar to *Texas v. Johnson, i.e.* protection for that which some Justices deem especially important as against free speech? Note: Of the five Justices remaining from *Johnson* three, Rehnquist, Stevens and O'Connor voted to deny protection to both *Johnson* and *Hill*, while Scalia and Kennedy voted to grant protection to both.

8. Should it have been relevant that a speaker could not approach within eight feet without first obtaining permission as opposed to merely being required to leave if the approached person indicated no desire to be counseled or educated? Shouldn't there at least be a presumption in favor of speech?

F. DISTINGUISHING THE MEDIUM FROM THE MESSENGER

p.   613 (Before AETC v. Forbes)

Although not a public forum case, the provocative and controversial case of *Boy Scouts of America v. Dale* involves some of the same problems as *Denver*. Specifically, the ultimate question in the case seems to be whether the Boy Scouts should be perceived as a First Amendment actor or a place of accommodation. The Court split five to four.

BOY SCOUTS OF AMERICA v. DALE

530 U.S. 640 (2000).

CHIEF JUSTICE REHNQUIST delivered the opinion of the Court.

Petitioners are the Boy Scouts of America and the Monmouth Council, a division of the Boy Scouts of America (collectively, Boy Scouts). The Boy Scouts is a private, not-for-profit organization engaged in instilling its system of values in young people. The Boy Scouts asserts that homosexual conduct is inconsistent with the values it seeks to instill. Respondent is James Dale, a former Eagle Scout whose adult membership in the Boy Scouts was revoked when the Boy Scouts learned that he is an avowed homosexual and gay rights activist. The New Jersey Supreme Court held that New Jersey's public accommodations law requires that the Boy Scouts admit Dale. This case presents the question whether applying New Jersey's public accommodations law in this way violates the Boy Scouts' First Amendment right of expressive association. We hold that it does.

I

James Dale entered scouting in 1978 at the age of eight by joining Monmouth Council's Cub Scout Pack 142. Dale became a Boy Scout in 1981 and remained a Scout until he turned 18. By all accounts, Dale was an exemplary Scout. In 1988, he achieved the rank of Eagle Scout, one of Scouting's highest honors.

Dale applied for adult membership in the Boy Scouts in 1989. The Boy Scouts approved his application for the position of assistant scoutmaster of Troop 73. Around the same time, Dale left home to attend Rutgers University. After arriving at Rutgers, Dale first acknowledged to himself and others that he is gay. He quickly became involved with, and eventually became the copresident of, the Rutgers University Lesbian/Gay Alliance. In 1990, Dale attended a seminar addressing the psychological and health needs of lesbian and gay teenagers. A newspaper covering the event interviewed Dale about his advocacy of homosexual teenagers' need for gay role models. In early July 1990, the newspaper published the interview and Dale's photograph over a caption identifying him as the copresident of the Lesbian/Gay Alliance.

Later that month, Dale received a letter from Monmouth Council Executive James Kay revoking his adult membership. Dale wrote to Kay requesting the reason for Monmouth Council's decision. Kay responded by letter that the Boy Scouts "specifically forbid membership to homosexuals."

In 1992, Dale filed a complaint against the Boy Scouts in the New Jersey Superior Court. The complaint alleged that the Boy Scouts had violated New Jersey's public accommodations statute and its common law by revoking Dale's membership based solely on his sexual orientation. New Jersey's public accommodations statute prohibits, among other things, discrimination on the basis of sexual orientation in places of public accommodation.

I

In *Roberts v. United States Jaycees*, 468 U.S. 609 (1984), we observed that "implicit in the right to engage in activities protected by the First Amendment" is "a corresponding right to associate with others in pursuit of a wide variety of political, social, economic, educational, religious, and cultural ends." This right is crucial in preventing the majority from imposing its views on groups that would rather express other, perhaps unpopular, ideas. (stating that protection of the right to expressive association is "especially important in preserving political and cultural diversity and in shielding dissident expression from suppression by the majority"). Government actions that may unconstitutionally burden this freedom may take many forms, one of which is "intrusion into the internal structure or affairs of an association" like a "regulation that forces the group to accept members it does not desire." Forcing a group to accept certain members may impair the ability of the group to express those views, and only those views, that it intends to express. Thus, "[f]reedom of association ... plainly presupposes a freedom not to associate."

The forced inclusion of an unwanted person in a group infringes the group's freedom of expressive association if the presence of that person affects in a significant way the group's ability to advocate public or private viewpoints. *New York State Club Assn., Inc. v. City of New York*, 487 U.S. 1 (1988). But the freedom of expressive association, like many freedoms, is not absolute. We have held that the freedom could be overridden "by regulations adopted to serve compelling state interests, unrelated to the suppression of ideas, that cannot be achieved through means significantly less restrictive of associational freedoms." *Roberts*.

To determine whether a group is protected by the First Amendment's expressive associational right, we must determine whether the group engages in "expressive association." The First Amendment's protection of expressive association is not reserved for advocacy groups. But to come within its ambit, a group must engage in some form of expression, whether it be public or private.

Because this is a First Amendment case where the ultimate conclusions of law are virtually inseparable from findings of fact, we are obligated to independently review the factual record to ensure that the state court's judgment does not unlawfully intrude on free expression. See *Hurley v. Irish–American Gay Lesbian and Bisexual Group of Boston*, 515 U.S. 557, 567–8 (1995). The record reveals the following. The Boy Scouts is a private, nonprofit organization. According to its mission statement:

> "It is the mission of the Boy Scouts of America to serve others by helping to instill values in young people and, in other ways, to prepare them to make ethical choices over their lifetime in achieving their full potential.

> "The values we strive to instill are based on those found in the Scout Oath and Law:

"Scout Oath

"On my honor I will do my best

To do my duty to God and my country

and to obey the Scout Law;

To help other people at all times;

To keep myself physically strong,

mentally awake, and morally straight.

"Scout Law

"A Scout is:

"Trustworthy	Obedient
Loyal	Cheerful
Helpful	Thrifty
Friendly	Brave
Courteous	Clean
Kind	Reverent."

Thus, the general mission of the Boy Scouts is clear: "[T]o instill values in young people." The Boy Scouts seeks to instill these values by having its adult leaders spend time with the youth members, instructing and engaging them in activities like camping, archery, and fishing. During the time spent with the youth members, the scoutmasters and assistant scoutmasters inculcate them with the Boy Scouts' values—both expressly and by example. It seems indisputable that an association that seeks to transmit such a system of values engages in expressive activity. See *Roberts*. (O'CONNOR, J., concurring) ("Even the training of outdoor survival skills or participation in community service might become expressive when the activity is intended to develop good morals, reverence, patriotism, and a desire for self-improvement").

Given that the Boy Scouts engages in expressive activity, we must determine whether the forced inclusion of Dale as an assistant scoutmaster would significantly affect the Boy Scouts' ability to advocate public or private viewpoints. This inquiry necessarily requires us first to explore, to a limited extent, the nature of the Boy Scouts' view of homosexuality.

The values the Boy Scouts seeks to instill are "based on" those listed in the Scout Oath and Law. The Boy Scouts explains that the Scout Oath and Law provide "a positive moral code for living; they are a list of 'do's' rather than 'don'ts.' " The Boy Scouts asserts that homosexual conduct is inconsistent with the values embodied in the Scout Oath and Law, particularly with the values represented by the terms "morally straight" and "clean."

Obviously, the Scout Oath and Law do not expressly mention sexuality or sexual orientation. And the terms "morally straight" and "clean" are by no means self-defining. Different people would attribute to those terms very different meanings. For example, some people may believe that engaging in homosexual conduct is not at odds with being "morally straight" and "clean." And others may believe that engaging in homosexual conduct is contrary to being "morally straight" and "clean." The Boy Scouts says it falls within the latter category.

The New Jersey Supreme Court analyzed the Boy Scouts' beliefs and found that the "exclusion of members solely on the basis of their sexual orientation is inconsistent with Boy Scouts' commitment to a diverse and 'representative' membership ... [and] contradicts Boy Scouts' overarching objective to reach 'all eligible youth.' " The court concluded that the exclusion of members like Dale "appears antithetical to the organization's goals and philosophy." But our cases reject this sort of inquiry; it is not the role of the courts to reject a group's expressed values because they disagree with those values or find them internally inconsistent. See *Democratic Party of United States v. Wisconsin ex rel. La Follette*, 450 U.S. 107, 124 (1981) ("As is true of all expressions of First Amendment freedoms, the courts may not interfere on the ground that they view a particular expression as unwise or irrational"); see also *Thomas v. Review Bd. of Indiana Employment Security Div.*, 450 U.S. 707, 714 (1981) ("Religious beliefs need not be acceptable, logical, consistent, or comprehensible to others to merit First Amendment protection").

The Boy Scouts asserts that it "teaches that homosexual conduct is not morally straight," and that it does "not want to promote homosexual conduct as a legitimate form of behavior." We accept the Boy Scouts' assertion. We need not inquire further to determine the nature of the Boy Scouts' expression with respect to homosexuality. But because the record before us contains written evidence of the Boy Scouts' viewpoint, we look to it as instructive, if only on the question of the sincerity of the professed beliefs.

A 1978 position statement to the Boy Scouts' Executive Committee, signed by Downing B. Jenks, the President of the Boy Scouts, and Harvey L. Price, the Chief Scout Executive, expresses the Boy Scouts' "official position" with regard to "homosexuality and Scouting":

> "Q. May an individual who openly declares himself to be a homosexual be a volunteer Scout leader?

"A. No. The Boy Scouts of America is a private, membership organization and leadership therein is a privilege and not a right. We do not
believe that homosexuality and leadership in Scouting are appropriate. We will continue to select only those who in our judgment meet
our standards and qualifications for leadership."

Thus, at least as of 1978—the year James Dale entered Scouting—the
official position of the Boy Scouts was that avowed homosexuals were not to
be Scout leaders.

A position statement promulgated by the Boy Scouts in 1991 (after Dale's
membership was revoked but before this litigation was filed) also supports its
current view:

"We believe that homosexual conduct is inconsistent with the requirement in the Scout Oath that a Scout be morally straight and in the Scout
Law that a Scout be clean in word and deed, and that homosexuals do not
provide a desirable role model for Scouts."

This position statement was redrafted numerous times but its core
message remained consistent. For example, a 1993 position statement, the
most recent in the record, reads, in part:

"The Boy Scouts of America has always reflected the expectations that
Scouting families have had for the organization. We do not believe that
homosexuals provide a role model consistent with these expectations.
Accordingly, we do not allow for the registration of avowed homosexuals
as members or as leaders of the BSA."

The Boy Scouts publicly expressed its views with respect to homosexual
conduct by its assertions in prior litigation. For example, throughout a
California case with similar facts filed in the early 1980's, the Boy Scouts
consistently asserted the same position with respect to homosexuality that it
asserts today. We cannot doubt that the Boy Scouts sincerely holds this view.

We must then determine whether Dale's presence as an assistant scoutmaster would significantly burden the Boy Scouts' desire to not "promote
homosexual conduct as a legitimate form of behavior." As we give deference to
an association's assertions regarding the nature of its expression, we must
also give deference to an association's view of what would impair its expression. See, *e.g., La Follette* (considering whether a Wisconsin law burdened the
National Party's associational rights and stating that "a State, or a court,
may not constitutionally substitute its own judgment for that of the Party").
That is not to say that an expressive association can erect a shield against
antidiscrimination laws simply by asserting that mere acceptance of a member
from a particular group would impair its message. But here Dale, by his own
admission, is one of a group of gay Scouts who have "become leaders in their
community and are open and honest about their sexual orientation." Dale was
the copresident of a gay and lesbian organization at college and remains a gay
rights activist. Dale's presence in the Boy Scouts would, at the very least,
force the organization to send a message, both to the youth members and the
world, that the Boy Scouts accepts homosexual conduct as a legitimate form of
behavior.

Hurley is illustrative on this point. There we considered whether the
application of Massachusetts' public accommodations law to require the

organizers of a private St. Patrick's Day parade to include among the marchers an Irish–American gay, lesbian, and bisexual group, GLIB, violated the parade organizers' First Amendment rights. We noted that the parade organizers did not wish to exclude the GLIB members because of their sexual orientations, but because they wanted to march behind a GLIB banner. We observed:

> "[A] contingent marching behind the organization's banner would at least bear witness to the fact that some Irish are gay, lesbian, or bisexual, and the presence of the organized marchers would suggest their view that people of their sexual orientations have as much claim to unqualified social acceptance as heterosexuals.... The parade's organizers may not believe these facts about Irish sexuality to be so, or they may object to unqualified social acceptance of gays and lesbians or have some other reason for wishing to keep GLIB's message out of the parade. But whatever the reason, it boils down to the choice of a speaker not to propound a particular point of view, and that choice is presumed to lie beyond the government's power to control."

Here, we have found that the Boy Scouts believes that homosexual conduct is inconsistent with the values it seeks to instill in its youth members; it will not "promote homosexual conduct as a legitimate form of behavior." As the presence of GLIB in Boston's St. Patrick's Day parade would have interfered with the parade organizers' choice not to propound a particular point of view, the presence of Dale as an assistant scoutmaster would just as surely interfere with the Boy Scout's choice not to propound a point of view contrary to its beliefs.

The New Jersey Supreme Court determined that the Boy Scouts' ability to disseminate its message was not significantly affected by the forced inclusion of Dale as an assistant scoutmaster because of the following findings:

> "Boy Scout members do not associate for the purpose of disseminating the belief that homosexuality is immoral; Boy Scouts discourages its leaders from disseminating *any* views on sexual issues; and Boy Scouts includes sponsors and members who subscribe to different views in respect of homosexuality."

We disagree with the New Jersey Supreme Court's conclusion drawn from these findings.

First, associations do not have to associate for the "purpose" of disseminating a certain message in order to be entitled to the protections of the First Amendment. An association must merely engage in expressive activity that could be impaired in order to be entitled to protection. For example, the purpose of the St. Patrick's Day parade in *Hurley* was not to espouse any views about sexual orientation, but we held that the parade organizers had a right to exclude certain participants nonetheless.

Second, even if the Boy Scouts discourages Scout leaders from disseminating views on sexual issues—a fact that the Boy Scouts disputes with contrary evidence—the First Amendment protects the Boy Scouts' method of expression. If the Boy Scouts wishes Scout leaders to avoid questions of sexuality and teach only by example, this fact does not negate the sincerity of its belief discussed above.

Third, the First Amendment simply does not require that every member of a group agree on every issue in order for the group's policy to be "expressive association." The Boy Scouts takes an official position with respect to homosexual conduct, and that is sufficient for First Amendment purposes. In this same vein, Dale makes much of the claim that the Boy Scouts does not revoke the membership of heterosexual Scout leaders that openly disagree with the Boy Scouts' policy on sexual orientation. But if this is true, it is irrelevant.[1] The presence of an avowed homosexual and gay rights activist in an assistant scoutmaster's uniform sends a distinctly different message from the presence of a heterosexual assistant scoutmaster who is on record as disagreeing with Boy Scouts policy. The Boy Scouts has a First Amendment right to choose to send one message but not the other. The fact that the organization does not trumpet its views from the housetops, or that it tolerates dissent within its ranks, does not mean that its views receive no First Amendment protection.

Having determined that the Boy Scouts is an expressive association and that the forced inclusion of Dale would significantly affect its expression, we inquire whether the application of New Jersey's public accommodations law to require that the Boy Scouts accept Dale as an assistant scoutmaster runs afoul of the Scouts' freedom of expressive association. We conclude that it does.

State public accommodations laws were originally enacted to prevent discrimination in traditional places of public accommodation—like inns and trains. Over time, the public accommodations laws have expanded to cover more places. New Jersey's statutory definition of " '[a] place of public accommodation' " is extremely broad. The term is said to "include, but not be limited to," a list of over 50 types of places. Many on the list are what one would expect to be places where the public is invited. For example, the statute includes as places of public accommodation taverns, restaurants, retail shops, and public libraries. But the statute also includes places that often may not carry with them open invitations to the public, like summer camps and roof gardens. In this case, the New Jersey Supreme Court went a step further and applied its public accommodations law to a private entity without even attempting to tie the term "place" to a physical location.[3] As the definition of "public accommodation" has expanded from clearly commercial entities, such as restaurants, bars, and hotels, to membership organizations such as the Boy Scouts, the potential for conflict between state public accommodations laws and the First Amendment rights of organizations has increased.

---

1. The record evidence sheds doubt on Dale's assertion. For example, the National Director of the Boy Scouts certified that *"any* persons who advocate to Scouting youth that homosexual conduct is" consistent with Scouting values will not be registered as adult leaders. (emphasis added). And the Monmouth Council Scout Executive testified that the advocacy of the morality of homosexuality to youth members by any adult member is grounds for revocation of the adult's membership.

3. Four State Supreme Courts and one United States Court of Appeals have ruled that the Boy Scouts is not a place of public accommodation. No federal appellate court or state supreme court—except the New Jersey Supreme Court in this case—has reached a contrary result.

We recognized in cases such as *Roberts* and *Bd. of Directors of Rotary Intl v. Rotary Club of Duarte* that States have a compelling interest in eliminating discrimination against women in public accommodations. But in each of these cases we went on to conclude that the enforcement of these statutes would not materially interfere with the ideas that the organization sought to express. In *Roberts*, we said "indeed, the Jaycees has failed to demonstrate . . . any serious burden on the male members' freedom of expressive association." In *Duarte*, we said:

> "Impediments to the exercise of one's right to choose one's associates can violate the right of association protected by the First Amendment. In this case, however, the evidence fails to demonstrate that admitting women to Rotary Clubs will affect in any significant way the existing members' ability to carry out their various purposes."

We thereupon concluded in each of these cases that the organizations' First Amendment rights were not violated by the application of the States' public accommodations laws.

In *Hurley,* we said that public accommodations laws "are well within the State's usual power to enact when a legislature has reason to believe that a given group is the target of discrimination, and they do not, as a general matter, violate the First or Fourteenth Amendments." But we went on to note that in that case "the Massachusetts [public accommodations] law has been applied in a peculiar way" because "any contingent of protected individuals with a message would have the right to participate in petitioners' speech, so that the communication produced by the private organizers would be shaped by all those protected by the law who wish to join in with some expressive demonstration of their own." And in the associational freedom cases such as *Roberts*, *Duarte*, and *New York State Club Assn.*, after finding a compelling state interest, the Court went on to examine whether or not the application of the state law would impose any "serious burden" on the organization's rights of expressive association. So in these cases, the associational interest in freedom of expression has been set on one side of the scale, and the State's interest on the other.

Dale contends that we should apply the intermediate standard of review enunciated in *United States v. O'Brien*, 391 U.S. 367 (1968), to evaluate the competing interests. There the Court enunciated a four-part test for review of a governmental regulation that has only an incidental effect on protected speech—in that case the symbolic burning of a draft card. A law prohibiting the destruction of draft cards only incidentally affects the free speech rights of those who happen to use a violation of that law as a symbol of protest. But New Jersey's public accommodations law directly and immediately affects associational rights, in this case associational rights that enjoy First Amendment protection. Thus, *O'Brien* is inapplicable.

In *Hurley,* we applied traditional First Amendment analysis to hold that the application of the Massachusetts public accommodations law to a parade violated the First Amendment rights of the parade organizers. Although we did not explicitly deem the parade in *Hurley* an expressive association, the analysis we applied there is similar to the analysis we apply here. We have already concluded that a state requirement that the Boy Scouts retain Dale as an assistant scoutmaster would significantly burden the organization's right to oppose or disfavor homosexual conduct. The state interests embodied in New Jersey's public accommodations law do not justify such a severe intrusion on the Boy Scouts' rights to freedom of expressive association. That being the case, we hold that the First Amendment prohibits the State from imposing such a requirement through the application of its public accommodations law.[4]

JUSTICE STEVENS' dissent makes much of its observation that the public perception of homosexuality in this country has changed. Indeed, it appears that homosexuality has gained greater societal acceptance. But this is scarcely an argument for denying First Amendment protection to those who refuse to accept these views. The First Amendment protects expression, be it of the popular variety or not. See, *e.g., Texas v. Johnson; Brandenburg v. Ohio.* And the fact that an idea may be embraced and advocated by increasing numbers of people is all the more reason to protect the First Amendment rights of those who wish to voice a different view.

JUSTICE STEVENS' extolling of Justice Brandeis' comments in *New State Ice Co. v. Liebmann,* 285 U.S. 262 (1932) (dissenting opinion); confuses two entirely different principles. In *New State Ice,* the Court struck down an Oklahoma regulation prohibiting the manufacture, sale, and distribution of ice without a license. Justice Brandeis, a champion of state experimentation in the economic realm, dissented. But Justice Brandeis was never a champion of state experimentation in the suppression of free speech. To the contrary, his First Amendment commentary provides compelling support for the Court's opinion in this case. In speaking of the Founders of this Nation, Justice Brandeis emphasized that they "believed that the freedom to think as you will and to speak as you think are means indispensable to the discovery and spread of political truth." *Whitney v. California,* 274 U.S. 357, 375 (concurring opinion). He continued:

> "Believing in the power of reason as applied through public discussion, they eschewed silence coerced by law—the argument of force in its worst form. Recognizing the occasional tyrannies of governing majorities, they amended the Constitution so that free speech and assembly should be guaranteed."

We are not, as we must not be, guided by our views of whether the Boy Scouts' teachings with respect to homosexual conduct are right or wrong; public or judicial disapproval of a tenet of an organization's expression does not justify the State's effort to compel the organization to accept members where such acceptance would derogate from the organization's expressive message. "While the law is free to promote all sorts of conduct in place of harmful behavior, it is not free to interfere with speech for no better reason than promoting an approved message or discouraging a disfavored one, however enlightened either purpose may strike the government." *Hurley.*

---

4. We anticipated this result in *Hurley* when we illustrated the reasons for our holding in that case by likening the parade to a private membership organization. We stated: "Assuming the parade to be large enough and a source of benefits (apart from its expression) that would generally justify a mandated access provision, GLIB could nonetheless be refused admission as an expressive contingent with its own message just as readily as a private club could exclude an applicant whose manifest views were at odds with a position taken by the club's existing members."

The judgment of the New Jersey Supreme Court is reversed, and the cause remanded for further proceedings not inconsistent with this opinion.

It is so ordered.

JUSTICE STEVENS, with whom JUSTICE SOUTER, JUSTICE GINSBURG and JUSTICE BREYER join, dissenting.

New Jersey "prides itself on judging each individual by his or her merits" and on being "in the vanguard in the fight to eradicate the cancer of unlawful discrimination of all types from our society." *Peper v. Princeton Univ. Bd. of Trustees*, 77 N. J. 55, 80, 389 A.2d 465, 478 (1978). Since 1945, it has had a law against discrimination. The law broadly protects the opportunity of all persons to obtain the advantages and privileges "of any place of public accommodation." And as amended in 1991, the law prohibits discrimination on the basis of nine different traits including an individual's "sexual orientation."[1] The question in this case is whether that expansive construction trenches on the federal constitutional rights of the Boy Scouts of America (BSA).

Because every state law prohibiting discrimination is designed to replace prejudice with principle, Justice Brandeis' comment on the States' right to experiment with "things social" is directly applicable to this case.

"To stay experimentation in things social and economic is a grave responsibility. Denial of the right to experiment may be fraught with serious consequences to the Nation. It is one of the happy incidents of the federal system that a single courageous State may, if its citizens choose, serve as a laboratory; and try novel social and economic experiments without risk to the rest of the country. This Court has the power to prevent an experiment. We may strike down the statute which embodies it on the ground that, in our opinion, the measure is arbitrary, capricious or unreasonable. We have power to do this, because the due process clause has been held by the Court applicable to matters of substantive law as well as to matters of procedure. But in the exercise of this high power, we must be ever on our guard, lest we erect our prejudices into legal principles. If we would guide by the light of reason, we must let our minds be bold." *New State Ice Co. v. Liebmann*, 285 U.S. 262, 311 (1932) (dissenting opinion).

In its "exercise of this high power" today, the Court does not accord this "courageous State" the respect that is its due.

I

James Dale joined BSA as a Cub Scout in 1978, when he was eight years old. Three years later he became a Boy Scout, and he remained a member until his 18th birthday. Along the way, he earned 25 merit badges, was admitted into the prestigious Order of the Arrow, and was awarded the rank

---

1. In 1992, the statute was again amended to add "familial status" as a tenth protected class. It now provides:

"10:5–4 Obtaining employment, accommodations and privileges without discrimination; civil right" "All persons shall have the opportunity to obtain employment, and to obtain all the accommodations, advantages, facilities, and privileges of any place of public accommodation, publicly assisted housing accommodation, and other real property without discrimination because of race, creed, color, national origin, ancestry, age, marital status, affectional or sexual orientation, familial status, or sex, subject only to conditions and limitations applicable alike to all persons. This opportunity is recognized as and declared to be a civil right."

of Eagle Scout—an honor given to only three percent of all Scouts. In 1989, BSA approved his application to be an Assistant Scoutmaster.

On July 19, 1990, after more than 12 years of active and honored participation, the Boys Scouts sent Dale a letter advising him of the revocation of his membership. The letter stated that membership in BSA "is a privilege" that may be denied "whenever there is a concern that an individual may not meet the high standards of membership which the BSA seeks to provide for American youth." Expressing surprise at his sudden expulsion, Dale sent a letter requesting an explanation of the decision. In response, BSA sent him a second letter stating that the grounds for the decision "are the standards for leadership established by the Boy Scouts of America, which specifically forbid membership to homosexuals." At that time, no such standard had been publicly expressed by BSA.

In this case, Boy Scouts of America contends that it teaches the young boys who are Scouts that homosexuality is immoral. Consequently, it argues, it would violate its right to associate to force it to admit homosexuals as members, as doing so would be at odds with its own shared goals and values. This contention, quite plainly, requires us to look at what, exactly, are the values that BSA actually teaches.

BSA's mission statement reads as follows: "It is the mission of the Boy Scouts of America to serve others by helping to instill values in young people and, in other ways, to prepare them to make ethical choices over their lifetime in achieving their full potential." Its federal charter declares its purpose is "to promote, through organization, and cooperation with other agencies, the ability of boys to do things for themselves and others, to train them in scoutcraft, and to teach them patriotism, courage, self-reliance, and kindred values, using the methods which were in common use by Boy Scouts on June 15, 1916." BSA describes itself as having a "representative membership," which it defines as "boy membership [that] reflects proportionately the characteristics of the boy population of its service area." In particular, the group emphasizes that "neither the charter nor the bylaws of the Boy Scouts of America permits the exclusion of any boy.... To meet these responsibilities we have made a commitment that our membership shall be representative of *all* the population in every community, district, and council." (emphasis in original).

To instill its shared values, BSA has adopted a "Scout Oath" and a "Scout Law" setting forth its central tenets. For example, the Scout Law requires a member to promise, among other things, that he will be "obedient." Accompanying definitions for the terms found in the Oath and Law are provided in the Boy Scout Handbook and the Scoutmaster Handbook. For instance, the Boy Scout Handbook defines "obedient" as follows:

> "A Scout is OBEDIENT. A Scout follows the rules of his family, school, and troop. He obeys the laws of his community and country. If he thinks these rules and laws are unfair, he tries to have them changed in an orderly manner rather than disobey them." (emphasis deleted).

To bolster its claim that its shared goals include teaching that homosexuality is wrong, BSA directs our attention to two terms appearing in the Scout Oath and Law. The first is the phrase "morally straight," which appears in the Oath ("On my honor I will do my best ... To keep myself ... morally straight"); the second term is the word "clean," which appears in a list of 12 characteristics together comprising the Scout Law.

The Boy Scout Handbook defines "morally straight," as such:

> "To be a person of strong character, guide your life with honesty, purity, and justice. Respect and defend the rights of all people. Your relationships with others should be honest and open. Be clean in your speech and actions, and faithful in your religious beliefs. The values you follow as a Scout will help you become virtuous and self-reliant."

The Scoutmaster Handbook emphasizes these points about being "morally straight":

> "In any consideration of moral fitness, a key word has to be 'courage.' A boy's courage to do what his head and his heart tell him is right. And the courage to refuse to do what his heart and his head say is wrong. Moral fitness, like emotional fitness, will clearly present opportunities for wise guidance by an alert Scoutmaster."

As for the term "clean," the Boy Scout Handbook offers the following:

> "A Scout is CLEAN. *A Scout keeps his body and mind fit and clean. He chooses the company of those who live by these same ideals. He helps keep his home and community clean.*

> "You never need to be ashamed of dirt that will wash off. If you play hard and work hard you can't help getting dirty. But when the game is over or the work is done, that kind of dirt disappears with soap and water.

> "There's another kind of dirt that won't come off by washing. It is the kind that shows up in foul language and harmful thoughts.

> "Swear words, profanity, and dirty stories are weapons that ridicule other people and hurt their feelings. The same is true of racial slurs and jokes making fun of ethnic groups or people with physical or mental limitations. A Scout knows there is no kindness or honor in such mean-spirited behavior. He avoids it in his own words and deeds. He defends those who are targets of insults." (emphasis in original).[2]

It is plain as the light of day that neither one of these principles—"morally straight" and "clean"—says the slightest thing about homosexuality. Indeed, neither term in the Boy Scouts' Law and Oath expresses any position whatsoever on sexual matters.

---

2. Scoutmasters are instructed to teach what it means to be "clean" using the following lesson:

"(Hold up two cooking pots, one shiny bright on the inside but sooty outside, the other shiny outside but dirty inside.) Scouts, which of these pots would you rather have your food cooked in? Did I hear somebody say, 'Neither one?'

"That's not a bad answer. We wouldn't have much confidence in a patrol cook who didn't have his pots shiny both inside and out.

"But if we had to make a choice, we would tell the cook to use the pot that's clean inside. The same idea applies to people.

"Most people keep themselves clean outside. But how about the inside? Do we try to keep our minds and our language clean? I think that's even more important than keeping the outside clean.

"A Scout, of course, should be clean inside and out. Water, soap, and a toothbrush take care of the outside. Only your determination will keep the inside clean. You can do it by following the Scout Law and the example of people you respect—your parents, your teachers, your clergyman, or a good buddy who is trying to do the same thing."

BSA's published guidance on that topic underscores this point. Scouts, for example, are directed to receive their sex education at home or in school, but not from the organization: "Your parents or guardian or a sex education teacher should give you the facts about sex that you must know." Boy Scout Handbook (1992). To be sure, Scouts are not forbidden from asking their Scoutmaster about issues of a sexual nature, but Scoutmasters are, literally, the last person Scouts are encouraged to ask: "If you have questions about growing up, about relationships, sex, or making good decisions, ask. Talk with your parents, religious leaders, teachers, or Scoutmaster." Moreover, Scoutmasters are specifically directed to steer curious adolescents to other sources of information:

> "If Scouts ask for information regarding ... sexual activity, answer honestly and factually, but stay within your realm of expertise and comfort. If a Scout has serious concerns that you cannot answer, refer him to his family, religious leader, doctor, or other professional." Scoutmaster Handbook (1990).

More specifically, BSA has set forth a number of rules for Scoutmasters when these types of issues come up:

> "You may have boys asking you for information or advice about sexual matters....

> "How should you handle such matters?

> "Rule number 1: *You do not undertake to instruct Scouts, in any formalized manner, in the subject of sex and family life. The reasons are that it is not construed to be Scouting's proper area*, and that you are probably not well qualified to do this.

> "Rule number 2: If Scouts come to you to ask questions or to seek advice, you would give it within your competence. A boy who appears to be asking about sexual intercourse, however, may really only be worried about his pimples, so it is well to find out just what information is needed.

> "Rule number 3: You should refer boys with sexual problems to persons better qualified than you [are] to handle them. If the boy has a spiritual leader or a doctor who can deal with them, he should go there. If such persons are not available, you may just have to do the best you can. But don't try to play a highly professional role. And at the other extreme, avoid passing the buck." Scoutmaster Handbook (1972) (emphasis added).

In light of BSA's self-proclaimed ecumenism, furthermore, it is even more difficult to discern any shared goals or common moral stance on homosexuality. Insofar as religious matters are concerned, BSA's bylaws state that it is "absolutely nonsectarian in its attitude toward ... religious training." "The BSA does not define what constitutes duty to God or the practice of religion. This is the responsibility of parents and religious leaders." In fact, many diverse religious organizations sponsor local Boy Scout troops. Because a number of religious groups do not view homosexuality as immoral or wrong and reject discrimination against homosexuals,[44] it is exceedingly difficult to

44. See, *e.g.*, Brief for Deans of Divinity Schools and Rabbinical Institutions as *Amicus*   *Curiae* 8 ("The diverse religi[ous] traditions of this country present no coherent moral mes-

believe that BSA nonetheless adopts a single particular religious or moral philosophy when it comes to sexual orientation. This is especially so in light of the fact that Scouts are advised to seek guidance on sexual matters from their religious leaders (and Scoutmasters are told to refer Scouts to them); BSA surely is aware that some religions do not teach that homosexuality is wrong.

II

The Court seeks to fill the void by pointing to a statement of "policies and procedures relating to homosexuality and Scouting" signed by BSA's President and Chief Scout Executive in 1978 and addressed to the members of the Executive Committee of the national organization. The letter says that the BSA does "not believe that homosexuality and leadership in Scouting are appropriate." But when the *entire* 1978 letter is read, BSA's position is far more equivocal:

> "4. Q. May an individual who openly declares himself to be a homosexual be employed by the Boy Scouts of America as a professional or non-professional?

> "A. Boy Scouts of America does not knowingly employ homosexuals as professionals or non-professionals. We are unaware of any present laws which would prohibit this policy.

> "5. Q. Should a professional or non-professional individual who openly declares himself to be a homosexual be terminated?

> "A. Yes, *in the absence of any law to the contrary.* At the present time we are unaware of any statute or ordinance in the United States which prohibits discrimination against individual's employment upon the basis of homosexuality. *In the event that such a law was applicable, it would be necessary for the Boy Scouts of America to obey it, in this case as in Paragraph 4 above.* It is our position, however, that homosexuality and professional or non-professional employment in Scouting are not appropriate." (emphasis added).

Four aspects of the 1978 policy statement are relevant to the proper disposition of this case. First, at most this letter simply adopts an exclusionary membership policy. But simply adopting such a policy has never been considered sufficient, by itself, to prevail on a right to associate claim.

Second, the 1978 policy was never publicly expressed—unlike, for example, the Scout's duty to be "obedient." It was an internal memorandum, never circulated beyond the few members of BSA's Executive Committee. It remained, in effect, a secret Boy Scouts policy. Far from claiming any intent to express an idea that would be burdened by the presence of homosexuals, BSA's *public* posture—to the world and to the Scouts themselves—remained what it had always been: one of tolerance, welcoming all classes of boys and

sage that excludes gays and lesbians from participating as full and equal members of those institutions. Indeed, the movement among a number of the nation's major religious institutions for many decades has been toward public recognition of gays and lesbians as full members of moral communities, and acceptance of gays and lesbians as religious leaders, elders and clergy"); Brief for General Board of Church and Society of the United Methodist Church et al. as *Amicus Curiae* 3 (describing views of The United Methodist Church, the Episcopal Church, the Religious Action Center of Reform Judaism, the United Church Board of Homeland Ministries, and the Unitarian Universalist Association, all of whom reject discrimination on the basis of sexual orientation).

young men. In this respect, BSA's claim is even weaker than those we have rejected in the past.

Third, it is apparent that the draftsmen of the policy statement foresaw the possibility that laws against discrimination might one day be amended to protect homosexuals from employment discrimination. Their statement clearly provided that, in the event such a law conflicted with their policy, a Scout's duty to be "obedient" and "obey the laws," even if "he thinks [the laws] are unfair" would prevail in such a contingency. In 1978, however, BSA apparently did not consider it to be a serious possibility that a State might one day characterize the Scouts as a "place of public accommodation" with a duty to open its membership to all qualified individuals. The portions of the statement dealing with membership simply assume that membership in the Scouts is a "privilege" that BSA is free to grant or to withhold. The statement does not address the question whether the publicly proclaimed duty to obey the law should prevail over the private discriminatory policy if, and when, a conflict between the two should arise—as it now has in New Jersey. At the very least, then, the statement reflects no unequivocal view on homosexuality. Indeed, the statement suggests that an appropriate way for BSA to preserve its unpublished exclusionary policy would include an open and forthright attempt to seek an amendment of New Jersey's statute. ("If he thinks these rules and laws are unfair, he tries to have them changed in an orderly manner rather than disobey them.")

Fourth, the 1978 statement simply says that homosexuality is not "appropriate." It makes no effort to connect that statement to a shared goal or expressive activity of the Boy Scouts. Whatever values BSA seeks to instill in Scouts, the idea that homosexuality is not "appropriate" appears entirely unconnected to, and is mentioned nowhere in, the myriad of publicly declared values and creeds of the BSA. That idea does not appear to be among any of the principles actually taught to Scouts. Rather, the 1978 policy appears to be no more than a private statement of a few BSA executives that the organization wishes to exclude gays—and that wish has nothing to do with any expression BSA actually engages in.

The majority also relies on four other policy statements that were issued between 1991 and 1993. All of them were written and issued *after* BSA revoked Dale's membership. Accordingly, they have little, if any, relevance to the legal question before this Court.[6]

At most the 1991 and 1992 statements declare only that BSA believed "homosexual *conduct* is inconsistent with the requirement in the Scout Oath that a Scout be morally straight and in the Scout Law that a Scout be clean in word and deed." (emphasis added). But New Jersey's law prohibits discrimination on the basis of sexual *orientation*. And when Dale was expelled from the Boy Scouts, BSA said it did so because of his sexual orientation, not because of his sexual conduct.[8]

6. Dale's complaint requested three forms of relief: (1) a declaration that his rights under the New Jersey statute had been violated when his membership was revoked; (2) an order reinstating his membership; and (3) compensatory and punitive damages. Nothing that BSA could have done after the revocation of his membership could affect Dale's first request for relief, though perhaps some possible post-revocation action could have influenced the other two requests for relief.

8. At oral argument, BSA's counsel was asked: "What if someone is homosexual in the sense of having a sexual orientation in that

It is clear, then, that nothing in these policy statements supports BSA's claim. The only policy written before the revocation of Dale's membership was an equivocal, undisclosed statement that evidences no connection between the group's discriminatory intentions and its expressive interests. The later policies demonstrate a brief—though ultimately abandoned—attempt to tie BSA's exclusion to its expression, but other than a single sentence, BSA fails to show that it ever taught Scouts that homosexuality is not "morally straight" or "clean," or that such a view was part of the group's collective efforts to foster a belief. Furthermore, BSA's policy statements fail to establish any clear, consistent, and unequivocal position on homosexuality. Nor did BSA have any reason to think Dale's sexual *conduct*, as opposed to his orientation, was contrary to the group's values.

III

BSA's claim finds no support in our cases. We have recognized "a right to associate for the purpose of engaging in those activities protected by the First Amendment—speech, assembly, petition for the redress of grievances, and the exercise of religion." And we have acknowledged that "when the State interferes with individuals' selection of those with whom they wish to join in a common endeavor, freedom of association . . . may be implicated." But "the right to associate for expressive purposes is not . . . absolute"; rather, "the nature and degree of constitutional protection afforded freedom of association may vary depending on the extent to which . . . the constitutionally protected liberty is at stake in a given case." Indeed, the right to associate does not mean "that in every setting in which individuals exercise some discrimination in choosing associates, their selective process of inclusion and exclusion is protected by the Constitution." *New York State Club Assn., Inc. v. City of New York*, 487 U.S. 1, 13 (1988). For example, we have routinely and easily rejected assertions of this right by expressive organizations with discriminatory membership policies, such as private schools,[10] law firms,[11] and labor organizations.[12] In fact, until today, we have never once found a claimed right

direction but does not engage in any homosexual conduct?" Counsel answered: "If that person also were to take the view that the reason they didn't engage in that conduct [was because] it would be morally wrong . . . that person would not be excluded."

10. *Runyon v. McCrary*, 427 U.S. 160, 175–176 (1976) ("The Court has recognized a First Amendment right 'to engage in association for the advancement of beliefs and ideas. . . .' From this principle it may be assumed that parents have a First Amendment right to send their children to educational institutions that promote the belief that racial segregation is desirable, and that the children have an equal right to attend such institutions. But it does not follow that the *practice* of excluding racial minorities from such institutions is also protected by the same principle" (internal citation omitted)).

11. *Hishon v. King & Spalding*, 467 U.S. 69 (1984) ("Respondent argues that application of Title VII in this case would infringe constitutional rights of . . . association. Although we

have recognized that the activities of lawyers may make a 'distinctive contribution . . . to the ideas and beliefs of our society,' respondent has not shown how its ability to fulfill such a function would be inhibited by a requirement that it consider petitioner for partnership on her merits. Moreover, as we have held in another context, 'invidious private discrimination may be characterized as a form of exercising freedom of association protected by the First Amendment, but it has never been accorded affirmative constitutional protections'" (internal citations omitted)).

12. *Railway Mail Assn. v. Corsi*, 326 U.S. 88, 93–94 (1945) ("Appellant first contends that [the law prohibiting racial discrimination by labor organizations] interferes with its right of selection to membership. . . . We see no constitutional basis for the contention that a state cannot protect workers from exclusion solely on the basis of race").

to associate in the selection of members to prevail in the face of a State's antidiscrimination law. To the contrary, we have squarely held that a State's antidiscrimination law does not violate a group's right to associate simply because the law conflicts with that group's exclusionary membership policy.

Several principles are made perfectly clear by *Jaycees* and *Rotary Club*. First, to prevail on a claim of expressive association in the face of a State's antidiscrimination law, it is not enough simply to engage in *some kind* of expressive activity. Both the Jaycees and the Rotary Club engaged in expressive activity protected by the First Amendment, yet that fact was not dispositive. Second, it is not enough to adopt an openly avowed exclusionary membership policy. Both the Jaycees and the Rotary Club did that as well. Third, it is not sufficient merely to articulate *some* connection between the group's expressive activities and its exclusionary policy. The Rotary Club, for example, justified its male-only membership policy by pointing to the " 'aspect of fellowship ... that is enjoyed by the [exclusively] male membership' " and by claiming that only with an exclusively male membership could it "operate effectively" in foreign countries. *Rotary Club*.

Rather, in *Jaycees*, we asked whether Minnesota's Human Rights Law requiring the admission of women "imposed any *serious burdens*" on the group's "collective effort on behalf of [its] *shared goals*." (emphases added). Notwithstanding the group's obvious publicly stated exclusionary policy, we did not view the inclusion of women as a "serious burden" on the Jaycees' ability to engage in the protected speech of its choice. The relevant question is whether the mere inclusion of the person at issue would "impose any serious burden," "affect in any significant way," or be "a substantial restraint upon" the organization's "shared goals," "basic goals," or "collective effort to foster beliefs." Accordingly, it is necessary to examine what, exactly, are BSA's shared goals and the degree to which its expressive activities would be burdened, affected, or restrained by including homosexuals.

The evidence before this Court makes it exceptionally clear that BSA has, at most, simply adopted an exclusionary membership policy and has no shared goal of disapproving of homosexuality. BSA's mission statement and federal charter say nothing on the matter; its official membership policy is silent; its Scout Oath and Law—and accompanying definitions—are devoid of any view on the topic; its guidance for Scouts and Scoutmasters on sexuality declare that such matters are "not construed to be Scouting's proper area," but are the province of a Scout's parents and pastor; and BSA's posture respecting religion tolerates a wide variety of views on the issue of homosexuality. Moreover, there is simply no evidence that BSA otherwise teaches anything in this area, or that it instructs Scouts on matters involving homosexuality in ways not conveyed in the Boy Scout or Scoutmaster Handbooks. In short, Boy Scouts of America is simply silent on homosexuality. There is no shared goal or collective effort to foster a belief about homosexuality at all—let alone one that is significantly burdened by admitting homosexuals.

IV

The majority pretermits this entire analysis. It finds that BSA in fact " 'teaches that homosexual conduct is not morally straight.' " This conclusion, remarkably, rests entirely on statements in BSA's briefs. Moreover, the majority insists that we must "give deference to an association's assertions regarding the nature of its expression" and "we must also give deference to an association's view of what would impair its expression." So long as the record "contains written evidence" to support a group's bare assertion, "we need not inquire further." Once the organization "asserts" that it engages in particular expression, "we cannot doubt" the truth of that assertion.

This is an astounding view of the law. I am unaware of any previous instance in which our analysis of the scope of a constitutional right was determined by looking at what a litigant asserts in his or her brief and inquiring no further. It is even more astonishing in the First Amendment area, because, as the majority itself acknowledges, "we are obligated to independently review the factual record." It is an odd form of independent review that consists of deferring entirely to whatever a litigant claims. But the majority insists that our inquiry must be "limited" because "it is not the role of the courts to reject a group's expressed values because they disagree with those values or find them internally inconsistent." ("The Constitution protects [BSA's] ability to control its own message").

There is, of course, a valid concern that a court's independent review may run the risk of paying too little heed to an organization's sincerely held views. But unless one is prepared to turn the right to associate into a free pass out of antidiscrimination laws, an independent inquiry is a necessity. Though the group must show that its expressive activities will be substantially burdened by the State's law, if that law truly has a significant effect on a group's speech, even the subtle speaker will be able to identify that impact.

In this case, no such concern is warranted. It is entirely clear that BSA in fact expresses no clear, unequivocal message burdened by New Jersey's law.

V

Even if BSA's right to associate argument fails, it nonetheless might have a First Amendment right to refrain from including debate and dialogue about homosexuality as part of its mission to instill values in Scouts. It can, for example, advise Scouts who are entering adulthood and have questions about sex to talk "with your parents, religious leaders, teachers, or Scoutmaster," and, in turn, it can direct Scoutmasters who are asked such questions "not undertake to instruct Scouts, in any formalized manner, in the subject of sex and family life" because "it is not construed to be Scouting's proper area." Dale's right to advocate certain beliefs in a public forum or in a private debate does not include a right to advocate these ideas when he is working as a Scoutmaster. And BSA cannot be compelled to include a message about homosexuality among the values it actually chooses to teach its Scouts, if it would prefer to remain silent on that subject.

"[O]ne important manifestation of the principle of free speech is that one who chooses to speak may also decide 'what not to say.' " *Hurley.* Though the majority mistakenly treats this statement as going to the right to associate, it actually refers to a free speech claim. As with the right to associate claim, though, the court is obligated to engage in an independent inquiry into whether the mere inclusion of homosexuals would actually force BSA to proclaim a message it does not want to send.

In its briefs, BSA implies, even if it does not directly argue, that Dale would use his Scoutmaster position as a "bully pulpit" to convey immoral messages to his troop, and therefore his inclusion in the group would compel BSA to include a message it does not want to impart. Even though the majority does not endorse that argument, I think it is important to explain why it lacks merit, before considering the argument the majority does accept.

BSA has not contended, nor does the record support, that Dale had ever advocated a view on homosexuality to his troop before his membership was revoked. Accordingly, BSA's revocation could only have been based on an assumption that he would do so in the future. But the only information BSA had at the time it revoked Dale's membership was a newspaper article describing a seminar at Rutgers University on the topic of homosexual teenagers that Dale attended. The relevant passage reads:

> "James Dale, 19, co-president of the Rutgers University Lesbian Gay Alliance with Sharice Richardson, also 19, said he lived a double life while in high school, pretending to be straight while attending a military academy.

> "He remembers dating girls and even laughing at homophobic jokes while at school, only admitting his homosexuality during his second year at Rutgers.

> " 'I was looking for a role model, someone who was gay and accepting of me,' Dale said, adding he wasn't just seeking sexual experiences, but a community that would take him in and provide him with a support network and friends."

Nothing in that article, however, even remotely suggests that Dale would advocate any views on homosexuality to his troop. The Scoutmaster Handbook instructs Dale, like all Scoutmasters, that sexual issues are not their "proper area," and there is no evidence that Dale had any intention of violating this rule. Indeed, from all accounts Dale was a model Boy Scout and Assistant Scoutmaster up until the day his membership was revoked, and there is no reason to believe that he would suddenly disobey the directives of BSA because of anything he said in the newspaper article.

The majority, though, does not rest its conclusion on the claim that Dale will use his position as a bully pulpit. Rather, it contends that Dale's mere presence among the Boy Scouts will itself force the group to convey a message about homosexuality—even if Dale has no intention of doing so. The majority holds that "the presence of an avowed homosexual and gay rights activist in an assistant scoutmaster's uniform sends a distinct ... message," and, accordingly, BSA is entitled to exclude that message. In particular, "Dale's presence in the Boy Scouts would, at the very least, force the organization to send a message, both to the youth members and the world, that the Boy Scouts accepts homosexual conduct as a legitimate form of behavior."See Brief for Petitioners 24 ("By donning the uniform of an adult leader in Scouting, he would 'celebrate [his] identity' as an openly gay Scout leader").

The majority's argument relies exclusively on *Hurley v. Irish–American Gay, Lesbian and Bisexual Group of Boston, Inc.*, 515 U.S. 557 (1995). In that case, petitioners John Hurley and the South Boston Allied War Veterans Council ran a privately operated St. Patrick's Day parade. Respondent, an organization known as "GLIB," represented a contingent of gays, lesbians, and bisexuals who sought to march in the petitioners' parade "as a way to express pride in their Irish heritage as openly gay, lesbian, and bisexual individuals." When the parade organizers refused GLIB's admission, GLIB brought suit under Massachusetts' antidiscrimination law. That statute, like New Jersey's law, prohibited discrimination on account of sexual orientation in any place of public accommodation, which the state courts interpreted to include the parade. Petitioners argued that forcing them to include GLIB in their parade would violate their free speech rights.

We agreed. We first pointed out that the St. Patrick's Day parade—like most every parade—is an inherently expressive undertaking. Next, we reaffirmed that the government may not compel anyone to proclaim a belief with which he or she disagrees. We then found that GLIB's marching in the parade would be an expressive act suggesting the view "that people of their sexual orientations have as much claim to unqualified social acceptance as heterosexuals." Finally, we held that GLIB's participation in the parade "would likely be perceived" as the parade organizers' own speech—or at least as a view which they approved—because of a parade organizer's customary control over who marches in the parade. Though *Hurley* has a superficial similarity to the present case, a close inspection reveals a wide gulf between that case and the one before us today.

First, it was critical to our analysis that GLIB was actually conveying a message by participating in the parade—otherwise, the parade organizers could hardly claim that they were being forced to include any unwanted message at all. Our conclusion that GLIB was conveying a message was inextricably tied to the fact that GLIB wanted to march in a parade, as well as the manner in which it intended to march. We noted the "inherent expressiveness of marching [in a parade] to make a point," and in particular that GLIB was formed for the purpose of making a particular point about gay pride. More specifically, GLIB "distributed a fact sheet describing the members' intentions" and, in a previous parade, had "marched behind a shamrock-strewn banner with the simple inscription 'Irish American Gay, Lesbian and Bisexual Group of Boston.'" "[A] contingent marching behind the organization's banner," we said, would clearly convey a message. Indeed, we expressly distinguished between the members of GLIB, who marched as a unit to express their views about their own sexual orientation, on the one hand, and homosexuals who might participate as individuals in the parade without intending to express anything about their sexuality by doing so.

Second, we found it relevant that GLIB's message "would likely be perceived" as the parade organizers' own speech. That was so because "parades and demonstrations ... are not understood to be so neutrally presented or selectively viewed" as, say, a broadcast by a cable operator, who is usually considered to be "merely 'a conduit' for the speech" produced by others. Rather, parade organizers are usually understood to make the "customary determination about a unit admitted to the parade."

Dale's inclusion in the Boy Scouts is nothing like the case in *Hurley*. His participation sends no cognizable message to the Scouts or to the world. Unlike GLIB, Dale did not carry a banner or a sign; he did not distribute any fact sheet; and he expressed no intent to send any message. If there is any kind of message being sent, then, it is by the mere act of joining the Boy Scouts. Such an act does not constitute an instance of symbolic speech under the First Amendment.[21]

It is true, of course, that some acts are so imbued with symbolic meaning that they qualify as "speech" under the First Amendment. See *United States v. O'Brien*. At the same time, however, "we cannot accept the view that an apparently limitless variety of conduct can be labeled 'speech' whenever the person engaging in the conduct intends thereby to express an idea." Though participating in the Scouts could itself conceivably send a message on some level, it is not the kind of act that we have recognized as speech. See *Dallas v. Stanglin*, 490 U.S. 19 (1989).[22] Indeed, if merely joining a group did constitute symbolic speech; and such speech were attributable to the group being joined; and that group has the right to exclude that speech (and hence, the right to exclude that person from joining), then the right of free speech effectively becomes a limitless right to exclude for every organization, whether or not it engages in *any* expressive activities. That cannot be, and never has been, the law.

Furthermore, it is not likely that BSA would be understood to send any message, either to Scouts or to the world, simply by admitting someone as a member. Over the years, BSA has generously welcomed over 87 million young Americans into its ranks. In 1992 over one million adults were active BSA members. The notion that an organization of that size and enormous prestige implicitly endorses the views that each of those adults may express in a non-Scouting context is simply mind boggling. Indeed, in this case there is no evidence that the young Scouts in Dale's troop, or members of their families, were even aware of his sexual orientation, either before or after his public statements at Rutgers University.[24] It is equally farfetched to assert that Dale's open declaration of his homosexuality, reported in a local newspaper, will effectively force BSA to send a message to anyone simply because it allows Dale to be an Assistant Scoutmaster. For an Olympic gold medal winner or a Wimbledon tennis champion, being "openly gay" perhaps communicates a message—for example, that openness about one's sexual orientation is more virtuous than concealment; that a homosexual person can be a capable and virtuous person who should be judged like anyone else; and that homosexuality is not immoral—but it certainly does not follow that they necessarily send a message on behalf of the organizations that sponsor the activities in which they excel. The fact that such persons participate in these organizations is not usually construed to convey a message on behalf of those

21. The majority might have argued (but it did not) that Dale had become so publicly and pervasively identified with a position advocating the moral legitimacy of homosexuality (as opposed to just being an individual who openly stated he is gay) that his leadership position in BSA would necessarily amount to using the organization as a conduit for publicizing his position. But as already noted, when BSA expelled Dale, it had nothing to go on beyond the one newspaper article quoted above, and one newspaper article does not convert Dale into a public symbol for a message. BSA simply has not provided a record that establishes the factual premise for this argument.

22. This is not to say that Scouts do not engage in expressive activity. It is only to say that the simple act of joining the Scouts—unlike joining a parade—is not inherently expressive.

24. For John Doe to make a public statement of his sexual orientation to the newspapers may, of course, be a matter of great importance to John Doe. Richard Roe, however, may be much more interested in the weekend weather forecast. Before Dale made his statement at Rutgers, the Scoutmaster of his troop did not know that he was gay.

organizations any more than does the inclusion of women, African–Americans, religious minorities, or any other discrete group.[25] Surely the organizations are not forced by antidiscrimination laws to take any position on the legitimacy of any individual's private beliefs or private conduct.

The State of New Jersey has decided that people who are open and frank about their sexual orientation are entitled to equal access to employment as school teachers, police officers, librarians, athletic coaches, and a host of other jobs filled by citizens who serve as role models for children and adults alike. Dozens of Scout units throughout the State are sponsored by public agencies, such as schools and fire departments, that employ such role models. BSA's affiliation with numerous public agencies that comply with New Jersey's law against discrimination cannot be understood to convey any particular message endorsing or condoning the activities of all these people.

VI

Unfavorable opinions about homosexuals "have ancient roots." *Bowers v. Hardwick*, 478 U.S. 186, 192 (1986). Like equally atavistic opinions about certain racial groups, those roots have been nourished by sectarian doctrine. Over the years, however, interaction with real people, rather than mere adherence to traditional ways of thinking about members of unfamiliar classes, have modified those opinions. A few examples: The American Psychiatric Association's and the American Psychological Association's removal of "homosexuality" from their lists of mental disorders; a move toward greater understanding within some religious communities; Justice Blackmun's classic opinion in *Bowers*; Georgia's invalidation of the statute upheld in *Bowers*;[31] and New Jersey's enactment of the provision at issue in this case. Indeed, the past month alone has witnessed some remarkable changes in attitudes about homosexuals.[32]

That such prejudices are still prevalent and that they have caused serious and tangible harm to countless members of the class New Jersey seeks to protect are established matters of fact that neither the Boy Scouts nor the Court disputes. That harm can only be aggravated by the creation of a constitutional shield for a policy that is itself the product of a habitual way of thinking about strangers. As Justice Brandeis so wisely advised, "we must be ever on our guard, lest we erect our prejudices into legal principles."

If we would guide by the light of reason, we must let our minds be bold. I respectfully dissent.

JUSTICE SOUTER, with whom JUSTICE GINSBURG and JUSTICE BREYER join, dissenting.

25. The majority simply announces, without analysis, that Dale's participation alone would "force the organization to send a message." "But ... these are merely conclusory words, barren of analysis.... For First Amendment principles to be implicated, the State must place the citizen in the position of either apparently or actually 'asserting as true' the message." *Wooley v. Maynard*, 430 U.S. 705, 721 (1977) (REHNQUIST, J., dissenting).

31. *Powell v. State*, 270 Ga. 327, 510 S. E. 2d 18 (1998).

32. See, *e.g.*, Bradsher, Big Carmakers Extend Benefits to Gay Couples, New York Times, June 9, 2000, p. C1; Marquis, Gay Pride Day is Observed By About 60 C. I. A. Workers, New York Times, June 9, 2000, p. A26; Zernike, Gay Couples are Accepted as Role Models at Exeter, New York Times, June 12, 2000, p. A18.

I join JUSTICE STEVENS's dissent but add this further word on the significance of Part VI of his opinion. There, JUSTICE STEVENS describes the changing attitudes toward gay people and notes a parallel with the decline of stereotypical thinking about race and gender. The legitimacy of New Jersey's interest in forbidding discrimination on all these bases by those furnishing public accommodations is, as JUSTICE STEVENS indicates, acknowledged by many to be beyond question. The fact that we are cognizant of this laudable decline in stereotypical thinking on homosexuality should not, however, be taken to control the resolution of this case.

Boy Scouts of America (BSA) is entitled, consistently with its own tenets and the open doors of American courts, to raise a federal constitutional basis for resisting the application of New Jersey's law. BSA has done that and has chosen to defend against enforcement of the state public accommodations law on the ground that the First Amendment protects expressive association: individuals have a right to join together to advocate opinions free from government interference. BSA has disclaimed any argument that Dale's past or future actions, as distinct from his unapologetic declaration of sexual orientation, would justify his exclusion from BSA.

The right of expressive association does not, of course, turn on the popularity of the views advanced by a group that claims protection. Whether the group appears to this Court to be in the vanguard or rearguard of social thinking is irrelevant to the group's rights. I conclude that BSA has not made out an expressive association claim, therefore, not because of what BSA may espouse, but because of its failure to make sexual orientation the subject of any unequivocal advocacy, using the channels it customarily employs to state its message. As JUSTICE STEVENS explains, no group can claim a right of expressive association without identifying a clear position to be advocated over time in an unequivocal way. To require less, and to allow exemption from a public accommodations statute based on any individual's difference from an alleged group ideal, however expressed and however inconsistently claimed, would convert the right of expressive association into an easy trump of any antidiscrimination law.[1]

If, on the other hand, an expressive association claim has met the conditions JUSTICE STEVENS describes as necessary, there may well be circumstances in which the antidiscrimination law must yield, as he says. It is certainly possible for an individual to become so identified with a position as to epitomize it publicly. When that position is at odds with a group's advocated position, applying an antidiscrimination statute to require the group's acceptance of the individual in a position of group leadership could so modify or muddle or frustrate the group's advocacy as to violate the expressive associational right. While it is not our business here to rule on any such hypothetical, it is at least clear that our estimate of the progressive character of the group's position will be irrelevant to the First Amendment analysis if such a case comes to us for decision.

---

1. An expressive association claim is in this respect unlike a basic free speech claim, as JUSTICE STEVENS points out; the later claim, *i.e.* the right to convey an individual's or group's position, if bona fide, may be taken at face value in applying the First Amendment. This case is thus unlike *Hurley v. Irish–American Gay, Lesbian and Bisexual Group of Boston, Inc.*, 515 U.S. 557 (1995).

QUESTIONS AND NOTES

1. Does retaining Dale as an Assistant Scoutmaster convey any message that the Boy Scouts don't wish to convey? What is the message?

2. Who should answer question 1? New Jersey? The Supreme Court? The Boy Scouts?

3. Are the Boy Scouts more like the Jaycees (who had no right to exclude women from club) or like the organizer of the parade in *Hurley* (right to exclude GLIB)? What does Rehnquist say? What does Stevens say? What would you say? Why?

4. Would (should) *Boy Scouts* be decided the same, if its policy called for excluding professed Atheists? Affirmative action supporters? People of a mixed-race descent? African–Americans? Explain.

5. Would (should) the case be decided the same if Dale were a twelve year old Boy Scout as opposed to a leader? Why? Why not?

Chapter VII

PRIOR RESTRAINTS

D. PRIOR RESTRAINT AND OBSCENITY

Insert p. 739 after *Freedman v. Maryland*

On *Thomas v. Chicago Park Dist.*, 534 U.S. 316 (2002):

"The Court unanimously held that *Freedman* does not apply to a content-neutral licensing scheme."

Chapter VIII

THE GOVERNMENT AS EDUCATOR
AND THE FIRST AMENDMENT

B. SUPPORT OF THE ARTS

Insert p. 817

Although usually arising in the high school context, the government as an educator issues can also arise in the university setting. It did so in *Southworth*.

BOARD OF REGENTS v. SOUTHWORTH
529 U.S. 217, 120 S.Ct. 1346 (2000).

JUSTICE KENNEDY delivered the opinion of the Court.

For the second time in recent years we consider constitutional questions arising from a program designed to facilitate extracurricular student speech at a public university. Respondents are a group of students at the University of Wisconsin. They brought a First Amendment challenge to a mandatory student activity fee imposed by petitioner Board of Regents of the University of Wisconsin and used in part by the University to support student organizations engaging in political or ideological speech. Respondents object to the speech and expression of some of the student organizations. Relying upon our precedents which protect members of unions and bar associations from being required to pay fees used for speech the members find objectionable, both the District Court and the Court of Appeals invalidated the University's student fee program. The University contends that its mandatory student activity fee and the speech which it supports are appropriate to further its educational mission.

We reverse. The First Amendment permits a public university to charge its students an activity fee used to fund a program to facilitate extracurricular student speech if the program is viewpoint neutral. We do not sustain, however, the student referendum mechanism of the University's program, which appears to permit the exaction of fees in violation of the viewpoint neutrality principle. As to that aspect of the program, we remand for further proceedings.

State law defines the University's mission in broad terms: "to develop human resources, to discover and disseminate knowledge, to extend knowledge and its application beyond the boundaries of its campuses and to serve and stimulate society by developing in students heightened intellectual, cultural and humane sensitivities . . . and a sense of purpose."

The responsibility for governing the University of Wisconsin System is vested by law with the board of regents. The same law empowers the students to share in aspects of the University's governance. One of those functions is to administer the student activities fee program. By statute the "students in consultation with the chancellor and subject to the final confirmation of the board [of regents] shall have the responsibility for the disposition of those student fees which constitute substantial support for campus student activities." The students do so, in large measure, through their student government, called the Associated Students of Madison (ASM), and various ASM subcommittees. The program the University maintains to support the extracurricular activities undertaken by many of its student organizations is the subject of the present controversy.

It seems that since its founding the University has required full-time students enrolled at its Madison campus to pay a nonrefundable activity fee. For the 1995–1996 academic year, when this suit was commenced, the activity fee amounted to $331.50 per year. The fee is segregated from the University's tuition charge. Once collected, the activity fees are deposited by the University into the accounts of the State of Wisconsin. The fees are drawn upon by the University to support various campus services and extracurricular student activities. In the University's view, the activity fees "enhance the educational experience" of its students by "promoting extracurricular activities," "stimulating advocacy and debate on diverse points of view," enabling "participation in political activity," "promoting student participation in campus administrative activity," and providing "opportunities to develop social skills," all consistent with the University's mission.

The board of regents classifies the segregated fee into allocable and nonallocable portions. The nonallocable portion approximates 80% of the total fee and covers expenses such as student health services, intramural sports, debt service, and the upkeep and operations of the student union facilities. Respondents did not challenge the purposes to which the University commits the nonallocable portion of the segregated fee.

The allocable portion of the fee supports extracurricular endeavors pursued by the University's registered student organizations or RSO's. To qualify for RSO status students must organize as a not-for-profit group, limit membership primarily to students, and agree to undertake activities related to student life on campus. During the 1995–1996 school year, 623 groups had RSO status on the Madison campus. To name but a few, RSO's included the Future Financial Gurus of America; the International Socialist Organization; the College Democrats; the College Republicans; and the American Civil Liberties Union Campus Chapter. As one would expect, the expressive activities undertaken by RSO's are diverse in range and content, from displaying posters and circulating newsletters throughout the campus, to hosting campus debates and guest speakers, and to what can best be described as political lobbying.

RSO's may obtain a portion of the allocable fees in one of three ways. Most do so by seeking funding from the Student Government Activity Fund

(SGAF), administered by the ASM. SGAF moneys may be issued to support an RSO's operations and events, as well as travel expenses "central to the purpose of the organization." As an alternative, an RSO can apply for funding from the General Student Services Fund (GSSF), administered through the ASM's finance committee. During the 1995–1996 academic year, 15 RSO's received GSSF funding. These RSO's included a campus tutoring center, the student radio station, a student environmental group, a gay and bisexual student center, a community legal office, an AIDS support network, a campus women's center, and the Wisconsin Student Public Interest Research Group (WISPIRG). The University acknowledges that, in addition to providing campus services (*e.g.,* tutoring and counseling), the GSSF-funded RSO's engage in political and ideological expression.

The GSSF, as well as the SGAF, consists of moneys originating in the allocable portion of the mandatory fee. The parties have stipulated that, with respect to SGAF and GSSF funding, "the process for reviewing and approving allocations for funding is administered in a viewpoint-neutral fashion," and that the University does not use the fee program for "advocating a particular point of view."

A student referendum provides a third means for an RSO to obtain funding. While the record is sparse on this feature of the University's program, the parties inform us that the student body can vote either to approve or to disapprove an assessment for a particular RSO. One referendum resulted in an allocation of $45,000 to WISPIRG during the 1995–1996 academic year. At oral argument, counsel for the University acknowledged that a referendum could also operate to defund an RSO or to veto a funding decision of the ASM. In October 1996, for example, the student body voted to terminate funding to a national student organization to which the University belonged. Both parties confirmed at oral argument that their stipulation regarding the program's viewpoint neutrality does not extend to the referendum process.

In March 1996, respondents, each of whom attended or still attend the University's Madison campus, filed suit in the United States District Court for the Western District of Wisconsin against members of the board of regents. Respondents alleged, *inter alia*, that imposition of the segregated fee violated their rights of free speech, free association, and free exercise under the First Amendment. They contended the University must grant them the choice not to fund those RSO's that engage in political and ideological expression offensive to their personal beliefs. Respondents requested both injunctive and declaratory relief.

II

The University of Wisconsin exacts the fee at issue for the sole purpose of facilitating the free and open exchange of ideas by, and among, its students. We conclude the objecting students may insist upon certain safeguards with respect to the expressive activities which they are required to support. Our public forum cases are instructive here by close analogy. This is true even though the student activities fund is not a public forum in the traditional sense of the term and despite the circumstance that those cases most often involve a demand for access, not a claim to be exempt from supporting speech.

The standard of viewpoint neutrality found in the public forum cases provides the standard we find controlling. We decide that the viewpoint neutrality requirement of the University program is in general sufficient to protect the rights of the objecting students. The student referendum aspect of the program for funding speech and expressive activities, however, appears to be inconsistent with the viewpoint neutrality requirement.

We must begin by recognizing that the complaining students are being required to pay fees which are subsidies for speech they find objectionable, even offensive. The *Abood* and *Keller* cases, then, provide the beginning point for our analysis. *Abood v. Detroit Bd. of Ed.*, 431 U.S. 209 (1977); *Keller v. State Bar of Cal.*, 496 U.S. 1 (1990). While those precedents identify the interests of the protesting students, the means of implementing First Amendment protections adopted in those decisions are neither applicable nor workable in the context of extracurricular student speech at a university.

In *Abood*, some nonunion public school teachers challenged an agreement requiring them, as a condition of their employment, to pay a service fee equal in amount to union dues. The objecting teachers alleged that the union's use of their fees to engage in political speech violated their freedom of association guaranteed by the First and Fourteenth Amendments. The Court agreed and held that any objecting teacher could "prevent the Union's spending a part of their required service fees to contribute to political candidates and to express political views unrelated to its duties as exclusive bargaining representative." The principles outlined in *Abood* provided the foundation for our later decision in *Keller*. There we held that lawyers admitted to practice in California could be required to join a state bar association and to fund activities "germane" to the association's mission of "regulating the legal profession and improving the quality of legal services." The lawyers could not, however, be required to fund the bar association's own political expression.

The proposition that students who attend the University cannot be required to pay subsidies for the speech of other students without some First Amendment protection follows from the *Abood* and *Keller* cases. Students enroll in public universities to seek fulfillment of their personal aspirations and of their own potential. If the University conditions the opportunity to receive a college education, an opportunity comparable in importance to joining a labor union or bar association, on an agreement to support objectionable, extracurricular expression by other students, the rights acknowledged in *Abood* and *Keller* become implicated. It infringes on the speech and beliefs of the individual to be required, by this mandatory student activity fee program, to pay subsidies for the objectionable speech of others without any recognition of the State's corresponding duty to him or her. Yet recognition must be given as well to the important and substantial purposes of the University, which seeks to facilitate a wide range of speech.

In *Abood* and *Keller* the constitutional rule took the form of limiting the required subsidy to speech germane to the purposes of the union or bar association. The standard of germane speech as applied to student speech at a university is unworkable, however, and gives insufficient protection both to the objecting students and to the University program itself. Even in the context of a labor union, whose functions are, or so we might have thought, well known and understood by the law and the courts after a long history of government regulation and judicial involvement, we have encountered difficulties in deciding what is germane and what is not. The difficulty manifested itself in our decision in *Lehnert v. Ferris Faculty Assn.*, 500 U.S. 507 (1991), where different members of the Court reached varying conclusions regarding what expressive activity was or was not germane to the mission of the association. If it is difficult to define germane speech with ease or precision where a union or bar association is the party, the standard becomes all the more unmanageable in the public university setting, particularly where the State undertakes to stimulate the whole universe of speech and ideas.

The speech the University seeks to encourage in the program before us is distinguished not by discernable limits but by its vast, unexplored bounds. To insist upon asking what speech is germane would be contrary to the very goal the University seeks to pursue. It is not for the Court to say what is or is not germane to the ideas to be pursued in an institution of higher learning.

Just as the vast extent of permitted expression makes the test of germane speech inappropriate for intervention, so too does it underscore the high potential for intrusion on the First Amendment rights of the objecting students. It is all but inevitable that the fees will result in subsidies to speech which some students find objectionable and offensive to their personal beliefs. If the standard of germane speech is inapplicable, then, it might be argued the remedy is to allow each student to list those causes which he or she will or will not support. If a university decided that its students' First Amendment interests were better protected by some type of optional or refund system it would be free to do so. We decline to impose a system of that sort as a constitutional requirement, however. The restriction could be so disruptive and expensive that the program to support extracurricular speech would be ineffective. The First Amendment does not require the University to put the program at risk.

The University may determine that its mission is well served if students have the means to engage in dynamic discussions of philosophical, religious, scientific, social, and political subjects in their extracurricular campus life outside the lecture hall. If the University reaches this conclusion, it is entitled to impose a mandatory fee to sustain an open dialogue to these ends.

The University must provide some protection to its students' First Amendment interests, however. The proper measure, and the principal standard of protection for objecting students, we conclude, is the requirement of viewpoint neutrality in the allocation of funding support. Viewpoint neutrality was the obligation to which we gave substance in *Rosenberger v. Rector and Visitors of Univ. of Va.*, 515 U.S. 819 (1995). There the University of Virginia feared that any association with a student newspaper advancing religious viewpoints would violate the Establishment Clause. We rejected the argument, holding that the school's adherence to a rule of viewpoint neutrality in administering its student fee program would prevent "any mistaken impression that the student newspapers speak for the University." While *Rosenberger* was concerned with the rights a student has to use an extracurricular speech program already in place, today's case considers the antecedent question, acknowledged but unresolved in *Rosenberger*: whether a public university may require its students to pay a fee which creates the mechanism for the extracurricular speech in the first instance. When a university requires its students to pay fees to support the extracurricular speech of other students, all in the interest of open discussion, it may not prefer some viewpoints to others. There is symmetry then in our holding here and in *Rosenberger*: Viewpoint neutrality is the justification for requiring the student to pay the fee in the first instance and for ensuring the integrity of the program's operation once the funds have been collected. We conclude that the University of Wisconsin may sustain the extracurricular dimensions of its programs by using mandatory student fees with viewpoint neutrality as the operational principle.

The parties have stipulated that the program the University has developed to stimulate extracurricular student expression respects the principle of viewpoint neutrality. If the stipulation is to continue to control the case, the University's program in its basic structure must be found consistent with the First Amendment.

We make no distinction between campus activities and the off-campus expressive activities of objectionable RSO's. Those activities, respondents tell us, often bear no relationship to the University's reason for imposing the segregated fee in the first instance, to foster vibrant campus debate among students. If the University shares those concerns, it is free to enact viewpoint neutral rules restricting off-campus travel or other expenditures by RSO's, for it may create what is tantamount to a limited public forum if the principles of viewpoint neutrality are respected. We find no principled way, however, to impose upon the University, as a constitutional matter, a requirement to adopt geographic or spatial restrictions as a condition for RSOs' entitlement to reimbursement. Universities possess significant interests in encouraging students to take advantage of the social, civic, cultural, and religious opportunities available in surrounding communities and throughout the country. Universities, like all of society, are finding that traditional conceptions of territorial boundaries are difficult to insist upon in an age marked by revolutionary changes in communications, information transfer, and the means of discourse. If the rule of viewpoint neutrality is respected, our holding affords the University latitude to adjust its extracurricular student speech program to accommodate these advances and opportunities.

III

It remains to discuss the referendum aspect of the University's program. While the record is not well developed on the point, it appears that by majority vote of the student body a given RSO may be funded or defunded. It is unclear to us what protection, if any, there is for viewpoint neutrality in this part of the process. To the extent the referendum substitutes majority determinations for viewpoint neutrality it would undermine the constitutional protection the program requires. The whole theory of viewpoint neutrality is that minority views are treated with the same respect as are majority views. Access to a public forum, for instance, does not depend upon majoritarian consent. That principle is controlling here. A remand is necessary and appropriate to resolve this point; and the case in all events must be reexamined in light of the principles we have discussed.

The judgment of the Court of Appeals is reversed, and the case is remanded for further proceedings consistent with this opinion. In this Court the parties shall bear their own costs.

It is so ordered

JUSTICE SOUTER, with whom JUSTICE STEVENS and JUSTICE BREYER join, concurring in the judgment.

The majority today validates the University's student activity fee after recognizing a new category of First Amendment interests and a new standard of viewpoint neutrality protection. I agree that the University's scheme is permissible, but do not believe that the Court should take the occasion to impose a cast-iron viewpoint neutrality requirement to uphold it. Instead, I would hold that the First Amendment interest claimed by the student respondents (hereinafter Southworth) here is simply insufficient to merit protection by anything more than the viewpoint neutrality already accorded by the University, and I would go no further.[2]

The parties have stipulated that the grant scheme is administered on a viewpoint neutral basis, and like the majority I take the case on that assumption. The question before us is thus properly cast not as whether viewpoint neutrality is required, but whether Southworth has a claim to relief from this specific viewpoint neutral scheme.[4] Two sources of law might be considered in answering this question.

The first comprises First Amendment and related cases grouped under the umbrella of academic freedom. Such law might be implicated by the University's proffered rationale, that the grant scheme funded by the student activity fee is an integral element in the discharge of its educational mission (excerpt from Dean of Students Office Student Organization Handbook noting that the activities of student groups constitute a " 'second curriculum' "); (statement of Associate Dean of Students of the UW–Madison noting academic importance of funding scheme). Our understanding of academic freedom has included not merely liberty from restraints on thought, expression, and association in the academy, but also the idea that universities and schools should have the freedom to make decisions about how and what to teach. In *Regents of Univ. of Mich. v. Ewing*, 474 U.S. 214 (1985), we recognized these related conceptions: "Academic freedom thrives not only on the independent and uninhibited exchange of ideas among teachers and students, but also, and somewhat inconsistently, on autonomous decisionmaking by the academy itself." Some of the opinions in our books emphasize broad conceptions of academic freedom that if accepted by the Court might seem to clothe the University with an immunity to any challenge to regulations made or obligations imposed in the discharge of its educational mission These broad statements on academic freedom do not dispose of the case here, however. *Ewing* addressed not the relationship between academic freedom and First

2. Under its own reasoning, the majority need not reach the question whether viewpoint neutrality is required to decide this case. The University program required viewpoint neutrality, and both parties have stipulated that the funds are disbursed accordingly. If viewpoint neutrality is a sufficient condition, the majority could uphold the scheme here on that limited ground without deciding whether it is a necessary one.

4. Our university cases have dealt with restrictions imposed from outside the academy on individual teachers' speech or associations, and cases dealing with the right of teaching institutions to limit expressive freedom of students have been confined to high schools, *Hazelwood School Dist. v. Kuhlmeier, Bethel School Dist. No. 403 v. Fraser, Tinker v. Des Moines Independent Community School Dist.*, whose students and their schools' relation to them are different and at least arguably distinguishable from their counterparts in college education.

Amendment burdens imposed by a university, but a due process challenge to a university's academic decisions, while as to them the case stopped short of recognizing absolute autonomy. Our other cases on academic freedom thus far have dealt with more limited subjects, and do not compel the conclusion that the objecting university student is without a First Amendment claim here. While we have spoken in terms of a wide protection for the academic freedom and autonomy that bars legislatures (and courts) from imposing conditions on the spectrum of subjects taught and viewpoints expressed in college teaching (as the majority recognizes), we have never held that universities lie entirely beyond the reach of students' First Amendment rights. Thus our prior cases do not go so far as to control the result in this one, and going beyond those cases would be out of order, simply because the University has not litigated on grounds of academic freedom. As to that freedom and university autonomy, then, it is enough to say that protecting a university's discretion to shape its educational mission may prove to be an important consideration in First Amendment analysis of objections to student fees.The second avenue for addressing Southworth's claim to a pro rata refund or the total abolition of the student activity fee is to see how closely the circumstances here resemble instances of governmental speech mandates found to require relief. As a threshold matter, it is plain that this case falls far afield of those involving compelled or controlled speech, apart from subsidy schemes. Indirectly transmitting a fraction of a student activity fee to an organization with an offensive message is in no sense equivalent to restricting or modifying the message a student wishes to express. Cf. *Hurley v. Irish–American Gay, Lesbian and Bisexual Group of Boston, Inc.*, 515 U.S. 557 (1995). Nor does it require an individual to bear an offensive statement personally, as in *Wooley v. Maynard*, 430 U.S. 705 (1977), let alone to affirm a moral or political commitment, as in *West Virginia Bd. of Ed. v. Barnette*. In each of these cases, the government was imposing far more directly and offensively on an objecting individual than collecting the fee that indirectly funds the jumble of other speakers' messages in this case.

Next, I agree with the majority that the *Abood* and *Keller* line of cases does not control the remedy here, the situation of the students being significantly different from that of union or bar association members.

Finally, the weakness of Southworth's claim is underscored by its setting within a university, whose students are inevitably required to support the expression of personally offensive viewpoints in ways that cannot be thought constitutionally objectionable unless one is prepared to deny the University its choice over what to teach. No one disputes that some fraction of students' tuition payments may be used for course offerings that are ideologically offensive to some students, and for paying professors who say things in the university forum that are radically at odds with the politics of particular students. Least of all does anyone claim that the University is somehow required to offer a spectrum of courses to satisfy a viewpoint neutrality requirement. See *Rosenberger* (SOUTER, J., dissenting). The University need not provide junior years abroad in North Korea as well as France, instruct in the theory of plutocracy as well as democracy, or teach Nietzsche as well as St. Thomas. Since uses of tuition payments (not optional for anyone who wishes to stay in college) may fund offensive speech far more obviously than the student activity fee does, it is difficult to see how the activity fee could present a stronger argument for a refund.

In sum, I see no basis to provide relief from the scheme being administered, would go no further, and respectfully concur in the judgment.

QUESTIONS AND NOTES

1. Is the Court holding that college students have fewer First Amendment rights than teachers or lawyers? If not, what is it holding? Explain.

2. If the plaintiffs had prevailed, could the University have continued to support the same programs? How? Why not?

3. What is wrong with the election process? Is the Court opposed to democracy? Cf. *Santa Fe v. Doe* (Next case in this supplement).

4. How, if at all, does Justice Souter's opinion differ from that of the Court? Had you been on the Court, which, if either, would you have joined? Explain.

Chapter IX

ESTABLISHMENT CLAUSE

C. RETURN TO THE SCHOOLS

Insert p. 1002 (First Amendment) p. 165 (Religion and the Constitution)

By the spring of 2000, the Court began showing some impatience with the various ingenious methods of returning prayer to the schools.

SANTA FE INDEPENDENT SCHOOL DISTRICT v. DOE

530 U.S. 290 (2000).

JUSTICE STEVENS delivered the opinion of the Court.

Prior to 1995, the Santa Fe High School student who occupied the school's elective office of student council chaplain delivered a prayer over the public address system before each varsity football game for the entire season. This practice, along with others, was challenged in District Court as a violation of the Establishment Clause of the First Amendment. While these proceedings were pending in the District Court, the school district adopted a different policy that permits, but does not require, prayer initiated and led by a student at all home games. The District Court entered an order modifying that policy to permit only nonsectarian, nonproselytizing prayer. The Court of Appeals held that, even as modified by the District Court, the football prayer policy was invalid. We granted the school district's petition for certiorari to review that holding.

I

The Santa Fe Independent School District (District) is a political subdivision of the State of Texas, responsible for the education of more than 4,000 students in a small community in the southern part of the State. The District includes the Santa Fe High School, two primary schools, an intermediate school and the junior high school. Respondents are two sets of current or former students and their respective mothers. One family is Mormon and the other is Catholic. The District Court permitted respondents (Does) to litigate anonymously to protect them from intimidation or harassment.[5]

5. A decision, the Fifth Circuit Court of Appeals noted, that many District officials: "apparently neither agreed with nor particularly respected." About a month after the

201

Respondents commenced this action in April 1995 and moved for a temporary restraining order to prevent the District from violating the Establishment Clause at the imminent graduation exercises. In their complaint the Does alleged that the District had engaged in several proselytizing practices, such as promoting attendance at a Baptist revival meeting, encouraging membership in religious clubs, chastising children who held minority religious beliefs, and distributing Gideon Bibles on school premises. They also alleged that the District allowed students to read Christian invocations and benedictions from the stage at graduation ceremonies,[6] and to deliver overtly Christian prayers over the public address system at home football games.

On May 10, 1995, the District Court entered an interim order addressing a number of different issues.[7] With respect to the impending graduation, the order provided that "non-denominational prayer" consisting of "an invocation and/or benediction" could be presented by a senior student or students selected by members of the graduating class. The text of the prayer was to be determined by the students, without scrutiny or preapproval by school officials. References to particular religious figures "such as Mohammed, Jesus, Buddha, or the like" would be permitted "as long as the general thrust of the prayer is non-proselytizing."

In response to that portion of the order, the District adopted a series of policies over several months dealing with prayer at school functions. The policies enacted in May and July for graduation ceremonies provided the format for the August and October policies for football games. The May policy provided:

complaint was filed, the District Court entered an order that provided, in part:

"[A]ny further attempt on the part of District or school administration, officials, counsellors, teachers, employees or servants of the School District, parents, students or anyone else, overtly or covertly to ferret out the identities of the Plaintiffs in this cause, by means of bogus petitions, questionnaires, individual interrogation, or downright 'snooping', will cease immediately. ANYONE TAKING ANY ACTION ON SCHOOL PROPERTY, DURING SCHOOL HOURS, OR WITH SCHOOL RESOURCES OR APPROVAL FOR PURPOSES OF ATTEMPTING TO ELICIT THE NAMES OR IDENTITIES OF THE PLAINTIFFS IN THIS CAUSE OF ACTION, BY OR ON BEHALF OF ANY OF THESE INDIVIDUALS, WILL FACE THE HARSHEST POSSIBLE CONTEMPT SANCTIONS FROM THIS COURT, AND MAY ADDITIONALLY FACE CRIMINAL LIABILITY. The Court wants these proceedings addressed on their merits, and not on the basis of intimidation or harassment of the participants on either side."

6. At the 1994 graduation ceremony the senior class president delivered this invocation:

"Please bow your heads.

"Dear heavenly Father, thank you for allowing us to gather here safely tonight. We thank you for the wonderful year you have allowed us to spend together as students of Santa Fe. We thank you for our teachers who have devoted many hours to each of us. Thank you, Lord, for our parents and may each one receive the special blessing. We pray also for a blessing and guidance as each student moves forward in the future. Lord, bless this ceremony and give us all a safe journey home. In Jesus' name we pray."

7. For example, it prohibited school officials from endorsing or participating in the baccalaureate ceremony sponsored by the Santa Fe Ministerial Alliance, and ordered the District to establish policies to deal with "manifest First Amendment infractions of teachers, counsellors, or other District or school officials or personnel, such as ridiculing, berating or holding up for inappropriate scrutiny or examination the beliefs of any individual students. Similarly, the School District will establish or clarify existing procedures for excluding overt or covert sectarian and proselytizing religious teaching, such as the use of blatantly denominational religious terms in spelling lessons, denominational religious songs and poems in English or choir classes, denominational religious stories and parables in grammar lessons and the like, while at the same time allowing for frank and open discussion of moral, religious, and societal views and beliefs, which are non-denominational and non-judgmental."

" 'The board has chosen to permit the graduating senior class, with the advice and counsel of the senior class principal or designee, to elect by secret ballot to choose whether an invocation and benediction shall be part of the graduation exercise. If so chosen the class shall elect by secret ballot, from a list of student volunteers, students to deliver nonsectarian, nonproselytizing invocations and benedictions for the purpose of solemnizing their graduation ceremonies.' "

The parties stipulated that after this policy was adopted, "the senior class held an election to determine whether to have an invocation and benediction at the commencement [and that the] class voted, by secret ballot, to include prayer at the high school graduation." In a second vote the class elected two seniors to deliver the invocation and benediction.[8]

In July, the District enacted another policy eliminating the requirement that invocations and benedictions be "nonsectarian and nonproselytising," but also providing that if the District were to be enjoined from enforcing that policy, the May policy would automatically become effective.

The August policy, which was titled "Prayer at Football Games," was similar to the July policy for graduations. It also authorized two student elections, the first to determine whether "invocations" should be delivered, and the second to select the spokesperson to deliver them. Like the July policy, it contained two parts, an initial statement that omitted any requirement that the content of the invocation be "nonsectarian and nonproselytising," and a fallback provision that automatically added that limitation if the preferred policy should be enjoined. On August 31, 1995, according to the parties' stipulation, "the district's high school students voted to determine whether a student would deliver prayer at varsity football games.... The students chose to allow a student to say a prayer at football games." A week later, in a separate election, they selected a student "to deliver the prayer at varsity football games."

The final policy (October policy) is essentially the same as the August policy, though it omits the word "prayer" from its title, and refers to "messages" and "statements" as well as "invocations."[9] It is the validity of that policy that is before us.[10]

---

8. The student giving the invocation thanked the Lord for keeping the class safe through 12 years of school and for gracing their lives with two special people and closed: "Lord, we ask that You keep Your hand upon us during this ceremony and to help us keep You in our hearts through the rest of our lives. In God's name we pray. Amen." The student benediction was similar in content and closed: "Lord, we ask for Your protection as we depart to our next destination and watch over us as we go our separate ways. Grant each of us a safe trip and keep us secure throughout the night. In Your name we pray. Amen."

9. Despite these changes, the school did not conduct another election, under the October policy, to supersede the results of the August policy election.

10. It provides:

"STUDENT ACTIVITIES:

"PRE–GAME CEREMONIES AT FOOTBALL GAMES

"The board has chosen to permit students to deliver a brief invocation and/or message to be delivered during the pre-game ceremonies of home varsity football games to solemnize the event, to promote good sportsmanship and student safety, and to establish the appropriate environment for the competition.

"Upon advice and direction of the high school principal, each spring, the high school student council shall conduct an election, by the high school student body, by secret ballot, to determine whether such a statement or invocation will be a part of the pre-game ceremonies and if so, shall elect a student, from a list of student volunteers, to deliver the statement or invocation. The student volunteer who is selected by his or her classmates may decide

The District Court did enter an order precluding enforcement of the first, open-ended policy. Relying on our decision in *Lee v. Weisman*, it held that the school's "action must not 'coerce anyone to support or participate in' a religious exercise." Applying that test, it concluded that the graduation prayers appealed "to distinctively Christian beliefs,"[11] and that delivering a prayer "over the school's public address system prior to each football and baseball game coerces student participation in religious events." Both parties appealed, the District contending that the enjoined portion of the October policy was permissible and the Does contending that both alternatives violated the Establishment Clause. The Court of Appeals majority agreed with the Does.

We granted the District's petition for certiorari, limited to the following question: "Whether petitioner's policy permitting student-led, student-initiated prayer at football games violates the Establishment Clause." We conclude, as did the Court of Appeals, that it does.

II

The first Clause in the First Amendment to the Federal Constitution provides that "Congress shall make no law respecting an establishment of religion, or prohibiting the free exercise thereof." The Fourteenth Amendment imposes those substantive limitations on the legislative power of the States and their political subdivisions. In *Lee*, we held that a prayer delivered by a rabbi at a middle school graduation ceremony violated that Clause. Although this case involves student prayer at a different type of school function, our analysis is properly guided by the principles that we endorsed in *Lee*.

As we held in that case:

"The principle that government may accommodate the free exercise of religion does not supersede the fundamental limitations imposed by the Establishment Clause. It is beyond dispute that, at a minimum, the Constitution guarantees that government may not coerce anyone to support or participate in religion or its exercise, or otherwise act in a way

what message and/or invocation to deliver, consistent with the goals and purposes of this policy.

"If the District is enjoined by a court order from the enforcement of this policy, then and only then will the following policy automatically become the applicable policy of the school district.

"The board has chosen to permit students to deliver a brief invocation and/or message to be delivered during the pre-game ceremonies of home varsity football games to solemnize the event, to promote good sportsmanship and student safety, and to establish the appropriate environment for the competition.

"Upon advice and direction of the high school principal, each spring, the high school student council shall conduct an election, by the high school student body, by secret ballot, to determine whether such a message or invocation will be a part of the pre-game ceremonies and if so, shall elect a student, from a list of student volunteers, to deliver the statement or invocation. The student volunteer who is selected by his or her classmates may decide what statement or invocation to deliver, consistent with the goals and purposes of this policy. Any message and/or invocation delivered by a student must be nonsectarian and nonproselytizing."

11. "The graduation prayers at issue in the instant case, in contrast, are infused with explicit references to Jesus Christ and otherwise appeal to distinctively Christian beliefs. The Court accordingly finds that use of these prayers during graduation ceremonies, considered in light of the overall manner in which they were delivered, violated the Establishment Clause."

which 'establishes a [state] religion or religious faith, or tends to do so' "
(quoting *Lynch v. Donnelly*).

In this case the District first argues that this principle is inapplicable to
its October policy because the messages are private student speech, not public
speech. It reminds us that "there is a crucial difference between *government*
speech endorsing religion, which the Establishment Clause forbids, and *private* speech endorsing religion, which the Free Speech and Free Exercise
Clauses protect." *Board of Ed. of Westside Community Schools (Dist.66) v.
Mergens*, 496 U.S. 226 (1990). We certainly agree with that distinction, but we
are not persuaded that the pregame invocations should be regarded as
"private speech."

These invocations are authorized by a government policy and take place
on government property at government-sponsored school-related events. Of
course, not every message delivered under such circumstances is the government's own. We have held, for example, that an individual's contribution to a
government-created forum was not government speech. See *Rosenberger v.
Rector and Visitors of Univ. of Va.*, 515 U.S. 819 (1995). Although the District
relies heavily on *Rosenberger* and similar cases involving such forums, it is
clear that the pregame ceremony is not the type of forum discussed in those
cases.[13] The Santa Fe school officials simply do not "evince either 'by policy or
by practice,' any intent to open the [pregame ceremony] to 'indiscriminate
use,' . . . by the student body generally." Rather, the school allows only one
student, the same student for the entire season, to give the invocation. The
statement or invocation, moreover, is subject to particular regulations that
confine the content and topic of the student's message. By comparison, in
Perry Ed. Assn. v. Perry we rejected a claim that the school had created a
limited public forum in its school mail system despite the fact that it had
allowed far more speakers to address a much broader range of topics than the
policy at issue here. As we concluded in *Perry*, "selective access does not
transform government property into a public forum."

Granting only one student access to the stage at a time does not, of
course, necessarily preclude a finding that a school has created a limited
public forum. Here, however, Santa Fe's student election system ensures that
only those messages deemed "appropriate" under the District's policy may be
delivered. That is, the majoritarian process implemented by the District
guarantees, by definition, that minority candidates will never prevail and that
their views will be effectively silenced.

Recently, in *Board of Regents of Univ. of Wis. System v. Southworth*, we
explained why student elections that determine, by majority vote, which
expressive activities shall receive or not receive school benefits are constitutionally problematic:

> "To the extent the referendum substitutes majority determinations for
> viewpoint neutrality it would undermine the constitutional protection the
> program requires. The whole theory of viewpoint neutrality is that

---

13. A conclusion that the District had created a public forum would help shed light on
whether the resulting speech is public or private, but we also note that we have never held
the mere creation of a public forum shields the
government entity from scrutiny under the
Establishment Clause. See, e.g., *Pinette*, [infra]
("I see no necessity to carve out . . . an exception to the endorsement test for the public
forum context").

minority views are treated with the same respect as are majority views. Access to a public forum, for instance, does not depend upon majoritarian consent. That principle is controlling here."

Like the student referendum for funding in *Southworth*, this student election does nothing to protect minority views but rather places the students who hold such views at the mercy of the majority.[15] Because "fundamental rights may not be submitted to vote; they depend on the outcome of no elections," *West Virginia Bd. of Ed. v. Barnette*, the District's elections are insufficient safeguards of diverse student speech.

In *Lee*, the school district made the related argument that its policy of endorsing only "civic or nonsectarian" prayer was acceptable because it minimized the intrusion on the audience as a whole. We rejected that claim by explaining that such a majoritarian policy "does not lessen the offense or isolation to the objectors. At best it narrows their number, at worst increases their sense of isolation and affront." Similarly, while Santa Fe's majoritarian election might ensure that most of the students are represented, it does nothing to protect the minority; indeed, it likely serves to intensify their offense.

Moreover, the District has failed to divorce itself from the religious content in the invocations. It has not succeeded in doing so, either by claiming that its policy is " 'one of neutrality rather than endorsement' " or by characterizing the individual student as the "circuit-breaker" in the process. Contrary to the District's repeated assertions that it has adopted a "hands-off" approach to the pregame invocation, the realities of the situation plainly reveal that its policy involves both perceived and actual endorsement of religion. In this case, as we found in *Lee*, the "degree of school involvement" makes it clear that the pregame prayers bear "the imprint of the State and thus put school-age children who objected in an untenable position."

The District has attempted to disentangle itself from the religious messages by developing the two-step student election process. The text of the October policy, however, exposes the extent of the school's entanglement. The elections take place at all only because the school "board *has chosen to permit* students to deliver a brief invocation and/or message"(emphasis added). The elections thus "shall" be conducted "by the high school student council" and "[u]pon advice and direction of the high school principal." The decision whether to deliver a message is first made by majority vote of the entire student body, followed by a choice of the speaker in a separate, similar majority election. Even though the particular words used by the speaker are not determined by those votes, the policy mandates that the "statement or invocation" be "consistent with the goals and purposes of this policy," which

---

15. If instead of a choice between an invocation and no pregame message, the first election determined whether a political speech should be made, and the second election determined whether the speaker should be a Democrat or a Republican, it would be rather clear that the public address system was being used to deliver a partisan message reflecting the viewpoint of the majority rather than a random statement by a private individual.

The fact that the District's policy provides for the election of the speaker only after the majority has voted on her message identifies an obvious distinction between this case and the typical election of a "student body president, or even a newly elected prom king or queen."

are "to solemnize the event, to promote good sportsmanship and student safety, and to establish the appropriate environment for the competition."

In addition to involving the school in the selection of the speaker, the policy, by its terms, invites and encourages religious messages. The policy itself states that the purpose of the message is "to solemnize the event." A religious message is the most obvious method of solemnizing an event. Moreover, the requirements that the message "promote good citizenship" and "establish the appropriate environment for competition" further narrow the types of message deemed appropriate, suggesting that a solemn, yet nonreligious, message, such as commentary on United States foreign policy, would be prohibited.[18] Indeed, the only type of message that is expressly endorsed in the text is an "invocation"—a term that primarily describes an appeal for divine assistance.[19] In fact, as used in the past at Santa Fe High School, an "invocation" has always entailed a focused religious message. Thus, the expressed purposes of the policy encourage the selection of a religious message, and that is precisely how the students understand the policy. The results of the elections described in the parties' stipulation make it clear that the students understood that the central question before them was whether prayer should be a part of the pregame ceremony. We recognize the important role that public worship plays in many communities, as well as the sincere desire to include public prayer as a part of various occasions so as to mark those occasions' significance. But such religious activity in public schools, as elsewhere, must comport with the First Amendment.

The actual or perceived endorsement of the message, moreover, is established by factors beyond just the text of the policy. Once the student speaker is selected and the message composed, the invocation is then delivered to a large audience assembled as part of a regularly scheduled, school-sponsored function conducted on school property. The message is broadcast over the school's public address system, which remains subject to the control of school officials. It is fair to assume that the pregame ceremony is clothed in the traditional indicia of school sporting events, which generally include not just the team, but also cheerleaders and band members dressed in uniforms sporting the school name and mascot. The school's name is likely written in large print across the field and on banners and flags. The crowd will certainly include many who display the school colors and insignia on their school T-shirts, jackets, or hats and who may also be waving signs displaying the school name. It is in a setting such as this that "[t]he board has chosen to permit" the elected student to rise and give the "statement or invocation."

In this context the members of the listening audience must perceive the pregame message as a public expression of the views of the majority of the student body delivered with the approval of the school administration. In cases involving state participation in a religious activity, one of the relevant questions is "whether an objective observer, acquainted with the text, legislative history, and implementation of the statute, would perceive it as a state

18. THE CHIEF JUSTICE's hypothetical of the student body president asked by the school to introduce a guest speaker with a biography of her accomplishments, obviously would pose no problems under the Establishment Clause.

19. *See, e.g.*, Webster's Third New International Dictionary 1190 (1993) (defining "invocation" as "a prayer of entreaty that is usu[ally] a call for the divine presence and is offered at the beginning of a meeting or service of worship").

endorsement of prayer in public schools." *Wallace* (O'CONNOR, J., concurring in judgment); see also *Capitol Square Review and Advisory Bd. v. Pinette* (O'CONNOR, J., concurring in part and concurring in judgment). Regardless of the listener's support for, or objection to, the message, an objective Santa Fe High School student will unquestionably perceive the inevitable pregame prayer as stamped with her school's seal of approval.

The text and history of this policy, moreover, reinforce our objective student's perception that the prayer is, in actuality, encouraged by the school. When a governmental entity professes a secular purpose for an arguably religious policy, the government's characterization is, of course, entitled to some deference. But it is nonetheless the duty of the courts to "distinguis[h] a sham secular purpose from a sincere one." *Wallace* (O'CONNOR, J., concurring in judgment).

According to the District, the secular purposes of the policy are to "foste[r] free expression of private persons . . . as well [as to] solemniz[e] sporting events, promot[e] good sportsmanship and student safety, and establis[h] an appropriate environment for competition." We note, however, that the District's approval of only one specific kind of message, an "invocation," is not necessary to further any of these purposes. Additionally, the fact that only one student is permitted to give a content-limited message suggests that this policy does little to "foste[r] free expression." Furthermore, regardless of whether one considers a sporting event an appropriate occasion for solemnity, the use of an invocation to foster such solemnity is impermissible when, in actuality, it constitutes prayer sponsored by the school. And it is unclear what type of message would be both appropriately "solemnizing" under the District's policy and yet non-religious.

Most striking to us is the evolution of the current policy from the long-sanctioned office of "Student Chaplain" to the candidly titled "Prayer at Football Games" regulation. This history indicates that the District intended to preserve the practice of prayer before football games. The conclusion that the District viewed the October policy simply as a continuation of the previous policies is dramatically illustrated by the fact that the school did not conduct a new election, pursuant to the current policy, to replace the results of the previous election, which occurred under the former policy. Given these observations, and in light of the school's history of regular delivery of a student-led prayer at athletic events, it is reasonable to infer that the specific purpose of the policy was to preserve a popular "state-sponsored religious practice." *Lee*.

School sponsorship of a religious message is impermissible because it sends the ancillary message to members of the audience who are nonadherents "that they are outsiders, not full members of the political community, and an accompanying message to adherents that they are insiders, favored members of the political community." *Lynch* (O'CONNOR, J., concurring). The delivery of such a message—over the school's public address system, by a speaker representing the student body, under the supervision of school faculty, and pursuant to a school policy that explicitly and implicitly encourages public prayer—is not properly characterized as "private" speech.

III

The District next argues that its football policy is distinguishable from the graduation prayer in *Lee* because it does not coerce students to participate in religious observances. Its argument has two parts: first, that there is no impermissible government coercion because the pregame messages are the product of student choices; and second, that there is really no coercion at all because attendance at an extracurricular event, unlike a graduation ceremony, is voluntary.

The reasons just discussed explaining why the alleged "circuit-breaker" mechanism of the dual elections and student speaker do not turn public speech into private speech also demonstrate why these mechanisms do not insulate the school from the coercive element of the final message. In fact, this aspect of the District's argument exposes anew the concerns that are created by the majoritarian election system. The parties' stipulation clearly states that the issue resolved in the first election was "whether a student would deliver prayer at varsity football games," and the controversy in this case demonstrates that the views of the students are not unanimous on that issue.

One of the purposes served by the Establishment Clause is to remove debate over this kind of issue from governmental supervision or control. We explained in *Lee* that the "preservation and transmission of religious beliefs and worship is a responsibility and a choice committed to the private sphere." The two student elections authorized by the policy, coupled with the debates that presumably must precede each, impermissibly invade that private sphere. The election mechanism, when considered in light of the history in which the policy in question evolved, reflects a device the District put in place that determines whether religious messages will be delivered at home football games. The mechanism encourages divisiveness along religious lines in a public school setting, a result at odds with the Establishment Clause. Although it is true that the ultimate choice of student speaker is "attributable to the students," the District's decision to hold the constitutionally problematic election is clearly "a choice attributable to the State." *Lee*.

The District further argues that attendance at the commencement ceremonies at issue in *Lee* "differs dramatically" from attendance at high school football games, which it contends "are of no more than passing interest to many students" and are "decidedly extracurricular," thus dissipating any coercion. Attendance at a high school football game, unlike showing up for class, is certainly not required in order to receive a diploma. Moreover, we may assume that the District is correct in arguing that the informal pressure to attend an athletic event is not as strong as a senior's desire to attend her own graduation ceremony.

There are some students, however, such as cheerleaders, members of the band, and, of course, the team members themselves, for whom seasonal commitments mandate their attendance, sometimes for class credit. The District also minimizes the importance to many students of attending and participating in extracurricular activities as part of a complete educational experience. As we noted in *Lee*, "[l]aw reaches past formalism." To assert that high school students do not feel immense social pressure, or have a truly genuine desire, to be involved in the extracurricular event that is American high school football is "formalistic in the extreme." We stressed in *Lee* the obvious observation that "adolescents are often susceptible to pressure from their peers towards conformity, and that the influence is strongest in matters of social convention." High school home football games are traditional gatherings of a school community; they bring together students and faculty as well as friends and family from years present and past to root for a common cause. Undoubtedly, the games are not important to some students, and they voluntarily choose not to attend. For many others, however, the choice between whether to attend these games or to risk facing a personally offensive religious ritual is in no practical sense an easy one. The Constitution, moreover, demands that the school may not force this difficult choice upon these students for "[i]t is a tenet of the First Amendment that the State cannot require one of its citizens to forfeit his or her rights and benefits as the price of resisting conformance to state-sponsored religious practice."

Even if we regard every high school student's decision to attend a home football game as purely voluntary, we are nevertheless persuaded that the delivery of a pregame prayer has the improper effect of coercing those present to participate in an act of religious worship. For "the government may no more use social pressure to enforce orthodoxy than it may use more direct means." As in *Lee*, "[w]hat to most believers may seem nothing more than a reasonable request that the nonbeliever respect their religious practices, in a school context may appear to the nonbeliever or dissenter to be an attempt to employ the machinery of the State to enforce a religious orthodoxy." The constitutional command will not permit the District "to exact religious conformity from a student as the price" of joining her classmates at a varsity football game.

The Religion Clauses of the First Amendment prevent the government from making any law respecting the establishment of religion or prohibiting the free exercise thereof. By no means do these commands impose a prohibition on all religious activity in our public schools. Indeed, the common purpose of the Religion Clauses "is to secure religious liberty" *Engel v. Vitale*. Thus, nothing in the Constitution as interpreted by this Court prohibits any public school student from voluntarily praying at any time before, during, or after the schoolday. But the religious liberty protected by the Constitution is abridged when the State affirmatively sponsors the particular religious practice of prayer.

IV

Finally, the District argues repeatedly that the Does have made a premature facial challenge to the October policy that necessarily must fail. The District emphasizes, quite correctly, that until a student actually delivers a solemnizing message under the latest version of the policy, there can be no certainty that any of the statements or invocations will be religious. Thus, it concludes, the October policy necessarily survives a facial challenge.

This argument, however, assumes that we are concerned only with the serious constitutional injury that occurs when a student is forced to participate in an act of religious worship because she chooses to attend a school event. But the Constitution also requires that we keep in mind "the myriad, subtle ways in which Establishment Clause values can be eroded," *Lynch* (O'CONNOR, J., concurring), and that we guard against other different, yet equally important, constitutional injuries. One is the mere passage by the District of a policy that has the purpose and perception of government establishment of religion. Another is the implementation of a governmental electoral process that subjects the issue of prayer to a majoritarian vote.

The District argues that the facial challenge must fail because "Santa Fe's Football Policy cannot be invalidated on the basis of some 'possibility or even likelihood' of an unconstitutional application." Our Establishment Clause cases involving facial challenges, however, have not focused solely on the possible applications of the statute, but rather have considered whether the statute has an unconstitutional purpose. Writing for the Court in *Bowen v. Kendrick*, THE CHIEF JUSTICE concluded that "[a]s in previous cases involving facial challenges on Establishment Clause grounds, we assess the constitutionality of an enactment by reference to the three factors first articulated in *Lemon v. Kurtzman*, ... which guides '[t]he general nature of our inquiry in this area.'" Under the *Lemon* standard, a court must invalidate a statute if it lacks "a secular legislative purpose." It is therefore proper, as part of this facial challenge, for us to examine the purpose of the October policy.

As discussed, the text of the October policy alone reveals that it has an unconstitutional purpose. The plain language of the policy clearly spells out the extent of school involvement in both the election of the speaker and the content of the message. Additionally, the text of the October policy specifies only one, clearly preferred message—that of Santa Fe's traditional religious "invocation." Finally, the extremely selective access of the policy and other content restrictions confirm that it is not a content-neutral regulation that creates a limited public forum for the expression of student speech. Our examination, however, need not stop at an analysis of the text of the policy.

This case comes to us as the latest step in developing litigation brought as a challenge to institutional practices that unquestionably violated the Establishment Clause. One of those practices was the District's long-established tradition of sanctioning student-led prayer at varsity football games. The narrow question before us is whether implementation of the October policy insulates the continuation of such prayers from constitutional scrutiny. It does not. Our inquiry into this question not only can, but must, include an examination of the circumstances surrounding its enactment. Whether a government activity violates the Establishment Clause is "in large part a legal question to be answered on the basis of judicial interpretation of social facts. . . . Every government practice must be judged in its unique circumstances. . . ." *Lynch* (O'CONNOR, J., concurring). Our discussion in the previous sections, demonstrates that in this case the District's direct involvement with school prayer exceeds constitutional limits.

The District, nevertheless, asks us to pretend that we do not recognize what every Santa Fe High School student understands clearly—that this policy is about prayer. The District further asks us to accept what is obviously untrue: that these messages are necessary to "solemnize" a football game and that this single-student, year-long position is essential to the protection of student speech. We refuse to turn a blind eye to the context in which this policy arose, and that context quells any doubt that this policy was implemented with the purpose of endorsing school prayer.

Therefore, the simple enactment of this policy, with the purpose and perception of school endorsement of student prayer, was a constitutional violation. We need not wait for the inevitable to confirm and magnify the constitutional injury. In *Wallace*, for example, we invalidated Alabama's as yet unimplemented and voluntary "moment of silence" statute based on our conclusion that it was enacted "for the sole purpose of expressing the State's endorsement of prayer activities for one minute at the beginning of each school day." Therefore, even if no Santa Fe High School student were ever to offer a religious message, the October policy fails a facial challenge because the attempt by the District to encourage prayer is also at issue. Government efforts to endorse religion cannot evade constitutional reproach based solely on the remote possibility that those attempts may fail.

This policy likewise does not survive a facial challenge because it impermissibly imposes upon the student body a majoritarian election on the issue of prayer. Through its election scheme, the District has established a governmental electoral mechanism that turns the school into a forum for religious debate. It further empowers the student body majority with the authority to subject students of minority views to constitutionally improper messages. The award of that power alone, regardless of the students' ultimate use of it, is not acceptable. Like the referendum in *Southworth*, the election mechanism established by the District undermines the essential protection of minority viewpoints. Such a system encourages divisiveness along religious lines and threatens the imposition of coercion upon those students not desiring to participate in a religious exercise. Simply by establishing this school-related procedure, which entrusts the inherently nongovernmental subject of religion to a majoritarian vote, a constitutional violation has occurred.[24] No further injury is required for the policy to fail a facial challenge.

To properly examine this policy on its face, we "must be deemed aware of the history and context of the community and forum." *Pinette* (O'CONNOR, J., concurring in part and concurring in judgment). Our examination of those circumstances above leads to the conclusion that this policy does not provide the District with the constitutional safe harbor it sought. The policy is invalid on its face because it establishes an improper majoritarian election on religion, and unquestionably has the purpose and creates the perception of encouraging the delivery of prayer at a series of important school events.

The judgment of the Court of Appeals is, accordingly, affirmed.

It is so ordered.

CHIEF JUSTICE REHNQUIST, with whom JUSTICE SCALIA and JUSTICE THOMAS join, dissenting.

The Court distorts existing precedent to conclude that the school district's student-message program is invalid on its face under the Establishment Clause. But even more disturbing than its holding is the tone of the Court's opinion; it bristles with hostility to all things religious in public life. Neither

---

24. THE CHIEF JUSTICE contends that we have "misconstrue[d] the nature ... [of] the policy as being an election on 'prayer' and 'religion.'" We therefore reiterate that the District has stipulated to the facts that the most recent election was held "to determine whether a student would deliver *prayer* at varsity football games," that the "students chose to allow a student to say a *prayer* at football games," and that a second election was then held "to determine which student would deliver the *prayer*." (emphases added). Furthermore, the policy was titled "*Prayer* at Football Games" (emphasis added). Although the District has since eliminated the word "prayer" from the policy, it apparently viewed that change as sufficiently minor as to make holding a new election unnecessary.

the holding nor the tone of the opinion is faithful to the meaning of the Establishment Clause, when it is recalled that George Washington himself, at the request of the very Congress which passed the Bill of Rights, proclaimed a day of "public thanksgiving and prayer, to be observed by acknowledging with grateful hearts the many and signal favors of Almighty God." Presidential Proclamation, 1 Messages and Papers of the Presidents, 1789–1897, p. 64 (J. Richardson ed. 1897).

We do not learn until late in the Court's opinion that respondents in this case challenged the district's student-message program at football games before it had been put into practice. As the Court explained in *United States v. Salerno*, 481 U.S. 739 (1987), the fact that a policy might "operate unconstitutionally under some conceivable set of circumstances is insufficient to render it wholly invalid." While there is an exception to this principle in the First Amendment overbreadth context because of our concern that people may refrain from speech out of fear of prosecution, there is no similar justification for Establishment Clause cases. No speech will be "chilled" by the existence of a government policy that might unconstitutionally endorse religion over nonreligion. Therefore, the question is not whether the district's policy may be applied in violation of the Establishment Clause, but whether it inevitably will be.

The Court, venturing into the realm of prophesy, decides that it "need not wait for the inevitable" and invalidates the district's policy on its face. To do so, it applies the most rigid version of the oft-criticized test of *Lemon v. Kurtzman*, 403 U.S. 602 (1971).

Lemon has had a checkered career in the decisional law of this Court. Indeed, in *Lee v. Weisman*, 505 U.S. 577 (1992), an opinion upon which the Court relies heavily today, we mentioned but did not feel compelled to apply the *Lemon* test.

Even if it were appropriate to apply the *Lemon* test here, the district's student-message policy should not be invalidated on its face. The Court applies *Lemon* and holds that the "policy is invalid on its face because it establishes an improper majoritarian election on religion, and unquestionably has the purpose and creates the perception of encouraging the delivery of prayer at a series of important school events." The Court's reliance on each of these conclusions misses the mark.

First, the Court misconstrues the nature of the "majoritarian election" permitted by the policy as being an election on "prayer" and "religion." To the contrary, the election permitted by the policy is a two-fold process whereby students vote first on whether to have a student speaker before football games at all, and second, if the students vote to have such a speaker, on who that speaker will be. It is conceivable that the election could become one in which student candidates campaign on platforms that focus on whether or not they will pray if elected. It is also conceivable that the election could lead to a Christian prayer before 90 percent of the football games. If, upon implementation, the policy operated in this fashion, we would have a record before us to review whether the policy, as applied, violated the Establishment Clause or unduly suppressed minority viewpoints. But it is possible that the students might vote not to have a pregame speaker, in which case there would be no threat of a constitutional violation. It is also possible that the election would not focus on prayer, but on public speaking ability or social popularity. And if student campaigning did begin to focus on prayer, the school might decide to implement reasonable campaign restrictions.[3]

But the Court ignores these possibilities by holding that merely granting the student body the power to elect a speaker that may choose to pray, "regardless of the students' ultimate use of it, is not acceptable." The Court so holds despite that any speech that may occur as a result of the election process here would be private, not government, speech. The elected student, not the government, would choose what to say. Support for the Court's holding cannot be found in any of our cases. And it essentially invalidates all student elections. A newly elected student body president, or even a newly elected prom king or queen, could use opportunities for public speaking to say prayers. Under the Court's view, the mere grant of power to the students to vote for such offices, in light of the fear that those elected might publicly pray, violates the Establishment Clause.

Second, with respect to the policy's purpose, the Court holds that "the simple enactment of this policy, with the purpose and perception of school endorsement of student prayer, was a constitutional violation." But the policy itself has plausible secular purposes: "[T]o solemnize the event, to promote good sportsmanship and student safety, and to establish the appropriate environment for the competition." Where a governmental body "expresses a plausible secular purpose" for an enactment, "courts should generally defer to that stated intent." *Wallace* (O'CONNOR, J., concurring in judgment). The Court grants no deference to—and appears openly hostile toward—the policy's stated purposes, and wastes no time in concluding that they are a sham.

For example, the Court dismisses the secular purpose of solemnization by claiming that it "invites and encourages religious messages." The Court so concludes based on its rather strange view that a "religious message is the most obvious means of solemnizing an event." But it is easy to think of solemn messages that are not religious in nature, for example urging that a game be fought fairly. And sporting events often begin with a solemn rendition of our national anthem, with its concluding verse "And this be our motto: 'In God is our trust.'" Under the Court's logic, a public school that sponsors the singing of the national anthem before football games violates the Establishment Clause. Although the Court apparently believes that solemnizing football games is an illegitimate purpose, the voters in the school district seem to disagree. Nothing in the Establishment Clause prevents them from making this choice.[4]

---

3. The Court's reliance on language regarding the student referendum in *Board of Regents of Univ. of Wis. System v. Southworth,* to support its conclusion with respect to the election process is misplaced. That case primarily concerned free speech, and, more particularly, mandated financial support of a public forum. But as stated above, if this case were in the "as applied" context and we were presented with the appropriate record, our language in *Southworth* could become more applicable. In fact, *Southworth* itself demonstrates the impropriety of making a decision with respect to the election process without a record of its opera-

tion. There we remanded in part for a determination of how the referendum functions.

4. The Court also determines that the use of the term "invocation" in the policy is an express endorsement of that type of message over all others. A less cynical view of the policy's text is that it permits many types of messages, including invocations. That a policy tolerates religion does not mean that it improperly endorses it. Indeed, as the majority reluctantly admits, the Free Exercise Clause mandates such tolerance.

The Court bases its conclusion that the true purpose of the policy is to endorse student prayer on its view of the school district's history of Establishment Clause violations and the context in which the policy was written, that is, as "the latest step in developing litigation brought as a challenge to institutional practices that unquestionably violated the Establishment Clause." But the context—attempted compliance with a District Court order—actually demonstrates that the school district was acting diligently to come within the governing constitutional law. The District Court ordered the school district to formulate a policy consistent with Fifth Circuit precedent, which permitted a school district to have a prayer-only policy. But the school district went further than required by the District Court order and eventually settled on a policy that gave the student speaker a choice to deliver either an invocation or a message. In so doing, the school district exhibited a willingness to comply with, and exceed, Establishment Clause restrictions. Thus, the policy cannot be viewed as having a sectarian purpose.

The Court also relies on our decision in *Lee v. Weisman* to support its conclusion. In *Lee*, we concluded that the content of the speech at issue, a graduation prayer given by a rabbi, was "directed and controlled" by a school official. In other words, at issue in *Lee* was *government* speech. Here, by contrast, the potential speech at issue, if the policy had been allowed to proceed, would be a message or invocation selected or created by a student. That is, if there were speech at issue here, it would be *private* speech. The "crucial difference between *government* speech endorsing religion, which the Establishment Clause forbids, and *private* speech endorsing religion, which the Free Speech and Free Exercise Clauses protect," applies with particular force to the question of endorsement. *Board of Ed. of Westside Community Schools (Dist. 66) v. Mergens*, 496 U.S. 226 (1990) (plurality opinion) (emphasis in original).

Had the policy been put into practice, the students may have chosen a speaker according to wholly secular criteria—like good public speaking skills or social popularity—and the student speaker may have chosen, on her own accord, to deliver a religious message. Such an application of the policy would likely pass constitutional muster.

Finally, the Court seems to demand that a government policy be completely neutral as to content or be considered one that endorses religion. This is undoubtedly a new requirement, as our Establishment Clause jurisprudence simply does not mandate "content neutrality." That concept is found in our First Amendment speech cases and is used as a guide for determining when we apply strict scrutiny. For example, we look to "content neutrality" in reviewing loudness restrictions imposed on speech in public forums, see *Ward v. Rock Against Racism*, 491 U.S. 781 (1989), and regulations against picketing, see *Boos v. Barry*, 485 U.S. 312 (1988). The Court seems to think that the fact that the policy is not content neutral somehow controls the Establishment Clause inquiry.

But even our speech jurisprudence would not require that all public school actions with respect to student speech be content neutral. See, e.g., *Bethel School Dist. No. 403 v. Fraser* (allowing the imposition of sanctions against a student speaker who, in nominating a fellow student for elective office during an assembly, referred to his candidate in terms of an elaborate

ually explicit metaphor). Schools do not violate the First Amendment every ᴜe they restrict student speech to certain categories. But under the Court's ᴇw, a school policy under which the student body president is to solemnize the graduation ceremony by giving a favorable introduction to the guest speaker would be facially unconstitutional. Solemnization "invites and encourages" prayer and the policy's content limitations prohibit the student body president from giving a solemn, yet non-religious, message like "commentary on United States foreign policy."

The policy at issue here may be applied in an unconstitutional manner, but it will be time enough to invalidate it if that is found to be the case. I would reverse the judgment of the Court of Appeals.

QUESTIONS AND NOTES

1. According to the Court, is the election an aggravating or mitigating factor insofar as the establishment clause is concerned? Which should it be? Why? Compare *Board of Regents v. Southworth* p. 192, *supra.*

2. Should the harassment of the plaintiffs have been relevant to the outcome of the case? Was it relevant? Why? Why not?

3. Is the Court's opinion "hostile to all things religious in public life" as the Chief Justice contends? Explain.

4. Does the dissent seem less strident than it was in *Lee*? If so, why?

5. Under the Court's decision, would the mention of God in the "Star Spangled Banner" be forbidden? Why? Why not?

6. The Court seemed to cite O'Connor concurrences with some frequency. Why do you suppose that it did that?

7. Suppose that the local radio station that broadcasts Santa Fe football games decides to announce a prayer on the radio just before each kickoff and encourages fans to turn their radios up so that the prayer will be heard all over the stadium. Suppose further that a large percentage of the crowd does that. Any constitutional violation? Explain.

8. Is there any way to return prayer to high school football games? Should there be? Explain.

9. Consider whether *Newdow* logically follows from the line of cases culminating in *Santa Fe.*

NEWDOW v. UNITED STATES CONGRESS
292 F.3d 597 (9th Cir.2002).

Goodwin, Circuit Judge:

Michael Newdow appeals a judgment dismissing his challenge to the constitutionality of the words "under God" in the Pledge of Allegiance to the Flag. Newdow argues that the addition of these words by a 1954 federal statute to the previous version of the Pledge of Allegiance (which made no reference to God) and the daily recitation in the classroom of the Pledge of Allegiance, with the added words included, by his daughter's public school teacher are violations of the Establishment Clause of the First Amendment to the United States Constitution.

FACTUAL AND PROCEDURAL BACKGROUND

Newdow is an atheist whose daughter attends public elementary school in the Elk Grove Unified School District ("EGUSD") in California. In accordance with state law and a school district rule, EGUSD teachers begin each school day by leading their students in a recitation of the Pledge of Allegiance ("the Pledge"). The California Education Code requires that public schools begin each school day with "appropriate patriotic exercises" and that [t]he giving of the Pledge of Allegiance to the Flag of the United States of "America shall satisfy" this requirement.

The classmates of Newdow's daughter in the EGUSD are led by their teacher in reciting the Pledge codified in federal law. On June 22, 1942, Congress first codified the Pledge as "I pledge allegiance to the flag of the United States of America and to the Republic for which it stands, one Nation indivisible, with liberty and justice for all."

The Pledge is currently codified as "I pledge allegiance to the Flag of the United States of America, and to the Republic for which it stands, one nation under God, indivisible, with liberty and justice for all."

Newdow does not allege that his daughter's teacher or school district requires his daughter to participate in reciting the Pledge.[1] Rather, he claims that his daughter is injured when she is compelled to "watch and listen as her state-employed teacher in her state-run school leads her classmates in a ritual proclaiming that there is a God, and that our's [sic] is 'one nation under God.'"

Newdow's complaint in the district court challenged the constitutionality, under the First Amendment, of the 1954 Act, the California statute, and the school district's policy requiring teachers to lead willing students in recitation of the Pledge. He sought declaratory and injunctive relief, but did not seek damages.

Over the last three decades, the Supreme Court has used three interrelated tests to analyze alleged violations of the Establishment Clause in the realm of public education: the three-prong test set forth in *Lemon v. Kurtzman*, the "endorsement" test, first articulated by Justice O'Connor in her concurring opinion in *Lynch*, and later adopted by a majority of the Court in County of *Allegheny v. ACLU*, and the "coercion" test first used by the Court in *Lee*.

In 1971, in the context of unconstitutional state aid to nonpublic schools, the Supreme Court in *Lemon* set forth the following test for evaluating alleged Establishment Clause violations. To survive the *"Lemon* test," the government conduct in question (1) must have a secular purpose, (2) must have a principal or primary effect that neither advances nor inhibits religion, and (3) must not foster an excessive government entanglement with religion.

The Supreme Court applied the *Lemon* test to every Establishment case it decided between 1971 and 1984, with the exception of *Marsh v. Chambers*. In the 1984 *Lynch* case, which upheld the inclusion of a nativity scene in a city's Christmas display, Justice O'Connor wrote a concurring opinion in order to suggest a "clarification" of Establishment Clause jurisprudence. Justice

---

1. Compelling students to recite the Pledge was held to be a First Amendment violation in West Virginia State Board of Education v. Barnette.

O'Connor's "endorsement" test effectively collapsed the first two prongs of the *Lemon* test:

> The Establishment Clause prohibits government from making adherence to a religion relevant in any way to a person's standing in the political community. Government can run afoul of that prohibition in two principal ways. One is excessive entanglement with religious institutions. The second and more direct infringement is government endorsement or disapproval of religion. Endorsement sends a message to non-adherents that they are outsiders, not full members of the political community, and an accompanying message to adherents that they are insiders, favored members of the political community.

The Court formulated the "coercion test" when it held unconstitutional the practice of including invocations and benedictions in the form of "nonsectarian" prayers at public school graduation ceremonies. Declining to reconsider the validity of the *Lemon* test, the Court in *Lee* found it unnecessary to apply the *Lemon* test to find the challenged practices unconstitutional. Rather, it relied on the principle that "at a minimum, the Constitution guarantees that government may not coerce anyone to support or participate in religion or its exercise, or otherwise to act in a way which establishes a state religion or religious faith, or tends to do so."[2] The Court first examined the degree of school involvement in the prayer, and found that "the graduation prayers bore the imprint of the State and thus put school-age children who objected in an untenable position." The next issue the Court considered was "the position of the students, both those who desired the prayer and she who did not." Noting that "there are heightened concerns with protecting freedom of conscience from subtle coercive pressure in the elementary and secondary public schools," the Court held that the school district's supervision and control of the graduation ceremony put impermissible pressure on students to participate in, or at least show respect during, the prayer. The Court concluded that primary and secondary school children may not be placed in the dilemma of either participating in a religious ceremony or protesting. Finally, in its most recent school prayer case, the Supreme Court applied the *Lemon* test, the endorsement test, and the coercion test to strike down a school district's policy of permitting student-led "invocations" before high school football games. Citing *Lee*, the Court held that "the delivery of a pregame prayer has the improper effect of coercing those present to participate in an act of religious worship." Applying the *Lemon* test, the Court found that the school district policy was facially unconstitutional because it did not have a secular purpose. The Court also used language associated with the endorsement test. "[T]his policy was implemented with the purpose of endorsing school prayer."); ("Government efforts to endorse religion cannot evade

---

2. Although this formulation is referred to as the "coercion" test, it should be noted that coercion is not a necessary element in finding an Establishment Clause violation. "The Establishment Clause, unlike the Free Exercise Clause, does not depend upon any showing of direct governmental compulsion...." Engel v. Vitale. "[T]his court has never relied on coercion alone as the touchstone of Establishment Clause analysis. To require a showing of coercion, even indirect coercion, as an essential element of an Establishment Clause violation would make the free Exercise Clause a redundancy." *Allegheny* (O'Connor, J., concurring). "Over the years, this Court has declared the invalidity of many non-coercive state laws and practices conveying a message of religious endorsement." *Lee* (Souter, J., concurring).

constitutional reproach based solely on the remote possibility that those attempts may fail.'').

We are free to apply any or all of the three tests, and to invalidate any measure that fails any one of them. The Supreme Court has not repudiated *Lemon*. In *Santa Fe*, it found that the application of each of the three tests provided an independent ground for invalidating the statute at issue in that case and in *Lee* the Court invalidated the policy solely on the basis of the coercion test. Although this court has typically applied the *Lemon* test to alleged Establishment Clause violations, we are not required to apply it if a practice fails one of the other tests.

Nevertheless, for purposes of completeness, we will analyze the school district policy and the 1954 Act under all three tests. We first consider whether the 1954 Act and the EGUSD's policy of teacher-led Pledge recitation survive the endorsement test. The magistrate judge found that "the ceremonial reference to God in the pledge does not convey endorsement of particular religious beliefs." Supreme Court precedent does not support that conclusion.

In the context of the Pledge, the statement that the United States is a nation "under God" is an endorsement of religion. It is a profession of a religious belief, namely, a belief in monotheism. The recitation that ours is a nation "under God" is not a mere acknowledgment that many Americans believe in a deity. Nor is it merely descriptive of the undeniable historical significance of religion in the founding of the Republic. Rather, the phrase "one nation under God" in the context of the Pledge is normative. To recite the Pledge is not to describe the United States; instead, it is to swear allegiance to the values for which the flag stands: unity, indivisibility, liberty, justice, and—since 1954—monotheism. The text of the official Pledge, codified in federal law, impermissibly takes a position with respect to the purely religious question of the existence and identity of God. A profession that we are a nation "under God" is identical, for Establishment Clause purposes, to a profession that we are a nation "under Jesus," a nation "under Vishnu," a nation "under Zeus," or a nation "under no god," because none of these professions can be neutral with respect to religion. "[T]he government must pursue a course of complete neutrality toward religion." *Wallace*. Furthermore, the school district's practice of teacher-led recitation of the Pledge aims to inculcate in students a respect for the ideals set forth in the Pledge, and thus amounts to state endorsement of these ideals. Although students cannot be forced to participate in recitation of the Pledge, the school district is nonetheless conveying a message of state endorsement of a religious belief when it requires public school teachers to recite, and lead the recitation of, the current form of the Pledge.

The Pledge, as currently codified, is an impermissible government endorsement of religion because it sends a message to unbelievers "that they are outsiders, not full members of the political community, and an accompanying message to adherents that they are insiders, favored members of the political community." *Lynch* (O'Connor, J., concurring). Justice Kennedy, in his dissent in *Allegheny*, agreed:

> [B]y statute, the Pledge of Allegiance to the Flag describes the United States as 'one nation under God.' To be sure, no one is obligated to recite this phrase, . . . but it borders on sophistry to suggest that the reasonable

atheist would not feel less than a full member of the political community every time his fellow Americans recited, as part of their expression of patriotism and love for country, a phrase he believed to be false.[3] Consequently, the policy and the Act fail the endorsement test.

Similarly, the policy and the Act fail the coercion test. Just as in *Lee*, the policy and the Act place students in the untenable position of choosing between participating in an exercise with religious content or protesting. As the Court observed with respect to the graduation prayer in that case: "What to most believers may seem nothing more than a reasonable request that the nonbeliever respect their religious practices, in a school context may appear to the nonbeliever or dissenter to be an attempt to employ the machinery of the State to enforce a religious orthodoxy." Although the defendants argue that the religious content of "one nation under God" is minimal, to an atheist or a believer in certain non–Judeo–Christian religions or philosophies, it may reasonably appear to be an attempt to enforce a "religious orthodoxy" of monotheism, and is therefore impermissible. The coercive effect of this policy is particularly pronounced in the school setting given the age and impressionability of schoolchildren, and their understanding that they are required to adhere to the norms set by their school, their teacher and their fellow students.[4] Furthermore, under *Lee*, the fact that students are not required to participate is no basis for distinguishing *Barnette* from the case at bar because, even without a recitation requirement for each child, the mere fact that a pupil is required to listen every day to the statement "one nation under God" has a coercive effect.[5] The coercive effect of the Act is apparent from its context and legislative history, which indicate that the Act was designed to result in the daily recitation of the words "under God" in school classrooms. President Eisenhower, during the Act's signing ceremony, stated: "From this day forward, the millions of our school children will daily proclaim in every city and town, every village and rural schoolhouse, the dedication of our Nation and our people to the Almighty." Therefore, the policy and the Act fail the coercion test.[6]

Finally we turn to the *Lemon* test, the first prong of which asks if the challenged policy has a secular purpose. Historically, the primary purpose of the 1954 Act was to advance religion, in conflict with the first prong of the

---

3. For Justice Kennedy, this result was a reason to reject the endorsement test.

4. The "subtle and indirect" social pressure which permeates the classroom also renders more acute the message sent to nonbelieving schoolchildren that they are outsiders. See *Lee*, (stating that "the risk of indirect coercion" from prayer exercises is particularly "pronounced" in elementary and secondary public school because students are subjected to peer pressure and public pressure which is "as real as any overt compulsion").

5. The objection to the Pledge in *Barnette*, like in the case at bar, was based upon a religious ground. The Pledge in the classroom context imposes upon schoolchildren the constitutionally unacceptable choice between participating and protesting. Recognizing the severity of the effect of this form of coercion on children, the Supreme Court in *Lee* stated,

"the State may not, consistent with the Establishment Clause, place primary and secondary school children in this position."

6. In Aronow v. United States, 432 F.2d 242 (9th Cir.1970), this court, without reaching the question of standing, upheld the inscription of the phrase "In God We Trust" on our coins and currency. But cf. Wooley v. Maynard, 430 U.S. 705, 722 (1977) (Rehnquist, J., dissenting) (stating that the majority's holding leads logically to the conclusion that "In God We Trust" is an unconstitutional affirmation of belief). In any event, *Aronow* is distinguishable in many ways from the present case. The most important distinction is that school children are not coerced into reciting or otherwise actively led to participating in an endorsement of the markings on the money in circulation.

Lemon test. The federal defendants "do not dispute that the words 'under God' were intended" "to recognize a Supreme Being," at a time when the government was publicly inveighing against atheistic communism. Nonetheless, the federal defendants argue that the Pledge must be considered as a whole when assessing whether it has a secular purpose. They claim that the Pledge has the secular purpose of "solemnizing public occasions, expressing confidence in the future, and encouraging the recognition of what is worthy of appreciation in society." The flaw in defendants' argument is that it looks at the text of the Pledge "as a whole," and glosses over the 1954 Act. The problem with this approach is apparent when one considers the Court's analysis in *Wallace*. There, the Court struck down Alabama's statute mandating a moment of silence for "meditation or voluntary prayer" not because the final version "as a whole" lacked a primary secular purpose, but because the state legislature had amended the statute specifically and solely to add the words "or voluntary prayer."

By analogy to *Wallace*, we apply the purpose prong of the *Lemon* test to the amendment that added the words "under God" to the Pledge, not to the Pledge in its final version. As was the case with the amendment to the Alabama statute in *Wallace*, the legislative history of the 1954 Act reveals that the Act's sole purpose was to advance religion, in order to differentiate the United States from nations under communist rule. "[T]he First Amendment requires that a statute must be invalidated if it is entirely motivated by a purpose to advance religion." As the legislative history of the 1954 Act sets forth:

> At this moment of our history the principles underlying our American Government and the American way of life are under attack by a system whose philosophy is at direct odds with our own. Our American Government is founded on the concept of the individuality and the dignity of the human being. Underlying this concept is the belief that the human person is important because he was created by God and endowed by Him with certain inalienable rights which no civil authority may usurp. The inclusion of God in our pledge therefore would further acknowledge the dependence of our people and our Government upon the moral directions of the Creator. At the same time it would serve to deny the atheistic and materialistic concepts of communism with its attendant subservience of the individual.

This language reveals that the purpose of the 1954 Act was to take a position on the question of theism, namely, to support the existence and moral authority of God, while "deny[ing] ... atheistic and materialistic concepts." Such a purpose runs counter to the Establishment Clause, which prohibits the government's endorsement or advancement not only of one particular religion at the expense of other religions, but also of religion at the expense of atheism.

In language that attempts to prevent future constitutional challenges, the sponsors of the 1954 Act expressly disclaimed a religious purpose. "This is not an act establishing a religion.... A distinction must be made between the existence of a religion as an institution and a belief in the sovereignty of God. The phrase 'under God' recognizes only the guidance of God in our national affairs." This alleged distinction is irrelevant for constitutional purposes. The

Act's affirmation of "a belief in the sovereignty of God" and its recognition of "the guidance of God" are endorsements by the government of religious beliefs. The Establishment Clause is not limited to "religion as an institution"; this is clear from cases such as *Santa Fe*, where the Court struck down student-initiated and student-led prayer at high school football games. The Establishment Clause guards not only against the establishment of "religion as an institution," but also against the endorsement of religious ideology by the government. Because the Act fails the purpose prong of *Lemon*, we need not examine the other prongs.

Similarly, the school district policy also fails the *Lemon* test. Although it survives the first prong of *Lemon* because, as even Newdow concedes, the school district had the secular purpose of fostering patriotism in enacting the policy, the policy fails the second prong. The second *Lemon* prong asks "whether the challenged government action is sufficiently likely to be perceived by adherents of the controlling denominations as an endorsement, and by the non-adherents as a disapproval, of their individual religious choices." Given the age and impressionability of schoolchildren, as discussed above, particularly within the confined environment of the classroom, the policy is highly likely to convey an impermissible message of endorsement to some and disapproval to others of their beliefs regarding the existence of a monotheistic God. Therefore the policy fails the effects prong of *Lemon*, and fails the *Lemon* test. In sum, both the policy and the Act fail the Lemon test as well as the endorsement and coercion tests.[7]

In conclusion, we hold that (1) the 1954 Act adding the words "under God" to the Pledge, and (2) EGUSD's policy and practice of teacher-led recitation of the Pledge, with the added words included, violate the Establishment Clause. The judgment of dismissal is vacated with respect to these two claims, and the cause is remanded for further proceedings consistent with our holding. Plaintiff is to recover costs on this appeal.

REVERSED AND REMANDED.

FERNANDEZ, CIRCUIT JUDGE, dissenting:

We are asked to hold that inclusion of the phrase "under God" in this nation's Pledge of Allegiance violates the religion clauses of the Constitution of the United States. We should do no such thing. We should, instead, recognize that those clauses were not designed to drive religious expression out of public thought; they were written to avoid discrimination.

We can run through the litany of tests and concepts which have floated to the surface from time to time. Were we to do so, the one that appeals most to me, the one I think to be correct, is the concept that what the religion clauses of the First Amendment require is neutrality; that those clauses are, in effect, an early kind of equal protection provision and assure that government will neither discriminate for nor discriminate against a religion or religions. But, legal world abstractions and ruminations aside, when all is said and done, the

---

7. We recognize that the Supreme Court has occasionally commented in dicta that the presence of "one nation under God" in the Pledge of Allegiance is constitutional. However, the Court has never been presented with the question directly, and has always clearly refrained from deciding it. Accordingly, it has never applied any of the three tests to the Act or to any school policy regarding the recitation of the Pledge. That task falls to us, although the final word, as always, remains with the Supreme Court.

danger that "under God" in our Pledge of Allegiance will tend to bring about a theocracy or suppress somebody's beliefs is so minuscule as to be *de minimis*. The danger that phrase presents to our First Amendment freedoms is picayune at most.

Judges, including Supreme Court Justices, have recognized the lack of danger in that and similar expressions for decades, if not for centuries, as have presidents and members of our Congress. In *County of Allegheny*, the Supreme Court had this to say: "Our previous opinions have considered in dicta the motto and the pledge, characterizing them as consistent with the proposition that government may not communicate an endorsement of religious belief." The Seventh Circuit, reacting in part to that statement, has wisely expressed the following thought:

> Plaintiffs observe that the Court sometimes changes its tune when it confronts a subject directly. True enough, but an inferior court had best respect what the majority says rather than read between the lines. If the Court proclaims that a practice is consistent with the Establishment Clause, we take its assurances seriously. If the Justices are just pulling our leg, let them say so. Sherman, 980 F.2d at 448.

Some, who rather choke on the notion of *de minimis*, have resorted to the euphemism "ceremonial deism." See, e.g., *Lynch* (Brennan, J., dissenting). But whatever it is called (I care not), it comes to this: such phrases as "In God We Trust," or "under God" have no tendency to establish a religion in this country or to suppress anyone's exercise, or non-exercise, of religion, except in the fevered eye of persons who most fervently would like to drive all tincture of religion out of the public life of our polity. Those expressions have not caused any real harm of that sort over the years since 1791, and are not likely to do so in the future.[8] As I see it, that is not because they are drained of meaning. Rather, as I have already indicated, it is because their tendency to establish religion (or affect its exercise) is exiguous. I recognize that some people may not feel good about hearing the phrases recited in their presence, but, then, others might not feel good if they are omitted. At any rate, the Constitution is a practical and balanced charter for the just governance of a free people in a vast territory. Thus, although we do feel good when we contemplate the effects of its inspiring phrasing and majestic promises, it is not primarily a feel-good prescription. In *Barnette*, for example, the Supreme Court did not say that the Pledge could not be recited in the presence of Jehovah's Witness children; it merely said that they did not have to recite it.[9] That fully protected their constitutional rights by precluding the government from trenching upon "the sphere of intellect and spirit." As the Court pointed out, their religiously based refusal "to participate in the ceremony [would] not interfere with or deny rights of others to do so." We should not permit Newdow's feel-good concept to change that balance.

My reading of the stelliscript suggests that upon Newdow's theory of our Constitution, accepted by my colleagues today, we will soon find ourselves

---

8. They have not led us down the long path to *kulturkampf* or worse. Those who are somehow beset by residual doubts and fears should find comfort in the reflection that no baleful religious effects have been generated by the existence of similar references to a deity throughout our history. More specifically, it is difficult to detect any signs of incipient theocracy springing up since the Pledge was amended in 1954.

9. I recognize that the Pledge did not then contain the phrase "under God."

prohibited from using our album of patriotic songs in many public settings. "God Bless America" and "America The Beautiful" will be gone for sure, and while use of the first and second stanzas of the Star Spangled Banner will still be permissible, we will be precluded from straying into the third.[10] And currency beware! Judges can accept those results if they limit themselves to elements and tests, while failing to look at the good sense and principles that animated those tests in the first place. But they do so at the price of removing a vestige of the awe we all must feel at the immenseness of the universe and our own small place within it, as well as the wonder we must feel at the good fortune of our country. That will cool the febrile nerves of a few at the cost of removing the healthy glow conferred upon many citizens when the forbidden verses, or phrases, are uttered, read, or seen.

In short, I cannot accept the eliding of the simple phrase "under God" from our Pledge of Allegiance, when it is obvious that its tendency to establish religion in this country or to interfere with the free exercise (or non-exercise) of religion is *de minimis*.[11]

Thus, I respectfully dissent.

QUESTIONS AND NOTES

1. As this supplement was going to press, Judge Goodwin stayed his order for sixty days.

2. Do you believe that the pledge in its current (post–1954) form endorses religion? Explain.

3. In terms of "purpose," is *Wallace v. Jaffree* distinguishable? If not, should *Wallace* be reconsidered?

4. Are patriotic songs with religious references different from the pledge in terms of endorsement? Why? Why not?

5. Is the concept of "Ceremonial Deism" meaningful? If so, does it justify the pledge? By that reasoning should *Lee v. Weisman* be overruled?

6. Does the following editorial by your casebook editor carry separation too far or does it accurately reflect what the Establishment Clause ought to mean?

SEPARATING GOD AND COUNTRY

Perceived judicial attacks on God or Country are not taken kindly by the populace or politicians. This point has been illustrated over and over again by constant attempts to amend the Constitution to allow school prayer and the punishment of flag burners. So it should come as no great surprise that when God AND Country appear to be under attack in one fell judicial swoop, the politicians will indeed become restless. Consequently, the senate's 99–0 rejection of the 9th Circuit's decision invalidating the phrase "under God" in the flag salute was not unexpected. It was, however, unfortunate.

---

10. Nor will we be able to stray into the fourth stanza of "My Country 'Tis of Thee" for that matter.

11. Lest I be misunderstood, I must emphasize that to decide this case it is not necessary to say, and I do not say, that there is such a thing as a *de minimis* constitutional violation. What I do say is that the *de minimis* tendency of the Pledge to establish a religion or to interfere with its free exercise is no constitutional violation at all.

I know of no more important duties than the support of God and Country. But they don't mix well. We elect Senators and Congressmen to enact laws describing reciprocal duties between ourselves and our Country. We do not elect them to prescribe our duty to God. For that we have Priests, Ministers, Rabbis, and other clerical or lay church leaders. Roger Williams, one of our most pious founders, insisted on separation of Church and State because of his firm belief that civil leaders were unqualified to lead us in the ways of God.

More recently, the Supreme Court has emphasized the importance of Government neither endorsing nor disapproving one's religious beliefs. Put differently, one's devotion (or lack thereof) to God is irrelevant to her status as a citizen. The phrase "under God" in a patriotic pledge certainly disapproves of Buddhists, Taoists, Ethical Culturalists, Secular Humanists and, of course, atheists. One might be tempted to respond: "So what, we're right and they're wrong. Who cares if a few heathen are offended." That, however, is just the point. You and I might know that we're right and they're wrong, but the Government is not permitted to know that. The Government must remain neutral.

In some ways, the public pledge in school is worse than public prayer. With prayer, the nonbeliever must identify herself as a nonbeliever by not participating. But with the pledge, a devoutly patriotic American atheist may appear to be unpatriotic when he was merely being ungodly. Compelling the atheistic patriot to either appear unpatriotic or betray his religious convictions is precisely the choice that the establishment clause forbids Government to impose on its citizens.

For those who think that "under God" is merely political and not religious, imagine a hypothetical future when America is controlled by a majority of atheists, who decide to substitute "without God" for "under God" in the flag salute. I would hope that the Supreme Court (even if then also controlled by atheists) would hold that phrase to be unconstitutional. I would argue that however atheistic the majority of the country may be, our fundamental charter demands that the majority's religious philosophy not be the basis of our country's politics.

Ironically, it was the Soviet Union's dictatorial infusion of atheism into the warp and woof of Soviet society that prompted us to add "under God" to the flag salute in the first place. Perhaps we should have added "with freedom of religion" instead. That would have properly highlighted the difference between us and the Soviet Union.

Those who worry that invalidation of "under God" in the pledge of allegiance might lead to the eventual demise of "In God we trust" on our coins and currency should recall Jesus' admonition in regard to the propriety of Caesar's likeness on the coins and currency of the realm. He famously remarked: "Render unto Caesar what is Caesar's and unto God what is God's." God most assuredly deserves our trust, but he doesn't need "Caesar" to provide it. Our alternative motto, e pluribus unum, from the many one, describes both our diversity and, in pledge terms, our indivisibility. And, it lacks the divisiveness of a motto spiritually offensive to some and theoretically offensive to others.

The love of both God and Country are characteristic of most good American citizens. It is my fondest hope that this will continue to be the way we are. But countries that seriously integrate the two are not among those that we like to emulate. The Shiites of Iran and Islamic Jihad are two recent examples of the harm that can come from excessive intermixing. While America would never go down that path, we would do well to remove ourselves as far as possible from the Theocratic State. As Justice Robert Jackson, the Nuremberg prosecutor, once observed: "It is possible to hold a faith with enough confidence to believe that what should be rendered to God does not need to be decided and collected by Caesar."

E. ARE SCHOOLS BECOMING PUBLIC SQUARES?

In the *Good News* case, the Court treated schools very much like public fora. Indeed, from the Court's perspective, *Good News* was a free speech case. It certainly brought the speech and religion clauses together.

GOOD NEWS CLUB v. MILFORD CENTRAL SCHOOL
533 U.S. 98 (2001).

JUSTICE THOMAS delivered the opinion of the Court.

This case presents two questions. The first question is whether Milford Central School violated the free speech rights of the Good News Club when it excluded the Club from meeting after hours at the school. The second question is whether any such violation is justified by Milford's concern that permitting the Club's activities would violate the Establishment Clause. We conclude that Milford's restriction violates the Club's free speech rights and that no Establishment Clause concern justifies that violation.

I

The State of New York authorizes local school boards to adopt regulations governing the use of their school facilities. In 1992, respondent Milford Central School (Milford) enacted a community use policy adopting seven purposes for which its building could be used after school. Two of the stated purposes are relevant here. First, district residents may use the school for "instruction in any branch of education, learning or the arts." Second, the school is available for "social, civic and recreational meetings and entertainment events, and other uses pertaining to the welfare of the community, provided that such uses shall be nonexclusive and shall be opened to the general public."

Stephen and Darleen Fournier reside within Milford's district and therefore are eligible to use the school's facilities as long as their proposed use is approved by the school. Together they are sponsors of the local Good News Club, a private Christian organization for children ages 6 to 12. Pursuant to Milford's policy, in September 1996 the Fourniers submitted a request to Dr. Robert McGruder, interim superintendent of the district, in which they sought permission to hold the Club's weekly afterschool meetings in the school cafeteria. The next month, McGruder formally denied the Fourniers' request on the ground that the proposed use—to have "a fun time of singing songs, hearing a Bible lesson and memorizing scripture,"—was "the equivalent of religious worship." According to McGruder, the community use policy, which prohibits use "by any individual or organization for religious purposes," foreclosed the Club's activities.

In response to a letter submitted by the Club's counsel, Milford's attorney requested information to clarify the nature of the Club's activities. The Club sent a set of materials used or distributed at the meetings and the following description of its meeting:

"The Club opens its session with Ms. Fournier taking attendance. As she calls a child's name, if the child recites a Bible verse the child receives a treat. After attendance, the Club sings songs. Next Club members engage in games that involve, *inter alia,* learning Bible verses. Ms. Fournier then relates a Bible story and explains how it applies to Club members' lives. The Club closes with prayer. Finally, Ms. Fournier distributes treats and the Bible verses for memorization."

McGruder and Milford's attorney reviewed the materials and concluded that "the kinds of activities proposed to be engaged in by the Good News Club were not a discussion of secular subjects such as child rearing, development of character and development of morals from a religious perspective, but were in fact the equivalent of religious instruction itself." In February 1997, the Milford Board of Education adopted a resolution rejecting the Club's request to use Milford's facilities "for the purpose of conducting religious instruction and Bible study."

In March 1997, petitioners, the Good News Club, Ms. Fournier, and her daughter Andrea Fournier (collectively, the Club), filed an action under 42 U.S.C. § 1983 against Milford in the United States District Court for the Northern District of New York. The Club alleged that Milford's denial of its application violated its free speech rights under the First and Fourteenth Amendments, its right to equal protection under the Fourteenth Amendment, and its right to religious freedom under the Religious Freedom Restoration Act of 1993, 107 Stat. 1488, 42 U.S.C. § 2000bb et seq.[1]

The Club moved for a preliminary injunction to prevent the school from enforcing its religious exclusion policy against the Club and thereby to permit the Club's use of the school facilities. On April 14, 1997, the District Court granted the injunction. The Club then held its weekly afterschool meetings from April 1997 until June 1998 in a high school resource and middle school special education room.

In August 1998, the District Court vacated the preliminary injunction and granted Milford's motion for summary judgment. The court found that the Club's "subject matter is decidedly religious in nature, and not merely a discussion of secular matters from a religious perspective that is otherwise permitted under [Milford's] use policies." Because the school had not permitted other groups that provided religious instruction to use its limited public forum, the court held that the school could deny access to the Club without engaging in unconstitutional viewpoint discrimination. The court also rejected the Club's equal protection claim.

---

1. The District Court dismissed the Club's claim under the Religious Freedom Restoration Act because we held the Act to be unconstitutional in *City of Boerne v. Flores, infra* ch. 11.

The Club appealed, and a divided panel of the United States Court of Appeals for the Second Circuit affirmed. Judge Jacobs filed a dissenting opinion in which he concluded that the school's restriction did constitute viewpoint discrimination under *Lamb's Chapel v. Center Moriches Union Free School Dist.*, 508 U.S. 384, 124 L.Ed.2d 352, 113 S.Ct. 2141 (1993).

There is a conflict among the Courts of Appeals on the question whether speech can be excluded from a limited public forum on the basis of the religious nature of the speech. We granted certiorari to resolve this conflict.

II

The standards that we apply to determine whether a State has unconstitutionally excluded a private speaker from use of a public forum depend on the nature of the forum. See *Perry Ed. Assn. v. Perry Local Educators' Assn.* If the forum is a traditional or open public forum, the State's restrictions on speech are subject to stricter scrutiny than are restrictions in a limited public forum. We have previously declined to decide whether a school district's opening of its facilities pursuant to N. Y. Educ. Law § 414 creates a limited or a traditional public forum. See *Lamb's Chapel.* Because the parties have agreed that Milford created a limited public forum when it opened its facilities in 1992, we need not resolve the issue here. Instead, we simply will assume that Milford operates a limited public forum.

When the State establishes a limited public forum, the State is not required to and does not allow persons to engage in every type of speech. The State may be justified "in reserving [its forum] for certain groups or for the discussion of certain topics." *Rosenberger v. Rector and Visitors of Univ. of Va.*, 515 U.S. 819, 829 (1995). The State's power to restrict speech, however, is not without limits. The restriction must not discriminate against speech on the basis of viewpoint, and the restriction must be "reasonable in light of the purpose served by the forum."

III

Applying this test, we first address whether the exclusion constituted viewpoint discrimination. We are guided in our analysis by two of our prior opinions, *Lamb's Chapel* and *Rosenberger.* In *Lamb's Chapel,* we held that a school district violated the Free Speech Clause of the First Amendment when it excluded a private group from presenting films at the school based solely on the films' discussions of family values from a religious perspective. Likewise, in *Rosenberger,* we held that a university's refusal to fund a student publication because the publication addressed issues from a religious perspective violated the Free Speech Clause. Concluding that Milford's exclusion of the Good News Club based on its religious nature is indistinguishable from the exclusions in these cases, we hold that the exclusion constitutes viewpoint discrimination. Because the restriction is viewpoint discriminatory, we need not decide whether it is unreasonable in light of the purposes served by the forum.[2]

2. Although Milford argued below that, under § 414, it could not permit its property to be used for the purpose of religious activity, here it merely asserts in one sentence that it has, "in accordance with state law, closed [its] limited open forum to purely religious instruction and services." Because Milford does not elaborate, it is difficult to discern whether it is

Milford has opened its limited public forum to activities that serve a variety of purposes, including events "pertaining to the welfare of the community." Milford interprets its policy to permit discussions of subjects such as child rearing, and of "the development of character and morals from a religious perspective." For example, this policy would allow someone to use Aesop's Fables to teach children moral values. Additionally, a group could sponsor a debate on whether there should be a constitutional amendment to permit prayer in public schools, and the Boy Scouts could meet "to influence a boy's character, development and spiritual growth." In short, any group that "promotes the moral and character development of children" is eligible to use the school building.

Just as there is no question that teaching morals and character development to children is a permissible purpose under Milford's policy, it is clear that the Club teaches morals and character development to children. For example, no one disputes that the Club instructs children to overcome feelings of jealousy, to treat others well regardless of how they treat the children, and to be obedient, even if it does so in a nonsecular way. Nonetheless, because Milford found the Club's activities to be religious in nature—"the equivalent of religious instruction itself"—it excluded the Club from use of its facilities.

Applying *Lamb's Chapel*,[3] we find it quite clear that Milford engaged in viewpoint discrimination when it excluded the Club from the afterschool forum. In *Lamb's Chapel*, the local New York school district similarly had adopted § 414's "social, civic or recreational use" category as a permitted use in its limited public forum. The district also prohibited use "by any group for religious purposes." Citing this prohibition, the school district excluded a church that wanted to present films teaching family values from a Christian perspective. We held that, because the films "no doubt dealt with a subject otherwise permissible" under the rule, the teaching of family values, the district's exclusion of the church was unconstitutional viewpoint discrimination.

Like the church in *Lamb's Chapel*, the Club seeks to address a subject otherwise permitted under the rule, the teaching of morals and character, from a religious standpoint. Certainly, one could have characterized the film presentations in *Lamb's Chapel* as a religious use, as the Court of Appeals did, *Lamb's Chapel v. Center Moriches Union Free School Dist., 959 F.2d 381,*

arguing that it is required by state law to exclude the Club's activities.

Before the Court of Appeals, Milford cited *Trietley v. Board of Ed. of Buffalo*, 65 A.D.2d 1, 409 N.Y.S.2d 912 (1978), in which a New York court held that a local school district could not permit a student Bible club to meet on school property because "religious purposes are not included in the enumerated purposes for which a school may be used under section 414 of the Education Law." Although the court conceded that the Bible clubs might provide incidental secular benefits, it nonetheless concluded that the school would have violated the Establishment Clause had it permitted the club's activities on campus. Because we hold that the exclusion of the Club on the basis of its religious perspective constitutes unconstitutional view-

point discrimination, it is no defense for Milford that purely religious purposes can be excluded under state law.

3. We find it remarkable that the Court of Appeals majority did not cite *Lamb's Chapel*, despite its obvious relevance to the case. We do not necessarily expect a court of appeals to catalog every opinion that reverses one of its precedents. Nonetheless, this oversight is particularly incredible because the majority's attention was directed to it at every turn. See, *e.g.*, (Jacobs, J., dissenting) ("I cannot square the majority's analysis in this case with *Lamb's Chapel*"); (District Court stating "that *Lamb's Chapel* and *Rosenberger* pinpoint the critical issue in this case");

388–389 (CA2 1992). And one easily could conclude that the films' purpose to instruct that " 'society's slide toward humanism ... can only be counterbalanced by a loving home where Christian values are instilled from an early age,' " was "quintessentially religious." The only apparent difference between the activity of Lamb's Chapel and the activities of the Good News Club is that the Club chooses to teach moral lessons from a Christian perspective through live storytelling and prayer, whereas Lamb's Chapel taught lessons through films. This distinction is inconsequential. Both modes of speech use a religious viewpoint. Thus, the exclusion of the Good News Club's activities, like the exclusion of Lamb's Chapel's films, constitutes unconstitutional viewpoint discrimination.

Our opinion in *Rosenberger* also is dispositive. In *Rosenberger,* a student organization at the University of Virginia was denied funding for printing expenses because its publication, Wide Awake, offered a Christian viewpoint. Just as the Club emphasizes the role of Christianity in students' morals and character, Wide Awake " 'challenged Christians to live, in word and deed, according to the faith they proclaim and ... encouraged students to consider what a personal relationship with Jesus Christ means.' " Because the university "selected for disfavored treatment those student journalistic efforts with religious editorial viewpoints," we held that the denial of funding was unconstitutional. Although in *Rosenberger* there was no prohibition on religion as a subject matter, our holding did not rely on this factor. Instead, we concluded simply that the university's denial of funding to print Wide Awake was viewpoint discrimination, just as the school district's refusal to allow Lamb's Chapel to show its films was viewpoint discrimination. Given the obvious religious content of Wide Awake, we cannot say that the Club's activities are any more "religious" or deserve any less First Amendment protection than did the publication of Wide Awake in *Rosenberger*.

Despite our holdings in *Lamb's Chapel* and *Rosenberger,* the Court of Appeals, like Milford, believed that its characterization of the Club's activities as religious in nature warranted treating the Club's activities as different in kind from the other activities permitted by the school. (the Club "is doing something other than simply teaching moral values"). The "Christian viewpoint" is unique, according to the court, because it contains an "additional layer" that other kinds of viewpoints do not. That is, the Club "is focused on teaching children how to cultivate their relationship with God through Jesus Christ," which it characterized as "quintessentially religious." With these observations, the court concluded that, because the Club's activities "fall outside the bounds of pure 'moral and character development,' " the exclusion did not constitute viewpoint discrimination.

We disagree that something that is "quintessentially religious" or "decidedly religious in nature" cannot also be characterized properly as the teaching of morals and character development from a particular viewpoint. See *202 F.3d at 512* (Jacobs, J., dissenting) ("When the subject matter is morals and character, it is quixotic to attempt a distinction between religious viewpoints and religious subject matters"). What matters for purposes of the Free Speech Clause is that we can see no logical difference in kind between the invocation of Christianity by the Club and the invocation of teamwork, loyalty, or patriotism by other associations to provide a foundation for their lessons. It is apparent that the unstated principle of the Court of Appeals' reasoning is its conclusion that any time religious instruction and prayer are used to discuss morals and character, the discussion is simply not a "pure" discussion of those issues. According to the Court of Appeals, reliance on Christian principles taints moral and character instruction in a way that other foundations for thought or viewpoints do not. We, however, have never reached such a conclusion. Instead, we reaffirm our holdings in *Lamb's Chapel* and *Rosenberger* that speech discussing otherwise permissible subjects cannot be excluded from a limited public forum on the ground that the subject is discussed from a religious viewpoint. Thus, we conclude that Milford's exclusion of the Club from use of the school, pursuant to its community use policy, constitutes impermissible viewpoint discrimination.[4]

JUSTICE SOUTER's recitation of the Club's activities is accurate. But in our view, religion is used by the Club in the same fashion that it was used by Lamb's Chapel and by the students in *Rosenberger*: religion is the viewpoint from which ideas are conveyed. We did not find the *Rosenberger* students' attempt to cultivate a personal relationship with Christ to bar their claim that religion was a viewpoint. And we see no reason to treat the Club's use of religion as something other than a viewpoint merely because of any evangelical message it conveys. According to JUSTICE SOUTER, the Club's activities constitute "an evangelical service of worship." Regardless of the label JUSTICE SOUTER wishes to use, what matters is the substance of the Club's activities, which we conclude are materially indistinguishable from the activities in *Lamb's Chapel* and *Rosenberger*.

IV

Milford argues that, even if its restriction constitutes viewpoint discrimination, its interest in not violating the Establishment Clause outweighs the Club's interest in gaining equal access to the school's facilities. In other words, according to Milford, its restriction was required to avoid violating the Establishment Clause. We disagree.

We have said that a state interest in avoiding an Establishment Clause violation "may be characterized as compelling," and therefore may justify content-based discrimination. *Widmar v. Vincent, 454 U.S. 263 (1981)*. However, it is not clear whether a State's interest in avoiding an Establishment Clause violation would justify viewpoint discrimination. See *Lamb's Chapel, 508 U.S. at 394–395* (noting the suggestion in *Widmar* but ultimately not finding an Establishment Clause problem). We need not, however, confront the issue in this case, because we conclude that the school has no valid Establishment Clause interest.

We rejected Establishment Clause defenses similar to Milford's in two previous free speech cases, *Lamb's Chapel* and *Widmar*. In particular, in *Lamb's Chapel*, we explained that "the showing of the film series would not have been during school hours, would not have been sponsored by the school, and would have been open to the public, not just to church members."

---

4. Despite Milford's insistence that the Club's activities constitute "religious worship," the Court of Appeals made no such determination. It did compare the Club's activities to "religious worship," but ultimately it concluded merely that the Club's activities "fall outside the bounds of pure 'moral and character development.' " In any event, we conclude that the Club's activities do not constitute mere religious worship, divorced from any teaching of moral values.

Accordingly, we found that "there would have been no realistic danger that the community would think that the District was endorsing religion or any particular creed." Likewise, in *Widmar*, where the university's forum was already available to other groups, this Court concluded that there was no Establishment Clause problem.

The Establishment Clause defense fares no better in this case. As in *Lamb's Chapel*, the Club's meetings were held after school hours, not sponsored by the school, and open to any student who obtained parental consent, not just to Club members. As in *Widmar*, Milford made its forum available to other organizations. The Club's activities are materially indistiguishable from those in *Lamb's Chapel* and *Widmar*. Thus, Milford's reliance on the Establishment Clause is unavailing.

Milford attempts to distinguish *Lamb's Chapel* and *Widmar* by emphasizing that Milford's policy involves elementary school children. According to Milford, children will perceive that the school is endorsing the Club and will feel coercive pressure to participate, because the Club's activities take place on school grounds, even though they occur during nonschool hours.[5] This argument is unpersuasive.

First, we have held that "a significant factor in upholding governmental programs in the face of Establishment Clause attack is their *neutrality* towards religion." *Rosenberger, 515 U.S. at 839* (emphasis added). See also *Mitchell v. Helms, infra* this supplement ("In distinguishing between indoctrination that is attributable to the State and indoctrination that is not, [the Court has] consistently turned to the principle of *neutrality,* upholding aid that is offered to a broad range of groups or persons without regard to their religion" (emphasis added)); (O'CONNOR, J., concurring in judgment) ("Neutrality is an important reason for upholding government-aid programs against Establishment Clause challenges"). Milford's implication that granting access to the Club would do damage to the neutrality principle defies logic. For the "guarantee of neutrality is respected, not offended, when the government, following neutral criteria and evenhanded policies, extends benefits to recipients whose ideologies and viewpoints, including religious ones, are broad and diverse." The Good News Club seeks nothing more than to be treated neutrally and given access to speak about the same topics as are other groups. Because allowing the Club to speak on school grounds would ensure neutrality, not threaten it, Milford faces an uphill battle in arguing that the Establishment Clause compels it to exclude the Good News Club.

Second, to the extent we consider whether the community would feel coercive pressure to engage in the Club's activities, cf. *Lee v. Weisman*, the relevant community would be the parents, not the elementary school children. It is the parents who choose whether their children will attend the Good News Club meetings. Because the children cannot attend without their parents' permission, they cannot be coerced into engaging in the Good News Club's

---

5. It is worth noting that, although Milford repeatedly has argued that the Club's meeting time directly after the schoolday is relevant to its Establishment Clause concerns, the record does not reflect any offer by the school district to permit the Club to use the facilities at a different time of day. The superintendent's stated reason for denying the applications was simply that the Club's activities were "religious instruction." In any event, consistent with *Lamb's Chapel* and *Widmar*, the school could not deny equal access to the Club for any time that is generally available for public use.

religious activities. Milford does not suggest that the parents of elementary school children would be confused about whether the school was endorsing religion. Nor do we believe that such an argument could be reasonably advanced.

Third, whatever significance we may have assigned in the Establishment Clause context to the suggestion that elementary school children are more impressionable than adults, we have never extended our Establishment Clause jurisprudence to foreclose private religious conduct during nonschool hours merely because it takes place on school premises where elementary school children may be present.

None of the cases discussed by Milford persuades us that our Establishment Clause jurisprudence has gone this far. For example, Milford cites *Lee* v. *Weisman* for the proposition that "there are heightened concerns with protecting freedom of conscience from subtle coercive pressure in the elementary and secondary public schools." In *Lee*, however, we concluded that attendance at the graduation exercise was obligatory. See also *Santa Fe Independent School Dist. v. Doe.* We did not place independent significance on the fact that the graduation exercise might take place on school premises. Here, where the school facilities are being used for a nonschool function and there is no government sponsorship of the Club's activities, *Lee* is inapposite.

Equally unsupportive is *Edwards v. Aguillard,* in which we held that a Louisiana law that proscribed the teaching of evolution as part of the public school curriculum, unless accompanied by a lesson on creationism, violated the Establishment Clause. In *Edwards,* we mentioned that students are susceptible to pressure in the classroom, particularly given their possible reliance on teachers as role models. But we did not discuss this concern in our application of the law to the facts. Moreover, we did note that mandatory attendance requirements meant that State advancement of religion in a school would be particularly harshly felt by impressionable students.[6] But we did not suggest that, when the school was not actually advancing religion, the impressionability of students would be relevant to the Establishment Clause issue. Even if *Edwards* had articulated the principle Milford believes it did, the facts in *Edwards* are simply too remote from those here to give the principle any weight. *Edwards* involved the content of the curriculum taught by state teachers *during the schoolday* to children required to attend. Obviously, when individuals who are not schoolteachers are giving lessons after school to children permitted to attend only with parental consent, the concerns expressed in *Edwards* are not present.[7]

---

6. Milford also cites *McCollum* for its position that the Club's religious element would be advanced by the State through compulsory attendance laws. In *McCollum*, the school district excused students from their normal classroom study during the regular schoolday to attend classes taught by sectarian religious teachers, who were subject to approval by the school superintendent. Under these circumstances, this Court found it relevant that "the operation of the State's compulsory education system ... assisted and was integrated with the program of religious instruction carried on by separate religious sects." In the present case, there is simply no integration and cooperation between the school district and the Club. The Club's activities take place *after* the time when the children are compelled by state law to be at the school.

7. Milford also refers to *Board of Ed. of Westside Community Schools (Dist. 66) v. Mergens, 496 U.S. 226, 110 L. Ed. 2d 191, 110 S. Ct. 2356 (1990),* to support its view that "assumptions about the ability of students to make ... subtle distinctions [between schoolteachers during the schoolday and Reverend Fournier after school] are less valid for elemen-

In further support of the argument that the impressionability of elementary school children even after school is significant, Milford points to several cases in which we have found Establishment Clause violations in public schools. For example, Milford relies heavily on *School Dist. of Abington Township v. Schempp,* in which we found unconstitutional Pennsylvania's practice of permitting public schools to read Bible verses at the opening of each schoolday. *Schempp,* however, is inapposite because this case does not involve activity by the school during the schoolday.

Fourth, even if we were to consider the possible misperceptions by schoolchildren in deciding whether Milford's permitting the Club's activities would violate the Establishment Clause, the facts of this case simply do not support Milford's conclusion. There is no evidence that young children are permitted to loiter outside classrooms after the schoolday has ended. Surely even young children are aware of events for which their parents must sign permission forms. The meetings were held in a combined high school resource room and middle school special education room, not in an elementary school classroom. The instructors are not schoolteachers. And the children in the group are not all the same age as in the normal classroom setting; their ages range from 6 to 12.[8] In sum, these circumstances simply do not support the theory that small children would perceive endorsement here.

Finally, even if we were to inquire into the minds of schoolchildren in this case, we cannot say the danger that children would misperceive the endorsement of religion is any greater than the danger that they would perceive a hostility toward the religious viewpoint if the Club were excluded from the public forum. This concern is particularly acute given the reality that Milford's building is not used only for elementary school children. Students, from kindergarten through the 12th grade, all attend school in the same building. There may be as many, if not more, upperclassmen than elementary school children who occupy the school after hours. For that matter, members of the public writ large are permitted in the school after hours pursuant to the community use policy. Any bystander could conceivably be aware of the school's use policy and its exclusion of the Good News Club, and could suffer as much from viewpoint discrimination as elementary school children could suffer from perceived endorsement. Cf. *Rosenberger* (expressing the concern that viewpoint discrimination can chill individual thought and expression).

We cannot operate, as Milford would have us do, under the assumption that any risk that small children would perceive endorsement should counsel in favor of excluding the Club's religious activity. We decline to employ

---

tary age children who tend to be less informed, more impressionable, and more subject to peer pressure than average adults." Four Justices in *Mergens* believed that high school students likely are capable of distinguishing between government and private endorsement of religion. (opinion of O'CONNOR, J.). The opinion, however, made no statement about how capable of discerning endorsement elementary school children would have been in the context of *Mergens,* where the activity at issue was *after school.* In any event, even to the extent elementary school children are more prone to peer pressure than are older children, it simply

is not clear what, in this case, they could be pressured to do.

8. Milford also relies on the Equal Access Act, 98 Stat. 1302, *20 U.S.C. §§ 4071–4074,* as evidence that Congress has recognized the vulnerability of elementary school children to misperceiving endorsement of religion. The Act, however, makes no express recognition of the impressionability of elementary school children. It applies only to public secondary schools and makes no mention of elementary schools. § 4071(a). We can derive no meaning from the choice by Congress not to address elementary schools.

Establishment Clause jurisprudence using a modified heckler's veto, in which a group's religious activity can be proscribed on the basis of what the youngest members of the audience might misperceive. Cf. *Capitol Square Review and Advisory Bd. v. Pinette* (O'CONNOR, J., concurring in part and concurring in judgment) ("Because our concern is with the political community writ large, the endorsement inquiry is *not about the perceptions of particular individuals* or saving isolated nonadherents from ... discomfort.... It is for this reason that the reasonable observer in the endorsement inquiry must be deemed aware of the history and context of the community and forum in which the religious [speech takes place]" (emphasis added)). There are countervailing constitutional concerns related to rights of other individuals in the community. In this case, those countervailing concerns are the free speech rights of the Club and its members. And, we have already found that those rights have been violated, not merely perceived to have been violated, by the school's actions toward the Club.

We are not convinced that there is any significance in this case to the possibility that elementary school children may witness the Good News Club's activities on school premises, and therefore we can find no reason to depart from our holdings in *Lamb's Chapel* and *Widmar*. Accordingly, we conclude that permitting the Club to meet on the school's premises would not have violated the Establishment Clause.[9]

V

When Milford denied the Good News Club access to the school's limited public forum on the ground that the Club was religious in nature, it discriminated against the Club because of its religious viewpoint in violation of the Free Speech Clause of the First Amendment. Because Milford has not raised a valid Establishment Clause claim, we do not address the question whether such a claim could excuse Milford's viewpoint discrimination.

The judgment of the Court of Appeals is reversed, and the case is remanded for further proceedings consistent with this opinion.

JUSTICE SCALIA, concurring.

I join the Court's opinion but write separately to explain further my views on two issues.

I

First, I join Part IV of the Court's opinion, regarding the Establishment Clause issue, with the understanding that its consideration of coercive pressure and perceptions of endorsement "to the extent" that the law makes such factors relevant, is consistent with the belief (which I hold) that in this case that extent is zero. As to coercive pressure: Physical coercion is not at issue

---

9. Both parties have briefed the Establishment Clause issue extensively, and neither suggests that a remand would be of assistance on this issue. Although JUSTICE SOUTER would prefer that a record be developed on several facts, and JUSTICE BREYER believes that development of those facts could yet be dispositive in this case, none of these facts is relevant to the Establishment Clause inquiry. For example, JUSTICE SOUTER suggests that we cannot determine whether there would be an Establishment Clause violation unless we know when, and to what extent, other groups use the facilities. When a limited public forum is available for use by groups presenting any viewpoint, however, we would not find an Establishment Clause violation simply because only groups presenting a religious viewpoint have opted to take advantage of the forum at a particular time.

here; and so-called "peer pressure," if it can even been considered coercion, is, when it arises from private activities, one of the attendant consequences of a freedom of association that is constitutionally protected. What is at play here is not coercion, but the compulsion of ideas—and the private right to exert and receive that compulsion (or to have one's children receive it) is *protected* by the Free Speech and Free Exercise Clauses, not banned by the Establishment Clause. A priest has as much liberty to proselytize as a patriot.

As to endorsement, I have previously written that "religious expression cannot violate the Establishment Clause where it (1) is purely private and (2) occurs in a traditional or designated public forum, publicly announced and open to all on equal terms." *Pinette.* The same is true of private speech that occurs in a limited public forum, publicly announced, whose boundaries are not drawn to favor religious groups but instead permit a cross-section of uses. In that context, which is this case, "erroneous conclusions [about endorsement] do not count." See *Lamb's Chapel v. Center Moriches Union Free School Dist.* (SCALIA, J., concurring in judgment) ("I would hold, simply and clearly, that giving [a private religious group] nondiscriminatory access to school facilities cannot violate [the Establishment Clause] because it does not signify state or local embrace of a particular religious sect").

II

Second, since we have rejected the only reason that respondent gave for excluding the Club's speech from a forum that clearly included it (the forum was opened to any "use pertaining to the welfare of the community"), I do not suppose it matters whether the exclusion is characterized as viewpoint or subject-matter discrimination. Lacking *any* legitimate reason for excluding the Club's speech from its forum—"because it's religious" will not do, see, *e.g., Church of Lukumi Babalu Aye, Inc. v. Hialeah, 508 U.S. 520, 532–533 (1993); Employment Div., Dept. of Human Resources of Ore. v. Smith, 494 U.S. 872, 877–878 (1990), infra* ch. 11—respondent would seem to fail First Amendment scrutiny regardless of how its action is characterized. Even subject-matter limits must at least be "reasonable in light of the purpose served by the forum," *Cornelius v. NAACP Legal Defense & Ed. Fund, Inc., 473 U.S. 788, 806 (1985).*[1] But I agree, in any event, that respondent did discriminate on the basis of viewpoint.

As I understand it, the point of disagreement between the Court and the dissenters (and the Court of Appeals) with regard to petitioner's Free Speech Clause claim is not whether the Good News Club must be permitted to present religious viewpoints on morals and character in respondent's forum,

1. In this regard, I should note the inaccuracy of the JUSTICE SOUTER'S claim that the reasonableness of the forum limitation is not properly before us. Petitioners argued, both in their papers filed in the District Court, Memorandum of Law in Support of Cross–Motion for Summary Judgment in No. 97–CV–0302 (NDNY), pp. 20–22, and in their brief filed on appeal, Brief for Appellants in No. 98–9494 (CA2), pp. 33–35, that respondent's exclusion of them from the forum was unreasonable in light of the purposes served by the forum. Although the District Court did say in passing that the reasonableness of respondent's general restriction on use of its facilities for religious purposes was not challenged, the Court of Appeals apparently decided that the particular reasonableness challenge brought by petitioners had been preserved, because it addressed the argument on the merits. ("Taking first the reasonableness criterion, the Club argues that the restriction is unreasonable.... This argument is foreclosed by precedent").

which has been opened to secular discussions of that subject.[2] The answer to that is established by our decision in *Lamb's Chapel*. The point of disagreement is not even whether *some* of the Club's religious speech fell within the protection of *Lamb's Chapel*. It certainly did (the Club's "teachings may involve secular values such as obedience or resisting jealousy").

The disagreement, rather, regards the portions of the Club's meetings that are not "purely" "discussions" of morality and character from a religious viewpoint. The Club, for example, urges children "who already believe in the Lord Jesus as their Savior" to "stop and ask God for the strength and the 'want' ... to obey Him," and it invites children who "don't know Jesus as Savior" to "trust the Lord Jesus to be [their] Savior from sin." The dissenters and the Second Circuit say that the presence of such additional speech, because it is purely religious, transforms the Club's meetings into something different in kind from other, nonreligious activities that teach moral and character development. Therefore, the argument goes, excluding the Club is not viewpoint discrimination. I disagree.

Respondent has opened its facilities to any "use pertaining to the welfare of the community, provided that such use shall be nonexclusive and shall be opened to the general public." Shaping the moral and character development of children certainly "pertains to the welfare of the community." Thus, respondent has agreed that groups engaged in the endeavor of developing character may use its forum. The Boy Scouts, for example, may seek "to influence a boy's character, development and spiritual growth," *Boy Scouts of America v. Dale* ("The general mission of the Boy Scouts is clear: 'to instill values in young people'" (quoting the Scouts' mission statement)), and a group may use Aesop's Fables to teach moral values. When the Club attempted to teach Biblical-based moral values, however, it was excluded because its activities "did not involve merely a religious perspective on the secular subject of morality" and because "it [was] clear from the conduct of the meetings that the Good News Club goes far beyond merely stating its viewpoint."

From no other group does respondent require the sterility of speech that it demands of petitioners. The Boy Scouts could undoubtedly buttress their exhortations to keep "morally straight" and live "clean" lives by giving *reasons* why that is a good idea—because parents want and expect it, because it will make the scouts "better" and "more successful" people, because it will emulate such admired past Scouts as former President Gerald Ford. The Club, however, may only discuss morals and character, and cannot give *its* reasons why they should be fostered—because God wants and expects it, because it will make the Club members "saintly" people, and because it emulates Jesus Christ. The Club may not, in other words, independently discuss the religious premise on which its views are based—that God exists and His assistance is necessary to morality. It may not defend the premise, and it absolutely must not seek to persuade the children that the premise is true. The children must, so to say, take it on faith. This is blatant viewpoint discrimination. Just as calls to character based on patriotism will go unanswered if the listeners do not believe their country is good and just, calls to moral behavior based on

---

2. Neither does the disagreement center on the mode of the Club's speech—the fact that it sings songs and plays games. Although a forum could perhaps be opened to lectures but not plays, debates but not concerts, respondent has placed no such restrictions on the use of its facilities. (allowing seminars, concerts, and plays).

God's will are useless if the listeners do not believe that God exists. Effectiveness in presenting a viewpoint rests on the persuasiveness with which the speaker defends his premise—and in respondent's facilities every premise but a religious one may be defended.

In *Rosenberger* we struck down a similar viewpoint restriction. There, a private student newspaper sought funding from a student-activity fund on the same basis as its secular counterparts. And though the paper printed such directly religious material as exhortations to belief, (quoting the paper's self-described mission " 'to encourage students to consider what a personal relationship with Jesus Christ means' "); (SOUTER, J., dissenting) (" 'The only way to salvation through Him is by confessing and repenting of sin. It is the Christian's duty to make sinners aware of their need for salvation' " (quoting the paper)); we held that refusing to provide the funds discriminated on the basis of viewpoint, because the religious speech had been used to "provide . . . a specific premise . . . from which a variety of subjects may be discussed and considered." The right to present a viewpoint based on a religion premise carried with it the right to defend the premise.

The dissenters emphasize that the religious speech used by the Club as the foundation for its views on morals and character is not just any type of religious speech—although they cannot agree exactly what type of religious speech it is. In JUSTICE STEVENS' view, it is speech "aimed principally at proselytizing or inculcating belief in a particular religious faith." This does not, to begin with, distinguish *Rosenberger,* which also involved proselytizing speech, as the above quotations show. But in addition, it does not distinguish the Club's activities from those of the other groups using respondent's forum—which have not, as JUSTICE STEVENS suggests, been restricted to roundtable "discussions" of moral issues. Those groups may seek to inculcate children with their beliefs, and they may furthermore "recruit others to join their respective groups." The Club must therefore have liberty to do the same, even if, as JUSTICE STEVENS fears without support in the record, its actions may prove (shudder!) divisive. See *Lamb's Chapel* (remarking that worries about "public unrest" caused by "proselytizing" are "difficult to defend as a reason to deny the presentation of a religious point of view"); cf. *Lynch v. Donnelly* (holding that "political divisiveness" could not invalidate inclusion of creche in municipal Christmas display).

JUSTICE SOUTER, while agreeing that the Club's religious speech "may be characterized as proselytizing," thinks that it is even more clearly excludable from respondent's forum because it is essentially "an evangelical service of worship." But we have previously rejected the attempt to distinguish worship from other religious speech, saying that "the distinction has [no] intelligible content," and further, no *"relevance"* to the constitutional issue. *Widmar v. Vincent, 454 U.S. 263, 269, n. 6 (1981).*[3] Those holdings are surely proved correct today by the dissenters' inability to agree, even between themselves, into which subcategory of religious speech the Club's activities fell. If the

---

3. We *have* drawn a different distinction—between religious speech generally and speech about religion—but only with regard to restrictions the State must place on its own speech, where pervasive state monitoring is unproblematic. See *School Dist. of Abington Township v. Schempp* (State schools in their official ca-pacity may not teach religion but may teach about religion). Whatever the rule there, licensing and monitoring private religious speech is an entirely different matter, see, *e.g., Kunz v. New York,* even in a limited public forum where the state has some authority to draw subject-matter distinctions.

distinction did have content, it would be beyond the courts' competence to administer. cf. *Lee v. Weisman* (SOUTER, J., concurring) ("I can hardly imagine a subject less amenable to the competence of the federal judiciary, or more deliberately to be avoided where possible," than "comparative theology"). And if courts (and other government officials) were competent, applying the distinction would require state monitoring of private, religious speech with a degree of pervasiveness that we have previously found unacceptable. I will not endorse an approach that suffers such a wondrous diversity of flaws.

With these words of explanation, I join the opinion of the Court.

JUSTICE BREYER, concurring in part.

I agree with the Court's conclusion and join its opinion to the extent that they are consistent with the following three observations. First, the government's "neutrality" in respect to religion is one, but only one, of the considerations relevant to deciding whether a public school's policy violates the Establishment Clause. See, *e.g.*, *Mitchell v. Helms, infra* p. 145 (O'CONNOR, J., concurring in judgment); *Capitol Square Review and Advisory Bd. v. Pinette* (O'CONNOR, J., concurring in part and concurring in judgment). As this Court previously has indicated, a child's perception that the school has endorsed a particular religion or religion in general may also prove critically important. Today's opinion does not purport to change that legal principle.

Second, the critical Establishment Clause question here may well prove to be whether a child, participating in the Good News Club's activities, could reasonably perceive the school's permission for the club to use its facilities as an endorsement of religion. ("An important concern of the effects test is whether ... the challenged government action is sufficiently likely to be perceived by adherents of the controlling denominations as an endorsement, and by the nonadherents as a disapproval, of their individual religious choices"). The time of day, the age of the children, the nature of the meetings, and other specific circumstances are relevant in helping to determine whether, in fact, the Club "so dominates" the "forum" that, in the children's minds, "a formal policy of equal access is transformed into a demonstration of approval." *Capitol Square Review and Advisory Bd.* (O'CONNOR, J., concurring in part and concurring in judgment).

Third, the Court cannot fully answer the Establishment Clause question this case raises, given its procedural posture. The specific legal action that brought this case to the Court of Appeals was the District Court's decision to grant

Milford Central School's motion for summary judgment. The Court of Appeals affirmed the grant of summary judgment. We now hold that the school was not entitled to summary judgment, either in respect to the Free Speech or the Establishment Clause issue. Our holding must mean that, *viewing the disputed facts* (including facts about the children's perceptions) *favorably to the Club* (the non moving party), the school has not shown an Establishment Clause violation.

To deny one party's motion for summary judgment, however, is not to grant summary judgment for the other side. There may be disputed "genuine issues" of "material fact," particularly about how a reasonable child participant would understand the school's role, cf. (SOUTER, J., dissenting). Indeed, the Court itself points to facts not in evidence ("There is no evidence that young children are permitted to loiter outside classrooms after the schoolday has ended"), ("There may be as many, if not more, upperclassmen than elementary school children who occupy the school after hours"), identifies facts in evidence which may, depending on other facts not in evidence, be of legal significance (discussing the type of room in which the meetings were held and noting that the Club's participants "are not all the same age as in the normal classroom setting"), and makes assumptions about other facts ("Surely even young children are aware of events for which their parents must sign permission forms"), ("Any bystander could conceivably be aware of the school's use policy and its exclusion of the Good News Club, and could suffer as much from viewpoint discrimination as elementary school children could suffer from perceived endorsement"). The Court's invocation of what is missing from the record and its assumptions about what is present in the record only confirm that both parties, if they so desire, should have a fair opportunity to fill the evidentiary gap in light of today's opinion.

JUSTICE STEVENS, dissenting.

The Milford Central School has invited the public to use its facilities for educational and recreational purposes, but not for "religious purposes." Speech for "religious purposes" may reasonably be understood to encompass three different categories. First, there is religious speech that is simply speech about a particular topic from a religious point of view. The film in *Lamb's Chapel v. Center Moriches Union Free School Dist.* illustrates this category. (observing that the film series at issue in that case "would discuss Dr. [James] Dobson's views on the undermining influences of the media that could only be counterbalanced by returning to traditional, Christian family values instilled at an early stage"). Second, there is religious speech that amounts to worship, or its equivalent. Our decision in *Widmar v. Vincent, 454 U.S. 263 (1981),* concerned such speech. Third, there is an intermediate category that is aimed principally at proselytizing or inculcating belief in a particular religious faith.

A public entity may not generally exclude even religious worship from an open public forum. Similarly, a public entity that creates a limited public forum for the discussion of certain specified topics may not exclude a speaker simply because she approaches those topics from a religious point of view. Thus, in *Lamb's Chapel* we held that a public school that permitted its facilities to be used for the discussion of family issues and child rearing could not deny access to speakers presenting a religious point of view on those issues.

But, while a public entity may not censor speech about an authorized topic based on the point of view expressed by the speaker, it has broad discretion to "preserve the property under its control for the use to which it is lawfully dedicated." Accordingly, "control over access to a nonpublic forum can be based on subject matter and speaker identity so long as the distinctions drawn are reasonable in light of the purpose served by the forum and are viewpoint neutral." *Cornelius v. NAACP Legal Defense & Ed. Fund, Inc., 473 U.S. 788, 806 (1985).* The novel question that this case presents concerns the constitutionality of a public school's attempt to limit the scope of a public forum it has created. More specifically, the question is whether a school can, consistently with the First Amendment, create a limited public forum that admits the first type of religious speech without allowing the other two.

Distinguishing speech from a religious viewpoint, on the one hand, from religious proselytizing, on the other, is comparable to distinguishing meetings to discuss political issues from meetings whose principal purpose is to recruit new members to join a political organization. If a school decides to authorize after school discussions of current events in its classrooms, it may not exclude people from expressing their views simply because it dislikes their particular political opinions. But must it therefore allow organized political groups—for example, the Democratic Party, the Libertarian Party, or the Ku Klux Klan—to hold meetings, the principal purpose of which is not to discuss the current-events topic from their own unique point of view but rather to recruit others to join their respective groups? I think not. Such recruiting meetings may introduce divisiveness and tend to separate young children into cliques that undermine the school's educational mission. Cf. *Lehman v. Shaker Heights, 418 U.S. 298 (1974)* (upholding a city's refusal to allow "political advertising" on public transportation).

School officials may reasonably believe that evangelical meetings designed to convert children to a particular religious faith pose the same risk. And, just as a school may allow meetings to discuss current events from a political perspective without also allowing organized political recruitment, so too can a school allow discussion of topics such as moral development from a religious (or nonreligious) perspective without thereby opening its forum to religious proselytizing or worship. *See, e.g., Campbell v. St. Tammany Parish School Board, 231 F.3d 937, 942 (CA5 2000)* ("Under the Supreme Court's jurisprudence, a government entity such as a school board has the opportunity to open its facilities to activity protected by the First Amendment, without inviting political or religious activities presented in a form that would disserve its efforts to maintain neutrality"). Moreover, any doubt on a question such as this should be resolved in a way that minimizes "intrusion by the Federal Government into the operation of our public schools."

The particular limitation of the forum at issue in this case is one that prohibits the use of the school's facilities for "religious purposes." It is clear that, by "religious purposes," the school district did not intend to exclude all speech from a religious point of view. (testimony of the superintendent for Milford schools indicating that the policy would permit people to teach "that man was created by God as described in the Book of Genesis" and that crime was caused by society's "lack of faith in God"). Instead, it sought only to exclude religious speech whose principal goal is to "promote the gospel." In other words, the school sought to allow the first type of religious speech while excluding the second and third types. As long as this is done in an even handed manner, I see no constitutional violation in such an effort.[1] The line between the various categories of religious speech may be difficult to draw, but I think that the distinctions are valid, and that a school, particularly an elementary school, must be permitted to draw them.[2]

1. The school district, for example, could not, consistently with its present policy, allow school facilities to be used by a group that affirmatively attempted to inculcate nonbelief in God or in the view that morality is wholly unrelated to belief in God. Nothing in the record, however, indicates that any such group was allowed to use school facilities.

2. "A perceptive observer sees a material difference between the light of day and the

This case is undoubtedly close. Nonetheless, regardless of whether the Good News Club's activities amount to "worship," it does seem clear, based on the facts in the record, that the school district correctly classified those activities as falling within the third category of religious speech and therefore beyond the scope of the school's limited public forum.[3] In short, I am persuaded that the school district could (and did) permissibly exclude from its limited public forum proselytizing religious speech that does not rise to the level of actual worship. I would therefore affirm the judgment of the Court of Appeals.

Even if I agreed with Part II of the majority opinion, however, I would not reach out, as it does in Part IV, to decide a constitutional question that was not addressed by either the District Court or the Court of Appeals. Accordingly, I respectfully dissent.

JUSTICE SOUTER, with whom JUSTICE GINSBURG joins, dissenting.

The majority rules on two issues. First, it decides that the Court of Appeals failed to apply the rule in *Lamb's Chapel*, which held that the government may not discriminate on the basis of viewpoint in operating a limited public forum. The majority applies that rule and concludes that Milford violated *Lamb's Chapel* in denying Good News the use of the school. The majority then goes on to determine that it would not violate the Establishment Clause of the First Amendment for the Milford School District to allow the Good News Club to hold its intended gatherings of public school children in Milford's elementary school. The majority is mistaken on both points. The Court of Appeals unmistakably distinguished this case from *Lamb's Chapel*, though not by name, and accordingly affirmed the application of a policy, unchallenged in the District Court, that Milford's public schools may not be used for religious purposes. As for the applicability of the Establishment Clause to the Good News Club's intended use of Milford's school, the majority commits error even in reaching the issue, which was addressed neither by the Court of Appeals nor by the District Court. I respectfully dissent.

I

Lamb's Chapel, a case that arose (as this one does) from application of N. Y. Educ. Law § 414 and local policy implementing it, built on the accepted

dark of night, and knows that difference to be a reality even though the two are separated not by a bright line but by a zone of twilight." *Buirkle v. Hanover Insurance Cos.*, 832 F. Supp. 469, 483 (Mass. 1993).

3. The majority elides the distinction between religious speech on a particular topic and religious speech that seeks primarily to inculcate belief. Thus, it relies on *Rosenberger* as if that case involved precisely the same type of speech that is at issue here. But, while both Wide Awake, the organization in *Rosenberger*, and the Good News Club engage in a mixture of different types of religious speech, the *Rosenberger* Court clearly believed that the first type of religious speech predominated in Wide Awake. It described that group's publications as follows:

"The first issue had articles about racism, crisis pregnancy, stress, prayer, C.S. Lewis' ideas about evil and free will, and reviews of religious music. In the next two issues, Wide Awake featured stories about homosexuality, Christian missionary work, and eating disorders, as well as music reviews and interviews with University professors."

In contrast to Wide Awake's emphasis on providing Christian commentary on such a diverse array of topics, Good News Club meetings are dominated by religious exhortation (SOUTER, J., dissenting). My position is therefore consistent with the Court's decision in *Rosenberger*.

rule that a government body may designate a public forum subject to a reasonable limitation on the scope of permitted subject matter and activity, so long as the government does not use the forum-defining restrictions to deny expression to a particular viewpoint on subjects open to discussion. Specifically, *Lamb's Chapel* held that the government could not "permit school property to be used for the presentation of all views about family issues and child rearing except those dealing with the subject matter from a religious standpoint.".

This case, like *Lamb's Chapel*, properly raises no issue about the reasonableness of Milford's criteria for restricting the scope of its designated public forum. Milford has opened school property for, among other things, "instruction in any branch of education, learning or the arts" and for "social, civic and recreational meetings and entertainment events and other uses pertaining to the welfare of the community, provided that such uses shall be nonexclusive and shall be opened to the general public." But Milford has done this subject to the restriction that "school premises shall not be used ... for religious purposes." As the District Court stated, Good News did "not object to the reasonableness of [Milford]'s policy that prohibits the use of [its] facilities for religious purposes."

The sole question before the District Court was, therefore, whether, in refusing to allow Good News's intended use, Milford was misapplying its unchallenged restriction in a way that amounted to imposing a viewpoint-based restriction on what could be said or done by a group entitled to use the forum for an educational, civic, or other permitted purpose. The question was whether Good News was being disqualified when it merely sought to use the school property the same way that the Milford Boy and Girl Scouts and the 4–H Club did. The District Court held on the basis of undisputed facts that Good News's activity was essentially unlike the presentation of views on secular issues from a religious standpoint held to be protected in *Lamb's Chapel*, and was instead activity precluded by Milford's unchallenged policy against religious use, even under the narrowest definition of that term.

The Court of Appeals understood the issue the same way. The Court of Appeals also realized that the *Lamb's Chapel* criterion was the appropriate measure: "The activities of the Good News Club do not involve merely a religious perspective on the secular subject of morality."[2] The appeals court agreed with the District Court that the undisputed facts in this case differ from those in *Lamb's Chapel*, as night from day. A sampling of those facts shows why both courts were correct.

Good News's classes open and close with prayer. In a sample lesson considered by the District Court, children are instructed that "the Bible tells us how we can have our sins forgiven by receiving the Lord Jesus Christ. It tells us how to live to please Him.... If you have received the Lord Jesus as your Saviour from sin, you belong to God's special group—His family." The lesson plan instructs the teacher to "lead a child to Christ," and, when reading a Bible verse, to "emphasize that this verse is from the Bible, God's

2. It is true, as the majority notes, at n. 3, that the Court of Appeals did not cite *Lamb's Chapel* by name. But it followed it in substance, and it did cite an earlier opinion written by the author of the panel opinion here, *Bronx Household of Faith v. Community School Dist. No. 10, 127 F.3d 207 (CA2 1997),* which discussed *Lamb's Chapel* at length.

Word" and is "important—and true—because God said it." The lesson further exhorts the teacher to "be sure to give an opportunity for the 'unsaved' children in your class to respond to the Gospel" and cautions against "neglecting this responsibility."

While Good News's program utilizes songs and games, the heart of the meeting is the "challenge" and "invitation," which are repeated at various times throughout the lesson. During the challenge, "saved" children who "already believe in the Lord Jesus as their Savior" are challenged to " 'stop and ask God for the strength and the "want" ... to obey Him.' " They are instructed that "if you know Jesus as your Savior, you need to place God first in your life. And if you don't know Jesus as Savior and if you would like to, then we will—we will pray with you separately, individually.... And the challenge would be, those of you who know Jesus as Savior, you can rely on God's strength to obey Him."

During the invitation, the teacher "invites" the "unsaved" children " 'to trust the Lord Jesus to be your Savior from sin,' " and " 'receive [him] as your Savior from sin.' " The children are then instructed that "if you believe what God's Word says about your sin and how Jesus died and rose again for you, you can have His forever life today. Please bow your heads and close your eyes. If you have never believed on the Lord Jesus as your Savior and would like to do that, please show me by raising your hand. If you raised your hand to show me you want to believe on the Lord Jesus, please meet me so I can show you from God's Word how you can receive His everlasting life."

It is beyond question that Good News intends to use the public school premises not for the mere discussion of a subject from a particular, Christian point of view, but for an evangelical service of worship calling children to commit themselves in an act of Christian conversion.[3] The majority avoids this reality only by resorting to the bland and general characterization of Good News's activity as "teaching of morals and character, from a religious standpoint." If the majority's statement ignores reality, as it surely does, then today's holding may be understood only in equally generic terms. Otherwise, indeed, this case would stand for the remarkable proposition that any public school opened for civic meetings must be opened for use as a church, synagogue, or mosque.

JUSTICE STEVENS distinguishes between proselytizing and worship (dissenting opinion), and distinguishes each from discussion reflecting a religious point of view. I agree with JUSTICE STEVENS that Good News's activities may be characterized as proselytizing and therefore as outside the purpose of Milford's limited forum. Like the Court of Appeals, I also believe Good News's meetings have elements of worship that put the club's activities further afield of Milford's limited forum policy, the legitimacy of which was unchallenged in the summary judgment proceeding.

---

3. The majority rejects Milford's contention that Good News's activities fall outside the purview of the limited forum because they constitute "religious worship" on the ground that the Court of Appeals made no such determination regarding the character of the club's program, see n. 4. This distinction is merely semantic, in light of the Court of Appeals's conclusion that "it is difficult to see how the Club's activities differ materially from the 'religious worship' described" in other case law and the record below.

II

I also respectfully dissent from the majority's refusal to remand on all other issues, insisting instead on acting as a court of first instance in reviewing Milford's claim that it would violate the Establishment Clause to grant Good News's application. Milford raised this claim to demonstrate a compelling interest for saying no to Good News, even on the erroneous assumption that *Lamb's Chapel*'s public forum analysis would otherwise require Milford to say yes. Whereas the District Court and Court of Appeals resolved this case entirely on the ground that Milford's actions did not offend the First Amendment's Speech Clause, the majority now sees fit to rule on the application of the Establishment Clause, in derogation of this Court's proper role as a court of review.

The Court's usual insistence on resisting temptations to convert itself into a trial court and on remaining a court of review is not any mere procedural nicety, and my objection to turning us into a district court here does not hinge on a preference for immutable procedural rules. Respect for our role as a reviewing court rests, rather, on recognizing that this Court can often learn a good deal from considering how a district court and a court of appeals have worked their way through a difficult issue. It rests on recognizing that an issue as first conceived may come to be seen differently as a case moves through trial and appeal; we are most likely to contribute something of value if we act with the benefit of whatever refinement may come in the course of litigation. And our customary refusal to become a trial court reflects the simple fact that this Court cannot develop a record as well as a trial court can. If I were a trial judge, for example, I would balk at deciding on summary judgment whether an Establishment Clause violation would occur here without having statements of undisputed facts or uncontradicted affidavits showing, for example, whether Good News conducts its instruction at the same time as school-sponsored extracurricular and athletic activities conducted by school staff and volunteers; whether any other community groups use school facilities immediately after classes end and how many students participate in those groups; and the extent to which Good News, with 28 students in its membership, may "dominate the forum" in a way that heightens the perception of official endorsement.

Of course, I am in no better position than the majority to perform an Establishment Clause analysis in the first instance. Like the majority, I lack the benefit that development in the District Court and Court of Appeals might provide, and like the majority I cannot say for sure how complete the record may be. I can, however, speak to the doubtful underpinnings of the majority's conclusion.

This Court has accepted the independent obligation to obey the Establishment Clause as sufficiently compelling to satisfy strict scrutiny under the First Amendment. ("The interest of the [government] in complying with its constitutional obligations may be characterized as compelling"); *Lamb's Chapel*. Milford's actions would offend the Establishment Clause if they carried the message of endorsing religion under the circumstances, as viewed by a reasonable observer. See *Pinette* (O'CONNOR, J., concurring). The majority concludes that such an endorsement effect is out of the question in Milford's case, because the context here is "materially indistinguishable" from the facts in *Lamb's Chapel* and *Widmar*. In fact, the majority is in no position to say that, for the principal grounds on which we based our Establishment Clause holdings in those cases are clearly absent here.

In *Widmar*, we held that the Establishment Clause did not bar a religious student group from using a public university's meeting space for worship as well as discussion. As for the reasonable observers who might perceive government endorsement of religion, we pointed out that the forum was used by university students, who "are, of course, young adults," and, as such, "are less impressionable than younger students and should be able to appreciate that the University's policy is one of neutrality toward religion." To the same effect, we remarked that the "large number of groups meeting on campus" negated "any reasonable inference of University support from the mere fact of a campus meeting place." Not only was the forum "available to a broad class of nonreligious as well as religious speakers," but there were, in fact, over 100 recognized student groups at the University, and an "absence of empirical evidence that religious groups [would] dominate [the University's] open forum." ("The provision of benefits to so broad a spectrum of groups is an important index of secular effect"). And if all that had not been enough to show that the university-student use would probably create no impression of religious endorsement, we pointed out that the university in that case had issued a student handbook with the explicit disclaimer that "the University's name will not 'be identified in any way with the aims, policies, programs, products, or opinions of any organization or its members.' "

Lamb's Chapel involved an evening film series on child-rearing open to the general public (and, given the subject matter, directed at an adult audience). There, school property "had repeatedly been used by a wide variety of private organizations," and we could say with some assurance that "under these circumstances ... there would have been no realistic danger that the community would think that the District was endorsing religion or any particular creed...." What we know about this case looks very little like *Widmar* or *Lamb's Chapel*. The cohort addressed by Good News is not university students with relative maturity, or even high school pupils, but elementary school children as young as six.[4] The Establishment Clause cases have consistently recognized the particular impressionability of schoolchildren, see *Edwards v. Aguillard*, and the special protection required for those in the elementary grades in the school forum. We have held the difference between college students and grade school pupils to be a "distinction [that] warrants a difference in constitutional results," *Edwards v. Aguillard*.

---

4. It is certainly correct that parents are required to give permission for their children to attend Good News's classes (as parents are often required to do for a host of official school extracurricular activities), and correct that those parents would likely not be confused as to the sponsorship of Good News's classes. But the proper focus of concern in assessing effects includes the elementary school pupils who are invited to meetings, who see peers heading into classrooms for religious instruction as other classes end, and who are addressed by the "challenge" and "invitation."

The fact that there may be no evidence in the record that individual students were confused during the time the Good News Club met on school premises pursuant to the District Court's preliminary injunction is immaterial. As JUSTICE O'CONNOR explained in *Capitol Square Review and Advisory Bd. v. Pinette, 515 U.S. 753 (1995)*, the endorsement test does not focus "on the actual perception of individual observers, who naturally have differing degrees of knowledge," but on "the perspective of a hypothetical observer."

Nor is Milford's limited forum anything like the sites for wide-ranging intellectual exchange that were home to the challenged activities in *Widmar* and *Lamb's Chapel*. See also *Rosenberger*. In *Widmar*, the nature of the university campus and the sheer number of activities offered precluded the reasonable college observer from seeing government endorsement in any one of them, and so did the time and variety of community use in the *Lamb's Chapel* case. See also *Rosenberger* ("Given this wide array of nonreligious, antireligious and competing religious viewpoints in the forum supported by the University, any perception that the University endorses one particular viewpoint would be illogical"), (emphasizing the array of university-funded magazines containing "widely divergent viewpoints" and the fact that believers in Christian evangelism competed on equal footing in the University forum with aficionados of "Plato, Spinoza, and Descartes," as well as "Karl Marx, Bertrand Russell, and Jean–Paul Sartre"); *Board of Ed. of Westside Community Schools (Dist. 66) v. Mergens, 496 U.S. 226, 252 (1990)* (plurality opinion) ("To the extent that a religious club is merely one of many different student-initiated voluntary clubs, students should perceive no message of government endorsement of religion").

The timing and format of Good News's gatherings, on the other hand, may well affirmatively suggest the *imprimatur* of officialdom in the minds of the young children. The club is open solely to elementary students (not the entire community, as in *Lamb's Chapel*), only four outside groups have been identified as meeting in the school, and Good News is, seemingly, the only one whose instruction follows immediately on the conclusion of the official school day. Although school is out at 2:56 p.m., Good News apparently requested use of the school beginning at 2:30 on Tuesdays "during the school year," so that instruction could begin promptly at 3:00, at which time children who are compelled by law to attend school surely remain in the building. Good News's religious meeting follows regular school activities so closely that the Good News instructor must wait to begin until "the room is clear," and "people are out of the room," before starting proceedings in the classroom located next to the regular third-and fourth-grade rooms. In fact, the temporal and physical continuity of Good News's meetings with the regular school routine seems to be the whole point of using the school. When meetings were held in a community church, 8 or 10 children attended; after the school became the site, the number went up three-fold.

Even on the summary judgment record, then, a record lacking whatever supplementation the trial process might have led to, and devoid of such insight as the trial and appellate judges might have contributed in addressing the Establishment Clause, we can say this: there is a good case that Good News's exercises blur the line between public classroom instruction and private religious indoctrination, leaving a reasonable elementary school pupil unable to appreciate that the former instruction is the business of the school while the latter evangelism is not. Thus, the facts we know (or think we know) point away from the majority's conclusion, and while the consolation may be that nothing really gets resolved when the judicial process is so truncated, that is not much to recommend today's result.

QUESTIONS AND NOTES

1. Is this case about speech, religion, or both?. What would Thomas, Scalia, Breyer, Stevens, and Souter each say? What do you think that the case should have been about?

2. Whatever else might be said about Milford's policy, do you believe that it constituted viewpoint discrimination? Why? Why not? Do you believe that the Court did a good job of justifying its conclusion on this question? Explain.

3. If the question were open, would you have characterized Milford as a public forum, limited public forum, or nonpublic forum? (Compare *Perry*, p. 485 [1st Amendment book] *supra*).

4. Was it wise of the Second Circuit to not cite *Lamb's Chapel*? Why? Why not?

5. How, if at all, is *Lamb's Chapel* different from this case?

6. Does *Good News* change establishment clause jurisprudence at all? Explain.

7. Would refusal to allow the Fourniers to meet in the activity room constitute disapproval of religion and be unconstitutional under the establishment clause for that reason?

8. Do you agree with Justice Scalia that singing songs and playing games constitutes speech? Is that consistent with the views he took in the nude dancing cases? *Cf. Dallas v. Stanglin* (490 U.S. 19) holding that ballroom dancing does not constitute speech.

9. With which, if any, of the opinions do you agree? Explain.

Chapter X

GOVERNMENT FINANCING
OF RELIGION

D. LEMON TODAY

Insert p. 1187 (First Amendment) p. 350 (Religion and the Constitution) after n.5

The *Helms* case alluded to at the close of Justice Ginsburg's opinion did indeed make it's way to the Supreme Court which upheld the program by a sharply divided 4–2–3 split.

MITCHELL v. HELMS

530 U.S. 793 (2000).

Justice Thomas announced the judgment of the court and delivered an opinion, in which The Chief Justice, Justice Scalia, and Justice Kennedy join.

As part of a longstanding school aid program known as Chapter 2, the Federal Government distributes funds to state and local governmental agencies, which in turn lend educational materials and equipment to public and private schools, with the enrollment of each participating school determining the amount of aid that it receives. The question is whether Chapter 2, as applied in Jefferson Parish, Louisiana, is a law respecting an establishment of religion, because many of the private schools receiving Chapter 2 aid in that parish are religiously affiliated. We hold that Chapter 2 is not such a law.

I

A

Chapter 2 of the Education Consolidation and Improvement Act of 1981, has its origins in the Elementary and Secondary Education Act of 1965 (ESEA), and is a close cousin of the provision of the ESEA that we recently considered in *Agostini v. Felton*. Like the provision at issue in *Agostini*, Chapter 2 channels federal funds to local educational agencies (LEA's), which are usually public school districts, via state educational agencies (SEA's), to implement programs to assist children in elementary and secondary schools. Among other things, Chapter 2 provides aid

"for the acquisition and use of instructional and educational materials, including library services and materials (including media materials), assessments, reference materials, computer software and hardware for instructional use, and other curricular materials."

LEA's and SEA's must offer assistance to both public and private schools (although any private school must be nonprofit). Participating private schools receive Chapter 2 aid based on the number of children enrolled in each school, and allocations of Chapter 2 funds for those schools must generally be "equal (consistent with the number of children to be served) to expenditures for programs ... for children enrolled in the public schools of the [LEA]." LEA's must in all cases "assure equitable participation" of the children of private schools "in the purposes and benefits" of Chapter 2. Further, Chapter 2 funds may only "supplement and, to the extent practical, increase the level of funds that would ... be made available from non-Federal sources." LEA's and SEA's may not operate their programs "so as to supplant funds from non-Federal sources."

Several restrictions apply to aid to private schools. Most significantly, the "services, materials, and equipment" provided to private schools must be "secular, neutral, and nonideological." In addition, private schools may not acquire control of Chapter 2 funds or title to Chapter 2 materials, equipment, or property. A private school receives the materials and equipment by submitting to the LEA an application detailing which items the school seeks and how it will use them; the LEA, if it approves the application, purchases those items from the school's allocation of funds, and then lends them to that school.

In Jefferson Parish (the Louisiana governmental unit at issue in this case), as in Louisiana as a whole, private schools have primarily used their allocations for nonrecurring expenses, usually materials and equipment. In the 1986–1987 fiscal year, for example, 44% of the money budgeted for private schools in Jefferson Parish was spent by LEA's for acquiring library and media materials, and 48% for instructional equipment. Among the materials and equipment provided have been library books, computers, and computer software, and also slide and movie projectors, overhead projectors, television sets, tape recorders, VCR's, projection screens, laboratory equipment, maps, globes, filmstrips, slides, and cassette recordings.

It appears that, in an average year, about 30% of Chapter 2 funds spent in Jefferson Parish are allocated for private schools. For the 1985–1986 fiscal year, 41 private schools participated in Chapter 2. For the following year, 46 participated, and the participation level has remained relatively constant since then. Of these 46, 34 were Roman Catholic; 7 were otherwise religiously affiliated; and 5 were not religiously affiliated.

II

The Establishment Clause of the First Amendment dictates that "Congress shall make no law respecting an establishment of religion." In the over 50 years since *Everson v. Bd. of Ed. of Ewing*, we have consistently struggled to apply these simple words in the context of governmental aid to religious schools.[4] As we admitted in *Tilton v. Richardson*, "candor compels the

---

4. Cases prior to *Everson* discussed the issue only indirectly, see *e.g., Vidal v. Philadelphia*, 2 How. 127 (1844); *Quick Bear v. Leupp*, 210 U.S. 50 (1908), or evaluated aid to schools under other provisions of the Constitution, see *Cochran v. Louisiana Bd. of Ed.*, 281 U.S. 370 (1930).

acknowledgment that we can only dimly perceive the boundaries of permissible government activity in this sensitive area."

In *Agostini*, however, we brought some clarity to our case law, by overruling two anomalous precedents (one in whole, the other in part) and by consolidating some of our previously disparate considerations under a revised test. Whereas in *Lemon* we had considered whether a statute (1) has a secular purpose, (2) has a primary effect of advancing or inhibiting religion, or (3) creates an excessive entanglement between government and religion, in *Agostini* we modified *Lemon* for purposes of evaluating aid to schools and examined only the first and second factors. We acknowledged that our cases discussing excessive entanglement had applied many of the same considerations as had our cases discussing primary effect, and we therefore recast *Lemon*'s entanglement inquiry as simply one criterion relevant to determining a statute's effect. We also acknowledged that our cases had pared somewhat the factors that could justify a finding of excessive entanglement. We then set out revised criteria for determining the effect of a statute:

> "To summarize, New York City's Title I program does not run afoul of any of three primary criteria we currently use to evaluate whether government aid has the effect of advancing religion: It does not result in governmental indoctrination; define its recipients by reference to religion; or create an excessive entanglement."

In this case, our inquiry under *Agostini*'s purpose and effect test is a narrow one. Because respondents do not challenge the District Court's holding that Chapter 2 has a secular purpose, and because the Fifth Circuit also did not question that holding, we will consider only Chapter 2's effect. Considering Chapter 2 in light of our more recent case law, we conclude that it neither results in religious indoctrination by the government nor defines its recipients by reference to religion. We therefore hold that Chapter 2 is not a "law respecting an establishment of religion." In so holding, we acknowledge what both the Ninth and Fifth Circuits saw was inescapable—*Meek v. Pittinger* and *Wolman v. Walter* are anomalies in our case law. We therefore conclude that they are no longer good law.

A

As we indicated in *Agostini*, and have indicated elsewhere, the question whether governmental aid to religious schools results in governmental indoctrination is ultimately a question whether any religious indoctrination that occurs in those schools could reasonably be attributed to governmental action. We have also indicated that the answer to the question of indoctrination will resolve the question whether a program of educational aid "subsidizes" religion, as our religion cases use that term.

In distinguishing between indoctrination that is attributable to the State and indoctrination that is not, we have consistently turned to the principle of neutrality, upholding aid that is offered to a broad range of groups or persons without regard to their religion. If the religious, irreligious, and areligious are all alike eligible for governmental aid, no one would conclude that any indoctrination that any particular recipient conducts has been done at the behest of the government. For attribution of indoctrination is a relative question. If the government is offering assistance to recipients who provide, so to speak, a broad range of indoctrination, the government itself is not thought responsible for any particular indoctrination. To put the point differently, if the government, seeking to further some legitimate secular purpose, offers aid on the same terms, without regard to religion, to all who adequately further that purpose, then it is fair to say that any aid going to a religious recipient only has the effect of furthering that secular purpose. The government, in crafting such an aid program, has had to conclude that a given level of aid is necessary to further that purpose among secular recipients and has provided no more than that same level to religious recipients.

As a way of assuring neutrality, we have repeatedly considered whether any governmental aid that goes to a religious institution does so "only as a result of the genuinely independent and private choices of individuals." We have viewed as significant whether the "private choices of individual parents," as opposed to the "unmediated" will of government, determine what schools ultimately benefit from the governmental aid, and how much. For if numerous private choices, rather than the single choice of a government, determine the distribution of aid pursuant to neutral eligibility criteria, then a government cannot, or at least cannot easily, grant special favors that might lead to a religious establishment.

The principles of neutrality and private choice, and their relationship to each other, were prominent not only in *Agostini*, but also in *Zobrest v. Cataline Foothills School Dist.*, *Witters v. Washington Dept. of Services for Blind*, and *Mueller v. Allen*.[5]

Agostini's second primary criterion for determining the effect of governmental aid is closely related to the first. The second criterion requires a court to consider whether an aid program "defines its recipients by reference to religion." As we briefly explained in *Agostini*, this second criterion looks to the same set of facts as does our focus, under the first criterion, on neutrality, but the second criterion uses those facts to answer a somewhat different question—whether the criteria for allocating the aid "create a financial incentive to undertake religious indoctrination." In *Agostini* we set out the following rule for answering this question:

> "This incentive is not present, however, where the aid is allocated on the basis of neutral, secular criteria that neither favor nor disfavor religion, and is made available to both religious and secular beneficiaries on a nondiscriminatory basis. Under such circumstances, the aid is less likely to have the effect of advancing religion."

The cases on which *Agostini* relied for this rule, and *Agostini* itself, make clear the close relationship between this rule, incentives, and private choice. For to say that a program does not create an incentive to choose religious schools is to say that the private choice is truly "independent." *Witters*.

We hasten to add, what should be obvious from the rule itself, that simply because an aid program offers private schools, and thus religious schools, a benefit that they did not previously receive does not mean that the program, by reducing the cost of securing a religious education, creates, under *Agosti-*

---

5. JUSTICE O'CONNOR acknowledges that "neutrality is an important reason for upholding government-aid programs," one that our recent cases have "emphasized ... repeatedly."

ni's second criterion, an "incentive" for parents to choose such an education for their children. For *any* aid will have some such effect.

B

Respondents inexplicably make no effort to address Chapter 2 under the *Agostini* test. Instead, dismissing *Agostini* as factually distinguishable, they offer two rules that they contend should govern our determination of whether Chapter 2 has the effect of advancing religion. They argue first, and chiefly, that "direct, nonincidental" aid to the primary educational mission of religious schools is always impermissible. Second, they argue that provision to religious schools of aid that is divertible to religious use is similarly impermissible. Respondents' arguments are inconsistent with our more recent case law, in particular *Agostini* and *Zobrest*, and we therefore reject them.

1

Although some of our earlier cases, particularly *School Dist. of Grand Rapids v. Ball*, did emphasize the distinction between direct and indirect aid, the purpose of this distinction was merely to prevent "subsidization" of religion. As even the dissent all but admits, our more recent cases address this purpose not through the direct/indirect distinction but rather through the principle of private choice, as incorporated in the first *Agostini* criterion (*i.e.*, whether any indoctrination could be attributed to the government). If aid to schools, even "direct aid," is neutrally available and, before reaching or benefiting any religious school, first passes through the hands (literally or figuratively) of numerous private citizens who are free to direct the aid elsewhere, the government has not provided any "support of religion." *Witters.* Although the presence of private choice is easier to see when aid literally passes through the hands of individuals—which is why we have mentioned directness in the same breath with private choice—there is no reason why the Establishment Clause requires such a form.

To the extent that respondents intend their direct/indirect distinction to require that any aid be literally placed in the hands of schoolchildren rather than given directly to the school for teaching those same children, the very cases on which respondents most rely, *Meek* and *Wolman*, demonstrate the irrelevance of such formalism. In *Meek*, we justified our rejection of a program that loaned instructional materials and equipment by, among other things, pointing out that the aid was loaned to the schools, and thus was "direct aid." The materials-and-equipment program in *Wolman* was essentially identical, except that the State, in an effort to comply with *Meek*, loaned the aid to the students. (The revised program operated much like the one we upheld in *Bd. of Ed. of Central School Dist. No. 1 v. Allen.* Compare *Wolman,* with *Allen.*) Yet we dismissed as "technical" the difference between the two programs: "It would exalt form over substance if this distinction were found to justify a result different from that in *Meek.*" *Wolman* thus, although purporting to reaffirm *Meek*, actually undermined that decision, as is evident from the similarity between the reasoning of *Wolman* and that of the *Meek* dissent. That *Meek* and *Wolman* reached the same result, on programs that were indistinguishable but for the direct/indirect distinction, shows that that distinction played no part in *Meek*.

Further, respondents' formalistic line breaks down in the application to real-world programs. In *Allen*, for example, although we did recognize that students themselves received and owned the textbooks, we also noted that the books provided were those that the private schools required for courses, that the schools could collect students' requests for books and submit them to the board of education, that the schools could store the textbooks, and that the textbooks were essential to the schools' teaching of secular subjects. Whether one chooses to label this program "direct" or "indirect" is a rather arbitrary choice, one that does not further the constitutional analysis.

Of course, we have seen "special Establishment Clause dangers" when *money* is given to religious schools or entities directly rather than, as in *Witters* and *Mueller*, indirectly. But direct payments of money are not at issue in this case, and we refuse to allow a "special" case to create a rule for all cases.

2

Respondents also contend that the Establishment Clause requires that aid to religious schools not be impermissibly religious in nature or be divertible to religious use. We agree with the first part of this argument but not the second. Respondents' "no divertibility" rule is inconsistent with our more recent case law and is unworkable. So long as the governmental aid is not itself "unsuitable for use in the public schools because of religious content," and eligibility for aid is determined in a constitutionally permissible manner, any use of that aid to indoctrinate cannot be attributed to the government and is thus not of constitutional concern. And, of course, the use to which the aid is put does not affect the criteria governing the aid's allocation and thus does not create any impermissible incentive under *Agostini*'s second criterion.

Our recent precedents, particularly *Zobrest*, require us to reject respondents' argument. For *Zobrest* gave no consideration to divertibility or even to actual diversion. Had such things mattered to the Court in *Zobrest*, we would have found the case to be quite easy—for *striking down* rather than, as we did, upholding the program—which is just how the dissent saw the case. Quite clearly, then, we did not, as respondents do, think that the *use* of governmental aid to further religious indoctrination was synonymous with religious indoctrination *by* the government or that such use of aid created any improper incentives.

Similarly, had we, in *Witters*, been concerned with divertibility or diversion, we would have unhesitatingly, perhaps summarily, struck down the tuition-reimbursement program, because it was certain that Witters sought to participate in it to acquire an education in a religious career from a sectarian institution. Diversion was guaranteed. *Mueller* took the same view as *Zobrest* and *Witters*, for we did not in *Mueller* require the State to show that the tax deductions were only for the costs of education in secular subjects. We declined to impose any such segregation requirement for either the tuition-expense deductions or the deductions for items strikingly similar to those at issue in *Meek* and *Wolman*, and here.

JUSTICE O'CONNOR acknowledges that the Court in *Zobrest* and *Witters* approved programs that involved actual diversion. The dissent likewise does not deny that *Witters* involved actual diversion. The dissent does claim that the aid in *Zobrest* "was not considered divertible," but the dissent in *Zobrest*, which the author of today's dissent joined, understood the case otherwise. As that dissent made clear, diversion is the use of government aid to further a religious message. By that definition, the government-provided interpreter in *Zobrest* was not only divertible, but actually diverted.

The issue is not divertibility of aid but rather whether the aid itself has an impermissible content. Where the aid would be suitable for use in a public school, it is also suitable for use in any private school. Similarly, the prohibition against the government providing impermissible content resolves the Establishment Clause concerns that exist if aid is actually diverted to religious uses.[9] In *Agostini*, we explained *Zobrest* by making just this distinction between the content of aid and the use of that aid: "Because the only *government* aid in *Zobrest* was the interpreter, who was *herself not inculcating* any religious messages, no *government* indoctrination took place." (second emphasis added). *Agostini* also acknowledged that what the dissenters in *Zobrest* had charged was essentially true: *Zobrest* did effect a "shift . . . in our Establishment Clause law." The interpreter herself, assuming that she fulfilled her assigned duties, had "no inherent religious significance." And just as a government interpreter does not herself inculcate a religious message— even when she is conveying one—so also a government computer or overhead projector does not itself inculcate a religious message, even when it is conveying one.

In *Agostini* itself, we approved the provision of public employees to teach secular remedial classes in private schools partly because we concluded that there was no reason to suspect that indoctrinating content would be part of such governmental aid. Relying on *Zobrest*, we refused to presume that the public teachers would " 'inject religious content' " into their classes, especially given certain safeguards that existed; we also saw no evidence that they had done so.

A concern for divertibility, as opposed to improper content, is misplaced not only because it fails to explain why the sort of aid that we have allowed is permissible, but also because it is boundless—enveloping all aid, no matter how trivial—and thus has only the most attenuated (if any) link to any realistic concern for preventing an "establishment of religion." Presumably, for example, government-provided lecterns, chalk, crayons, pens, paper, and paintbrushes would have to be excluded from religious schools under respondents' proposed rule. But we fail to see how indoctrination by means of (*i.e.,* diversion of) such aid could be attributed to the government. In fact, the risk of improper attribution is *less* when the aid *lacks* content, for there is no risk (as there is with books), of the government inadvertently providing improper content. Finally, *any* aid, with or without content, is "divertible" in the sense that it allows schools to "divert" resources. Yet we have " 'not accepted the

---

9. The dissent would find an establishment of religion if a government-provided projector were used in a religious school to show a privately purchased religious film, even though a public school that possessed the same kind of projector would likely be constitutionally barred from *refusing* to allow a student bible club to use that projector in a classroom to show the very same film, where the classrooms and projectors were generally available to student groups. See *Lamb's Chapel v. Center Moriches Union Free School Dist.,* 508 U.S. 384 (1993).

recurrent argument that all aid is forbidden because aid to one aspect of an institution frees it to spend its other resources on religious ends.' "

C

The dissent serves up a smorgasbord of 11 factors that, depending on the facts of each case "in all its particularity," could be relevant to the constitutionality of a school-aid program. And those 11 are a bare minimum. We are reassured that there are likely more.[12] Presumably they will be revealed in future cases, as needed, but at least one additional factor is evident from the dissent itself: The dissent resurrects the concern for political divisiveness that once occupied the Court but that post-*Aguilar* cases have rightly disregarded.

One of the dissent's factors deserves special mention: whether a school that receives aid (or whose students receive aid) is pervasively sectarian. The dissent is correct that there was a period when this factor mattered, particularly if the pervasively sectarian school was a primary or secondary school. But that period is one that the Court should regret, and it is thankfully long past.

There are numerous reasons to formally dispense with this factor. First, its relevance in our precedents is in sharp decline. Although our case law has consistently mentioned it even in recent years, we have not struck down an aid program in reliance on this factor since 1985, in *Aguilar* and *Ball*. *Agostini* of course overruled *Aguilar* in full and *Ball* in part, and today JUSTICE O'CONNOR distances herself from the part of *Ball* with which she previously agreed, by rejecting the distinction between public and private employees that was so prominent in *Agostini*.

Second, the religious nature of a recipient should not matter to the constitutional analysis, so long as the recipient adequately furthers the government's secular purpose. If a program offers permissible aid to the religious (including the pervasively sectarian), the areligious, and the irreligious, it is a mystery which view of religion the government has established, and thus a mystery what the constitutional violation would be. The pervasively sectarian recipient has not received any special favor, and it is most bizarre that the Court would, as the dissent seemingly does, reserve special hostility for those who take their religion seriously, who think that their religion should affect the whole of their lives, or who make the mistake of being effective in transmitting their views to children.

Third, the inquiry into the recipient's religious views required by a focus on whether a school is pervasively sectarian is not only unnecessary but also offensive. It is well established, in numerous other contexts, that courts should refrain from trolling through a person's or institution's religious beliefs. See *Employment Div., Dept. of Human Resources of Ore. v. Smith*, 494 U.S. 872 (1990) (collecting cases). Yet that is just what this factor requires, as was evident before the District Court. Although the dissent welcomes such probing, we find it profoundly troubling. In addition, and related, the application of the "pervasively sectarian" factor collides with our decisions that have prohibited governments from discriminating in the distribution of public

---

12. It is thus surprising for the dissent to accuse us of following a rule of "breathtaking   . . . manipulability."

benefits based upon religious status or sincerity. See *Rosenberger v. Rector and Visitors of Univ. of Va.*, 515 U.S. 819 (1995); *Lamb's Chapel v. Center Moriches Union Free School Dist.*, 508 U.S. 384 (1993); *Widmar v. Vincent*, 454 U.S. 263 (1981).

Finally, hostility to aid to pervasively sectarian schools has a shameful pedigree that we do not hesitate to disavow. Although the dissent professes concern for "the implied exclusion of the less favored," the exclusion of pervasively sectarian schools from government-aid programs is just that, particularly given the history of such exclusion. Opposition to aid to "sectarian" schools acquired prominence in the 1870's with Congress's consideration (and near passage) of the Blaine Amendment, which would have amended the Constitution to bar any aid to sectarian institutions. Consideration of the amendment arose at a time of pervasive hostility to the Catholic Church and to Catholics in general, and it was an open secret that "sectarian" was code for "Catholic." Notwithstanding its history, of course, "sectarian" could, on its face, describe the school of any religious sect, but the Court eliminated this possibility of confusion when, in *Hunt v. McNair,* 413 U.S. 734, 743 (1973), it coined the term "pervasively sectarian"—a term which, at that time, could be applied almost exclusively to Catholic parochial schools and which even today's dissent exemplifies chiefly by reference to such schools.

In short, nothing in the Establishment Clause requires the exclusion of pervasively sectarian schools from otherwise permissible aid programs, and other doctrines of this Court bar it. This doctrine, born of bigotry, should be buried now.

III

Applying the two relevant *Agostini* criteria, we see no basis for concluding that Jefferson Parish's Chapter 2 program "has the effect of advancing religion." Chapter 2 does not result in governmental indoctrination, because it determines eligibility for aid neutrally, allocates that aid based on the private choices of the parents of schoolchildren, and does not provide aid that has an impermissible content. Nor does Chapter 2 define its recipients by reference to religion.

Taking the second criterion first, it is clear that Chapter 2 aid "is allocated on the basis of neutral, secular criteria that neither favor nor disfavor religion, and is made available to both religious and secular beneficiaries on a nondiscriminatory basis." Aid is allocated based on enrollment: "Private schools receive Chapter 2 materials and equipment based on the per capita number of students at each school," and allocations to private schools must "be equal (consistent with the number of children to be served) to expenditures for programs under this subchapter for children enrolled in the public schools of the [LEA]."

Chapter 2 also satisfies the first *Agostini* criterion. The program makes a broad array of schools eligible for aid without regard to their religious affiliations or lack thereof. We therefore have no difficulty concluding that Chapter 2 is neutral with regard to religion.

The ultimate beneficiaries of Chapter 2 aid are the students who attend the schools that receive that aid, and this is so regardless of whether individual students lug computers to school each day or, as Jefferson Parish has more sensibly provided, the schools receive the computers. Like the Ninth Circuit, and unlike the dissent, we "see little difference in loaning science kits to students who then bring the kits to school as opposed to loaning science kits to the school directly."

Finally, Chapter 2 satisfies the first *Agostini* criterion because it does not provide to religious schools aid that has an impermissible content. The statute explicitly bars anything of the sort, providing that all Chapter 2 aid for the benefit of children in private schools shall be "secular, neutral, and nonideological," and the record indicates that the Louisiana SEA and the Jefferson Parish LEA have faithfully enforced this requirement insofar as relevant to this case. The chief aid at issue is computers, computer software, and library books. The computers presumably have no pre-existing content, or at least none that would be impermissible for use in public schools. Respondents do not contend otherwise. Respondents also offer no evidence that religious schools have received software from the government that has an impermissible content.

There is evidence that equipment has been, or at least easily could be, diverted for use in religious classes. JUSTICE O'CONNOR, however, finds the safeguards against diversion adequate to prevent and detect actual diversion. The safeguards on which she relies reduce to three: (1) signed assurances that Chapter 2 aid will be used only for secular, neutral, and nonideological purposes, (2) monitoring visits, and (3) the requirement that equipment be labeled as belonging to Chapter 2. As to the first, JUSTICE O'CONNOR rightly places little reliance on it. As to the second, monitoring by SEA and LEA officials is highly unlikely to prevent or catch diversion. As to the third, compliance with the labeling requirement is haphazard, and, even if the requirement were followed, we fail to see how a label prevents diversion. In addition, we agree with the dissent that there is evidence of actual diversion and that, were the safeguards anything other than anemic, there would almost certainly be more such evidence. In any event, for reasons we discussed in Part II–B–2, *supra*, the evidence of actual diversion and the weakness of the safeguards against actual diversion are not relevant to the constitutional inquiry, whatever relevance they may have under the statute and regulations.

Respondents do, however, point to some religious books that the LEA improperly allowed to be loaned to several religious schools, and they contend that the monitoring programs of the SEA and the Jefferson Parish LEA are insufficient to prevent such errors. The evidence, however, establishes just the opposite, for the improper lending of library books occurred—and was discovered and remedied—before this litigation began almost 15 years ago. In other words, the monitoring system worked. Further, the violation by the LEA and the private schools was minor and, in the view of the SEA's coordinator, inadvertent. There were approximately 191 improper book requests over three years (the 1982–1983 through 1984–1985 school years); these requests came from fewer than half of the 40 private schools then participating; and the cost of the 191 books amounted to "less than one percent of the total allocation over all those years."

The District Court found that prescreening by the LEA coordinator of requested library books was sufficient to prevent statutory violations, and the

Fifth Circuit did not disagree. Further, as noted, the monitoring system appears adequate to catch those errors that do occur. We are unwilling to elevate scattered *de minimis* statutory violations, discovered and remedied by the relevant authorities themselves prior to any litigation, to such a level as to convert an otherwise unobjectionable parishwide program into a law that has the effect of advancing religion.

IV

In short, Chapter 2 satisfies both the first and second primary criteria of *Agostini*. It therefore does not have the effect of advancing religion. For the same reason, Chapter 2 also "cannot reasonably be viewed as an endorsement of religion." Accordingly, we hold that Chapter 2 is not a law respecting an establishment of religion. Jefferson Parish need not exclude religious schools from its Chapter 2 program. To the extent that *Meek* and *Wolman* conflict with this holding, we overrule them.

The judgment of the Fifth Circuit is reversed.

It is so ordered.

JUSTICE O'CONNOR, with whom JUSTICE BREYER joins, concurring in the judgment.

Three Terms ago, we held in *Agostini v. Felton* that Title I, as applied in New York City, did not violate the Establishment Clause. I believe that *Agostini* likewise controls the constitutional inquiry respecting Title II presented here, and requires the reversal of the Court of Appeals' judgment that the program is unconstitutional as applied in Jefferson Parish, Louisiana. To the extent our decisions in *Meek* and *Wolman* are inconsistent with the Court's judgment today, I agree that those decisions should be overruled. I therefore concur in the judgment.

I

I write separately because, in my view, the plurality announces a rule of unprecedented breadth for the evaluation of Establishment Clause challenges to government school-aid programs. Reduced to its essentials, the plurality's rule states that government aid to religious schools does not have the effect of advancing religion so long as the aid is offered on a neutral basis and the aid is secular in content. The plurality also rejects the distinction between direct and indirect aid, and holds that the actual diversion of secular aid by a religious school to the advancement of its religious mission is permissible. Although the expansive scope of the plurality's rule is troubling, two specific aspects of the opinion compel me to write separately. First, the plurality's treatment of neutrality comes close to assigning that factor singular importance in the future adjudication of Establishment Clause challenges to government school-aid programs. Second, the plurality's approval of actual diversion of government aid to religious indoctrination is in tension with our precedents and, in any event, unnecessary to decide the instant case.

The clearest example of the plurality's near-absolute position with respect to neutrality is found in its following statement:

"If the religious, irreligious, and areligious are all alike eligible for governmental aid, no one would conclude that any indoctrination that any particular recipient conducts has been done at the behest of the government. For attribution of indoctrination is a relative question. If the government is offering assistance to recipients who provide, so to speak, a broad range of indoctrination, the government itself is not thought responsible for any particular indoctrination. To put the point differently, if the government, seeking to further some legitimate secular purpose, offers aid on the same terms, without regard to religion, to all who adequately further that purpose, then it is fair to say that any aid going to a religious recipient only has the effect of furthering that secular purpose."

I agree with JUSTICE SOUTER that the plurality, by taking such a stance, "appears to take evenhandedness neutrality and in practical terms promote it to a single and sufficient test for the establishment constitutionality of school aid."

I do not quarrel with the plurality's recognition that neutrality is an important reason for upholding government-aid programs against Establishment Clause challenges. Our cases have described neutrality in precisely this manner, and we have emphasized a program's neutrality repeatedly in our decisions approving various forms of school aid. Nevertheless, we have never held that a government-aid program passes constitutional muster *solely* because of the neutral criteria it employs as a basis for distributing aid. For example, in *Agostini*, neutrality was only one of several factors we considered in determining that New York City's Title I program did not have the impermissible effect of advancing religion (noting lack of evidence of inculcation of religion by Title I instructors, legal requirement that Title I services be supplemental to regular curricula, and that no Title I funds reached religious schools' coffers). Indeed, given that the aid in *Agostini* had secular content and was distributed on the basis of wholly neutral criteria, our consideration of additional factors demonstrates that the plurality's rule does not accurately describe our recent Establishment Clause jurisprudence. See also *Zobrest* (noting that no government funds reached religious school's coffers, aid did not relieve school of expense it otherwise would have assumed, and aid was not distributed to school but to the child).

I also disagree with the plurality's conclusion that actual diversion of government aid to religious indoctrination is consistent with the Establishment Clause. Although "our cases have permitted some government funding of secular functions performed by sectarian organizations," our decisions "provide no precedent for the use of public funds to finance religious activities." At least two of the decisions at the heart of today's case demonstrate that we have long been concerned that secular government aid not be diverted to the advancement of religion. In both *Agostini*, our most recent school-aid case, and *Allen*, we rested our approval of the relevant programs in part on the fact that the aid had not been used to advance the religious missions of the recipient schools.

The plurality bases its holding that actual diversion is permissible on *Witters* and *Zobrest*. Those decisions, however, rested on a significant factual premise missing from this case, as well as from the majority of cases thus far considered by the Court involving Establishment Clause challenges to school-aid programs. Specifically, we decided *Witters* and *Zobrest* on the understanding that the aid was provided directly to the individual student who, in turn, made the choice of where to put that aid to use. Accordingly, our approval of the aid in both cases relied to a significant extent on the fact that "any aid ... that ultimately flows to religious institutions does so only as a result of the genuinely independent and private choices of aid recipients."

Recognizing this distinction, the plurality nevertheless finds *Witters* and *Zobrest*—to the extent those decisions might permit the use of government aid for religious purposes—relevant in any case involving a neutral, per-capita-aid program. Like JUSTICE SOUTER, I do not believe that we should treat a per-capita-aid program the same as the true private-choice programs considered in *Witters* and *Zobrest*. First, when the government provides aid directly to the student beneficiary, that student can attend a religious school and yet retain control over whether the secular government aid will be applied toward the religious education. The fact that aid flows to the religious school and is used for the advancement of religion is therefore *wholly* dependent on the student's private decision.

Second, I believe the distinction between a per-capita school-aid program and a true private-choice program is significant for purposes of endorsement. *See, e.g., Lynch v. Donnelly*, (O'CONNOR, J., concurring). In terms of public perception, a government program of direct aid to religious schools based on the number of students attending each school differs meaningfully from the government distributing aid directly to individual students who, in turn, decide to use the aid at the same religious schools. In the former example, if the religious school uses the aid to inculcate religion in its students, it is reasonable to say that the government has communicated a message of endorsement. Because the religious indoctrination is supported by government assistance, the reasonable observer would naturally perceive the aid program as *government* support for the advancement of religion. That the amount of aid received by the school is based on the school's enrollment does not separate the government from the endorsement of the religious message. The aid formula does not—and could not—indicate to a reasonable observer that the inculcation of religion is endorsed only by the individuals attending the religious school, who each affirmatively choose to direct the secular government aid to the school and its religious mission. No such choices have been made. In contrast, when government aid supports a school's religious mission only because of independent decisions made by numerous individuals to guide their secular aid to that school, "[n]o reasonable observer is likely to draw from the facts ... an inference that the State itself is endorsing a religious practice or belief." Rather, endorsement of the religious message is reasonably attributed to the individuals who select the path of the aid.

Finally, the distinction between a per-capita-aid program and a true private-choice program is important when considering aid that consists of direct monetary subsidies. This Court has "recognized special Establishment Clause dangers where the government makes direct money payments to sectarian institutions." If, as the plurality contends, a per-capita-aid program is identical in relevant constitutional respects to a true private-choice program, then there is no reason that, under the plurality's reasoning, the government should be precluded from providing direct money payments to religious organizations (including churches) based on the number of persons belonging to each organization. And, because actual diversion is permissible under the plurality's holding, the participating religious organizations (including churches) could use that aid to support religious indoctrination. To be sure, the plurality does not actually hold that its theory extends to direct money payments. That omission, however, is of little comfort. In its logic—as well as its specific advisory language,—the plurality opinion foreshadows the approval of direct monetary subsidies to religious organizations, even when they use the money to advance their religious objectives.

Our school-aid cases often pose difficult questions at the intersection of the neutrality and no-aid principles and therefore defy simple categorization under either rule. As I explained in *Rosenberger*, "resolution instead depends on the hard task of judging—sifting through the details and determining whether the challenged program offends the Establishment Clause. Such judgment requires courts to draw lines, sometimes quite fine, based on the particular facts of each case."

II

In *Agostini*, after reexamining our jurisprudence since *School Dist. of Grand Rapids v. Ball*, we explained that the general principles used to determine whether government aid violates the Establishment Clause have remained largely unchanged. Thus, we still ask "whether the government acted with the purpose of advancing or inhibiting religion" and "whether the aid has the 'effect' of advancing or inhibiting religion." We also concluded in *Agostini*, however, that the specific criteria used to determine whether government aid has an impermissible effect had changed. Looking to our recently decided cases, we articulated three primary criteria to guide the determination whether a government-aid program impermissibly advances religion: (1) whether the aid results in governmental indoctrination, (2) whether the aid program defines its recipients by reference to religion, and (3) whether the aid creates an excessive entanglement between government and religion. Finally, we noted that the same criteria could be reviewed to determine whether a government-aid program constitutes an endorsement of religion.

Respondents neither question the secular purpose of the Chapter 2 (Title II) program nor contend that it creates an excessive entanglement. Accordingly, for purposes of deciding whether Chapter 2, as applied in Jefferson Parish, Louisiana, violates the Establishment Clause, we need ask only whether the program results in governmental indoctrination or defines its recipients by reference to religion.

Taking the second inquiry first, it is clear that Chapter 2 does not define aid recipients by reference to religion. In *Agostini*, we explained that scrutiny of the manner in which a government-aid program identifies its recipients is important because "the criteria might themselves have the effect of advancing religion by creating a financial incentive to undertake religious indoctrination." We then clarified that this financial incentive is not present "where the aid is allocated on the basis of neutral, secular criteria that neither favor nor disfavor religion, and is made available to both religious and secular beneficiaries on a nondiscriminatory basis." Under Chapter 2, the Secretary of Education allocates funds to the States based on each State's share of the Nation's school-age population.

Agostini next requires us to ask whether Chapter 2 "results in governmental indoctrination." Because this is a more complex inquiry under our case law, it is useful first to review briefly the basis for our decision in *Agostini* that New York City's Title I program did not result in governmental indoctrination. Under that program, public-school teachers provided Title I instruction to eligible students on private school premises during regular school hours. Twelve years earlier, in *Aguilar v. Felton*, we had held the same New York City program unconstitutional. In *Ball*, a companion case to *Aguilar*, we also held that a similar program in Grand Rapids, Michigan, violated the Constitution. Our decisions in *Aguilar* and *Ball* were both based on a presumption, drawn in large part from *Meek*, that public-school instructors who teach secular classes on the campuses of religious schools will inevitably inculcate religion in their students.

In *Agostini*, we recognized that "our more recent cases [had] undermined the assumptions upon which *Ball* and *Aguilar* relied." First, we explained that the Court had since abandoned "the presumption erected in *Meek* and *Ball* that the placement of public employees on parochial school grounds inevitably results in the impermissible effect of state-sponsored indoctrination or constitutes a symbolic union between government and religion."

Second, we noted that the Court had "departed from the rule relied on in *Ball* that all government aid that directly assists the educational function of religious schools is invalid." Relying on *Witters* and *Zobrest*, we noted that our cases had taken a more forgiving view of neutral government programs that make aid available generally without regard to the religious or nonreligious character of the recipient school.

The Chapter 2 program at issue here bears the same hallmarks of the New York City Title I program that we found important in *Agostini*. First, as explained above, Chapter 2 aid is distributed on the basis of neutral, secular criteria. The aid is available to assist students regardless of whether they attend public or private nonprofit religious schools. Second, the statute requires participating SEA's and LEA's to use and allocate Chapter 2 funds only to supplement the funds otherwise available to a religious school. Chapter 2 funds must in no case be used to supplant funds from non-Federal sources. Third, no Chapter 2 funds ever reach the coffers of a religious school. Like the Title I program considered in *Agostini*, all Chapter 2 funds are controlled by public agencies—the SEA's and LEA's. Although respondents claim that Chapter 2 aid has been diverted to religious instruction, that evidence is *de minimis*, as I explain at greater length below.

III

Respondents contend that *Agostini* is distinguishable, pointing to the distinct character of the aid program considered there. In *Agostini*, federal funds paid for public-school teachers to provide secular instruction to eligible children on the premises of their religious schools. Here, in contrast, federal funds pay for instructional materials and equipment that LEA's lend to religious schools for use by those schools' own teachers in their classes. Because we held similar programs unconstitutional in *Meek* and *Wolman*, respondents contend that those decisions, and not *Agostini*, are controlling.

The inconsistency between the two strands of the Court's jurisprudence did not go unnoticed, as Justices on both sides of the *Meek* and *Wolman* decisions relied on the contradiction to support their respective arguments. See, *e.g.*, *Meek*, (Brennan, J., concurring in part and dissenting in part) ("What the Court says of the instructional materials and equipment may be said perhaps even more accurately of the textbooks"); (REHNQUIST, J., concurring in judgment in part and dissenting in part) ("The failure of the majority to justify the differing approaches to textbooks and instructional materials and equipment in the above respect is symptomatic of its failure even to attempt to distinguish the ... textbook loan program, which the plurality upholds, from the ... instructional materials and equipment loan program, which the majority finds unconstitutional"). The irrationality of this distinction is patent. As one Member of our Court has noted, it has meant that "a State may lend to parochial school children geography textbooks that contain maps of the United States, but the State may not lend maps of the United States for use in geography class." *Wallace v. Jaffree*, (Rehnquist, J., DISSENTING).

Indeed, technology's advance since the *Allen*, *Meek*, and *Wolman* decisions has only made the distinction between textbooks and instructional materials and equipment more suspect. In this case, for example, we are asked to draw a constitutional line between lending textbooks and lending computers. Because computers constitute instructional equipment, adherence to *Meek* and *Wolman* would require the exclusion of computers from any government school aid program that includes religious schools. Yet, computers are now as necessary as were schoolbooks 30 years ago, and they play a somewhat similar role in the educational process. That *Allen*, *Meek*, and *Wolman* would permit the constitutionality of a school-aid program to turn on whether the aid took the form of a computer rather than a book further reveals the inconsistency inherent in their logic.

Respondents insist that there is a reasoned basis under the Establishment Clause for the distinction between textbooks and instructional materials and equipment. They claim that the presumption that religious schools will use instructional materials and equipment to inculcate religion is sound because such materials and equipment, unlike textbooks, are reasonably divertible to religious uses. For example, no matter what secular criteria the government employs in selecting a film projector to lend to a religious school, school officials can always divert that projector to religious instruction. Respondents therefore claim that the Establishment Clause prohibits the government from giving or lending aid to religious schools when that aid is reasonably divertible to religious uses. JUSTICE SOUTER also states that the divertibility of secular government aid is an important consideration under the Establishment Clause, although he apparently would not ascribe it the constitutionally determinative status that respondents do.

I would reject respondents' proposed divertibility rule. First, respondents cite no precedent of this Court that would require it. The only possible direct precedential support for such a rule is a single sentence contained in a footnote from our *Wolman* decision. There, the Court described *Allen* as having been "premised on the view that the educational content of textbooks is something that can be ascertained in advance and cannot be diverted to sectarian uses." To the extent this simple description of *Allen* is even correct, it certainly does not constitute an actual holding that the Establishment Clause prohibits the government from lending any divertible aid to religious schools. Rather, as explained above, the *Wolman* Court based its holding invalidating the lending of instructional materials and equipment to religious schools on the rationale adopted in *Meek*—that the secular educational function of a religious school is inseparable from its religious mission. Indeed, if anything, the *Wolman* footnote confirms the irrationality of the distinction between textbooks and instructional materials and equipment. After the *Wolman* Court acknowledged that its holding with respect to instructional materials and equipment was in tension with *Allen*, the Court explained the continuing validity of *Allen* solely on the basis of *stare decisis*: "*Board of Education* v. *Allen* has remained law, and we now follow as a matter of *stare decisis* the principle that restriction of textbooks to those provided the public schools is sufficient to ensure that the books will not be used for religious purposes." Thus, the *Wolman* Court never justified the inconsistent treatment it accorded the lending of textbooks and the lending of instructional materials and equipment based on the items' reasonable divertibility.

In any event, even if *Meek* and *Wolman* had articulated the divertibility rationale urged by respondents and JUSTICE SOUTER, I would still reject it for a more fundamental reason. Stated simply, the theory does not provide a logical distinction between the lending of textbooks and the lending of instructional materials and equipment. An educator can use virtually any instructional tool, whether it has ascertainable content or not, to teach a religious message. In this respect, I agree with the plurality that "it is hard to imagine any book that could not, in even moderately skilled hands, serve to illustrate a religious message." In today's case, for example, we are asked to draw a constitutional distinction between lending a textbook and lending a library book. JUSTICE SOUTER's try at justifying that distinction only demonstrates the absurdity on which such a difference must rest. He states that "although library books, like textbooks, have fixed content, religious teachers can assign secular library books for religious critique." Regardless of whether that explanation is even correct (for a student surely could be given a religious assignment in connection with a textbook too), it is hardly a distinction on which constitutional law should turn. Moreover, if the mere ability of a teacher to devise a religious lesson involving the secular aid in question suffices to hold the provision of that aid unconstitutional, it is difficult to discern any limiting principle to the divertibility rule. For example, even a publicly financed lunch would apparently be unconstitutional under a divertibility rationale because religious-school officials conceivably could use the lunch to lead the students in a blessing over the bread.

To the extent JUSTICE SOUTER believes several related Establishment Clause decisions require application of a divertibility rule in the context of this case, I respectfully disagree. JUSTICE SOUTER is correct to note our continued recognition of the special dangers associated with direct money grants to religious institutions. It does not follow, however, that we should treat as constitutionally suspect any form of secular aid that might conceivably be diverted to a religious use. As the cases JUSTICE SOUTER cites demonstrate, our concern with direct monetary aid is based on more than just diversion. In fact, the most important reason for according special treatment to direct money grants is that this form of aid falls precariously close to the original object of the Establishment Clause's prohibition.

IV

Because divertibility fails to explain the distinction our cases have drawn between textbooks and instructional materials and equipment, there remains the question of which of the two irreconcilable strands of our Establishment Clause jurisprudence we should now follow. Between the two, I would adhere to the rule that we have applied in the context of textbook lending programs: To establish a First Amendment violation, plaintiffs must prove that the aid in question actually is, or has been, used for religious purposes. Just as we held in *Agostini* that our more recent cases had undermined the assumptions underlying *Ball* and *Aguilar*, I would now hold that *Agostini* and the cases on which it relied have undermined the assumptions underlying *Meek* and *Wolman*. To be sure, *Agostini* only addressed the specific presumption that public-school employees teaching on the premises of religious schools would inevitably inculcate religion. Nevertheless, I believe that our definitive rejection of that presumption also stood for—or at least strongly pointed to—the broader proposition that such presumptions of religious indoctrination are normally inappropriate when evaluating neutral school-aid programs under the Establishment Clause. In *Agostini*, we repeatedly emphasized that it would be inappropriate to presume inculcation of religion; rather, plaintiffs raising an Establishment Clause challenge must present evidence that the government aid in question has resulted in religious indoctrination. We specifically relied on our statement in *Zobrest* that a presumption of indoctrination, because it constitutes an absolute bar to the aid in question regardless of the religious school's ability to separate that aid from its religious mission, constitutes a "flat rule, smacking of antiquated notions of 'taint,' [that] would indeed exalt form over substance." That reasoning applies with equal force to the presumption in *Meek* and *Ball* concerning instructional materials and equipment. As we explained in *Agostini*, "we have departed from the rule relied on in *Ball* that all government aid that directly assists the educational function of religious schools is invalid."

V

Respondents do not rest, however, on their divertibility argument alone. Rather, they also contend that the evidence respecting the actual administration of Chapter 2 in Jefferson Parish demonstrates that the program violated the Establishment Clause. First, respondents claim that the program's safeguards are insufficient to uncover instances of actual diversion. Second, they contend that the record shows that some religious schools in Jefferson Parish may have used their Chapter 2 aid to support religious education (*i.e.*, that they diverted the aid). Third, respondents highlight violations of Chapter 2's secular content restrictions. And, finally, they note isolated examples of potential violations of Chapter 2's supplantation restriction. Based on the evidence underlying the first and second claims, the plurality appears to contend that the Chapter 2 program can be upheld only if actual diversion of government aid to the advancement of religion is permissible under the Establishment Clause. Relying on the evidence underlying all but the last of the above claims, JUSTICE SOUTER concludes that the Chapter 2 program, as applied in Jefferson Parish, violated the Establishment Clause. I disagree with both the plurality and JUSTICE SOUTER. The limited evidence amassed by respondents during 4 years of discovery (which began approximately 15 years ago) is at best *de minimis* and therefore insufficient to affect the constitutional inquiry.

The plurality and JUSTICE SOUTER direct the primary thrust of their arguments at the alleged inadequacy of the program's safeguards. Respondents, the plurality, and JUSTICE SOUTER all appear to proceed from the premise that, so long as actual diversion presents a constitutional problem, the government must have a failsafe mechanism capable of detecting *any* instance of diversion. We rejected that very assumption, however, in *Agostini*. There, we explained that because we had "abandoned the assumption that properly instructed public employees will fail to discharge their duties faithfully, we must also discard the assumption that *pervasive* monitoring of Title I teachers is required." (emphasis in original). Because I believe that the Court should abandon the presumption adopted in *Meek* and *Wolman* respecting the use of instructional materials and equipment by religious-school teachers, I see no constitutional need for *pervasive* monitoring under the Chapter 2 program.

The safeguards employed by the program are constitutionally sufficient. At the federal level, the statute limits aid to "secular, neutral, and nonideological services, materials, and equipment," requires that the aid only supplement and not supplant funds from non-Federal sources, and prohibits "any payment . . . for religious worship or instruction." At the state level, the Louisiana Department of Education (the relevant SEA for Louisiana) requires all nonpublic schools to submit signed assurances that they will use Chapter 2 aid only to supplement and not to supplant non-Federal funds, and that the instructional materials and equipment "will only be used for secular, neutral and nonideological purposes." Although there is some dispute concerning the mandatory nature of these assurances, Dan Lewis, the director of Louisiana's Chapter 2 program, testified that all of the State's nonpublic schools had thus far been willing to sign the assurances, and that the State retained the power to cut off aid to any school that breached an assurance. The Louisiana SEA also conducts monitoring visits to each of the State's LEA's—and one or two of the nonpublic schools covered by the relevant LEA—once every three years. In addition to other tasks performed on such visits, SEA representatives conduct a random review of a school's library books for religious content.

At the local level, the Jefferson Parish Public School System (JPPSS) requires nonpublic schools seeking Chapter 2 aid to submit applications, complete with specific project plans, for approval. The JPPSS then conducts annual monitoring visits to each of the nonpublic schools receiving Chapter 2 aid. As part of this process, a JPPSS employee examines the titles of requested library books and rejects any book whose title reveals (or suggests) a religious subject matter. As the above description of the JPPSS monitoring process should make clear, JUSTICE SOUTER's citation of a statewide report finding a lack of monitoring in some Louisiana LEA's is irrelevant as far as Jefferson Parish is concerned.

Respondents, the plurality, and JUSTICE SOUTER all fault the above-described safeguards primarily because they depend on the good faith of participating religious school officials. For example, both the plurality and JUSTICE SOUTER repeatedly cite testimony by state and parish officials acknowledging that the safeguards depend to a certain extent on the religious schools' self-reporting and that, therefore, there is no way for the State or Jefferson Parish to say definitively that no Chapter 2 aid is diverted to religious purposes. These admissions, however, do not prove that the safeguards are inadequate. To find that actual diversion will flourish, one must presume bad faith on the part of the religious school officials who report to the JPPSS monitors regarding the use of Chapter 2 aid. I disagree with the plurality and JUSTICE SOUTER on this point and believe that it is entirely proper to presume that these school officials will act in good faith. That presumption is especially appropriate in this case, since there is no proof that religious school officials have breached their schools' assurances or failed to tell government officials the truth.

The evidence proffered by respondents, and relied on by the plurality and JUSTICE SOUTER, concerning actual diversion of Chapter 2 aid in Jefferson Parish is *de minimis*. Respondents first cite the following statement from a Jefferson Parish religious school teacher: "Audio-visual materials are a very necessary and enjoyable tool used when teaching young children. As a second grade teacher I use them in all subjects and see a very positive result." Respondents' only other evidence consists of a chart concerning one Jefferson Parish religious school, which shows that the school's theology department was a significant user of audiovisual equipment. Although an accompanying letter indicates that much of the school's equipment was purchased with federal funds, the chart does not provide a breakdown identifying specific Chapter 2 usage. Indeed, unless we are to relieve respondents of their evidentiary burden and presume a violation of Chapter 2, we should assume that the school used its own equipment in the theology department and the Chapter 2 equipment elsewhere. The more basic point, however, is that neither piece of evidence demonstrates that Chapter 2 aid actually was diverted to religious education. At most, it proves the possibility that, out of the more than 40 nonpublic schools in Jefferson Parish participating in Chapter 2, aid may have been diverted in one school's second-grade class and another school's theology department.

JUSTICE SOUTER also relies on testimony by one religious school principal indicating that a computer lent to her school under Chapter 2 was connected through a network to non-Chapter 2 computers. The principal testified that the Chapter 2 computer would take over the network if another non-Chapter 2 computer were to break down. To the extent the principal's testimony even proves that Chapter 2 funds were diverted to the school's religious mission, the evidence is hardly compelling.

JUSTICE SOUTER contends that *any* evidence of actual diversion requires the Court to declare the Chapter 2 program unconstitutional as applied in Jefferson Parish. For support, he quotes my concurring opinion in *Bowen* and the statement therein that "*any* use of public funds to promote religious doctrines violates the Establishment Clause." That principle of course remains good law, but the next sentence in my opinion is more relevant to the case at hand: "*Extensive* violations—if they can be proved in this case—will be highly relevant in shaping an appropriate remedy that ends such abuses." I know of no case in which we have declared an entire aid program unconstitutional on Establishment Clause grounds solely because of violations on the miniscule scale of those at issue here.

Respondents' next evidentiary argument concerns an admitted violation of Chapter 2's secular content restriction. Over three years, Jefferson Parish religious schools ordered approximately 191 religious library books through Chapter 2. Dan Lewis, the director of Louisiana's Chapter 2 program, testified that he discovered some of the religious books while performing a random check during a state monitoring visit to a Jefferson Parish religious school. The discovery prompted the State to notify the JPPSS, which then reexamined book requests dating back to 1982, discovered the 191 books in question, and recalled them. This series of events demonstrates not that the Chapter 2 safeguards are inadequate, but rather that the program's monitoring system succeeded. Even if I were instead willing to find this incident to be evidence of a likelihood of future violations, the evidence is insignificant. The 191 books constituted less than one percent of the total allocation of Chapter 2 aid in Jefferson Parish during the relevant years. JUSTICE SOUTER understandably concedes that the book incident constitutes "only limited evidence." I agree with the plurality that, like the above evidence of actual diversion, the borrowing of the religious library books constitutes only *de minimis* evidence.

Given the important similarities between the Chapter 2 program here and the Title I program at issue in *Agostini*, respondents' Establishment Clause challenge must fail. As in *Agostini*, the Chapter 2 aid is allocated on the basis of neutral, secular criteria; the aid must be supplementary and cannot supplant non-Federal funds; no Chapter 2 funds ever reach the coffers of religious schools; the aid must be secular; any evidence of actual diversion is *de minimis*; and the program includes adequate safeguards. Regardless of whether these factors are constitutional requirements, they are surely sufficient to find that the program at issue here does not have the impermissible effect of advancing religion. For the same reasons, "this carefully constrained program also cannot reasonably be viewed as an endorsement of religion." Accordingly, I concur in the judgment.

JUSTICE SOUTER, with whom JUSTICE STEVENS and JUSTICE GINSBURG join, dissenting.

The First Amendment's Establishment Clause prohibits Congress (and, by incorporation, the States) from making any law respecting an establishment of religion. It has been held to prohibit not only the institution of an official church, but any government act favoring religion, a particular religion, or for that matter irreligion. Thus it bars the use of public funds for religious aid.

The establishment prohibition of government religious funding serves more than one end. It is meant to guarantee the right of individual conscience against compulsion, to protect the integrity of religion against the corrosion of secular support, and to preserve the unity of political society against the implied exclusion of the less favored and the antagonism of controversy over public support for religious causes.

These objectives are always in some jeopardy since the substantive principle of no aid to religion is not the only limitation on government action toward religion. Because the First Amendment also bars any prohibition of individual free exercise of religion, and because religious organizations cannot be isolated from the basic government functions that create the civil environment, it is as much necessary as it is difficult to draw lines between forbidden aid and lawful benefit. For more than 50 years, this Court has been attempting to draw these lines. Owing to the variety of factual circumstances in which the lines must be drawn, not all of the points creating the boundary have enjoyed self-evidence.

So far as the line drawn has addressed government aid to education, a few fundamental generalizations are nonetheless possible. There may be no aid supporting a sectarian school's religious exercise or the discharge of its religious mission, while aid of a secular character with no discernible benefit to such a sectarian objective is allowable. Because the religious and secular spheres largely overlap in the life of many such schools, the Court has tried to identify some facts likely to reveal the relative religious or secular intent or effect of the government benefits in particular circumstances. We have asked whether the government is acting neutrally in distributing its money, and about the form of the aid itself, its path from government to religious institution, its divertibility to religious nurture, its potential for reducing traditional expenditures of religious institutions, and its relative importance to the recipient, among other things.

In all the years of its effort, the Court has isolated no single test of constitutional sufficiency, and the question in every case addresses the substantive principle of no aid: what reasons are there to characterize this benefit as aid to the sectarian school in discharging its religious mission? Particular factual circumstances control, and the answer is a matter of judgment.

In what follows I will flesh out this summary, for this case comes at a time when our judgment requires perspective on how the Establishment Clause has come to be understood and applied. It is not just that a majority today mistakes the significance of facts that have led to conclusions of unconstitutionality in earlier cases, though I believe the Court commits error in failing to recognize the divertibility of funds to the service of religious objectives. What is more important is the view revealed in the plurality opinion, which espouses a new conception of neutrality as a practically sufficient test of constitutionality that would, if adopted by the Court, eliminate enquiry into a law's effects. The plurality position breaks fundamentally with Establishment Clause principle, and with the methodology painstakingly worked out in support of it. I mean to revisit that principle and describe the methodology at some length, lest there be any question about the rupture that the plurality view would cause. From that new view of the law, and from a majority's mistaken application of the old, I respectfully dissent.

I

The prohibition that "Congress shall make no law respecting an establishment of religion," eludes elegant conceptualization simply because the prohibition applies to such distinct phenomena as state churches and aid to religious schools, and as applied to school aid has prompted challenges to programs ranging from construction subsidies to hearing aids to textbook loans. Any criteria, moreover, must not only define the margins of the establishment prohibition, but must respect the succeeding Clause of the First Amendment guaranteeing religion's free exercise. It is no wonder that the complementary constitutional provisions and the inexhaustably various circumstances of their applicability have defied any simple test and have instead produced a combination of general rules often in tension at their edges. If coherence is to be had, the Court has to keep in mind the principal objectives served by the Establishment Clause, and its application to school aid, and their recollection may help to explain the misunderstandings that underlie the majority's result in this case.

A

At least three concerns have been expressed since the founding and run throughout our First Amendment jurisprudence. First, compelling an individual to support religion violates the fundamental principle of freedom of conscience. Madison's and Jefferson's now familiar words establish clearly that liberty of personal conviction requires freedom from coercion to support religion, n1 and this means that the government can compel no aid to fund it. Madison put it simply: "The same authority which can force a citizen to contribute three pence only of his property for the support of any one establishment, may force him to conform to any other establishment." Second, government aid corrupts religion. See *Engel v. Vitale* ("[The Establishment Clause's] first and most immediate purpose rested on the belief that a union of government and religion tends to destroy government and to degrade religion"). Third, government establishment of religion is inextricably linked with conflict.

B

These concerns are reflected in the Court's classic summation delivered in *Everson v. Board of Education*, its first opinion directly addressing standards governing aid to religious schools:

> "The 'establishment of religion' clause of the First Amendment means at least this: Neither a state nor the Federal Government can set up a church. Neither can pass laws which aid one religion, aid all religions, or prefer one religion over another. Neither can force nor influence a person to go to or to remain away from church against his will or force him to profess a belief or disbelief in any religion. No person can be punished for entertaining or professing religious beliefs or disbeliefs, for church attendance or non-attendance. No tax in any amount, large or small, can be levied to support any religious activities or institutions, whatever they may be called, or whatever form they may adopt to teach or practice religion. Neither a state nor the Federal Government can, openly or secretly, participate in the affairs of any religious organizations or groups and vice versa. In the words of Jefferson, the clause against establishment of religion by law was intended to erect 'a wall of separation between Church and State.' "

The most directly pertinent doctrinal statements here are these: no government "can pass laws which aid one religion [or] all religions.... No tax in any amount ... can be levied to support any religious activities or institutions ... whatever form they may adopt to teach ... religion." Thus, the principle of "no aid," with which no one in *Everson* disagreed.[4]

___

4. While *Everson*'s dissenters parted com-   pany with the majority over the specific ques-

Immediately, however, there was the difficulty over what might amount to "aid" or "support." The problem for the *Everson* Court was not merely the imprecision of the words, but the "other language of the [First Amendment that] commands that [government] cannot hamper its citizens in the free exercise of their own religion," with the consequence that government must "be a neutral in its relations with groups of religious believers and non-believers." Since withholding some public benefits from religious groups could be said to "hamper" religious exercise indirectly, and extending other benefits said to aid it, an argument-proof formulation of the no-aid principle was impossible, and the Court wisely chose not to attempt any such thing. Instead it gave definitive examples of public benefits provided pervasively throughout society that would be of some value to organized religion but not in a way or to a degree that could sensibly be described as giving it aid or violating the neutrality requirement: there was no Establishment Clause concern with "such general government services as ordinary police and fire protection, connections for sewage disposal, public highways and sidewalks." These "benefits of public welfare legislation," extended in modern times to virtually every member of the population and valuable to every person and association, were the paradigms of advantages that religious organizations could enjoy consistently with the prohibition against aid, and that governments could extend without deserting their required position of neutrality.

But paradigms are not perfect fits very often, and government spending resists easy classification as between universal general service or subsidy of favoritism. The 5-to-4 division of the *Everson* Court turned on the inevitable question whether reimbursing all parents for the cost of transporting their children to school was close enough to police protection to tolerate its indirect benefit in some degree to religious schools, with the majority in *Everson* thinking the reimbursement statute fell on the lawful side of the line. Although the state scheme reimbursed parents for transporting children to sectarian schools, among others, it gave "no money to the schools. It [did] not support them. Its legislation [did] no more than provide a general program to help parents get their children, regardless of their religion, safely and expeditiously to and from accredited schools." The dissenters countered with factual analyses showing the limitation of the law's benefits in fact to private school pupils who were Roman Catholics, (Jackson, J., dissenting), and indicating the inseparability of transporting pupils to school from support for the religious instruction that was the school's *raison d'etre*.

Everson is usefully understood in the light of a successor case two decades later, *Board of Ed. Allen*. As *Everson* had rested on the understanding that no money and no support went to the school, *Allen* emphasized that the savings to parents were devoid of any measurable effect in teaching religion. Justice Harlan, concurring, summed up the approach with his observations that the required government "[n]eutrality is . . . a coat of many colors," and quoted Justice Goldberg's conclusion, that there was " 'no simple and clear measure' . . . by which this or any [religious school aid] case may readily be decided," (quoting *Schempp*).

tion of school buses, the Court stood as one   teaching.
behind the principle of no aid for religious

After *Everson* and *Allen*, the state of the law applying the Establishment Clause to public expenditures producing some benefit to religious schools was this:

1. Government aid to religion is forbidden, and tax revenue may not be used to support a religious school or religious teaching.

2. Government provision of such paradigms of universally general welfare benefits as police and fire protection does not count as aid to religion.

3. Whether a law's benefit is sufficiently close to universally general welfare paradigms to be classified with them, as distinct from religious aid, is a function of the purpose and effect of the challenged law in all its particularity. The judgment is not reducible to the application of any formula. Evenhandedness of distribution as between religious and secular beneficiaries is a relevant factor, but not a sufficiency test of constitutionality. There is no rule of religious equal protection to the effect that any expenditure for the benefit of religious school students is necessarily constitutional so long as public school pupils are favored on ostensibly identical terms.

4. Government must maintain neutrality as to religion, "neutrality" being a conclusory label for the required position of government as neither aiding religion nor impeding religious exercise by believers. "Neutrality" was not the name of any test to identify permissible action, and in particular, was not synonymous with evenhandedness in conferring benefit on the secular as well as the religious.

Today, the substantive principle of no aid to religious mission remains the governing understanding of the Establishment Clause as applied to public benefits inuring to religious schools. The governing opinions on the subject in the 35 years since *Allen* have never challenged this principle. The cases have, however, recognized that in actual Establishment Clause litigation over school aid legislation, there is no pure aid to religion and no purely secular welfare benefit; the effects of the laws fall somewhere in between, with the judicial task being to make a realistic allocation between the two possibilities. The Court's decisions demonstrate its repeated attempts to isolate considerations relevant in classifying particular benefits as between those that do not discernibly support or threaten support of a school's religious mission, and those that cross or threaten to cross the line into support for religion.

II

A

The most deceptively familiar of those considerations is "neutrality," the presence or absence of which, in some sense, we have addressed from the moment of *Everson* itself. I say "some sense," for we have used the term in at least three ways in our cases, and an understanding of the term's evolution will help to explain the concept as it is understood today, as well as the limits of its significance in Establishment Clause analysis. "Neutrality" has been employed as a term to describe the requisite state of government equipoise between the forbidden encouragement and discouragement of religion; to characterize a benefit or aid as secular; and to indicate evenhandedness in distributing it.

As already mentioned, the Court first referred to neutrality in *Everson*, simply stating that government is required "to be a neutral" among religions and between religion and nonreligion. Although "neutral" may have carried a hint of inaction when we indicated that the First Amendment "does not require the state to be [the] adversary" of religious believers, or to cut off general government services from religious organizations, *Everson* provided no explicit definition of the term or further indication of what the government was required to do or not do to be a "neutral" toward religion. In practical terms, "neutral" in *Everson* was simply a term for government in its required median position between aiding and handicapping religion. The second major case on aid to religious schools, *Allen*, used "neutrality" to describe an adequate state of balance between government as ally and as adversary to religion ([by] discussing line between "state neutrality to religion and state support of religion"). The term was not further defined, and a few subsequent school cases used "neutrality" simply to designate the required relationship to religion, without explaining how to attain it.

The Court began to employ "neutrality" in a sense different from equipoise, however, as it explicated the distinction between "religious" and "secular" benefits to religious schools, the latter being in some circumstances permissible. Even though both *Everson* and *Allen* had anticipated some such distinction, neither case had used the term "neutral" in this way. In *Everson*, Justice Black indicated that providing police, fire, and similar government services to religious institutions was permissible, in part because they were "so separate and so indisputably marked off from the religious function." *Allen* similarly focused on the fact that the textbooks lent out were "secular" and approved by secular authorities, and assumed that the secular textbooks and the secular elements of education they supported were not so intertwined with religious instruction as "in fact [to be] instrumental in the teaching of religion." Such was the Court's premise in *Lemon* for shifting the use of the word "neutral" from labeling the required position of the government to describing a benefit that was nonreligious.

In sum, "neutrality" originally entered this field of jurisprudence as a conclusory term, a label for the required relationship between the government and religion as a state of equipoise between government as ally and government as adversary. Reexamining *Everson*'s paradigm cases to derive a prescriptive guideline, we first determined that "neutral" aid was secular, nonideological, or unrelated to religious education. Our subsequent reexamination of *Everson* and *Allen*, beginning in *Comm. for Pub. Ed. & Religious Liberty v. Nyquist* and culminating in *Mueller* and most recently in *Agostini*, recast neutrality as a concept of "evenhandedness."

There is, of course, good reason for considering the generality of aid and the evenhandedness of its distribution in making close calls between benefits that in purpose or effect support a school's religious mission and those that do not. This is just what *Everson* did. Even when the disputed practice falls short of *Everson*'s paradigms, the breadth of evenhanded distribution is one pointer toward the law's purpose, since on the face of it aid distributed generally and without a religious criterion is less likely to be meant to aid religion than a benefit going only to religious institutions or people. And, depending on the breadth of distribution, looking to evenhandedness is a way of asking whether a benefit can reasonably be seen to aid religion in fact; we do not regard the postal system as aiding religion, even though parochial schools get mail. Given the legitimacy of considering evenhandedness, then, there is no reason to avoid the term "neutrality" to refer to it. But one crucial point must be borne in mind.

In the days when "neutral" was used in *Everson*'s sense of equipoise, neutrality was tantamount to constitutionality; the term was conclusory, but when it applied it meant that the government's position was constitutional under the Establishment Clause. This is not so at all, however, under the most recent use of "neutrality" to refer to generality or evenhandedness of distribution. This kind of neutrality is relevant in judging whether a benefit scheme so characterized should be seen as aiding a sectarian school's religious mission, but this neutrality is not alone sufficient to qualify the aid as constitutional. It is to be considered only along with other characteristics of aid, its administration, its recipients, or its potential that have been emphasized over the years as indicators of just how religious the intent and effect of a given aid scheme really is. Thus, the basic principle of establishment scrutiny of aid remains the principle as stated in *Everson*, that there may be no public aid to religion or support for the religious mission of any institution.

B

The insufficiency of evenhandedness neutrality as a stand-alone criterion of constitutional intent or effect has been clear from the beginning of our interpretative efforts, for an obvious reason. Evenhandedness in distributing a benefit approaches the equivalence of constitutionality in this area only when the term refers to such universality of distribution that it makes no sense to think of the benefit as going to any discrete group. Conversely, when evenhandedness refers to distribution to limited groups within society, like groups of schools or schoolchildren, it does make sense to regard the benefit as aid to the recipients.

Hence, if we looked no further than evenhandedness, and failed to ask what activities the aid might support, or in fact did support, religious schools could be blessed with government funding as massive as expenditures made for the benefit of their public school counterparts, and religious missions would thrive on public money. This is why the consideration of less than universal neutrality has never been recognized as dispositive and has always been teamed with attention to other facts bearing on the substantive prohibition of support for a school's religious objective.

At least three main lines of enquiry addressed particularly to school aid have emerged to complement evenhandedness neutrality. First, we have noted that two types of aid recipients heighten Establishment Clause concern: pervasively religious schools and primary and secondary religious schools. Second, we have identified two important characteristics of the method of distributing aid: directness or indirectness of distribution and distribution by genuinely independent choice. Third, we have found relevance in at least five characteristics of the aid itself: its religious content; its cash form; its divertibility or actually diversion to religious support; its supplantation of traditional items of religious school expense; and its substantiality.

1

Two types of school aid recipients have raised special concern. First, we have recognized the fact that the overriding religious mission of certain schools, those sometimes called "pervasively sectarian," is not confined to a discrete element of the curriculum. Based on record evidence and long experience, we have concluded that religious teaching in such schools is at the core of the instructors' individual and personal obligations. As religious teaching cannot be separated from secular education in such schools or by such teachers, we have concluded that direct government subsidies to such schools are prohibited because they will inevitably and impermissibly support religious indoctrination.

Second, we have expressed special concern about aid to primary and secondary religious schools. On the one hand, we have understood how the youth of the students in such schools makes them highly susceptible to religious indoctrination. On the other, we have recognized that the religious element in the education offered in most sectarian primary and secondary schools is far more intertwined with the secular than in university teaching, where the natural and academic skepticism of most older students may separate the two. Thus, government benefits accruing to these pervasively religious primary and secondary schools raise special dangers of diversion into support for the religious indoctrination of children and the involvement of government in religious training and practice.

2

We have also evaluated the portent of support to an organization's religious mission that may be inherent in the method by which aid is granted, finding pertinence in at least two characteristics of distribution. First, we have asked whether aid is direct or indirect, observing distinctions between government schemes with individual beneficiaries and those whose beneficiaries in the first instance might be religious schools. Direct aid obviously raises greater risks, although recent cases have discounted this risk factor, looking to other features of the distribution mechanism.[8]

Second, we have distinguished between indirect aid that reaches religious schools only incidentally as a result of numerous individual choices and aid that is in reality directed to religious schools by the government or in practical terms selected by religious schools themselves. *Mueller*; *Witters*; *Zobrest*. In these cases, we have declared the constitutionality of programs providing aid directly to parents or students as tax deductions or scholarship money, where such aid may pay for education at some sectarian institutions,

---

8. In *Agostini*, the Court indicated that "we have departed from the rule relied on in *Ball* that all government aid that directly assists the educational function of religious schools is invalid," and cited *Witters* and *Zobrest*. However, *Agostini* did not rely on this dictum, instead clearly stating that "[w]hile it is true that individual students may not directly apply for Title I services, it does not follow from this premise that those services are distributed 'directly to the religious schools.' In fact, they are not. No Title I funds ever reach the coffers of religious schools, and Title I services may not be provided to religious schools on a school-wide basis." Until today, this Court has never permitted aid to go directly to schools on a school-wide basis.

but only as the result of "genuinely independent and private choices of aid recipients." We distinguished this path of aid from the route in *Ball* and *Wolman*, where the opinions indicated that "[w]here ... no meaningful distinction can be made between aid to the student and aid to the school, the concept of a loan to individuals is a transparent fiction."

3

In addition to the character of the school to which the benefit accrues, and its path from government to school, a number of features of the aid itself have figured in the classifications we have made. First, we have barred aid with actual religious content, which would obviously run afoul of the ban on the government's participation in religion.

Second, we have long held government aid invalid when circumstances would allow its diversion to religious education. The risk of diversion is obviously high when aid in the form of government funds makes its way into the coffers of religious organizations, and so from the start we have understood the Constitution to bar outright money grants of aid to religion.[11]

Divertibility is not, of course, a characteristic of cash alone, and when examining provisions for ostensibly secular supplies we have considered their susceptibility to the service of religious ends. In upholding a scheme to provide students with secular textbooks, we emphasized that "each book loaned must be approved by the public school authorities; only secular books may receive approval." By the same token, we could not sustain provisions for instructional materials adaptable to teaching a variety of subjects.[14] While the textbooks had a known and fixed secular content not readily divertible to religious teaching purposes, the adaptable materials did not. So, too, we explained the permissibility of busing on public routes to schools but not busing for field trips designed by religious authorities specifically because the latter trips were components of teaching in a pervasively religious school. With the same point in mind, we held that buildings constructed with government grants to universities with religious affiliation must be barred from religious use indefinitely to prevent the diversion of government funds to religious objectives. *Tilton v. Richardson*, 403 U.S. 672, 683 (1971) (plurality opinion) ("If, at the end of 20 years, the building is, for example, converted into a chapel or otherwise used to promote religious interests, the original federal

---

11. We have similarly noted that paying salaries of parochial school teachers creates too much of a risk that such support will aid the teaching of religion, striking down such programs because of the need for pervasive monitoring that would be required. See *Lemon* ("We do not assume, however, that parochial school teachers will be unsuccessful in their attempts to segregate their religious beliefs from their secular educational responsibilities. But the potential for impermissible fostering of religion is present. The [state legislature] has not, and could not, provide state aid on the basis of a mere assumption that secular teachers under religious discipline can avoid conflicts. The State must be certain, given the Religion Clauses, that subsidized teachers do not inculcate religion.... A comprehensive,

discriminating, and continuing state surveillance will inevitably be required to ensure that these restrictions are obeyed and the First Amendment otherwise respected").

14. Contrary to the plurality's apparent belief, *Lamb's Chapel v. Center Moriches Union Free School Dist.*, 508 U.S. 384 (1993), sheds no light on the question of divertibility and school aid. The Court in that case clearly distinguished the question of after-school access to public facilities from anything resembling the school aid cases: "The showing of this film series would not have been during school hours, would not have been sponsored by the school, and would have been open to the public, not just to church members."

grant will in part have the effect of advancing religion. To this extent the Act therefore trespasses on the Religion Clauses").

Third, our cases have recognized the distinction, adopted by statute in the Chapter 2 legislation, between aid that merely supplements and aid that supplants expenditures for offerings at religious schools, the latter being barred. Although we have never adopted the position that any benefit that flows to a religious school is impermissible because it frees up resources for the school to engage in religious indoctrination, from our first decision holding it permissible to provide textbooks for religious schools we have repeatedly explained the unconstitutionality of aid that supplants an item of the school's traditional expense. See, *e.g., Cochran v. Louisiana Bd. of Ed.,* 281 U.S. 370, 375 (1930) (noting that religious schools "are not the beneficiaries of these appropriations. They obtain nothing from them, nor are they relieved of a single obligation because of them").

Finally, we have recognized what is obvious (however imprecise), in holding "substantial" amounts of aid to be unconstitutional whether or not a plaintiff can show that it supplants a specific item of expense a religious school would have borne.[18]

C

This stretch of doctrinal history leaves one point clear beyond peradventure: together with James Madison we have consistently understood the Establishment Clause to impose a substantive prohibition against public aid to religion and, hence, to the religious mission of sectarian schools. Evenhandedness neutrality is one, nondispositive pointer toward an intent and (to a lesser degree) probable effect on the permissible side of the line between forbidden aid and general public welfare benefit. Other pointers are facts about the religious mission and education level of benefited schools and their pupils, the pathway by which a benefit travels from public treasury to educational effect, the form and content of the aid, its adaptability to religious ends, and its effects on school budgets. The object of all enquiries into such matters is the same whatever the particular circumstances: is the benefit intended to aid in providing the religious element of the education and is it likely to do so?

The substance of the law has thus not changed since *Everson*. Emphasis on one sort of fact or another has varied depending on the perceived utility of the enquiry, but all that has been added is repeated explanation of relevant considerations, confirming that our predecessors were right in their prophecies that no simple test would emerge to allow easy application of the establishment principle.

The plurality, however, would reject that lesson. The majority misapplies it.

---

18. I do not read the plurality to question the prohibition on substantial aid. The plurality challenges any rule based on the proportion of aid that a program provides to religious recipients, citing *Witters* and *Agostini*. I reject the plurality's reasoning. The plurality misreads *Witters*; Justice Marshall, writing for the Court in *Witters*, emphasized that only a small amount of aid was provided to religious institutions, and no controlling majority rejected the importance of this fact. The plurality also overreads *Agostini*, which simply declined to adopt a rule based on proportionality. Moreover, regardless of whether the proportion of aid actually provided to religious schools is relevant, we have never questioned our holding in *Meek* that substantial aid to religious schools is prohibited.

III

A

The nub of the plurality's new position is this:

> "[I]f the government, seeking to further some legitimate secular purpose, offers aid on the same terms, without regard to religion, to all who adequately further that purpose, then it is fair to say that any aid going to a religious recipient only has the effect of furthering that secular purpose. The government, in crafting such an aid program, has had to conclude that a given level of aid is necessary to further that purpose among secular recipients and has provided no more than that same level to religious recipients."

As a break with consistent doctrine the plurality's new criterion is unequaled in the history of Establishment Clause interpretation. Simple on its face, it appears to take evenhandedness neutrality and in practical terms promote it to a single and sufficient test for the establishment constitutionality of school aid. Even on its own terms, its errors are manifold, and attention to at least three of its mistaken assumptions will show the degree to which the plurality's proposal would replace the principle of no aid with a formula for generous religious support.

First, the plurality treats an external observer's attribution of religious support to the government as the sole impermissible effect of a government aid scheme. While perceived state endorsement of religion is undoubtedly a relevant concern under the Establishment Clause, it is certainly not the only one. *Everson* made this clear from the start: secret aid to religion by the government is also barred. State aid not attributed to the government would still violate a taxpayer's liberty of conscience, threaten to corrupt religion, and generate disputes over aid.[19]

Second, the plurality apparently assumes as a fact that equal amounts of aid to religious and nonreligious schools will have exclusively secular and equal effects, on both external perception and on incentives to attend different schools. But there is no reason to believe that this will be the case; the effects of same-terms aid may not be confined to the secular sphere at all. This is the reason that we have long recognized that unrestricted aid to religious schools will support religious teaching in addition to secular education, a fact that would be true no matter what the supposedly secular purpose of the law might be.

Third, the plurality assumes that per capita distribution rules safeguard the same principles as independent, private choices. But that is clearly not so. We approved university scholarships in *Witters* because we found them close to giving a government employee a paycheck and allowing him to spend it as he chose, but a per capita aid program is a far cry from awarding scholarships

---

19. Adopting the plurality's rule would permit practically any government aid to religion so long as it could be supplied on terms ostensibly comparable to the terms under which aid was provided to nonreligious recipients. As a principle of constitutional sufficiency, the manipulability of this rule is breathtaking. A legislature would merely need to state a secular objective in order to legalize massive aid to all religions, one religion, or even one sect, to which its largess could be directed through the easy exercise of crafting facially neutral terms under which to offer aid favoring that religious group. Short of formally replacing the Establishment Clause, a more dependable key to the public fisc or a cleaner break with prior law would be difficult to imagine.

to individuals, one of whom makes an independent private choice. Not the least of the significant differences between per capita aid and aid individually determined and directed is the right and genuine opportunity of the recipient to choose not to give the aid. To hold otherwise would be to license the government to donate funds to churches based on the number of their members, on the patent fiction of independent private choice.

The plurality's mistaken assumptions explain and underscore its sharp break with the Framers' understanding of establishment and this Court's consistent interpretative course. Under the plurality's regime, little would be left of the right of conscience against compelled support for religion; the more massive the aid the more potent would be the influence of the government on the teaching mission; the more generous the support, the more divisive would be the resentments of those resisting religious support, and those religions without school systems ready to claim their fair share.

B

The plurality's conception of evenhandedness does not, however, control the case, whose disposition turns on the misapplication of accepted categories of school aid analysis. The facts most obviously relevant to the Chapter 2 scheme in Jefferson Parish are those showing divertibility and actual diversion in the circumstance of pervasively sectarian religious schools. The type of aid, the structure of the program, and the lack of effective safeguards clearly demonstrate the divertibility of the aid. While little is known about its use, owing to the anemic enforcement system in the parish, even the thin record before us reveals that actual diversion occurred.

The aid that the government provided was highly susceptible to unconstitutional use. Much of the equipment provided under Chapter 2 was not of the type provided for individual students, but included "slide projectors, movie projectors, overhead projectors, television sets, tape recorders, projection screens, maps, globes, filmstrips, cassettes, computers," and computer software and peripherals. The videocassette players, overhead projectors, and other instructional aids were of the sort that we have found can easily be used by religious teachers for religious purposes. The same was true of the computers, which were as readily employable for religious teaching as the other equipment, and presumably as immune to any countervailing safeguard. Although library books, like textbooks, have fixed content, religious teachers can assign secular library books for religious critique, and books for libraries may be religious, as any divinity school library would demonstrate. The sheer number and variety of books that could be and were ordered gave ample opportunity for such diversion.

The divertibility thus inherent in the forms of Chapter 2 aid was enhanced by the structure of the program in Jefferson Parish. Requests for specific items under Chapter 2 came not from secular officials, but from officials of the religious schools (and even parents of religious school pupils).

The concern with divertibility thus predicated is underscored by the fact that the religious schools in question here covered the primary and secondary grades, the grades in which the sectarian nature of instruction is characteristically the most pervasive, and in which pupils are the least critical of the schools' religious objectives. No one, indeed, disputes the trial judge's findings, based on a detailed record, that the Roman Catholic schools, which made up the majority of the private schools participating, were pervasively sectarian, that their common objective and mission was to engage in religious education, and that their teachers taught religiously, making them precisely the kind of primary and secondary religious schools that raise the most serious Establishment Clause concerns.

The plurality has already noted at length the ineffectiveness of the government's monitoring program. Government officials themselves admitted that there was no way to tell whether instructional materials had been diverted, and, as the plurality notes, the only screening mechanism in the library book scheme was a review of titles by a single government official. The government did not even have a policy on the consequences of noncompliance.

Providing such governmental aid without effective safeguards against future diversion itself offends the Establishment Clause, and even without evidence of actual diversion, our cases have repeatedly held that a "substantial risk" of it suffices to invalidate a government aid program on establishment grounds. A substantial risk of diversion in this case was more than clear, as the plurality has conceded. The First Amendment was violated.

But the record here goes beyond risk, to instances of actual diversion. What one would expect from such paltry efforts at monitoring and enforcement naturally resulted, and the record strongly suggests that other, undocumented diversions probably occurred as well. First, the record shows actual diversion in the library book program. Although only limited evidence exists, it contrasts starkly with the records of the numerous textbook programs that we have repeatedly upheld, where there was no evidence of any actual diversion. Here, discovery revealed that under Chapter 2, nonpublic schools requested and the government purchased at least 191 religious books with taxpayer funds by December 1985. Books such as A Child's Book of Prayers, and The Illustrated Life of Jesus, were discovered among others that had been ordered under the program.

The evidence persuasively suggests that other aid was actually diverted as well. The principal of one religious school testified, for example, that computers lent with Chapter 2 funds were joined in a network with other non-Chapter 2 computers in some schools, and that religious officials and teachers were allowed to develop their own unregulated software for use on this network. She admitted that the Chapter 2 computer took over the support of the computing system whenever there was a breakdown of the master computer purchased with the religious school's own funds. Moreover, as the plurality observes, comparing the records of considerable federal funding of audiovisual equipment in religious schools with records of the schools' use of unidentified audiovisual equipment in religion classes strongly suggests that film projectors and videotape machines purchased with public funds were used in religious indoctrination over a period of at least seven years.

Indeed, the plurality readily recognizes that the aid in question here was divertible and that substantial evidence of actual diversion exists. Although JUSTICE O'CONNOR attributes limited significance to the evidence of divertibility and actual diversion, she also recognizes that it exists. The Court has no choice but to hold that the program as applied violated the Establishment Clause.

IV

The plurality would break with the law. The majority misapplies it. That misapplication is, however, the only consolation in the case, which reaches an erroneous result but does not stage a doctrinal coup. But there is no mistaking the abandonment of doctrine that would occur if the plurality were to become a majority. It is beyond question that the plurality's notion of evenhandedness neutrality as a practical guarantee of the validity of aid to sectarian schools would be the end of the principle of no aid to the schools' religious mission. And if that were not so obvious it would become so after reflecting on the plurality's thoughts about diversion and about giving attention to the pervasiveness of a school's sectarian teaching.

The plurality is candid in pointing out the extent of actual diversion of Chapter 2 aid to religious use in the case before us, and equally candid in saying it does not matter. To the plurality there is nothing wrong with aiding a school's religious mission; the only question is whether religious teaching obtains its tax support under a formally evenhanded criterion of distribution. The principle of no aid to religious teaching has no independent significance.

And if this were not enough to prove that no aid in religious school aid is dead under the plurality's First Amendment, the point is nailed down in the plurality's attack on the legitimacy of considering a school's pervasively sectarian character when judging whether aid to the school is likely to aid its religious mission. The relevance of this consideration is simply a matter of common sense: where religious indoctrination pervades school activities of children and adolescents, it takes great care to be able to aid the school without supporting the doctrinal effort. This is obvious. The plurality nonetheless condemns any enquiry into the pervasiveness of doctrinal content as a remnant of anti-Catholic bigotry (as if evangelical Protestant schools and Orthodox Jewish yeshivas were never pervasively sectarian[29]), and it equates a refusal to aid religious schools with hostility to religion (as if aid to religious teaching were not opposed in this very case by at least one religious respondent[30] and numerous religious *amici curiae* in a tradition claiming descent from Roger Williams). My concern with these arguments goes not so much to their details as it does to the fact that the plurality's choice to employ imputations of bigotry and irreligion as terms in the Court's debate makes one point clear: that in rejecting the principle of no aid to a school's religious mission the plurality is attacking the most fundamental assumption underlying the Establishment Clause, that government can in fact operate with

---

29. Indeed, one group of *amici curiae*, which consists of "religious and educational leaders from a broad range of both Eastern and Western religious traditions, and Methodist, Jewish and Seventh-day Adventist individuals" including "church administrators, administrators of religious elementary and secondary school systems; elementary and secondary school teachers at religious schools; and pastors and laity who serve on church school boards," identifies its members as having "broad experience teaching in and administering pervasively sectarian schools." Brief for Interfaith Religious Liberty Foundation et al. as *Amici Curiae* 1.

30. One of the respondents describes herself as a "life-long, committed member of the Roman Catholic Church" who "objects to the government providing benefits to her parish school" because "she has seen the chilling effect such entangling government aid has on the religious mission of schools run by her church." She has been a member of the church for about 36 years, and six of her children attended different Jefferson Parish Catholic run schools.

neutrality in its relation to religion. I believe that it can, and so respectfully dissent.

QUESTIONS AND NOTES

1. Is the dispute among the Justices a question of rules vs. standards? Justice Thomas, for the plurality, seems to be pushing for a simple rule of neutrality; while O'Connor and Souter seem to prefer ad hoc balancing of many factors. In general, which is better? In this case, which is better? Why?

2. Is the concept of neutrality congruent with the concept of neutrality that prevailed in *Santa Fe* (p. 1002 *supra*)? In *Santa Fe*, Justices Souter and O'Connor were on the side *favoring* neutrality while Justice Thomas was on the side *opposing* it. Is there any consistency or does it all depend on whose ox is gored?

3. Should divertibility be relevant? Determinative? How about actual diversion? With which of the three opinions do you most agree? With which do you most disagree? Explain.

4. Has the Court traditionally been hostile to pervasively sectarian institutions? Should it be?

5. In the future, what factors are likely to be relevant in regard to financial aid? Determinative? Will anybody be sure before five Justices vote?

6. Should there be a presumption for or against including religious schools in programs that aid other public and private schools?

7. Will (should) tuition grants by the State to students attending private religious school be permitted?

ZELMAN v. SIMMONS–HARRIS

122 S.Ct. 2460 (2002).

CHIEF JUSTICE REHNQUIST delivered the opinion of the Court.

The State of Ohio has established a pilot program designed to provide educational choices to families with children who reside in the Cleveland City School District. The question presented is whether this program offends the Establishment Clause of the United States Constitution. We hold that it does not. There are more than 75,000 children enrolled in the Cleveland City School District. The majority of these children are from low-income and minority families. Few of these families enjoy the means to send their children to any school other than an inner-city public school. For more than a generation, however, Cleveland's public schools have been among the worst performing public schools in the Nation. In 1995, a Federal District Court declared a "crisis of magnitude" and placed the entire Cleveland school district under state control. Shortly thereafter, the state auditor found that Cleveland's public schools were in the midst of a "crisis that is perhaps unprecedented in the history of American education." The district had failed to meet any of the 18 state standards for minimal acceptable performance. Only 1 in 10 ninth graders could pass a basic proficiency examination, and students at all levels performed at a dismal rate compared with students in other Ohio public schools. More than two-thirds of high school students either dropped or failed out before graduation. Of those students who managed to reach their senior year, one of every four still failed to graduate. Of those students who did graduate, few could read, write, or compute at levels comparable to their counterparts in other cities.

It is against this backdrop that Ohio enacted, among other initiatives, its Pilot Project Scholarship Program. The program provides financial assistance to families in any Ohio school district that is or has been "under federal court order requiring supervision and operational management of the district by the state superintendent." Cleveland is the only Ohio school district to fall within that category.

The program provides two basic kinds of assistance to parents of children in a covered district. First, the program provides tuition aid for students in kindergarten through third grade, expanding each year through eighth grade, to attend a participating public or private school of their parent's choosing. Second, the program provides tutorial aid for students who choose to remain enrolled in public school.

The tuition aid portion of the program is designed to provide educational choices to parents who reside in a covered district. Any private school, whether religious or nonreligious, may participate in the program and accept program students so long as the school is located within the boundaries of a covered district and meets statewide educational standards. Participating private schools must agree not to discriminate on the basis of race, religion, or ethnic background, or to "advocate or foster unlawful behavior or teach hatred of any person or group on the basis of race, ethnicity, national origin, or religion." Any public school located in a school district adjacent to the covered district may also participate in the program. Adjacent public schools are eligible to receive a $2,250 tuition grant for each program student accepted in addition to the full amount of per-pupil state funding attributable to each additional student.[1] All participating schools, whether public or private, are required to accept students in accordance with rules and procedures established by the state superintendent.

Tuition aid is distributed to parents according to financial need. Families with incomes below 200% of the poverty line are given priority and are eligible to receive 90% of private school tuition up to $2,250. For these lowest-income families, participating private schools may not charge a parental co-payment greater than $250. For all other families, the program pays 75% of tuition costs, up to $1,875, with no co-payment cap. These families receive tuition aid only if the number of available scholarships exceeds the number of low-income children who choose to participate. Where tuition aid is spent depends solely upon where parents who receive tuition aid choose to enroll their child. If parents choose a private school, checks are made payable to the parents who then endorse the checks over to the chosen school.

The tutorial aid portion of the program provides tutorial assistance through grants to any student in a covered district who chooses to remain in

---

1. Although the parties dispute the precise amount of state funding received by suburban school districts adjacent to the Cleveland City School District, there is no dispute that any suburban district agreeing to participate in the program would receive a $2,250 tuition grant plus the ordinary allotment of per-pupil state funding for each program student enrolled in a suburban public school. See Brief for Respondents Simmons-Harris (suburban schools would receive "on average, approximately, $4,750" per program student); Brief for Petitioners in (suburban schools would receive "about $6,544" per program student).

public school. Parents arrange for registered tutors to provide assistance to their children and then submit bills for those services to the State for payment. Students from low-income families receive 90% of the amount charged for such assistance up to $360. All other students receive 75% of that amount. The number of tutorial assistance grants offered to students in a covered district must equal the number of tuition aid scholarships provided to students enrolled at participating private or adjacent public schools.

The program has been in operation within the Cleveland City School District since the 1996–1997 school year. In the 1999–2000 school year, 56 private schools participated in the program, 46 (or 82%) of which had a religious affiliation. None of the public schools in districts adjacent to Cleveland have elected to participate. More than 3,700 students participated in the scholarship program, most of whom (96%) enrolled in religiously affiliated schools. Sixty percent of these students were from families at or below the poverty line. In the 1998–1999 school year, approximately 1,400 Cleveland public school students received tutorial aid. This number was expected to double during the 1999–2000 school year. The program is part of a broader undertaking by the State to enhance the educational options of Cleveland's schoolchildren in response to the 1995 takeover. That undertaking includes programs governing community and magnet schools. Community schools are funded under state law but are run by their own school boards, not by local school districts. These schools enjoy academic independence to hire their own teachers and to determine their own curriculum. They can have no religious affiliation and are required to accept students by lottery. During the 1999–2000 school year, there were 10 start-up community schools in the Cleveland City School District with more than 1,900 students enrolled. For each child enrolled in a community school, the school receives state funding of $4,518, twice the funding a participating program school may receive.

Magnet schools are public schools operated by a local school board that emphasize a particular subject area, teaching method, or service to students. For each student enrolled in a magnet school, the school district receives $7,746, including state funding of $4,167, the same amount received per student enrolled at a traditional public school. As of 1999, parents in Cleveland were able to choose from among 23 magnet schools, which together enrolled more than 13,000 students in kindergarten through eighth grade. These schools provide specialized teaching methods, such as Montessori, or a particularized curriculum focus, such as foreign language, computers, or the arts.

The Establishment Clause of the First Amendment, applied to the States through the Fourteenth Amendment, prevents a State from enacting laws that have the "purpose" or "effect" of advancing or inhibiting religion. There is no dispute that the program challenged here was enacted for the valid secular purpose of providing educational assistance to poor children in a demonstrably failing public school system. Thus, the question presented is whether the Ohio program nonetheless has the forbidden "effect" of advancing or inhibiting religion.

To answer that question, our decisions have drawn a consistent distinction between government programs that provide aid directly to religious schools, and programs of true private choice, in which government aid reaches religious schools only as a result of the genuine and independent choices of private individuals. While our jurisprudence with respect to the constitutionality of direct aid programs has "changed significantly" over the past two decades, our jurisprudence with respect to true private choice programs has remained consistent and unbroken. Three times we have confronted Establishment Clause challenges to neutral government programs that provide aid directly to a broad class of individuals, who, in turn, direct the aid to religious schools or institutions of their own choosing. Three times we have rejected such challenges.

In *Mueller*, we rejected an Establishment Clause challenge to a Minnesota program authorizing tax deductions for various educational expenses, including private school tuition costs, even though the great majority of the program's beneficiaries (96%) were parents of children in religious schools. We began by focusing on the class of beneficiaries, finding that because the class included "all parents," including parents with "children [who] attend nonsectarian private schools or sectarian private schools," 463 U.S. at 397 (emphasis in original), the program was "not readily subject to challenge under the Establishment Clause," Then, viewing the program as a whole, we emphasized the principle of private choice, noting that public funds were made available to religious schools "only as a result of numerous, private choices of individual parents of school-age children." This, we said, ensured that " 'no imprimatur of state approval' can be deemed to have been conferred on any particular religion, or on religion generally." We thus found it irrelevant to the constitutional inquiry that the vast majority of beneficiaries were parents of children in religious schools, saying:

> "We would be loath to adopt a rule grounding the constitutionality of a facially neutral law on annual reports reciting the extent to which various classes of private citizens claimed benefits under the law."

That the program was one of true private choice, with no evidence that the State deliberately skewed incentives toward religious schools, was sufficient for the program to survive scrutiny under the Establishment Clause.

In *Witters*, we used identical reasoning to reject an Establishment Clause challenge to a vocational scholarship program that provided tuition aid to a student studying at a religious institution to become a pastor.

Five Members of the Court, in separate opinions, emphasized the general rule from *Mueller* that the amount of government aid channeled to religious institutions by individual aid recipients was not relevant to the constitutional inquiry. Our holding thus rested not on whether few or many recipients chose to expend government aid at a religious school but, rather, on whether recipients generally were empowered to direct the aid to schools or institutions of their own choosing.

Finally, in *Zobrest*, we applied *Mueller* and *Witters* to reject an Establishment Clause challenge to a federal program that permitted sign-language interpreters to assist deaf children enrolled in religious schools. Reviewing our earlier decisions, we stated that "government programs that neutrally provide benefits to a broad class of citizens defined without reference to religion are not readily subject to an Establishment Clause challenge." Looking once again to the challenged program as a whole, we observed that the program "distributes benefits neutrally to any child qualifying as 'disabled.' " Its "primary beneficiaries," we said, were "disabled children, not sectarian schools."

Mueller, *Witters*, and *Zobrest* thus make clear that where a government aid program is neutral with respect to religion, and provides assistance directly to a broad class of citizens who, in turn, direct government aid to religious schools wholly as a result of their own genuine and independent private choice, the program is not readily subject to challenge under the Establishment Clause. A program that shares these features permits government aid to reach religious institutions only by way of the deliberate choices of numerous individual recipients. The incidental advancement of a religious mission, or the perceived endorsement of a religious message, is reasonably attributable to the individual recipient, not to the government, whose role ends with the disbursement of benefits. As a plurality of this Court recently observed:

> "[I]f numerous private choices, rather than the single choice of a government, determine the distribution of aid, pursuant to neutral eligibility criteria, then a government cannot, or at least cannot easily, grant special favors that might lead to a religious establishment." *Mitchell*.

(See also, O'CONNOR, J., concurring in judgment: "[W]hen government aid supports a school's religious mission only because of independent decisions made by numerous individuals to guide their secular aid to that school, 'no reasonable observer is likely to draw from the facts ... an inference that the State itself is endorsing a religious practice or belief' " It is precisely for these reasons that we have never found a program of true private choice to offend the Establishment Clause.

We believe that the program challenged here is a program of true private choice, consistent with *Mueller*, *Witters*, and *Zobrest*, and thus constitutional. As was true in those cases, the Ohio program is neutral in all respects toward religion. It is part of a general and multifaceted undertaking by the State of Ohio to provide educational opportunities to the children of a failed school district. It confers educational assistance directly to a broad class of individuals defined without reference to religion, i.e., any parent of a school-age child who resides in the Cleveland City School District. The program permits the participation of all schools within the district, religious or nonreligious. Adjacent public schools also may participate and have a financial incentive to do so. Program benefits are available to participating families on neutral terms, with no reference to religion. The only preference stated anywhere in the program is a preference for low-income families, who receive greater assistance and are given priority for admission at participating schools.

There are no "financial incentive[s]" that "ske[w]" the program toward religious schools. The program here in fact creates financial disincentives for religious schools, with private schools receiving only half the government assistance given to community schools and one-third the assistance given to magnet schools. Adjacent public schools, should any choose to accept program students, are also eligible to receive two to three times the state funding of a private religious school. Families too have a financial disincentive to choose a private religious school over other schools. Parents that choose to participate in the scholarship program and then to enroll their children in a private school (religious or nonreligious) must copay a portion of the school's tuition.

Families that choose a community school, magnet school, or traditional public school pay nothing. Although such features of the program are not necessary to its constitutionality, they clearly dispel the claim that the program "creates . . . financial incentive[s] for parents to choose a sectarian school."[2]

Respondents suggest that even without a financial incentive for parents to choose a religious school, the program creates a "public perception that the State is endorsing religious practices and beliefs." But we have repeatedly recognized that no reasonable observer would think a neutral program of private choice, where state aid reaches religious schools solely as a result of the numerous independent decisions of private individuals, carries with it the imprimatur of government endorsement. The argument is particularly misplaced here since "the reasonable observer in the endorsement inquiry must be deemed aware" of the "history and context" underlying a challenged program. *Good News Club v. Milford Central School.* See also *Capitol Square Review and Advisory Bd. v. Pinette* (O'CONNOR, J., concurring in part and concurring in judgment). Any objective observer familiar with the full history and context of the Ohio program would reasonably view it as one aspect of a broader undertaking to assist poor children in failed schools, not as an endorsement of religious schooling in general.

There also is no evidence that the program fails to provide genuine opportunities for Cleveland parents to select secular educational options for their school-age children. Cleveland schoolchildren enjoy a range of educational choices: They may remain in public school as before, remain in public school with publicly funded tutoring aid, obtain a scholarship and choose a religious school, obtain a scholarship and choose a nonreligious private school, enroll in a community school, or enroll in a magnet school. That 46 of the 56 private schools now participating in the program are religious schools does not condemn it as a violation of the Establishment Clause. The Establishment Clause question is whether Ohio is coercing parents into sending their children to religious schools, and that question must be answered by evaluating all options Ohio provides Cleveland schoolchildren, only one of which is to obtain a program scholarship and then choose a religious school.

Justice SOUTER speculates that because more private religious schools currently participate in the program, the program itself must somehow discourage the participation of private nonreligious schools. *Post,* at 19–21 (dissenting opinion).[3] But Cleveland's preponderance of religiously affiliated private schools certainly did not arise as a result of the program; it is a

2. Justice SOUTER suggests the program is not "neutral" because program students cannot spend scholarship vouchers at traditional public schools. Post, at 2491–2492 (dissenting opinion). This objection is mistaken: Public schools in Cleveland already receive $7,097 in public funding per pupil—$4,167 of which is attributable to the State. Program students who receive tutoring aid and remain enrolled in traditional public schools therefore direct almost twice as much state funding to their chosen school as do program students who receive a scholarship and attend a private school. Justice SOUTER does not seriously claim that the program differentiates based on

the religious status of beneficiaries or providers of services, the touchstone of neutrality under the Establishment Clause. Mitchell v. Helms.

3. Justice SOUTER appears to base this claim on the unfounded assumption that capping the amount of tuition charged to low-income students (at $2,500) favors participation by religious schools. Post, at 21–22 (dissenting opinion). But elsewhere he claims that the program spends too much money on private schools and chides the state legislature for even proposing to raise the scholarship amount for low-income recipients.

phenomenon common to many American cities. Indeed, by all accounts the program has captured a remarkable cross-section of private schools, religious and nonreligious. It is true that 82% of Cleveland's participating private schools are religious schools, but it is also true that 81% of private schools in Ohio are religious schools. To attribute constitutional significance to this figure, moreover, would lead to the absurd result that a neutral school-choice program might be permissible in some parts of Ohio, such as Columbus, where a lower percentage of private schools are religious schools, but not in inner-city Cleveland, where Ohio has deemed such programs most sorely needed, but where the preponderance of religious schools happens to be greater. Likewise, an identical private choice program might be constitutional in some States, such as Maine or Utah, where less than 45% of private schools are religious schools, but not in other States, such as Nebraska or Kansas, where over 90% of private schools are religious schools.

Respondents and Justice SOUTER claim that even if we do not focus on the number of participating schools that are religious schools, we should attach constitutional significance to the fact that 96% of scholarship recipients have enrolled in religious schools. They claim that this alone proves parents lack genuine choice, even if no parent has ever said so. We need not consider this argument in detail, since it was flatly rejected in *Mueller*, where we found it irrelevant that 96% of parents taking deductions for tuition expenses paid tuition at religious schools. Indeed, we have recently found it irrelevant even to the constitutionality of a direct aid program that a vast majority of program benefits went to religious schools. See *Agostini*. The constitutionality of a neutral educational aid program simply does not turn on whether and why, in a particular area, at a particular time, most private schools are run by religious organizations, or most recipients choose to use the aid at a religious school. As we said in *Mueller*, "[s]uch an approach would scarcely provide the certainty that this field stands in need of, nor can we perceive principled standards by which such statistical evidence might be evaluated."

This point is aptly illustrated here. The 96% figure upon which respondents and Justice SOUTER rely discounts entirely (1) the more than 1,900 Cleveland children enrolled in alternative community schools, (2) the more than 13,000 children enrolled in alternative magnet schools, and (3) the more than 1,400 children enrolled in traditional public schools with tutorial assistance. Including some or all of these children in the denominator of children enrolled in nontraditional schools during the 1999–2000 school year drops the percentage enrolled in religious schools from 96% to under 20%. The 96% figure also represents but a snapshot of one particular school year. In the 1997–1998 school year, by contrast, only 78% of scholarship recipients attended religious schools. The difference was attributable to two private nonreligious schools that had accepted 15% of all scholarship students electing instead to register as community schools, in light of larger per-pupil funding for community schools and the uncertain future of the scholarship program generated by this litigation. Many of the students enrolled in these schools as scholarship students remained enrolled as community school students, thus demonstrating the arbitrariness of counting one type of school but not the other to assess primary effect. In spite of repeated questioning from the Court at oral argument, respondents offered no convincing justification for their approach, which relies entirely on such arbitrary classifications.[4]

Respondents finally claim that we should look to *Nyquist* to decide these cases. We disagree for two reasons. First, the program in *Nyquist* was quite different from the program challenged here. *Nyquist* involved a New York program that gave a package of benefits exclusively to private schools and the parents of private school enrollees. Although the program was enacted for ostensibly secular purposes, we found that its "function" was "*unmistakably* to provide desired financial support for nonpublic, sectarian institutions," (emphasis added). Its genesis, we said, was that private religious schools faced "increasingly grave fiscal problems." The program thus provided direct money grants to religious schools. It provided tax benefits "unrelated to the amount of money actually expended by any parent on tuition," ensuring a windfall to parents of children in religious schools. It similarly provided tuition reimbursements designed explicitly to "offe[r] . . . an incentive to parents to send their children to sectarian schools." Indeed, the program flatly prohibited the participation of any public school, or parent of any public school enrollee. Ohio's program shares none of these features.

Second, were there any doubt that the program challenged in *Nyquist* is far removed from the program challenged here, we expressly reserved judgment with respect to "a case involving some form of public assistance (e.g., scholarships) made available generally without regard to the sectarian-nonsectarian, or public-nonpublic nature of the institution benefited." That, of course, is the very question now before us, and it has since been answered, first in *Mueller,* then in *Witters,* and again in *Zobrest.* To the extent the scope of *Nyquist* has remained an open question in light of these later decisions, we now hold that *Nyquist* does not govern neutral educational assistance programs that, like the program here, offer aid directly to a broad class of individual recipients defined without regard to religion.[5]

In sum, the Ohio program is entirely neutral with respect to religion. It provides benefits directly to a wide spectrum of individuals, defined only by financial need and residence in a particular school district. It permits such individuals to exercise genuine choice among options public and private, secular and religious. The program is therefore a program of true private choice. In keeping with an unbroken line of decisions rejecting challenges to

---

4. Justice SOUTER and Justice STEVENS claim that community schools and magnet schools are separate and distinct from program schools, simply because the program itself does not include community and magnet school options. But none of the dissenting opinions explain how there is any perceptible difference between scholarship schools, community schools, or magnet schools from the perspective of Cleveland parents looking to choose the best educational option for their school-age children. Parents who choose a program school in fact receive from the State precisely what parents who choose a community or magnet school receive—the opportunity to send their children largely at state expense to schools they prefer to their local public school. (Cleveland parents who enroll their children in

schools other than local public schools typically explore all state-funded options before choosing an alternative school).

5. Justice BREYER would raise the invisible specters of "divisiveness" and "religious strife" to find the program unconstitutional. It is unclear exactly what sort of principle Justice BREYER has in mind, considering that the program has ignited no "divisiveness" or "strife" other than this litigation. Nor is it clear where Justice BREYER would locate this presumed authority to deprive Cleveland residents of a program that they have chosen but that we subjectively find "divisive." We quite rightly have rejected the claim that some speculative potential for divisiveness bears on the constitutionality of educational aid programs.

similar programs, we hold that the program does not offend the Establishment Clause.

The judgment of the Court of Appeals is reversed.

JUSTICE O'CONNOR, concurring.

While I join the Court's opinion, I write separately for two reasons. First, although the Court takes an important step, I do not believe that today's decision, when considered in light of other longstanding government programs that impact religious organizations and our prior Establishment Clause jurisprudence, marks a dramatic break from the past. Second, given the emphasis the Court places on verifying that parents of voucher students in religious schools have exercised "true private choice," I think it is worth elaborating on the Court's conclusion that this inquiry should consider all reasonable educational alternatives to religious schools that are available to parents. To do otherwise is to ignore how the educational system in Cleveland actually functions.

I

These cases are different from prior indirect aid cases in part because a significant portion of the funds appropriated for the voucher program reach religious schools without restrictions on the use of these funds. The share of public resources that reach religious schools is not, however, as significant as respondents suggest. Data from the 1999–2000 school year indicate that 82 percent of schools participating in the voucher program were religious and that 96 percent of participating students enrolled in religious schools, but these data are incomplete. These statistics do not take into account all of the reasonable educational choices that may be available to students in Cleveland public schools. When one considers the option to attend community schools, the percentage of students enrolled in religious schools falls to 62.1 percent. If magnet schools are included in the mix, this percentage falls to 16.5 percent.

Even these numbers do not paint a complete picture. The Cleveland program provides voucher applicants from low-income families with up to $2,250 in tuition assistance and provides the remaining applicants with up to $1,875 in tuition assistance. In contrast, the State provides community schools $4,518 per pupil and magnet schools, on average, $7,097 per pupil. Even if one assumes that all voucher students came from low-income families and that each voucher student used up the entire $2,250 voucher, at most $8.2 million of public funds flowed to religious schools under the voucher program in 1999–2000. Although just over one-half as many students attended community schools as religious private schools on the state fisc, the State spent over $1 million more—$9.4 million—on students in community schools than on students in religious private schools because per-pupil aid to community schools is more than double the per-pupil aid to private schools under the voucher program. Moreover, the amount spent on religious private schools is minor compared to the $114.8 million the State spent on students in the Cleveland magnet schools.

Although $8.2 million is no small sum, it pales in comparison to the amount of funds that federal, state, and local governments already provide religious institutions. Religious organizations may qualify for exemptions from the federal corporate income tax, the corporate income tax in many

States, and property taxes in all 50 States, and clergy qualify for a federal tax break on income used for housing expenses. In addition, the Federal Government provides individuals, corporations, trusts, and estates a tax deduction for charitable contributions to qualified religious groups. Finally, the Federal Government and certain state governments provide tax credits for educational expenses, many of which are spent on education at religious schools.

Most of these tax policies are well established, yet confer a significant relative benefit on religious institutions. The state property tax exemptions for religious institutions alone amount to very large sums annually. For example, available data suggest that Colorado's exemption lowers that State's tax revenues by more than $40 million annually. Maryland's exemption lowers revenues by more than $60 million. Wisconsin's exemption lowers revenues by approximately $122 million and Louisiana's exemption, looking just at the city of New Orleans, lowers revenues by over $36 million. As for the Federal Government, the tax deduction for charitable contributions reduces federal tax revenues by nearly $25 billion annually. Even the relatively minor exemptions lower federal tax receipts by substantial amounts. The parsonage exemption, for example, lowers revenues by around $500 million.

These tax exemptions, which have "much the same effect as [cash grants] . . . of the amount of tax [avoided]," are just part of the picture. Federal dollars also reach religiously affiliated organizations through public health programs such as Medicare and Medicaid, through educational programs such as the Pell Grant program and the G.I. Bill of Rights, and through child care programs such as the Child Care and Development Block Grant Program.

A significant portion of the funds appropriated for these programs reach religiously affiliated institutions, typically without restrictions on its subsequent use. For example, it has been reported that religious hospitals, which account for 18 percent of all hospital beds nationwide, rely on Medicare funds for 36 percent of their revenue. Moreover, taking into account both Medicare and Medicaid, religious hospitals received nearly $45 billion from the federal fisc in 1998. Federal aid to religious schools is also substantial. Although data for all States is not available, data from Minnesota, for example, suggest that a substantial share of Pell Grant and other federal funds for college tuition reach religious schools. Roughly one-third or $27.1 million of the federal tuition dollars spent on students at schools in Minnesota were used at private 4–year colleges. The vast majority of these funds—$23.5 million—flowed to religiously affiliated institutions.

Against this background, the support that the Cleveland voucher program provides religious institutions is neither substantial nor atypical of existing government programs. While this observation is not intended to justify the Cleveland voucher program under the Establishment Clause, it places in broader perspective alarmist claims about implications of the Cleveland program and the Court's decision in these cases.

II

Nor does today's decision signal a major departure from this Court's prior Establishment Clause jurisprudence. A central tool in our analysis of cases in this area has been the *Lemon* test. As originally formulated, a statute passed this test only if it had "a secular legislative purpose," if its "principal or primary effect" was one that "neither advance[d] nor inhibit [ed] religion," and if it did "not foster an excessive government entanglement with religion." In *Agostini*, we folded the entanglement inquiry into the primary effect inquiry. This made sense because both inquiries rely on the same evidence and the degree of entanglement has implications for whether a statute advances or inhibits religion. The test today is basically the same as that set forth in *School Dist. of Abington Township v. Schempp* (citing *Everson*).

The Court's opinion in these cases focuses on a narrow question related to the Lemon test: how to apply the primary effects prong in indirect aid cases? Specifically, it clarifies the basic inquiry when trying to determine whether a program that distributes aid to beneficiaries, rather than directly to service providers, has the primary effect of advancing or inhibiting religion, or, as I have put it, of "endors[ing] or disapprov[ing] ... religion." Courts are instructed to consider two factors: first, whether the program administers aid in a neutral fashion, without differentiation based on the religious status of beneficiaries or providers of services; second, and more importantly, whether beneficiaries of indirect aid have a genuine choice among religious and nonreligious organizations when determining the organization to which they will direct that aid. If the answer to either query is "no," the program should be struck down under the Establishment Clause.

Justice SOUTER portrays this inquiry as a departure from *Everson*. A fair reading of the holding in that case suggests quite the opposite. Justice Black's opinion for the Court held that the "[First] Amendment requires the state to be a neutral in its relations with groups of religious believers and non-believers; it does not require the state to be their adversary." How else could the Court have upheld a state program to provide students transportation to public and religious schools alike? What the Court clarifies in these cases is that the Establishment Clause also requires that state aid flowing to religious organizations through the hands of beneficiaries must do so only at the direction of those beneficiaries. Such a refinement of the Lemon test surely does not betray *Everson*.

III

There is little question in my mind that the Cleveland voucher program is neutral as between religious schools and nonreligious schools. Justice SOUTER rejects the Court's notion of neutrality, proposing that the neutrality of a program should be gauged not by the opportunities it presents but rather by its effects. In particular, a "neutrality test ... [should] focus on a category of aid that may be directed to religious as well as secular schools, and ask whether the scheme favors a religious direction." Justice SOUTER doubts that the Cleveland program is neutral under this view. He surmises that the cap on tuition that voucher schools may charge low-income students encourages these students to attend religious rather than nonreligious private voucher schools. But Justice SOUTER's notion of neutrality is inconsistent with that in our case law. As we put it in *Agostini*, government aid must be "made available to both religious and secular beneficiaries on a nondiscriminatory basis."

I do not agree that the nonreligious schools have failed to provide Cleveland parents reasonable alternatives to religious schools in the voucher program. For nonreligious schools to qualify as genuine options for parents, they need not be superior to religious schools in every respect. They need only be adequate substitutes for religious schools in the eyes of parents. The District Court record demonstrates that nonreligious schools were able to compete effectively with Catholic and other religious schools in the Cleveland voucher program. The best evidence of this is that many parents with vouchers selected nonreligious private schools over religious alternatives and an even larger number of parents send their children to community and magnet schools rather than seeking vouchers at all. Moreover, there is no record evidence that any voucher-eligible student was turned away from a nonreligious private school in the voucher program, let alone a community or magnet school.

To support his hunch about the effect of the cap on tuition under the voucher program, Justice SOUTER cites national data to suggest that, on average, Catholic schools have a cost advantage over other types of schools. Even if national statistics were relevant for evaluating the Cleveland program, Justice SOUTER ignores evidence which suggests that, at a national level, nonreligious private schools may target a market for different, if not higher, quality of education. For example, nonreligious private schools are smaller, have more highly educated teachers, and have principals with longer job tenure than Catholic schools.

Additionally, Justice SOUTER's theory that the Cleveland voucher program's cap on the tuition encourages low-income student to attend religious schools ignores that these students receive nearly double the amount of tuition assistance under the community schools program than under the voucher program and that none of the community schools is religious.

In my view the more significant finding in these cases is that Cleveland parents who use vouchers to send their children to religious private schools do so as a result of true private choice. The Court rejects, correctly, the notion that the high percentage of voucher recipients who enroll in religious private schools necessarily demonstrates that parents do not actually have the option to send their children to nonreligious schools. Likewise, the mere fact that some parents enrolled their children in religious schools associated with a different faith than their own, says little about whether these parents had reasonable nonreligious options. Indeed, no voucher student has been known to be turned away from a nonreligious private school participating in the voucher program. This is impressive given evidence in the record that the present litigation has discouraged the entry of some nonreligious private schools into the voucher program. Finally, as demonstrated above, the Cleveland program does not establish financial incentives to undertake a religious education.

I find the Court's answer to the question whether parents of students eligible for vouchers have a genuine choice between religious and nonreligious schools persuasive. In looking at the voucher program, all the choices available to potential beneficiaries of the government program should be considered. In these cases, parents who were eligible to apply for a voucher also had the option, at a minimum, to send their children to community schools. Yet the Court of Appeals chose not to look at community schools, let alone magnet schools, when evaluating the Cleveland voucher program.

Considering all the educational options available to parents whose children are eligible for vouchers, including community and magnet schools, the Court finds that parents in the Cleveland schools have an array of nonreligious options. Not surprisingly, respondents present no evidence that any students who were candidates for a voucher were denied slots in a community school or a magnet school. Indeed, the record suggests the opposite with respect to community schools.

Justice SOUTER nonetheless claims that, of the 10 community schools operating in Cleveland during the 1999–2000 school year, 4 were unavailable to students with vouchers and 4 others reported poor test scores. But that analysis unreasonably limits the choices available to Cleveland parents. It is undisputed that Cleveland's 24 magnet schools are reasonable alternatives to voucher schools. And of the four community schools Justice SOUTER claims are unavailable to voucher students, he is correct only about one (Life Skills Center of Cleveland). Justice SOUTER rejects the three other community schools (Horizon Science Academy, Cleveland Alternative Learning, and International Preparatory School) because they did not offer primary school classes, were targeted towards poor students or students with disciplinary or academic problems, or were not in operation for a year. But a community school need not offer primary school classes to be an alternative to religious middle schools, and catering to impoverished or otherwise challenged students may make a school more attractive to certain inner-city parents. Moreover, the one community school that was closed in 1999–2000 was merely looking for a new location and was operational in other years.

Of the six community schools that Justice SOUTER admits as alternatives to the voucher program in 1999–2000, he notes that four (the Broadway, Cathedral, Chapelside, and Lincoln Park campuses of the Hope Academy) reported lower test scores than public schools during the school year after the District Court's grant of summary judgment to respondents, according to report cards prepared by the Ohio Department of Education. These report cards underestimate the value of the four Hope Academy schools. Before they entered the community school program, two of them participated in the voucher program. Although they received far less state funding in that capacity, they had among the highest rates of parental satisfaction of all voucher schools, religious or nonreligious. This is particularly impressive given that a Harvard University study found that the Hope Academy schools attracted the "poorest and most educationally disadvantaged students." Moreover, Justice SOUTER's evaluation of the Hope Academy schools assumes that the only relevant measure of school quality is academic performance. It is reasonable to suppose, however, that parents in the inner city also choose schools that provide discipline and a safe environment for their children. On these dimensions some of the schools that Justice SOUTER derides have performed quite ably.

Ultimately, Justice SOUTER relies on very narrow data to draw rather broad conclusions. One year of poor test scores at four community schools targeted at the most challenged students from the inner city says little about the value of those schools, let alone the quality of the 6 other community schools and 24 magnet schools in Cleveland. Justice SOUTER's use of statistics confirms the Court's wisdom in refusing to consider them when assessing the Cleveland program's constitutionality. What appears to motivate

Justice SOUTER's analysis is a desire for a limiting principle to rule out certain nonreligious schools as alternatives to religious schools in the voucher program. But the goal of the Court's Establishment Clause jurisprudence is to determine whether, after the Cleveland voucher program was enacted, parents were free to direct state educational aid in either a nonreligious or religious direction. That inquiry requires an evaluation of all reasonable educational options Ohio provides the Cleveland school system, regardless of whether they are formally made available in the same section of the Ohio Code as the voucher program.

Based on the reasoning in the Court's opinion, which is consistent with the realities of the Cleveland educational system, I am persuaded that the Cleveland voucher program affords parents of eligible children genuine nonreligious options and is consistent with the Establishment Clause.

JUSTICE THOMAS, concurring.

Frederick Douglass once said that "[e]ducation ... means emancipation. It means light and liberty. It means the uplifting of the soul of man into the glorious light of truth, the light by which men can only be made free." Today many of our inner-city public schools deny emancipation to urban minority students. Despite this Court's observation nearly 50 years ago in *Brown v. Board of Education*, that "it is doubtful that any child may reasonably be expected to succeed in life if he is denied the opportunity of an education," urban children have been forced into a system that continually fails them. These cases present an example of such failures. Besieged by escalating financial problems and declining academic achievement, the Cleveland City School District was in the midst of an academic emergency when Ohio enacted its scholarship program.

The dissents and respondents wish to invoke the Establishment Clause of the First Amendment, as incorporated through the Fourteenth, to constrain a State's neutral efforts to provide greater educational opportunity for underprivileged minority students. Today's decision properly upholds the program as constitutional, and I join it in full.

I

This Court has often considered whether efforts to provide children with the best educational resources conflict with constitutional limitations. Attempts to provide aid to religious schools or to allow some degree of religious involvement in public schools have generated significant controversy and litigation as States try to navigate the line between the secular and the religious in education. We have recently decided several cases challenging federal aid programs that include religious schools. To determine whether a federal program survives scrutiny under the Establishment Clause, we have considered whether it has a secular purpose and whether it has the primary effect of advancing or inhibiting religion. I agree with the Court that Ohio's program easily passes muster under our stringent test, but, as a matter of first principles, I question whether this test should be applied to the States.

The Establishment Clause of the First Amendment states that "Congress shall make no law respecting an establishment of religion." On its face, this provision places no limit on the States with regard to religion. The Establishment Clause originally protected States, and by extension their citizens, from the imposition of an established religion by the Federal Government. Whether and how this Clause should constrain state action under the Fourteenth Amendment is a more difficult question.

The Fourteenth Amendment fundamentally restructured the relationship between individuals and the States and ensured that States would not deprive citizens of liberty without due process of law. It guarantees citizenship to all individuals born or naturalized in the United States and provides that "[n]o State shall make or enforce any law which shall abridge the privileges or immunities of citizens of the United States; nor shall any State deprive any person of life, liberty, or property, without due process of law; nor deny to any person within its jurisdiction the equal protection of the laws." As Justice Harlan noted, the Fourteenth Amendment "added greatly to the dignity and glory of American citizenship, and to the security of personal liberty." *Plessy v. Ferguson*, 163 U.S. 537, 555 (1896) (dissenting opinion). When rights are incorporated against the States through the Fourteenth Amendment they should advance, not constrain, individual liberty.

Consequently, in the context of the Establishment Clause, it may well be that state action should be evaluated on different terms than similar action by the Federal Government. "States, while bound to observe strict neutrality, should be freer to experiment with involvement [in religion]—on a neutral basis—than the Federal Government." *Walz v. Tax Comm'n of City of New York*, 397 U.S. 664, 699 (1970) (Harlan, J., concurring). Thus, while the Federal Government may "make no law respecting an establishment of religion," the States may pass laws that include or touch on religious matters so long as these laws do not impede free exercise rights or any other individual religious liberty interest. By considering the particular religious liberty right alleged to be invaded by a State, federal courts can strike a proper balance between the demands of the Fourteenth Amendment on the one hand and the federalism prerogatives of States on the other.[6]

Whatever the textual and historical merits of incorporating the Establishment Clause, I can accept that the Fourteenth Amendment protects religious liberty rights. But I cannot accept its use to oppose neutral programs of school choice through the incorporation of the Establishment Clause. There would be a tragic irony in converting the Fourteenth Amendment's guarantee of individual liberty into a prohibition on the exercise of educational choice.

II

The wisdom of allowing States greater latitude in dealing with matters of religion and education can be easily appreciated in this context. Respondents

---

6. Several Justices have suggested that rights incorporated through the Fourteenth Amendment apply in a different manner to the States than they do to the Federal Government. For instance, Justice Jackson stated, "[t]he inappropriateness of a single standard for restricting State and Nation is indicated by the disparity between their functions and duties in relation to those freedoms." Beauharnais v. Illinois, 343 U.S. 250, 294 (1952) (dissenting opinion). Justice Harlan noted: "The Constitution differentiates between those areas of human conduct subject to the regulation of the States and those subject to the powers of the Federal Government. The substantive powers of the two governments, in many instances, are distinct. And in every case where we are called upon to balance the interest in free expression against other interests, it seems to me important that we should keep in the forefront the question of whether those other interests are state or federal." Roth v. United States, 354 U.S. 476, 503–504 (1957) (dissenting opinion). See also, Gitlow v. New York, 268 U.S. 652, 672 (1925) (Holmes, J., dissenting).

advocate using the Fourteenth Amendment to handcuff the State's ability to experiment with education. But without education one can hardly exercise the civic, political, and personal freedoms conferred by the Fourteenth Amendment. Faced with a severe educational crisis, the State of Ohio enacted wide-ranging educational reform that allows voluntary participation of private and religious schools in educating poor urban children otherwise condemned to failing public schools. The program does not force any individual to submit to religious indoctrination or education. It simply gives parents a greater choice as to where and in what manner to educate their children.[7] This is a choice that those with greater means have routinely exercised.

Cleveland parents now have a variety of educational choices. There are traditional public schools, magnet schools, and privately run community schools, in addition to the scholarship program. Currently, 46 of the 56 private schools participating in the scholarship program are church affiliated (35 are Catholic), and 96 percent of students in the program attend religious schools. Thus, were the Court to disallow the inclusion of religious schools, Cleveland children could use their scholarships at only 10 private schools.

In addition to expanding the reach of the scholarship program, the inclusion of religious schools makes sense given Ohio's purpose of increasing educational performance and opportunities. Religious schools, like other private schools, achieve far better educational results than their public counterparts. For example, the students at Cleveland's Catholic schools score significantly higher on Ohio proficiency tests than students at Cleveland public schools. Of Cleveland eighth graders taking the 1999 Ohio proficiency test, 95 percent in Catholic schools passed the reading test, whereas only 57 percent in public schools passed. And 75 percent of Catholic school students passed the math proficiency test, compared to only 22 percent of public school students. But the success of religious and private schools is in the end beside the point, because the State has a constitutional right to experiment with a variety of different programs to promote educational opportunity. That Ohio's program includes successful schools simply indicates that such reform can in fact provide improved education to underprivileged urban children. Although one of the purposes of public schools was to promote democracy and a more egalitarian culture, failing urban public schools disproportionately affect minority children most in need of educational opportunity. At the time of Reconstruction, blacks considered public education "a matter of personal liberation and a necessary function of a free society." Today, however, the promise of public school education has failed poor inner-city blacks. While in theory providing education to everyone, the quality of public schools varies significantly across districts. Just as blacks supported public education during Reconstruction, many blacks and other minorities now support school choice programs because they provide the greatest educational opportunities for their children in struggling communities.[8] Opponents of the program raise

7. This Court has held that parents have the fundamental liberty to choose how and in what manner to educate their children. Pierce v. Society of Sisters, 268 U.S. 510, 535 (1925). But see Troxel v. Granville, 530 U.S. 57, 80 (2000) (THOMAS, J., concurring in judgment).

8. Minority and low-income parents express the greatest support for parental choice and are most interested in placing their children in private schools. "[T]he appeal of private schools is especially strong among parents who are low in income, minority, and live in low-performing districts: precisely the parents who

formalistic concerns about the Establishment Clause but ignore the core purposes of the Fourteenth Amendment.

While the romanticized ideal of universal public education resonates with the cognoscenti who oppose vouchers, poor urban families just want the best education for their children, who will certainly need it to function in our high-tech and advanced society. As Thomas Sowell noted 30 years ago: "Most black people have faced too many grim, concrete problems to be romantics. They want and need certain tangible results, which can be achieved only by developing certain specific abilities." Black Education: Myths and Tragedies 228 (1972). The same is true today. An individual's life prospects increase dramatically with each successfully completed phase of education. For instance, a black high school dropout earns just over $13,500, but with a high school degree the average income is almost $21,000. Blacks with a bachelor's degree have an average annual income of about $37,500, and $75,500 with a professional degree. Staying in school and earning a degree generates real and tangible financial benefits, whereas failure to obtain even a high school degree essentially relegates students to a life of poverty and, all too often, of crime.[9] The failure to provide education to poor urban children perpetuates a vicious cycle of poverty, dependence, criminality, and alienation that continues for the remainder of their lives. If society cannot end racial discrimination, at least it can arm minorities with the education to defend themselves from some of discrimination's effects.

* * *

Ten States have enacted some form of publicly funded private school choice as one means of raising the quality of education provided to underprivileged urban children. These programs address the root of the problem with failing urban public schools that disproportionately affect minority students. Society's other solution to these educational failures is often to provide racial preferences in higher education. Such preferences, however, run afoul of the Fourteenth Amendment's prohibition against distinctions based on race. See *Plessy* (Harlan, J., dissenting). By contrast, school choice programs that involve religious schools appear unconstitutional only to those who would twist the Fourteenth Amendment against itself by expansively incorporating the Establishment Clause. Converting the Fourteenth Amendment from a guarantee of opportunity to an obstacle against education reform distorts our constitutional values and disserves those in the greatest need.

As Frederick Douglass poignantly noted "no greater benefit can be bestowed upon a long benighted people, than giving to them, as we are here earnestly this day endeavoring to do, the means of an education."

JUSTICE STEVENS, dissenting.

Is a law that authorizes the use of public funds to pay for the indoctrination of thousands of grammar school children in particular religious faiths a

---

are the most disadvantaged under the current system." T. Moe, Schools, Vouchers, and the American Public 164 (2001). Nearly three-fourths of all public school parents with an annual income less than $20,000 support vouchers, compared to 57 percent of public school parents with an annual income of over $60,000. In addition, 75 percent of black public school parents support vouchers, as do 71 percent of Hispanic public school parents.

9. In 1997, approximately 68 percent of prisoners in state correctional institutions did not have a high school degree.

"law respecting an establishment of religion" within the meaning of the First Amendment? In answering that question, I think we should ignore three factual matters that are discussed at length by my colleagues.

First, the severe educational crisis that confronted the Cleveland City School District when Ohio enacted its voucher program is not a matter that should affect our appraisal of its constitutionality. In the 1999–2000 school year, that program provided relief to less than five percent of the students enrolled in the district's schools. The solution to the disastrous conditions that prevented over 90 percent of the student body from meeting basic proficiency standards obviously required massive improvements unrelated to the voucher program.[10] Of course, the emergency may have given some families a powerful motivation to leave the public school system and accept religious indoctrination that they would otherwise have avoided, but that is not a valid reason for upholding the program.

Second, the wide range of choices that have been made available to students within the public school system has no bearing on the question whether the State may pay the tuition for students who wish to reject public education entirely and attend private schools that will provide them with a sectarian education. The fact that the vast majority of the voucher recipients who have entirely rejected public education receive religious indoctrination at state expense does, however, support the claim that the law is one "respecting an establishment of religion." The State may choose to divide up its public schools into a dozen different options and label them magnet schools, community schools, or whatever else it decides to call them, but the State is still required to provide a public education and it is the State's decision to fund private school education over and above its traditional obligation that is at issue in these cases.[11]

Third, the voluntary character of the private choice to prefer a parochial education over an education in the public school system seems to me quite irrelevant to the question whether the government's choice to pay for religious indoctrination is constitutionally permissible. Today, however, the Court seems to have decided that the mere fact that a family that cannot afford a private education wants its children educated in a parochial school is a sufficient justification for this use of public funds. For the reasons stated by Justice SOUTER and Justice BREYER, I am convinced that the Court's decision is profoundly misguided. Admittedly, in reaching that conclusion I have been influenced by my understanding of the impact of religious strife on the decisions of our forbears to migrate to this continent, and on the decisions of neighbors in the Balkans, Northern Ireland, and the Middle East to mistrust one another. Whenever we remove a brick from the wall that was designed to separate religion and government, we increase the risk of religious strife and weaken the foundation of our democracy.

10. Ohio is currently undergoing a major overhaul of its public school financing pursuant to an order of the Ohio Supreme Court in DeRolph v. State, 93 Ohio St.3d 309, 754 N.E.2d 1184 (2001). The Court ought, at least, to allow that reform effort and the district's experimentation with alternative public schools to take effect before relying on Cleveland's educational crisis as a reason for state financed religious education.

11. The Court suggests that an education at one of the district's community or magnet schools is provided "largely at state expense." But a public education at either of these schools is provided entirely at State expense— as the State is required to do.

I respectfully dissent.

JUSTICE SOUTER, with whom JUSTICE STEVENS, JUSTICE GINSBURG, and JUSTICE BREYER join, dissenting.

The Court's majority holds that the Establishment Clause is no bar to Ohio's payment of tuition at private religious elementary and middle schools under a scheme that systematically provides tax money to support the schools' religious missions. The occasion for the legislation thus upheld is the condition of public education in the city of Cleveland. The record indicates that the schools are failing to serve their objective, and the vouchers in issue here are said to be needed to provide adequate alternatives to them. If there were an excuse for giving short shrift to the Establishment Clause, it would probably apply here. But there is no excuse. Constitutional limitations are placed on government to preserve constitutional values in hard cases, like these. "[C]onstitutional lines have to be drawn, and on one side of every one of them is an otherwise sympathetic case that provokes impatience with the Constitution and with the line. But constitutional lines are the price of constitutional government." *Agostini v. Felton* (SOUTER, J., dissenting). I therefore respectfully dissent.

The applicability of the Establishment Clause to public funding of benefits to religious schools was settled in *Everson v. Board of Ed. of Ewing*, 330 U.S. 1 (1947), which inaugurated the modern era of establishment doctrine. The Court stated the principle in words from which there was no dissent:

> "No tax in any amount, large or small, can be levied to support any religious activities or institutions, whatever they may be called, or whatever form they may adopt to teach or practice religion."

The Court has never in so many words repudiated this statement, let alone, in so many words, overruled *Everson*.

Today, however, the majority holds that the Establishment Clause is not offended by Ohio's Pilot Project Scholarship Program, under which students may be eligible to receive as much as $2,250 in the form of tuition vouchers transferable to religious schools. In the city of Cleveland the overwhelming proportion of large appropriations for voucher money must be spent on religious schools if it is to be spent at all, and will be spent in amounts that cover almost all of tuition. The money will thus pay for eligible students' instruction not only in secular subjects but in religion as well, in schools that can fairly be characterized as founded to teach religious doctrine and to imbue teaching in all subjects with a religious dimension. Public tax money will pay at a systemic level for teaching the covenant with Israel and Mosaic law in Jewish schools, the primacy of the Apostle Peter and the Papacy in Catholic schools, the truth of reformed Christianity in Protestant schools, and the revelation to the Prophet in Muslim schools, to speak only of major religious groupings in the Republic.

How can a Court consistently leave *Everson* on the books and approve the Ohio vouchers? The answer is that it cannot. It is only by ignoring *Everson* that the majority can claim to rest on traditional law in its invocation of neutral aid provisions and private choice to sanction the Ohio law. It is, moreover, only by ignoring the meaning of neutrality and private choice themselves that the majority can even pretend to rest today's decision on those criteria.

I

The majority's statements of Establishment Clause doctrine cannot be appreciated without some historical perspective on the Court's announced limitations on government aid to religious education, and its repeated repudiation of limits previously set. My object here is not to give any nuanced exposition of the cases, which I tried to classify in some detail in an earlier opinion, see *Mitchell v. Helms* (dissenting opinion), but to set out the broad doctrinal stages covered in the modern era, and to show that doctrinal bankruptcy has been reached today.

Viewed with the necessary generality, the cases can be categorized in three groups. In the period from 1947 to 1968, the basic principle of no aid to religion through school benefits was unquestioned. Thereafter for some 15 years, the Court termed its efforts as attempts to draw a line against aid that would be divertible to support the religious, as distinct from the secular, activity of an institutional beneficiary. Then, starting in 1983, concern with divertibility was gradually lost in favor of approving aid in amounts unlikely to afford substantial benefits to religious schools, when offered evenhandedly without regard to a recipient's religious character, and when channeled to a religious institution only by the genuinely free choice of some private individual. Now, the three stages are succeeded by a fourth, in which the substantial character of government aid is held to have no constitutional significance, and the espoused criteria of neutrality in offering aid, and private choice in directing it, are shown to be nothing but examples of verbal formalism.

A

Everson inaugurated the modern development of Establishment Clause doctrine at the behest of a taxpayer challenging state provision of "tax-raised funds to pay the bus fares of parochial school pupils" on regular city buses as part of a general scheme to reimburse the public-transportation costs of children attending both public and private nonprofit schools. Although the Court split, no Justice disagreed with the basic doctrinal principle already quoted, that "[n]o tax in any amount ... can be levied to support any religious activities or institutions, ... whatever form they may adopt to teach ... religion." Nor did any Member of the Court deny the tension between the New Jersey program and the aims of the Establishment Clause. The majority upheld the state law on the strength of rights of religious-school students under the Free Exercise Clause, which was thought to entitle them to free public transportation when offered as a "general government servic[e]" to all schoolchildren. Despite the indirect benefit to religious education, the transportation was simply treated like "ordinary police and fire protection, connections for sewage disposal, public highways and sidewalks," and, most significantly, "state-paid policemen, detailed to protect children going to and from church schools from the very real hazards of traffic." The dissenters, however, found the benefit to religion too pronounced to survive the general principle of no establishment, no aid, and they described it as running counter to every objective served by the establishment ban.

The difficulty of drawing a line that preserved the basic principle of no aid was no less obvious some 20 years later in Allen, which upheld a New York law authorizing local school boards to lend textbooks in secular subjects to children attending religious schools, a result not self-evident from Everson's "general government services" rationale. The Court relied instead on the theory that the in-kind aid could only be used for secular educational purposes, and found it relevant that "no funds or books are furnished [directly] to parochial schools, and the financial benefit is to parents and children, not to schools." Justice Black, who wrote *Everson*, led the dissenters. Textbooks, even when " 'secular,' realistically will in some way inevitably tend to propagate the religious views of the favored sect."

Transcending even the sharp disagreement, however, was

"the consistency in the way the Justices went about deciding the case. . . . Neither side rested on any facile application of the 'test' or any simplistic reliance on the generality or evenhandedness of the state law. Disagreement concentrated on the true intent inferrable behind the law, the feasibility of distinguishing in fact between religious and secular teaching in church schools, and the reality or sham of lending books to pupils instead of supplying books to schools. . . .[T]he stress was on the practical significance of the actual benefits received by the schools."

B

Allen recognized the reality that "religious schools pursue two goals, religious instruction and secular education," if state aid could be restricted to serve the second, it might be permissible under the Establishment Clause. But in the retrenchment that followed, the Court saw that the two educational functions were so intertwined in religious primary and secondary schools that aid to secular education could not readily be segregated, and the intrusive monitoring required to enforce the line itself raised Establishment Clause concerns about the entanglement of church and state. See *Lemon*. To avoid the entanglement, the Court's focus in the post-*Allen* cases was on the principle of divertibility, on discerning when ostensibly secular government aid to religious schools was susceptible to religious uses. The greater the risk of diversion to religion (and the monitoring necessary to avoid it), the less legitimate the aid scheme was under the no-aid principle. On the one hand, the Court tried to be practical, and when the aid recipients were not so "pervasively sectarian" that their secular and religious functions were inextricably intertwined, the Court generally upheld aid earmarked for secular use. See, e.g *Tilton v. Richardson*. But otherwise the principle of nondivertibility was enforced strictly, with its violation being presumed in most cases, even when state aid seemed secular on its face. Compare, e.g., *Levitt v. Committee for Public Ed. & Religious Liberty*, 413 U.S. 472, 480 (1973) (striking down state program reimbursing private schools' administrative costs for teacher-prepared tests in compulsory secular subjects), with *Wolman v. Walter* (upholding similar program using standardized tests); and *Meek v. Pittenger*, (no public funding for staff and materials for "auxiliary services" like guidance counseling and speech and hearing services), with *Wolman* (permitting state aid for diagnostic speech, hearing, and psychological testing).

The fact that the Court's suspicion of divertibility reflected a concern with the substance of the no-aid principle is apparent in its rejection of stratagems invented to dodge it. In *Nyquist*, for example, the Court struck down a New York program of tuition grants for poor parents and tax deductions for more affluent ones who sent their children to private schools. The *Nyquist* Court dismissed warranties of a "statistical guarantee," that the scheme provided at most 15% of the total cost of an education at a religious school, which could presumably be matched to a secular 15% of a child's education at the school. And it rejected the idea that the path of state aid to religious schools might be dispositive: "far from providing a per se immunity from examination of the substance of the State's program, the fact that aid is disbursed to parents rather than to the schools is only one among many factors to be considered." The point was that "the effect of the aid is unmistakably to provide desired financial support for nonpublic, sectarian institutions." *Nyquist* thus held that aid to parents through tax deductions was no different from forbidden direct aid to religious schools for religious uses. The focus remained on what the public money bought when it reached the end point of its disbursement.

C

Like all criteria requiring judicial assessment of risk, divertibility is an invitation to argument, but the object of the arguments provoked has always been a realistic assessment of facts aimed at respecting the principle of no aid. In *Mueller v. Allen*, however, that object began to fade, for *Mueller* started down the road from realism to formalism. The aid in *Mueller* was in substance indistinguishable from that in *Nyquist*, and both were substantively difficult to distinguish from aid directly to religious schools. But the Court upheld the Minnesota tax deductions in *Mueller*, emphasizing their neutral availability for religious and secular educational expenses and the role of private choice in taking them. The Court relied on the same two principles in *Witters*.

School Dist. of Grand Rapids v. Ball, overruled in part by *Agostini*, clarified that the notions of evenhandedness neutrality and private choice in *Mueller* did not apply to cases involving direct aid to religious schools, which were still subject to the divertibility test. But in *Agostini*, where the substance of the aid was identical to that in *Ball*, public employees teaching remedial secular classes in private schools, the Court rejected the 30–year-old presumption of divertibility, and instead found it sufficient that the aid "supplement[ed]" but did not "supplant" existing educational services.

In the 12 years between *Ball* and *Agostini*, the Court decided not only *Witters*, but two other cases emphasizing the form of neutrality and private choice over the substance of aid to religious uses, but always in circumstances where any aid to religion was isolated and insubstantial. *Zobrest*, like *Witters*, involved one student's choice to spend funds from a general public program at a religious school (to pay for a sign-language interpreter). As in *Witters*, the Court reasoned that "[d]isabled children, not sectarian schools, [were] the primary beneficiaries ...; to the extent sectarian schools benefit at all ..., they are only incidental beneficiaries." 509 U.S. at 12. *Rosenberger v. Rector*, like *Zobrest* and *Witters*, involved an individual and insubstantial use of neutrally available public funds for a religious purpose (to print an evangelical magazine). To be sure, the aid in *Agostini* was systemic and arguably substantial, but, as I have said, the majority there chose to view it as a bare "supplement." And this was how the controlling opinion described the systemic aid in our most recent case, *Mitchell v. Helms*, as aid going merely to a "portion" of the religious schools' budgets, (O'CONNOR, J., concurring in judgment). The plurality in that case did not feel so uncomfortable about jettisoning substance entirely in favor of form, finding it sufficient that the aid was neutral and that there was virtual private choice, since any aid "first passes through the hands (literally or figuratively) of numerous private citizens who are free to direct the aid elsewhere." But that was only the plurality view.

Hence it seems fair to say that it was not until today that substantiality of aid has clearly been rejected as irrelevant by a majority of this Court, just as it has not been until today that a majority, not a plurality, has held purely formal criteria to suffice for scrutinizing aid that ends up in the coffers of religious schools. Today's cases are notable for their stark illustration of the inadequacy of the majority's chosen formal analysis.

II

Although it has taken half a century since *Everson* to reach the majority's twin standards of neutrality and free choice, the facts show that, in the majority's hands, even these criteria cannot convincingly legitimize the Ohio scheme.

A

Consider first the criterion of neutrality. As recently as two Terms ago, a majority of the Court recognized that neutrality conceived of as evenhandedness toward aid recipients had never been treated as alone sufficient to satisfy the Establishment Clause, *Mitchell* (O'CONNOR, J., concurring in judgment); (SOUTER, J., dissenting). But at least in its limited significance, formal neutrality seemed to serve some purpose. Today, however, the majority employs the neutrality criterion in a way that renders it impossible to understand.

Neutrality in this sense refers, of course, to evenhandedness in setting eligibility as between potential religious and secular recipients of public money. Thus, for example, the aid scheme in *Witters* provided an eligible recipient with a scholarship to be used at any institution within a practically unlimited universe of schools; it did not tend to provide more or less aid depending on which one the scholarship recipient chose, and there was no indication that the maximum scholarship amount would be insufficient at secular schools. Neither did any condition of *Zobrest's* interpreter's subsidy favor religious education.

In order to apply the neutrality test, then, it makes sense to focus on a category of aid that may be directed to religious as well as secular schools, and ask whether the scheme favors a religious direction. Here, one would ask whether the voucher provisions, allowing for as much as $2,250 toward private school tuition (or a grant to a public school in an adjacent district), were written in a way that skewed the scheme toward benefiting religious schools.

This, however, is not what the majority asks. The majority looks not to the provisions for tuition vouchers, but to every provision for educational opportunity: "The program permits the participation of *all* schools within the district, [as well as public schools in adjacent districts], religious or nonreligious." (emphasis in original). The majority then finds confirmation that "participation of all schools" satisfies neutrality by noting that the better part of total state educational expenditure goes to public schools, thus showing there is no favor of religion.

The illogic is patent. If regular, public schools (which can get no voucher payments) "participate" in a voucher scheme with schools that can, and public expenditure is still predominantly on public schools, then the majority's reasoning would find neutrality in a scheme of vouchers available for private tuition in districts with no secular private schools at all. "Neutrality" as the majority employs the term is, literally, verbal and nothing more. This, indeed, is the only way the majority can gloss over the very nonneutral feature of the total scheme covering "all schools": public tutors may receive from the State no more than $324 per child to support extra tutoring (that is, the State's 90% of a total amount of $360), whereas the tuition voucher schools (which turn out to be mostly religious) can receive up to $2,250.

Why the majority does not simply accept the fact that the challenge here is to the more generous voucher scheme and judge its neutrality in relation to religious use of voucher money seems very odd. It seems odd, that is, until one recognizes that comparable schools for applying the criterion of neutrality are also the comparable schools for applying the other majority criterion, whether the immediate recipients of voucher aid have a genuinely free choice of religious and secular schools to receive the voucher money. And in applying this second criterion, the consideration of "all schools" is ostensibly helpful to the majority position.

B

The majority addresses the issue of choice the same way it addresses neutrality, by asking whether recipients or potential recipients of voucher aid have a choice of public schools among secular alternatives to religious schools. Again, however, the majority asks the wrong question and misapplies the criterion. The majority has confused choice in spending scholarships with choice from the entire menu of possible educational placements, most of them open to anyone willing to attend a public school. I say "confused" because the majority's new use of the choice criterion, which it frames negatively as "whether Ohio is coercing parents into sending their children to religious schools" ignores the reason for having a private choice enquiry in the first place. Cases since Mueller have found private choice relevant under a rule that aid to religious schools can be permissible so long as it first passes through the hands of students or parents. The majority's view that all educational choices are comparable for purposes of choice thus ignores the whole point of the choice test: it is a criterion for deciding whether indirect aid to a religious school is legitimate because it passes through private hands that can spend or use the aid in a secular school. The question is whether the private hand is genuinely free to send the money in either a secular direction or a religious one. The majority now has transformed this question about private choice in channeling aid into a question about selecting from examples of state spending (on education) including direct spending on magnet and community public schools that goes through no private hands and could never reach a religious school under any circumstance. When the choice test is transformed from where to spend the money to where to go to school, it is cut loose from its very purpose.

Defining choice as choice in spending the money or channeling the aid is, moreover, necessary if the choice criterion is to function as a limiting principle at all. If "choice" is present whenever there is any educational alternative to the religious school to which vouchers can be endorsed, then there will always be a choice and the voucher can always be constitutional, even in a system in which there is not a single private secular school as an alternative to the religious school. And because it is unlikely that any participating private religious school will enroll more pupils than the generally available public system, it will be easy to generate numbers suggesting that aid to religion is not the significant intent or effect of the voucher scheme. That is, in fact, just the kind of rhetorical argument that the majority accepts in these cases. In addition to secular private schools (129 students), the majority considers public schools with tuition assistance (roughly 1,400 students), magnet schools (13,000 students), and community schools (1,900 students), and concludes that fewer than 20% of pupils receive state vouchers to attend religious schools. (In fact, the numbers would seem even more favorable to the majority's argument if enrollment in traditional public schools without tutoring were considered, an alternative the majority thinks relevant to the private choice enquiry). Justice O'CONNOR focuses on how much money is spent on each educational option and notes that at most $8.2 million is spent on vouchers for students attending religious schools (concurring opinion), which is only 6% of the State's expenditure if one includes separate funding for Cleveland's community ($9.4 million) and magnet ($114.8 million) public schools. The variations show how results may shift when a judge can pick and choose the alternatives to use in the comparisons, and they also show what dependably comfortable results the choice criterion will yield if the identification of relevant choices is wide open. If the choice of relevant alternatives is an open one, proponents of voucher aid will always win, because they will always be able to find a "choice" somewhere that will show the bulk of public spending to be secular. The choice enquiry will be diluted to the point that it can screen out nothing, and the result will always be determined by selecting the alternatives to be treated as choices. Confining the relevant choices to spending choices, on the other hand, is not vulnerable to comparable criticism. Although leaving the selection of alternatives for choice wide open, as the majority would, virtually guarantees the availability of a "choice" that will satisfy the criterion, limiting the choices to spending choices will not guarantee a negative result in every case. There may, after all, be cases in which a voucher recipient will have a real choice, with enough secular private school desks in relation to the number of religious ones, and a voucher amount high enough to meet secular private school tuition levels. But, even to the extent that choice-to-spend does tend to limit the number of religious funding options that pass muster, the choice criterion has to be understood this way in order, as I have said, for it to function as a limiting principle.[12] Otherwise there is surely no point in requiring the choice to be a true or real or genuine one.[13]

It is not, of course, that I think even a genuine choice criterion is up to the task of the Establishment Clause when substantial state funds go to religious teaching; the discussion in Part III, *infra*, shows that it is not. The point is simply that if the majority wishes to claim that choice is a criterion, it must define choice in a way that can function as a criterion with a practical capacity to screen something out.

If, contrary to the majority, we ask the right question about genuine choice to use the vouchers, the answer shows that something is influencing choices in a way that aims the money in a religious direction: of 56 private schools in the district participating in the voucher program (only 53 of which accepted voucher students in 1999–2000), 46 of them are religious; 96.6% of all voucher recipients go to religious schools, only 3.4% to nonreligious ones. Unfortunately for the majority position, there is no explanation for this that suggests the religious direction results simply from free choices by parents. One answer to these statistics, for example, which would be consistent with the genuine choice claimed to be operating, might be that 96.6% of families choosing to avail themselves of vouchers choose to educate their children in

12. The need for a limit is one answer to Justice O'CONNOR, who argues at length that community schools should factor in the "private choice" calculus. To be fair, community schools do exhibit some features of private schools: they are autonomously managed without any interference from the school district or State and two have prior histories as private schools. It may be, then, that community schools might arguably count as choices because they are not like other public schools run by the State or municipality, but in substance merely private schools with state funding outside the voucher program.

But once any public school is deemed a relevant object of choice, there is no stopping this progression. For example, both the majority and Justice O'CONNOR characterize public magnet schools as an independent category of genuine educational options, simply because they are "nontraditional" public schools. But they do not share the "private school" features of community schools, and the only thing that distinguishes them from "traditional" public schools is their thematic focus, which in some cases appears to be nothing more than creative marketing.

13. And how should we decide which "choices" are "genuine" if the range of relevant choices is theoretically wide open? The showcase educational options that the majority and Justice O'CONNOR trumpet are Cleveland's 10 community schools, but they are hardly genuine choices. Two do not even enroll students in kindergarten through third grade, and thus parents contemplating participation in the voucher program cannot select those schools. ("[N]o new students may receive scholarships unless they are enrolled in grade

kindergarten, one, two, or three"). One school was not "in operation" as of 1999, and in any event targeted students below the federal poverty line, not all voucher-eligible students. Another school was a special population school for students with "numerous suspensions, behavioral problems and who are a grade level below their peers," which, as Justice O'CONNOR points out, may be "more attractive to certain inner-city parents," but is probably not an attractive "choice" for most parents.

Of the six remaining schools, the most recent statistics on fourth-grade student performance (unavailable for one school) indicate: three scored well below the Cleveland average in each of five tested subjects on state proficiency examinations, one scored above in one subject, and only one community school, Old Brooklyn Montessori School, was even an arguable competitor, scoring slightly better than traditional public schools in three subjects, and somewhat below in two.

I think that objective academic excellence should be the benchmark in comparing schools under the majority's test; Justice O'CONNOR prefers comparing educational options on the basis of subjective "parental satisfaction," and I am sure there are other plausible ways to evaluate "genuine choices." Until now, our cases have never talked about the quality of educational options by whatever standard, but now that every educational option is a relevant "choice," this is what the "genuine and independent private choice" enquiry, (opinion of the Court), would seem to require if it is to have any meaning at all. But if that is what genuine choice means, what does this enquiry have to do with the Establishment Clause?

schools of their own religion. This would not, in my view, render the scheme constitutional, but it would speak to the majority's choice criterion. Evidence shows, however, that almost two out of three families using vouchers to send their children to religious schools did not embrace the religion of those schools.[14] The families made it clear they had not chosen the schools because they wished their children to be proselytized in a religion not their own, or in any religion, but because of educational opportunity.[15]

Even so, the fact that some 2,270 students chose to apply their vouchers to schools of other religions, might be consistent with true choice if the students "chose" their religious schools over a wide array of private nonreligious options, or if it could be shown generally that Ohio's program had no effect on educational choices and thus no impermissible effect of advancing religious education. But both possibilities are contrary to fact. First, even if all existing nonreligious private schools in Cleveland were willing to accept large numbers of voucher students, only a few more than the 129 currently enrolled in such schools would be able to attend, as the total enrollment at all nonreligious private schools in Cleveland for kindergarten through eighth grade is only 510 children, see Brief for California Alliance for Public Schools as Amicus Curiae 15, and there is no indication that these schools have many open seats. Second, the $2,500 cap that the program places on tuition for participating low-income pupils has the effect of curtailing the participation of nonreligious schools: "nonreligious schools with higher tuition (about $4,000) stated that they could afford to accommodate just a few voucher students." By comparison, the average tuition at participating Catholic schools in Cleveland in 1999–2000 was $1,592, almost $1,000 below the cap.

Of course, the obvious fix would be to increase the value of vouchers so that existing nonreligious private and non-Catholic religious schools would be able to enroll more voucher students, and to provide incentives for educators to create new such schools given that few presently exist. Private choice, if as robust as that available to the seminarian in *Witters*, would then be "true private choice" under the majority's criterion. But it is simply unrealistic to presume that parents of elementary and middle schoolchildren in Cleveland will have a range of secular and religious choices even arguably comparable to the statewide program for vocational and higher education in *Witters*. And to get to that hypothetical point would require that such massive financial support be made available to religion as to disserve every objective of the Establishment Clause even more than the present scheme does. See Part III–B, *infra*.[16]

14. For example, 40% of families who sent their children to private schools for the first time under the voucher program were Baptist, but only one school, enrolling 44 voucher students, is Baptist.

15. When parents were surveyed as to their motives for enrolling their children in the voucher program, 96.4% cited a better education than available in the public schools, and 95% said their children's safety. When asked specifically in one study to identify the most important factor in selecting among participating private schools, 60% of parents mentioned academic quality, teacher quality, or the sub-

stance of what is taught (presumably secular); only 15% mentioned the religious affiliation of the school as even a consideration.

16. The majority notes that I argue both that the Ohio program is unconstitutional because the voucher amount is too low to create real private choice and that any greater expenditure would be unconstitutional as well. The majority is dead right about this, and there is no inconsistency here: any voucher program that satisfied the majority's requirement of "true private choice" would be even more egregiously unconstitutional than the current

There is, in any case, no way to interpret the 96.6% of current voucher money going to religious schools as reflecting a free and genuine choice by the families that apply for vouchers. The 96.6% reflects, instead, the fact that too few nonreligious school desks are available and few but religious schools can afford to accept more than a handful of voucher students. And contrary to the majority's assertion, public schools in adjacent districts hardly have a financial incentive to participate in the Ohio voucher program, and none has. For the overwhelming number of children in the voucher scheme, the only alternative to the public schools is religious. And it is entirely irrelevant that the State did not deliberately design the network of private schools for the sake of channeling money into religious institutions. The criterion is one of genuinely free choice on the part of the private individuals who choose, and a Hobson's choice is not a choice, whatever the reason for being Hobsonian.

III

I do not dissent merely because the majority has misapplied its own law, for even if I assumed *arguendo* that the majority's formal criteria were satisfied on the facts, today's conclusion would be profoundly at odds with the Constitution. Proof of this is clear on two levels. The first is circumstantial, in the now discarded symptom of violation, the substantial dimension of the aid. The second is direct, in the defiance of every objective supposed to be served by the bar against establishment.

A

The scale of the aid to religious schools approved today is unprecedented, both in the number of dollars and in the proportion of systemic school expenditure supported. Each measure has received attention in previous cases. On one hand, the sheer quantity of aid, when delivered to a class of religious primary and secondary schools, was suspect on the theory that the greater the aid, the greater its proportion to a religious school's existing expenditures, and the greater the likelihood that public money was supporting religious as well as secular instruction. As we said in Meek, "it would simply ignore reality to attempt to separate secular educational functions from the predominantly religious role" as the object of aid that comes in "substantial amounts." Conversely, the more "attenuated [the] financial benefit ... that eventually flows to parochial schools," the more the Court has been willing to find a form of state aid permissible.[17]

On the other hand, the Court has found the gross amount unhelpful for Establishment Clause analysis when the aid afforded a benefit solely to one individual, however substantial as to him, but only an incidental benefit to the religious school at which the individual chose to spend the State's money. See *Witters*, cf. *Zobrest*. When neither the design nor the implementation of an aid scheme channels a series of individual students' subsidies toward religious

---

scheme due to the substantial amount of aid to religious teaching that would be required.

17. The majority relies on *Mueller*, *Agostini*, and *Mitchell* to dispute the relevance of the large number of students that use vouchers to attend religious schools, but the reliance is inapt because each of those cases involved insubstantial benefits to the religious schools,

regardless of the number of students that benefited. See, e.g., *Mueller*, 463 U.S., at 391 ($112 in tax benefit to the highest-bracket taxpayer), *Agostini* (aid "must 'supplement, and in no case supplant' "), *Mitchell*, 530 U.S., at 866 (O'CONNOR, J., concurring in judgment) ("*de minimis*").

recipients, the relevant beneficiaries for establishment purposes, the Establishment Clause is unlikely to be implicated. The majority's reliance on the observations of five Members of the Court in *Witters* as to the irrelevance of substantiality of aid in that case is therefore beside the point in the matter before us, which involves considerable sums of public funds systematically distributed through thousands of students attending religious elementary and middle schools in the city of Cleveland.

The Cleveland voucher program has cost Ohio taxpayers $33 million since its implementation in 1996 ($28 million in voucher payments, $5 million in administrative costs), and its cost was expected to exceed $8 million in the 2001–2002 school year. The gross amounts of public money contributed are symptomatic of the scope of what the taxpayers' money buys for a broad class of religious-school students. In paying for practically the full amount of tuition for thousands of qualifying students, the scholarships purchase everything that tuition purchases, be it instruction in math or indoctrination in faith. The consequences of "substantial" aid hypothesized in *Meek* are realized here: the majority makes no pretense that substantial amounts of tax money are not systematically underwriting religious practice and indoctrination.

B

It is virtually superfluous to point out that every objective underlying the prohibition of religious establishment is betrayed by this scheme, but something has to be said about the enormity of the violation. I anticipated these objectives earlier, in discussing *Everson*, which cataloged them, the first being respect for freedom of conscience. Jefferson described it as the idea that no one "shall be compelled to ... support any religious worship, place, or ministry whatsoever," even a "teacher of his own religious persuasion," and Madison thought it violated by any " 'authority which can force a citizen to contribute three pence ... of his property for the support of any ... establishment.' " Memorial and Remonstrance ¶ 3, reprinted in *Everson*. "Any tax to establish religion is antithetical to the command that the minds of men always be wholly free." Madison's objection to three pence has simply been lost in the majority's formalism.

As for the second objective, to save religion from its own corruption, Madison wrote of the " 'experience ... that ecclesiastical establishments, instead of maintaining the purity and efficacy of Religion, have had a contrary operation.' " In Madison's time, the manifestations were "pride and indolence in the Clergy; ignorance and servility in the laity[,] in both, superstition, bigotry and persecution," in the 21st century, the risk is one of "corrosive secularism" to religious schools, and the specific threat is to the primacy of the schools' mission to educate the children of the faithful according to the unaltered precepts of their faith. Even "[t]he favored religion may be compromised as political figures reshape the religion's beliefs for their own purposes; it may be reformed as government largesse brings government regulation." *Lee v. Weisman* (Blackmun, J., concurring).

The risk is already being realized. In Ohio, for example, a condition of receiving government money under the program is that participating religious schools may not "discriminate on the basis of ... religion," which means the school may not give admission preferences to children who are members of the patron faith; children of a parish are generally consigned to the same admission lotteries as non-believers. This indeed was the exact object of a 1999 amendment repealing the portion of a predecessor statute that had allowed an admission preference for "[c]hildren ... whose parents are affiliated with any organization that provides financial support to the school, at the discretion of the school." Nor is the State's religious antidiscrimination restriction limited to student admission policies: by its terms, a participating religious school may well be forbidden to choose a member of its own clergy to serve as teacher or principal over a layperson of a different religion claiming equal qualification for the job.[18] Indeed, a separate condition that "[t]he school ... not ... teach hatred of any person or group on the basis of ... religion," could be understood (or subsequently broadened) to prohibit religions from teaching traditionally legitimate articles of faith as to the error, sinfulness, or ignorance of others,[19] if they want government money for their schools.

For perspective on this foot-in-the-door of religious regulation, it is well to remember that the money has barely begun to flow. Prior examples of aid, whether grants through individuals or in-kind assistance, were never significant enough to alter the basic fiscal structure of religious schools; state aid was welcome, but not indispensable. But given the figures already involved here, there is no question that religious schools in Ohio are on the way to becoming bigger businesses with budgets enhanced to fit their new stream of tax-raised income. The administrators of those same schools are also no doubt following the politics of a move in the Ohio State Senate to raise the current maximum value of a school voucher from $2,250 to the base amount of current state spending on each public school student ($4,814 for the 2001 fiscal year). Ohio, in fact, is merely replicating the experience in Wisconsin, where a similar increase in the value of educational vouchers in Milwaukee has induced the creation of some 23 new private schools, some of which, we may safely surmise, are religious. New schools have presumably pegged their financial prospects to the government from the start, and the odds are that increases in government aid will bring the threshold voucher amount closer to the tuition at even more expensive religious schools.

When government aid goes up, so does reliance on it; the only thing likely to go down is independence. If Justice Douglas in *Allen* was concerned with

---

18. And the courts will, of course, be drawn into disputes about whether a religious school's employment practices violated the Ohio statute. In part precisely to avoid this sort of involvement, some Courts of Appeals have held that religious groups enjoy a First Amendment exemption for clergy from state and federal laws prohibiting discrimination on the basis of race or ethnic origin.

19. See, e.g., Christian New Testament (2 Corinthians 6:14) (King James Version) ("Be ye not unequally yoked together with unbelievers: for what fellowship hath righteousness with unrighteousness? and what communion hath light with darkness?"); The Book of Mormon (2 Nephi 9:24) ("And if they will not repent and believe in his name, and be baptized in his name, and endure to the end, they

must be damned; for the Lord God, the Holy One of Israel, has spoken it"); Pentateuch (Deut.29:18) (The New Jewish Publication Society Translation) (for one who converts to another faith, "[t]he LORD will never forgive him; rather will the LORD's anger and passion rage against that man, till every sanction recorded in this book comes down upon him, and the LORD blots out his name from under heaven"); The Koran 334 (The Cow Ch. 2:1) (N. Dawood transl. 4th rev. ed. 1974) ("As for the unbelievers, whether you forewarn them or not, they will not have faith. Allah has set a seal upon their hearts and ears; their sight is dimmed and a grievous punishment awaits them").

state agencies, influenced by powerful religious groups, choosing the textbooks that parochial schools would use (dissenting opinion), how much more is there reason to wonder when dependence will become great enough to give the State of Ohio an effective veto over basic decisions on the content of curriculums? A day will come when religious schools will learn what political leverage can do, just as Ohio's politicians are now getting a lesson in the leverage exercised by religion.

Increased voucher spending is not, however, the sole portent of growing regulation of religious practice in the school, for state mandates to moderate religious teaching may well be the most obvious response to the third concern behind the ban on establishment, its inextricable link with social conflict.

Justice BREYER has addressed this issue in his own dissenting opinion, which I join, and here it is enough to say that the intensity of the expectable friction can be gauged by realizing that the scramble for money will energize not only contending sectarians, but taxpayers who take their liberty of conscience seriously. Religious teaching at taxpayer expense simply cannot be cordoned from taxpayer politics, and every major religion currently espouses social positions that provoke intense opposition. Not all taxpaying Protestant citizens, for example, will be content to underwrite the teaching of the Roman Catholic Church condemning the death penalty.[20] Nor will all of America's Muslims acquiesce in paying for the endorsement of the religious Zionism taught in many religious Jewish schools, which combines "a nationalistic sentiment" in support of Israel with a "deeply religious" element. Nor will every secular taxpayer be content to support Muslim views on differential treatment of the sexes,[21] or, for that matter, to fund the espousal of a wife's obligation of obedience to her husband, presumably taught in any schools adopting the articles of faith of the Southern Baptist Convention.[22] Views like these, and innumerable others, have been safe in the sectarian pulpits and classrooms of this Nation not only because the Free Exercise Clause protects them directly, but because the ban on supporting religious establishment has protected free exercise, by keeping it relatively private. With the arrival of vouchers in religious schools, that privacy will go, and along with it will go confidence that religious disagreement will stay moderate.

* * *

If the divisiveness permitted by today's majority is to be avoided in the short term, it will be avoided only by action of the political branches at the state and national levels. Legislatures not driven to desperation by the problems of public education may be able to see the threat in vouchers negotiable in sectarian schools. Perhaps even cities with problems like Cleveland's will perceive the danger, now that they know a federal court will not save them from it.

20. See R. Martino, Abolition of the Death Penalty (Nov. 2, 1999) ("The position of the Holy See, therefore, is that authorities, even for the most serious crimes, should limit themselves to non-lethal means of punishment") (citing John Paul II, Evangelium Vitae n. 56

21. See R. Martin, Islamic Studies 224 (2d ed.1996) (interpreting the Koran to mean that "[m]en are responsible to earn a living and

provide for their families; women bear children and run the household").

22. See The Baptist Faith and Message, Art. XVIII, available at www.sbc.net ("A wife is to submit herself graciously to the servant leadership of her husband even as the church willingly submits to the headship of Christ").

My own course as a judge on the Court cannot, however, simply be to hope that the political branches will save us from the consequences of the majority's decision. *Everson's* statement is still the touchstone of sound law, even though the reality is that in the matter of educational aid the Establishment Clause has largely been read away. True, the majority has not approved vouchers for religious schools alone, or aid earmarked for religious instruction. But no scheme so clumsy will ever get before us, and in the cases that we may see, like these, the Establishment Clause is largely silenced. I do not have the option to leave it silent, and I hope that a future Court will reconsider today's dramatic departure from basic Establishment Clause principle.

Justice Breyer, with whom Justice Stevens and Justice Souter join, dissenting.

I join Justice SOUTER's opinion, and I agree substantially with Justice STEVENS. I write separately, however, to emphasize the risk that publicly financed voucher programs pose in terms of religiously based social conflict. I do so because I believe that the Establishment Clause concern for protecting the Nation's social fabric from religious conflict poses an overriding obstacle to the implementation of this well-intentioned school voucher program. And by explaining the nature of the concern, I hope to demonstrate why, in my view, "parental choice" cannot significantly alleviate the constitutional problem.

I

The First Amendment begins with a prohibition, that "Congress shall make no law respecting an establishment of religion," and a guarantee, that the government shall not prohibit "the free exercise thereof." These Clauses embody an understanding, reached in the 17th century after decades of religious war, that liberty and social stability demand a religious tolerance that respects the religious views of all citizens, permits those citizens to "worship God in their own way," and allows all families to "teach their children and to form their characters" as they wish. The Clauses reflect the Framers' vision of an American Nation free of the religious strife that had long plagued the nations of Europe. Whatever the Framers might have thought about particular 18th century school funding practices, they undeniably intended an interpretation of the Religion Clauses that would implement this basic First Amendment objective.

In part for this reason, the Court's 20th century Establishment Clause cases—both those limiting the practice of religion in public schools and those limiting the public funding of private religious education—focused directly upon social conflict, potentially created when government becomes involved in religious education. In *Engel v. Vitale*, the Court held that the Establishment Clause forbids prayer in public elementary and secondary schools. It did so in part because it recognized the "anguish, hardship and bitter strife that could come when zealous religious groups struggl[e] with one another to obtain the Government's stamp of approval . . . ." And it added:

"The history of governmentally established religion, both in England and in this country, showed that whenever government had allied itself with one particular form of religion, the inevitable result had been that it had incurred the hatred, disrespect and even contempt of those who held contrary beliefs."

In *Lemon v. Kurtzman*, the Court held that the Establishment Clause forbids state funding, through salary supplements, of religious school teachers. It did so in part because of the "threat" that this funding would create religious "divisiveness" that would harm "the normal political process." The Court explained:

"[P]olitical debate and division ... are normal and healthy manifestations of our democratic system of government, but political division along religious lines was one of the principal evils against which [the First Amendment's religious clauses were] ... intended to protect."

And in *Nyquist*, the Court struck down a state statute that, much like voucher programs, provided aid for parents whose children attended religious schools, explaining that the "assistance of the sort here involved carries grave potential for ... continuing political strife over aid to religion."

When it decided these 20th century Establishment Clause cases, the Court did not deny that an earlier American society might have found a less clear-cut church/state separation compatible with social tranquility. Indeed, historians point out that during the early years of the Republic, American schools—including the first public schools—were Protestant in character. Their students recited Protestant prayers, read the King James version of the Bible, and learned Protestant religious ideals. Those practices may have wrongly discriminated against members of minority religions, but given the small number of such individuals, the teaching of Protestant religions in schools did not threaten serious social conflict. (Catholics constituted less than 2% of American church-affiliated population at time of founding).

The 20th century Court was fully aware, however, that immigration and growth had changed American society dramatically since its early years. By 1850, 1.6 million Catholics lived in America, and by 1900 that number rose to 12 million. There were similar percentage increases in the Jewish population. Not surprisingly, with this increase in numbers, members of non-Protestant religions, particularly Catholics, began to resist the Protestant domination of the public schools. Scholars report that by the mid–19th century religious conflict over matters such as Bible reading "grew intense," as Catholics resisted and Protestants fought back to preserve their domination. "Dreading Catholic domination," native Protestants "terrorized Catholics." In some States "Catholic students suffered beatings or expulsions for refusing to read from the Protestant Bible, and crowds ... rioted over whether Catholic children could be released from the classroom during Bible reading."

The 20th century Court was also aware that political efforts to right the wrong of discrimination against religious minorities in primary education had failed; in fact they had exacerbated religious conflict. Catholics sought equal government support for the education of their children in the form of aid for private Catholic schools. But the "Protestant position" on this matter, scholars report, "was that public schools must be 'nonsectarian' (which was usually understood to allow Bible reading and other Protestant observances) and public money must not support 'sectarian' schools (which in practical terms meant Catholic)." And this sentiment played a significant role in creating a movement that sought to amend several state constitutions (often successfully), and to amend the United States Constitution (unsuccessfully) to make certain that government would not help pay for "sectarian" (i.e., Catholic) schooling for children.

These historical circumstances suggest that the Court, applying the Establishment Clause through the Fourteenth Amendment to 20th century American society, faced an interpretive dilemma that was in part practical. The Court appreciated the religious diversity of contemporary American society. It realized that the status quo favored some religions at the expense of others. And it understood the Establishment Clause to prohibit (among other things) any such favoritism. Yet how did the Clause achieve that objective? Did it simply require the government to give each religion an equal chance to introduce religion into the primary schools—a kind of "equal opportunity" approach to the interpretation of the Establishment Clause? Or, did that Clause avoid government favoritism of some religions by insisting upon "separation"—that the government achieve equal treatment by removing itself from the business of providing religious education for children? This interpretive choice arose in respect both to religious activities in public schools and government aid to private education.

In both areas the Court concluded that the Establishment Clause required "separation," in part because an "equal opportunity" approach was not workable. With respect to religious activities in the public schools, how could the Clause require public primary and secondary school teachers, when reading prayers or the Bible, only to treat all religions alike? In many places there were too many religions, too diverse a set of religious practices, too many whose spiritual beliefs denied the virtue of formal religious training. This diversity made it difficult, if not impossible, to devise meaningful forms of "equal treatment" by providing an "equal opportunity" for all to introduce their own religious practices into the public schools.

With respect to government aid to private education, did not history show that efforts to obtain equivalent funding for the private education of children whose parents did not hold popular religious beliefs only exacerbated religious strife? As Justice Rutledge recognized:

> "Public money devoted to payment of religious costs, educational or other, brings the quest for more. It brings too the struggle of sect against sect for the larger share or for any. Here one [religious sect] by numbers [of adherents] alone will benefit most, there another. This is precisely the history of societies which have had an established religion and dissident groups." *Everson* (dissenting opinion).

The upshot is the development of constitutional doctrine that reads the Establishment Clause as avoiding religious strife, *not* by providing every religion with an *equal opportunity* (say, to secure state funding or to pray in the public schools), but by drawing fairly clear lines of *separation* between church and state—at least where the heartland of religious belief, such as primary religious education, is at issue.

II

The principle underlying these cases—avoiding religiously based social conflict—remains of great concern. As religiously diverse as America had become when the Court decided its major 20th century Establishment Clause cases, we are exponentially more diverse today. America boasts more than 55 different religious groups and subgroups with a significant number of members. Major religions include, among others, Protestants, Catholics, Jews, Muslims, Buddhists, Hindus, and Sikhs. And several of these major religions contain different subsidiary sects with different religious beliefs. Newer Christian immigrant groups are "expressing their Christianity in languages, customs, and independent churches that are barely recognizable, and often controversial, for European-ancestry Catholics and Protestants."

Under these modern-day circumstances, how is the "equal opportunity" principle to work—without risking the "struggle of sect against sect" against which Justice Rutledge warned? School voucher programs finance the religious education of the young. And, if widely adopted, they may well provide billions of dollars that will do so. Why will different religions not become concerned about, and seek to influence, the criteria used to channel this money to religious schools? Why will they not want to examine the implementation of the programs that provide this money—to determine, for example, whether implementation has biased a program toward or against particular sects, or whether recipient religious schools are adequately fulfilling a program's criteria? If so, just how is the State to resolve the resulting controversies without provoking legitimate fears of the kinds of religious favoritism that, in so religiously diverse a Nation, threaten social dissension? Consider the voucher program here at issue. That program insists that the religious school accept students of all religions. Does that criterion treat fairly groups whose religion forbids them to do so? The program also insists that no participating school "advocate or foster unlawful behavior or teach hatred of any person or group on the basis of race, ethnicity, national origin, or religion." And it requires the State to "revoke the registration of any school if, after a hearing, the superintendent determines that the school is in violation" of the program's rules. As one *amicus* argues, "it is difficult to imagine a more divisive activity" than the appointment of state officials as referees to determine whether a particular religious doctrine "teaches hatred or advocates lawlessness."

How are state officials to adjudicate claims that one religion or another is advocating, for example, civil disobedience in response to unjust laws, the use of illegal drugs in a religious ceremony, or resort to force to call attention to what it views as an immoral social practice? What kind of public hearing will there be in response to claims that one religion or another is continuing to teach a view of history that casts members of other religions in the worst possible light? How will the public react to government funding for schools that take controversial religious positions on topics that are of current popular interest—say, the conflict in the Middle East or the war on terrorism? Yet any major funding program for primary religious education will require criteria. And the selection of those criteria, as well as their application, inevitably pose problems that are divisive. Efforts to respond to these problems not only will seriously entangle church and state, but also will promote division among religious groups, as one group or another fears (often legitimately) that it will receive unfair treatment at the hands of the government.

I recognize that other nations, for example Great Britain and France, have in the past reconciled religious school funding and religious freedom without creating serious strife. Yet British and French societies are religiously more homogeneous—and it bears noting that recent waves of immigration have begun to create problems of social division there as well. See, e.g., The Muslims of France, 75 Foreign Affairs 78 (1996) (describing increased religious strife in France, as exemplified by expulsion of teenage girls from school for wearing traditional Muslim scarves); Ahmed, Extreme Prejudice; Muslims in Britain, The Times of London, May 2, 1992, p. 10 (describing religious strife in connection with increased Muslim immigration in Great Britain).

In a society as religiously diverse as ours, the Court has recognized that we must rely on the Religion Clauses of the First Amendment to protect against religious strife, particularly when what is at issue is an area as central to religious belief as the shaping, through primary education, of the next generation's minds and spirits.

III

I concede that the Establishment Clause currently permits States to channel various forms of assistance to religious schools, for example, transportation costs for students, computers, and secular texts. States now certify the nonsectarian educational content of religious school education. Yet the consequence has not been great turmoil. But see, e.g., May, Charter School's Religious Tone; Operation of South Bay Academy Raises Church–State Questions, San Francisco Chronicle, Dec. 17, 2001, p. A1 (describing increased government supervision of charter schools after complaints that students were "studying Islam in class and praying with their teachers," and Muslim educators complaining of " 'post-Sept. 11 anti-Muslim sentiment' ").

School voucher programs differ, however, in both kind and degree from aid programs upheld in the past. They differ in kind because they direct financing to a core function of the church: the teaching of religious truths to young children. For that reason the constitutional demand for "separation" is of particular constitutional concern.

Private schools that participate in Ohio's program, for example, recognize the importance of primary religious education, for they pronounce that their goals are to "communicate the gospel," "provide opportunities to ... experience a faith community," "provide ... for growth in prayer," and "provide instruction in religious truths and values." History suggests, not that such private school teaching of religion is undesirable, but that government funding of this kind of religious endeavor is far more contentious than providing funding for secular textbooks, computers, vocational training, or even funding for adults who wish to obtain a college education at a religious university. Contrary to Justice O'CONNOR's opinion, history also shows that government involvement in religious primary education is far more divisive than state property tax exemptions for religious institutions or tax deductions for charitable contributions, both of which come far closer to exemplifying the neutrality that distinguishes, for example, fire protection on the one hand from direct monetary assistance on the other. Federal aid to religiously based hospitals is even further removed from education, which lies at the heartland of religious belief.

Vouchers also differ in *degree*. The aid programs recently upheld by the Court involved limited amounts of aid to religion. But the majority's analysis here appears to permit a considerable shift of taxpayer dollars from public secular schools to private religious schools. That fact, combined with the use to which these dollars will be put, exacerbates the conflict problem. State aid that takes the form of peripheral secular items, with prohibitions against diversion of funds to religious teaching, holds significantly less potential for social division. In this respect as well, the secular aid upheld in Mitchell differs dramatically from the present case. Although it was conceivable that minor amounts of money could have, contrary to the statute, found their way to the religious activities of the recipients, that case is at worst the camel's nose, while the litigation before us is the camel itself.

IV

I do not believe that the "parental choice" aspect of the voucher program sufficiently offsets the concerns I have mentioned. Parental choice cannot help the taxpayer who does not want to finance the religious education of children. It will not always help the parent who may see little real choice between inadequate nonsectarian public education and adequate education at a school whose religious teachings are contrary to his own. It will not satisfy religious minorities unable to participate because they are too few in number to support the creation of their own private schools. It will not satisfy groups whose religious beliefs preclude them from participating in a government-sponsored program, and who may well feel ignored as government funds primarily support the education of children in the doctrines of the dominant religions. And it does little to ameliorate the entanglement problems or the related problems of social division that Part II describes. Consequently, the fact that the parent may choose which school can cash the government's voucher check does not alleviate the Establishment Clause concerns associated with voucher programs.

V

The Court, in effect, turns the clock back. It adopts, under the name of "neutrality," an interpretation of the Establishment Clause that this Court rejected more than half a century ago. In its view, the parental choice that offers each religious group a kind of equal opportunity to secure government funding overcomes the Establishment Clause concern for social concord. An earlier Court found that "equal opportunity" principle insufficient; it read the Clause as insisting upon greater separation of church and state, at least in respect to primary education. In a society composed of many different religious creeds, I fear that this present departure from the Court's earlier understanding risks creating a form of religiously based conflict potentially harmful to the Nation's social fabric. Because I believe the Establishment Clause was written in part to avoid this kind of conflict, and for reasons set forth by Justice SOUTER and Justice STEVENS, I respectfully dissent.

QUESTIONS AND NOTES

1. Is *Zelman* likely to uphold vouchers everywhere, or was the deplorable state of Cleveland schools the deciding factor?

2. How should Justice Thomas' plea for racial justice factor into the *Zelman* question? Is the establishment clause more compromised by vouchers or the equal protection clause by affirmative action? Explain.

3. Are you impressed by Justice Breyer's attempt to bring political divisiveness back into the mix? Is the Cleveland program any more politically divisive that the Louisiana program that he voted to sustain a year earlier?

4. Assuming that available alternatives are to be measured, should the alternatives include charter and magnet schools or only non-religious private schools? Explain.

5. Would Justice Souter uphold *any* aid that benefits religious schools directly or indirectly? Would he have dissented in *Everson*?

6. Is the wisdom of vouchers relevant to their constitutionality? Are they wise? Should they have been found constitutional?

7. Is it relevant that vouchers may prompt a non-Catholic parent to send her child to a Catholic school (where Catholic prayers are said) because that is the place where the parent believes the child will receive the best possible education? Would that not be State money spent to proselytize the child in a religion not of her choosing?

†